THE PROMISE OF FREEDOM FOR SLAVES ESCAPING IN BRITISH SHIPS

Dedicated to the Memory of Jane Corbett Floyd

THE PROMISE OF FREEDOM FOR SLAVES ESCAPING IN BRITISH SHIPS

THE EMANCIPATION REVOLUTION, 1740–1807

Theodore Corbett

PEN & SWORD
MARITIME

First published in Great Britain in 2024 by
PEN AND SWORD MARITIME
an imprint of
Pen and Sword Books Ltd
Yorkshire – Philadelphia

Typeset in Times New Roman 9.5/12 by
SJmagic DESIGN SERVICES, India.
Printed and bound in the UK by CPI Group (UK) Ltd.

Pen & Sword Books Ltd incorporates the imprints of Pen & Sword
Archaeology, Atlas, Aviation, Battleground, Discovery,
Family History, History, Maritime, Military, Naval, Politics, Railways,
Select, Social History, Transport, True Crime, Claymore Press,
Frontline Books, Leo Cooper, Praetorian Press, Remember When,
Seaforth Publishing and Wharncliffe.

For a complete list of Pen & Sword titles please contact
PEN & SWORD BOOKS LIMITED
George House, Units 12 & 13, Beevor Street, Off Pontefract Road,
Barnsley, South Yorkshire, S71 1HN, England
E-mail: enquiries@pen-and-sword.co.uk
Website: www.pen-and-sword.co.uk

or

PEN AND SWORD BOOKS
1950 Lawrence Rd, Havertown, PA 19083, USA
E-mail: uspen-and-sword@casematepublishers.com
Website: www.penandswordbooks.com

Contents

Preface

This project began as I completed a now published book for Pen and Sword, *The Atlantic-wide Conflict over Independence and Empire: A Maritime History of the American Revolutionary War*. Editor Tara Moran suggested that my final chapter be expanded into another book on black emancipation. I took on the new challenge.

My journey to writing this book has been long and indirect. I have always been interested in the American War for Independence because I grew up in upstate New York among many historic sites from the conflict. I began working on the war in 2003, speaking at Fort Ticonderoga's war colleges, held annually before a broad audience on Lake Champlain. Ultimately, I published *No Turning Point*, covering the Saratoga Campaign. For this I visited and used the manuscript collections of the National Library and Archives of Canada in Ottawa to develop a British perspective on the war.

Still the task of writing about black emancipation was very different from writing about the war's military or maritime history. Tracing a new revolution in what has been called 'the Age of Revolution' that encompassed the American and French Revolutions requires considerable rethinking. I had to explore conceptions of slavery and the genesis of its abolition over a long period. The public already had an impression of certain events which had been recently enshrined in movies about William Wilberforce and Lord Mansfield as abolitionists.

I did find that some historians thought that black emancipation came of age during the era of the War for Independence. Here is eminent American historian David Brion Davis:

> It is indisputable that the American Revolution opened the way for Britain's
> emancipation of 780,000 colonial slaves. The worthy achievement celebrated
> as the dawning of a millennial era of universal emancipation confirmed Britain
> self-image as the world's altruistic champion of liberty and civilization.[1]

This is further substantiated by intellectual historian Christopher Brown who, in tracking the failure of early anti-slavery initiatives, sees attempts to abolish slavery as a product of the American, rather than the Industrial, Revolution.

Confident of the War for Independence's importance, I had to place it within the Atlantic-wide context it deserves. This expanse was almost too much for me. I was able to focus on areas with which I was familiar but am aware that I could not cover every aspect of Britain's colonial empire.

Since I had just finished an account of the War for Independence focusing on the Royal Navy, its role was fresh in my mind. At first, I thought the navy was not a logical partner for reforming evangelists and abolitionists. After all, the navy could not tolerate even occasional pacifism and its impress recruiting was regarded by some as a fate worse than slavery. Sources show, however, that there was another side to the navy. Here I have made an effort to portray the navy's officers and crews as being enlightened enough to accept blacks who chose to join or appear on their ships. This meant I had to be able to explain to what degree they were evangelized and to what extent crews were color-blind.

I had already looked at the navy through the lens of the Hamond Papers at the University of Virginia, the most extensive source on Captain Andrew Snape Hamond's career. They are readily available at several research libraries because they were microfilmed in 1966 and a guide to the papers published the same year. Most of Hamond's papers were put together by himself in scrapbook, for he was interested in producing an autobiography which was never completed or published. In the manuscript, pagination is often lacking and loose inserts exist, while Hamond inverted the notebook pages into which his material was placed. This collection also includes Hamond-Hans Stanley correspondence, the only personal papers, which were purchased separately by the university to enhance the collection.

Still, as with any historian who wants to comprehend naval history, Britain beckoned. In 2017 and 2022, I had the pleasure of working with staff of several research facilities. In Greenwich, the Caird Library of the National Maritime Museum offered a rich collection of ships' log books. One Caird librarian in particular, Mark Benson, was especially accommodating. Across London at Kew, The National Archives provided access to the Admiralty Papers.

As I also wanted to pay attention to the other side, especially in the Southern United States, I had published two histories of communities during the war: *Revolutionary New Castle* and *Revolutionary Chestertown*. Research would ultimately take me to the NABB Center of Salisbury University, Maryland, where I became acquainted with Director Ray Thompson and his staff, who were ever helpful. It was here that I first read manuscripts covering Delmarva history. An instructive and pleasurable experience was lively discussion with students in my Eastern Shore Maritime History classes, sponsored by Salisbury University.

Further south on the Virginia Shore, Archivist Miles Barnes of the Eastern Shore Public Library, Accomac, Virginia proved to be supportive, not only with new sources on Virginia's maritime history but also in opening his home library, where I spent many an afternoon in discussion. I was not going to allow this opportunity to be missed and I cajoled him into reading every word of this manuscript.

This book was crafted during 2021–2022, when the Covid pandemic was surging in the United States and Britain. In order to fight the pandemic, many archives were closed or limited their hours. This handicap was offset by efforts to place collections online. Some collections used here, like the Maryland Archives or the Naval Documents of the American Revolution, were already online, but new additions appeared. In my notes, I have tried to continue my respect for modern technology by citing sources which are available online.

The works of certain historians on both sides of the Atlantic have also guided my task. Two works can be singled out as indispensable in crafting this history, namely Cassandra Pybus's *Epic Journeys of Freedom* and Simon Schama's *Rough Crossings*. They must be recognized for breaking the ground on which I was able to build this book. For naval history, the writings of Nicholas Andrew Martin Rodger are magisterial. No one has revolutionized the study of the eighteenth-century Royal Navy as much as he, based on his unprecedented knowledge of documentary sources. On the British side of the Atlantic, I found Richard Bake's *Evangelicals in the Royal Navy* helpful, while the story of Britain's blacks is covered in Kathleen Charter's

Untold Histories and Stephen Braidwood's *Black Poor and White Philanthropists*. As to the American side, my best choices were Philip Morgan's *Slave Counterpoint* and Dee Andrews *The Methodists*, along with two case studies, Judith Van Buskirk's *Generous Enemies* about the New York area and Robert Olwell's *Masters, Slaves, and Subjects* about the South Carolina Low Country. Finally, an overall recommendation is the pioneering works of the late Ellen Wilson, including *The Loyal Blacks* and *John Clarkson and the African Adventure*.

Ground rules must be set for what follows. It should be clear that the judgements are made in the context of the eighteenth century. I will judge George Washington and Thomas Jefferson by the standards of the eighteenth century, not those of Martin Luther King and the Civil Rights Movement. This is why I have tried to provide the context of past institutions and social mores, so that my analysis minimizes twenty-first-century concerns. Words like racism or even slavery and freedom explain nothing unless they are defined and seen within the context of this past era and fully explained.

When looking for sources on American runaway slaves, I lacked the options of historians of nineteenth-century runaways with their networks of anti-slavery sympathizers and the Underground Railway. The vast majority of eighteenth-century blacks were illiterate and alone. Thus, the difficulty is to find sources that allow blacks to speak for themselves rather than having the perspective of more literate whites. I have come to depend on the eighteenth-century works of authors of African birth or descent in the Atlantic world. These precious few sources are invaluable because they offer us their detailed lives, thoughts and motives. Their literacy was a demonstration that members of their race were capable of expressing their ideas in written and spoken English.

Admittedly, as sources these authors require special handling for the conditions in the eighteenth-century literature were different from today. Valuable anthologies by Henry Lewis Gates Jr and Vincent Carretta have popularized them, but they have also led to further research, which challenges their authorship and veracity. Scholars have questioned Olaudah Equiano's African nativity, Briton Hammon's ability to write, and Quobna Cugoano's unidentified appropriations from other authors.[2] Reasons for these supposed lapses vary; certainly memories can be inadequate, authors may have felt they needed to exaggerate their experiences, and we must remember that most narratives were meant to encourage the abolition of slavery. With this in mind, I have chosen to use them carefully but still find them crucial for the black perspective, regardless of biographical errors.

Recently, historians have taken the origins of British abolition as far back as the mid-seventeenth and the English Civil War. This can only be done by viewing slavery as an Atlantic-wide phenomenon in which the temporary bondage of white indentured servitude is as important as the perpetual bondage of African slaves.[3] Here I have separated them, but it is understandable that these early abolitionist views made little distinction between what they regarded as the two forms of slavery.

As expected the Pen & Sword editorial team, including Harriet Fielding and Gaynor Haliday, has done a superb job in making this book. One of the necessities of scholarships is time and funding for research and reflection. I am grateful for awards received from the Gilder Lehrman Foundation, the National Endowment for the Humanities and Handsell Historic Site.

As the 'Black Lives Matter' movement has again called on historians to reassess African American history, it should come as no surprise that blacks were left out of the American Founding Fathers' Revolutionary decisions, beginning a trend that has continued. Hopefully, this history of slavery and abolitionism will help us to make progress with racial problems in our time.

Introduction

Another revolution existed in the late eighteenth-century world, not the familiar movement for independence of the United States or even the French Revolution, but rather the effort for freedom from slavery, opposed by most in the thirteen British colonies that sought independence. Although Africans and African Americans were left out of most accounts of these momentous years, we will piece together their emerging path towards freedom. Here our concern will be their part in the revolution which advanced from the slave trade to the American War for Independence, ending in the abolition of the slave trade throughout the British Empire. To blacks, this Emancipation Revolution on the part of Britain rang out more loudly than the Declaration of Independence.

Here the Old Regime was neither the salutary neglect of the British colonial administration nor the French monarchy's support of the War for Independence. Instead, it consisted of planters who struggled to maintain plantation society in coastal North America and the West Indies. Essential to managing a plantation was a master-slave relationship to produce staples like sugar or tobacco, which were exported to Europe. Plantation masters gained control of their local legislatures and vestries and passed slave codes to restrict slave movement, catch runaways and prevent insurrections. Before and during the War for Independence, the planters continued to fear their slaves would rebel against them, thus they sought to obstruct them from gathering or arming themselves. They also feared that their slaves would become Christians, implying the status of freeman and offering the possibility that a slave could be more pious than his master. Preventing Christianity amongst slaves was tied to restricting educational opportunities so that slaves would not be able to read the Bible.

Still, from Britain came the Great Awakening, the advent of evangelism in America, which would provide slaves with hope for future freedom.[1] In the 1740s, white British evangelists like George Whitefield asked for the better treatment of slaves, but later black evangelists like David Margrett or John Marrant carried the concern a step further, asserting that freedom was more important than kind treatment and they inspired slaves to runaway to freedom. Plantation masters would justify slavery by claiming slaves were not Christians, but rather African heathens. Their conversion to Christianity, including crucial baptism, would not be welcomed by plantation masters.

By the time of the War for Independence, many planters in the West Indies and American mainland came to see Britain as a dangerous place, where their valuable slaves were likely to be freed. The planters' ability to retain and recover their slaves was threatened by English Common Law and Anglican and Methodist evangelism, which respected blacks as members of the human race. A benevolence movement expanded among British merchants, Royal Navy officers and literary figures, which would focus on giving opportunities to black Loyalists, who had arrived in British ports during and after the War for Independence. This would be the beginning of British anti-slavery agitation which would ultimately lead to planters in all British territory losing their valuable property in slaves. Whites and blacks would come together in the British emancipation movement.

Black writer Ignatius Sancho summed up the War for Independence in a letter of 1778: 'What is worse, we have politics – and a detestable Brothers' war – where the right hand is hacking and hewing the left – whilst Angels weep at our madness – and Devils rejoice at the ruinous prospect.'[2] As will become evident, eighteenth-century people treated religion more seriously than we do today. Blacks would become as knowledgeable as whites in their command of Christian scripture. Evangelism was a force which spread the Christian gospel by public preaching or individual witness in which blacks were as active as whites. Rather than politics, the evangelical foment before and during the war should be seen as the discord that caused the Emancipation Revolution.

During the War for Independence, plantations would be attacked and suffer loss of their slaves who received freedom from the British military. In 1775, black emancipation commenced in Chesapeake Bay with Lord Dunmore's proclamation and the resulting fleet, which attracted black recruits and even extended families, creating the first mass emancipation of slaves in British colonial history. Dunmore did not act alone as he was supported by a growing Royal Navy squadron. From then on, the navy would have an almost constant presence in the bay, so that rebel authorities regarded its ships as a very cause of black and white Loyalist disaffection.

The emancipation of blacks was a matter of smaller incidents, rather than focusing on a major upheaval. Blacks would find their way to Royal Navy ships or behind British lines in New York, Charleston, Savannah or the Chesapeake. While many blacks had already served in the Royal Navy, they also could join a group of irregular raiders, usually including white Loyalists, or a provincial unit like the Black Pioneers. Although mostly land-based, irregular raids required watermen and their craft to carry out stealthy forays. Sometimes they freed slaves, who became part of their contingent.

At the end of the war, the British evacuations of loyal subjects from 1782 to 1785 were the turning point in the Emancipation Revolution. Blacks who had joined the British would not be returned to their masters to be punished and re-enslaved. Blacks no longer saw themselves as the property of anyone, when offered the possibility of freedom within the new British Empire. This perspective has taken historians some time to recognize. In 1961, black historian Benjamin Quarles was at pains to describe the effort of rebel masters to find and re-enslave their valuable property before it was evacuated. Forty-five years later this perspective no longer held, when Cassandra Pybus's work over the same ground emphasized the journeys that free black refugees would take on Royal Navy ships in 'Their Global Quest for Liberty'.[3]

A majority of free and enslaved blacks would remain where the Royal Navy ships and transports landed them in Jamaica, the Bahamas, Nova Scotia, or Britain. Despite obstacles, they would involve themselves in a concerted effort to settle or integrate, in which some succeeded remarkably, while others failed. A vocal minority would not be happy in their new homes and it is their plight that has gained many historians' attention. Their discontent was expressed in their own petitions and demand for audiences concerning the allocation of British government resources to support their resettlement. The appearance of black leadership in these communities promoted the abolitionist belief that blacks could be equal to whites in their ability to settle and develop new territories.

However, this black outburst produced what all revolutions seem to have, a counter revolution. This would be created by black migration from Nova Scotia to the existing black colony of Sierra Leone in West Africa. A conservative business board of directors in London would turn the clock back to create a Sierra Leone colony that they wanted to be a commercial success. Their well-intentioned effort to replace the slave economy of the West Indies as a source of tropical products with a plantation economy in Sierra Leone would cause a revolt of its black settlers against their authority. The colony again failed to live up to expectations and it was left to the British government to pick up the pieces and create a Crown colony.

The Emancipation Revolution is a contribution to Black History, although sources for the extraction of their eighteenth-century history are sparse. Many thousands joined the British during the War for Independence, some of them serving on Royal Navy ships. Consistently, blacks become evangelical Christians, some even as charismatic preachers with a growing following. This required the most pious to struggle to read the Bible, offering them a moral equality to their supposedly Christian masters. It is evident that their support of the British was based on their understanding of Biblical scripture, rather than natural rights or the Founding Fathers.

Blacks' love of freedom would always surpass their need for economic security or even the bonds of family. In this revolution, comfort was not what blacks sought. Former Africans found that the British Isles offered an environment which was more conducive to their freedom than any American colony. The possibility of free blacks being returned to slavery, under any circumstance, was dreaded by them throughout the Emancipation Revolution.

This book is also meant to add to our knowledge of Maritime History as best seen through the activities of the Royal Navy in fostering the Emancipation Revolution. Historian Benjamin Quarles has rightly claimed, 'The British were more inclined to use Negros at sea than on land.'[4] The navy and Loyalist privateers and raiders caused the first liberation of significant numbers of enslaved Americans. On its ships, the Royal Navy perpetuated opportunities for blacks to escape and have their freedom protected. Only from the standpoint of these ships can movement between diverging Atlantic societies and communities be seen. The British Isles, the mainland American colonies, the West Indies and West Africa are the geographical setting for this Emancipation Revolution.

Some historians have seen the navy as a corrupting and morally bankrupt organization, not so different from the pirates it had obliterated in the early eighteenth century.[5] On land, sailors were known to be dangerous to civilians, actually rioting in favor of their prostitutes and taverns where they resided in dissipation. Some reformers saw the navy's impress service to seize sailors as abusive.

Here a different picture of the maritime world will be presented. Featured will be relationships between Britain's maritime captains and their crews, which contained slave and free blacks. To blacks, the Royal Navy offered opportunities. At sea they were not discriminated against because sailors of diverse race and origin had to work together, developing a common respect for the captain and their ship's preservation, forming a unified ship's company. In this effort, skill was more valued than any skin color. A recent assessment claims that since the Royal Navy 'demanded technical skills, the navy accidently became the most color-blind institution in Europe'.[6]

The history of religion also plays a part in our narrative. Evangelism did not undermine any existing churches like the established Anglican Church, but it did radically reform them. It allowed unordained black preachers to appear among slaves and inspire them to become Christians and run away to freedom. Evangelism also appeared in the Royal Navy, the result of officers becoming convinced that it improved the discipline, literacy and quality of their crews. Some officers who were humanitarians acted as early abolitionists. They were exposed to anti-slavery literature and became supporters of black freedom, especially when they shipped refugees to various parts of the British Empire. Overall, this evangelistic upheaval is not usually treated as part of the War for Independence, but here it will be shown as a significant transatlantic movement, causing the need for moral reform, which inspired the Emancipation Revolution.

Lastly, this account of the Emancipation Revolution is meant to offer a comparative history of the British American Past. Too often, the perspectives of the American War for Independence and the evolving British Empire have been treated as incompatible. This book is as much about American as it is British imperial history. Attempt is made to show American slaveholders' varying convictions, even though emancipation may seem inevitable. America's great planters and Continental generals are seen as perpetuating slavery as a right of property. So also are their West Indies counterparts. As a result of the War for Independence, 'The institution of chattel slavery was not dead, ... nor would it be for many years to come ... as long as the institution of slavery lasted, the burden of proof would lie with its advocates to show why the statement 'all men are created equal' did not mean precisely what it said: all men, 'white or black'.[7]

PART 1

THE OLD REGIME OF PLANTATION SLAVERY

Chapter 1

Slave Trade in
British and American Ports

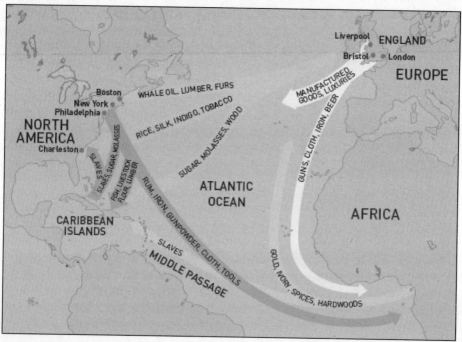

Atlantic Slave Trade.

We start with the forcible migration of thousands of black Africans across the Atlantic Ocean to be enslaved for work on plantations in the West Indies and the North American mainland. The trade involved Britons and British Americans and was regarded as a mainstay of their ports and maritime economies. In the seventeenth century, a triangular trade had developed in British ports like London and Bristol by which ships left Britain and sailed to West Africa carrying arms and goods desired by African kings to be exchanged for African captives.[1] The European traders went no further than the African coast where factories had been established by Africans, who fed these posts with people who they had violently taken from the African interior. From there, slavers sailed with their human cargo to the Americas (the infamous

Middle Passage) where slaves were sold to white colonials to produce plantation staples like sugar, molasses, tobacco and wheat. These commodities were purchased for the return voyage to be sold in the British Isles. The entire voyage lasted between nine and twelve months.

As the eighteenth century developed, other British and colonial ports like Liverpool or Newport entered into this trade. American plantation owners regarded the enslaved Africans as their personal property, to be made into field hands as productive as possible. They sold and separated slaves from their family and friends at will, and punished them for infractions by the lash, or worse.

Africans were certainly not passive victims of the slave trade. Remembering his suffering in being forcibly taken from Africa as a child, Quobna Cugoano wrote in 1787, 'Every man that has any claim … to the name of Christian knows that the base treatment which the African Slaves undergo ought to be abolished and that … the iniquitous traffic of slavery, can nowhere, or in any degree, be admitted.'[2] On the slave ships, many slaves refused food, tried to throw themselves overboard, or sought to blow up the vessel, thereby choosing death over slavery. They also launched concerted rebellions, in the hope that they could seize the ship and regain their freedom.

Newport's slave trade

Eighteenth-century Newport, Rhode Island had the distinction of being more heavily involved in the slave trade than any other American colonial port.[3]

Actually, all the merchants located on Rhode Island's Narragansett Bay participated in the slave trade, including Providence's Brown family. The trade required rum distilled in Newport from molasses imported from the Caribbean. This liquid currency was used to purchase slaves on the African coast, which then were sold in the Caribbean or American colonies. Rum was in great demand in Africa, giving Newport an advantage over British competition from Bristol or Liverpool, whose merchants offered fabrics or manufactures in trade for slaves. Newport's shipbuilding expanded to support the trade so that it was constructing five times as much tonnage as its rival Boston. Newport's slave trade vessels were swift and small because slaves had to be collected rapidly at several African factories and then exported immediately to reach a market without the impediments of sickness, injury or rebellion. By 1774, the trade had affected Newport's population as it was one-ninth black, a high percentage for a New England community. Also, the number of adult males involved in the trade or lost at the sea was high, so the Newport's sex ratio was heavily in favor of women. While women were brought up to be dependent on their men, the absence of husbands on slaving voyages forced wives to be independent in making day-to-day decisions for their households.

Charleston's slave trade

Colonial South Carolina needed slaves for plantations growing rice and indigo (processed to make a blue dyestuff), the staples for trade from Charleston to the wider world. It became the British American mainland's largest entrepot for slaves, taking a quarter of all slaves imported into the colonies. From 1751 to 1775 over 56,000 slaves were brought from Africa for the colony's plantations.[4]

Approaching 12,000 souls, Charleston was the largest city in the Southern colonies and the wealthiest in the mainland colonies, with elegant planter and merchant houses; its families were interrelated through marriage. The city was built on a peninsula between the Ashley and Cooper Rivers, with the port on the latter river. To reach the port, ships had to enter the harbor's mouth, which was obstructed by a bar, then navigate through an extensive expanse protected by occasional fortifications. On Sullivan's Island, slaves were washed then rubbed with beeswax to look their best and be sold to the highest bidder at the public vendues held on the wharves along the Cooper River. The rivers offered access to the immediate interior and along them were plantations, growing the exports which were the source of city's wealth. It was no accident that over half the city's population was black and that the plantations continued to need more slaves. In contrast to the other American ports, it had a decidedly West Indies flavor, as it had been settled in part from Barbados and the bulk of its slaves came from the islands. Ultimately, 6,000 blacks would outnumber whites in Charleston, but since the slaves' mortality rate was high, the plantations would require a continued import of slaves.

Liverpool's slave trade

The first slave ship left the port of Liverpool in 1696, but the business only exploded after 1740, when the town's merchants aggressively searched the African coast for new sources of slaves. The slave trade benefited from the building of the first enclosed wet dock in 1715, which allowed ships to berth against a quay and load irrespective of the River Mersey's tides. For the next half century, Liverpool would become responsible for 80 per cent of the slaving voyages from British ports. Liverpool's merchants, captains and sailors forcibly transported more than a million and a half Africans across the Atlantic to the plantations of mainland America and the Caribbean Islands. By the end of the eighteenth century, as many ports had ceased trading, Liverpool accounted for 46 per cent of the entire transatlantic slave trade.

With its location on the River Mersey leading to the Irish Sea and beyond, Liverpool's later eighteenth-century success was built on its lower shipping costs. Crucially, seamen were available as they already were a large portion of Liverpool's workforce. In 1760 there were 4,870 seamen in a total population of 25,787 and by 1773, 6,000 seamen existed in a population of almost 35,000.[5] Its merchants were also willing to illicitly supply the Spanish colonies in America with slaves.

Liverpool's merchant oligarchy supported the slave trade continuously for many generations. One of the leading Liverpool merchant houses was headed by Foster Cunliffe. He would be mayor of Liverpool three times. It helped that Foster and his sons, Robert and Ellis, were zealous supporters of the Hanover dynasty, and rendered military service during the uprising of Bonnie Prince Charlie in 1745, the king rewarding them with knighthoods. They came to dominate the slave trade in many parts of America, especially providing slaves for the Chesapeake tobacco trade, and had ships plying between the Chesapeake and River Mersey, with stops at Madeira, the coast of Africa and the West Indies. Most of their slaving voyages went to Barbados or Jamaica, but on the way back to Liverpool some stopped in the Chesapeake. They supplied other commodities besides slaves, their largest import into the Chesapeake Eastern Shore was actually salt. They also offered indentured servants and convicts under judicial sentence.

Cunliffe created a trading hub on the Chesapeake's Eastern Shore with a large number of retail stores.[6] They aimed at supplying Oxford, Maryland's shipwrights with articles needed for the construction and equipment of vessels. The families of the workmen in the shipyards were furnished with necessities from their stores, creating another source of gain. The Liverpool firm was a customer as it bought ships from the surrounding shipyards. It had factories, as their warehouses and stores were called, seated along the shores of the Chesapeake and its tributaries. In 1738, Liverpool's Robert Morris was placed in charge of the principal factory at Oxford. Besides this factory, subsidiaries were placed under his supervision, conducted by factors who were responsible to him and drew their supplies from his store. After the mid-century, the Chesapeake's slave trade began to falter, not through any fault of Cunliffe, but because conditions were so healthy that slave women were now bearing enough offspring to fill labor needs. When Foster Cunliffe died in 1758, his sons decided to withdraw from the Chesapeake as it was no longer profitable. In the future, Robert Morris's son and namesake would be important as a financier to Congress during the War for Independence.

Whitehaven's slave trade

To the north of Liverpool on the Irish Sea, Whitehaven's port was only moderately involved in the slave trade and had ceased to be involved before the War for Independence. From 1710 to 1769, it sent 69 slave voyages, carrying about 14,000 slaves. Briefly then, Whitehaven ranked fifth in the number of slave voyages, after London, Liverpool, Bristol and Lancaster. Whitehaven vessels were outfitted to go to West Africa with goods that would be traded for slaves. These ships would then take slaves to sell in America, returning to Whitehaven with rum, sugar, tobacco and wood. Investors at Whitehaven were established merchants diversifying their Atlantic commercial activities because competition from Glasgow merchants was cutting into their profits from tobacco trade with Virginia and Maryland. The slave trade was thus an alternative investment opportunity, not the fundamental basis of Whitehaven's trade. In the late 1740s, Whitehaven merchants also faced renewed competition in their French and Dutch markets.

Exceptionally, in 1758, Whitehaven merchant Anthony Bacon was contracted by the British government to provision the forts crucial to the slave trade in Senegal, West Africa, which had recently been won from the French. Bacon actually managed this contract from London and continued to be involved in provisioning the forts until 1778. Whitehaven merchant Walter Lutwidge was most involved in the slave trade, purchasing slaves in Angola in the 1730s, but later he and others sent their slave voyages from nearby Liverpool, explaining that 'people here being strangers to it'.[7] Whitehaven ships then went to the Gold and Bonny Coasts to obtain larger consignments of slaves. Most Whitehaven ships confined their sales to the established slave markets of Jamaica and Barbados. Whitehaven families like the Lowthers and Senhouses acquired West Indies plantations with slaves in Barbados as a result of the trade. The Jefferson family purchased a plantation in Antigua to assure it would have supplies of rum. An enameled goblet in Whitehaven commemorates the launching in 1763 of the *King George* on which is inscribed, 'Success to the African Trade of Whitehaven'. However, in only a few years, the slave trade ended as Whitehaven merchants were unable to complete with Liverpool slavers and found other enterprises more profitable.

Glasgow

Glasgow has to be put alongside Liverpool and Whitehaven as cities that profited from the slave trade. It was not so much a matter of slaving voyages; surprisingly most came from smaller Scottish places like Kirkcudbright and Dumfries.[8] However, the Union of 1707 opened the English colonies to Scots and Scottish enterprise, which was protected by the Royal Navy. On the River Clyde, which emptied into the Firth of Clyde, the navigation had to be improved to allow shipping to reach Glasgow. Its rising connection with the tobacco trade in the Chesapeake and the city's 'tobacco lords' is well documented, but its connection with the slave-owning sugar plantations in Jamaica and the West Indies is less known. It was common for the younger sons of wealthy Scots to migrate to these plantations in the hope of making a fortune to bring back to Scotland. Capital for the plantations came from Glasgow banks and private investors. Families from Glasgow and the surrounding area such as the Smiths of Jordanhill, the Stirlings of Keir, the Cunninghams of Craigend, the Glassfords of Dougalston and the Speirs of Elderslie were heavily involved in the sugar and tobacco industries. Investment in Glasgow's emerging tanneries, bottleworks, breweries, and iron works came from these profits. Atlantic-wide slave markets were vital to Scottish herring fishermen and linen producers.

Sailors on slavers

From these ports, many sailors began their career in a slaver. Slave ships had a high rate of crew per ton as they had to be large in number to control the slaves. Typical of the sailors was John Newton, born in London's East End at Wapping in 1725, the son of John Newton the Elder, a shipmaster in the Mediterranean service, and Elizabeth, the only daughter of Simon Scatliff, a London instrument maker.[9] At age 11, John first went to sea with his father, sailing six voyages before his father retired in 1742. His father made plans for him to work at a sugar cane plantation in Jamaica, but Newton avoided it, instead signing on with a merchant ship sailing to the Mediterranean Sea.

Now age 18, while going to visit friends, Newton was pressed into the Royal Navy as he was an experienced seaman. He became a midshipman aboard the *Harwich*. When he tried to desert, he was disciplined in front of the crew, by being stripped to the waist, tied to a grating and receiving eight dozen lashes, also being reduced to the rank of a common seaman. He initially contemplated murdering the captain and committing suicide by throwing himself overboard, but he recovered, both physically and mentally. Later, as the *Harwich* was en route to India, his captain got rid of who he felt was a trouble maker, by exchanging him for a prime seaman, transferring him to *Pegasus*, a slave ship bound for West Africa. The ship carried goods to Africa and traded them for slaves to be shipped to the Caribbean and North America. Out of the navy, Newton was now a seaman in the slave trade.

Newton's hostility to authority made it impossible for him to get along with his ships' captains. In 1745, the *Pegasus*'s captain left him in West Africa with Amos Clowe, an unscrupulous slave dealer. Clowe took him to the African coast and gave him a wife, Princess Peye of the Sherbro people. She mistreated him as much as she did her other slaves. Newton saw this period as the time he was 'once an infidel and libertine, a servant of slaves in West Africa'.[10] Three years later, he was rescued by a sea captain who had been commissioned by his father to search for him and he returned to England on the merchant ship *Greyhound*, with a cargo of beeswax. Thus, he had become a mariner with a knowledge of the West African slave trade.

In 1748, Newton came back to Liverpool and found his father's friend Joseph Manesty, who gave him a position as first mate aboard his slaver *Brownlow*, bound for the West Indies via the coast of Guinea. In two years, he returned to England and he made three voyages as captain of the Liverpool slavers *Duke of Argyle* and *African*. On these voyages, he feared slave insurrection, placing carriage guns on his deck to overawe them and punishing 'them with the thumb screws and afterwards put them in neck yokes'.[11] After suffering a severe stroke in 1754, however, Newton gave up seafaring, while continuing to invest in Manesty's slaving operations.

At this point, Newton came to understand the importance of spiritual accountability and friendship. Now in Liverpool, he spent seven frustrating years in the company of Calvinist Baptists and other Dissenters, striving towards ordination as an Anglican priest. He organized a regular Sunday evening meeting for a few friends to discuss spiritual matters. His first literary venture was entitled 'Thoughts on Religious Associations'. His new-found belief in Christ would connect him to other evangelistic Christians in London.

Ordained, Newton became the parson of a church in Olney, Bucks, close enough to visit and form a friendship with the Wilberforce family in London. His tales of the sea also made a great impression on bright 11-year-old Billy Wilberforce. Despite his experiences in West Africa and Liverpool, it would be a while before Newton came to believe that the slave trade should be abolished.

Others in the slave trade

Newton was not alone in being caught up with the slave trade in his early years. In America, many future Continental Navy captains began their maritime career navigating a slave ship. In September 1764, Captain Esek Hopkins took command of the slave ship *Sally*, owned by the influential Nicholas Brown and Company of Providence. Hopkins had no prior experience in sailing a slaver and as a result the fifteen-month voyage would end with the death of 109 out of 196 slaves he carried.[12] When *Sally* arrived in the West Indies, the surviving African captives were in such poor condition that most sold below expectation. Hopkins' failure with the slaver contributed to the Brown brothers reconsidering their participation in Rhode Island's slave trade.

Another was a 16-year-old Scot, John Paul, who had sailing skills, but like most seamen he was out of work when the Seven Years' War ended. In 1764, he went into the slave trade as third mate on the *King George* of Whitehaven. Two years later he was at the end of 'the Middle Passage' in Jamaica. He was now first mate of the brigantine *Two Friends* of Kingston, Jamaica. Only 50 feet long with a crew of six, it had carried seventy-seven Africans to Jamaica. The smell from 'black-birders', as the slavers were called, could be detected for 10 miles distance. When paid off for this voyage in Jamaica, Paul quitted the slave traffic calling it an 'abominable trade'.[13] Left in the Caribbean where he might have dissipated, he was saved by being given free passage home by a friendly Scot on the new brigantine *John* of Kirkcudbright.

Possible nursery of seamen

Defenders of the slave trade argued that it should be retained because it was the great nursery of seamen. Advocates of this idea felt that the slavers' crews provided the navy with a ready supply of seamen, especially when war broke out as they were immediately needed. Certainly, the careers of Newton, Hopkins and Jones were examples of this contention, requiring a review of mariners' conditions on slavers.

What actually happened in wartime, however, was the demand for mariners caused their pay rate to rise, making the merchant ship's higher wage better than could be obtained from the Royal Navy.[14] For young singles without a family, it was an attractive option – but it left the navy with a continued scarcity of sailors.

Furthermore, from 1729, mariners were protected from abuses as British merchant ships were required to offer mariners like Newton or Paul a contract, which stipulated wages and terms of service and was signed or marked by the mariner.[15] This contract made it more difficult for captains and owners to cheat the mariner. The main concern of sailors was their wages. While wages might be accumulated on a monthly basis, the actual payment was governed by the maxim that no pay would be released until the cargo had been sold. Slave ships were considered to be trading port to port, especially if they followed the triangular trade pattern. This meant that sailors could leave if they desired at the second delivery port, where the slaves were sold, usually in the West Indies or the mainland colonies. Sailors would then be paid, but would not necessarily do the return leg of the journey to the British Isles leaving their ship short of hands.

In a slaver, fitting himself out was the sailor's responsibility. His captain cut into his pay constantly, deducting for clothing, tobacco and spirits, as well as infractions like a chicken being chased overboard. If a ship were wrecked or captured and the cargo lost, it was unlikely he would receive any pay. As a sailor, he did have the option of suing his employers in the High Court of Admiralty for wages lost – but court cases took time and were expensive.

Slavers had other drawbacks, which make it impossible to think of them as a source of sailors. As seen, captains and their crews were disgusted by the responsibility for the human cargo, involving them in the death of excessive numbers of Africans on the Middle Passage. The captain was responsible for keeping alive as many as possible, while once landed, the crew was delegated to prepare them for sale. A captain or sailor experienced first-hand how dangerous life on a slave ship really was. Crew mortality in the triangular trade was eight times higher than those who simply sailed back and forth between England and Caribbean. It was claimed that 'a mortality among [the] crew in the middle passage is a pleasant thing to a Guinea captain … it saves the ship a great expense in wages'.[16] When the slaver *Enterprise* left Jamaica it had only twenty of the original forty-six crew members that had left Liverpool: nine had died, eight had run, one had been impressed by the Royal Navy, and eight had been discharged in Jamaica. While the Royal Navy normally had to press for seamen, desertions from the slave ships to enlist in the navy were so strong in the West Indies, that the press was unnecessary.

Slavers and their crews spent much time in the West Indies, a drawback in itself. Officers and crews alike tried to circumvent sailing in the warm waters and tropical shores of the Indies because of the risk of fever. On account of its climate, a crew could not be worked as hard and the usual drinking had to be strictly limited because of heat exhaustion. The teredo worm played havoc with the ship's wooden sheathing as weeds accumulated, cutting down the speed of the vessel. The hurricane season, lasting from the end of July to the beginning of November, forced ships to escape from the Indies altogether, heading for North America or Europe.

Still, for those sailors who needed an opportunity, especially if they were out of work, they could gravitate to the nearest slave trade port. Black mariners were actually employed on slavers. From 1748 to 1807, documents show that many seamen originally from Africa and the West Indians served on slave ships originating in Liverpool, Bristol and Rhode Island. It is assumed that they were free blacks.[17] Those who felt that the slave trade was nursery for seamen would have to navigate many contradictions.

Chapter 2

The Rise of American Plantation Slavery

The slave trade was mixed with trade in staples produced on plantations, such as sugar, tobacco, wheat and rice. By the end of the century, planters found that an investment in African slave labor was their best choice. Expanding plantations would depend upon field slaves, who lived in designated quarters and were restricted from leaving the plantation.[1]

The labor transition

In the Chesapeake, the transformation from white to black labor on plantations came about gradually. In the seventeenth century, the main source of a labor was white indentured servants along with a few slave and free blacks. The line between white servants and African slaves or freemen was fluid, so that white and black laborers commonly lived and worked together, and formed sexual unions. Mixed-race children born to white mothers were considered free because they took the social status of their mothers, a principle of Maryland's slave law, which followed Virginia's law of 1662.[2] As a result, families of free people of color were formed by unions of white women and African men. In 1681, the Maryland legislature passed a law which released white servant women and their mixed-race children from slavery, if the marriage was permitted or encouraged by their master.

Eleven years later, however, the Maryland legislature changed its attitude, now enacting a law to promote plantation slavery. White women who had children by slaves were to be punished. The case of Mary Chambers, an indentured white servant of William Frisby of Kent County, is illuminating. In November 1716, she appeared in court and confessed to having two 'Mollatoe Children' by a 'Negro'.[3] As they were not married, the court ordered her to serve an additional seven years on her indenture and bound her children, a boy and a girl, to her master until the age of 31. Only then were her mulatto children to be free.

Free black labor now faced a crisis. Leaving Maryland became the chief means for free blacks to improve their lot. They migrated to avoid planter efforts to return and hold them in some form of bondage. Free black families were able to migrate to nearby Delaware or North Carolina, where land was cheaper and they could afford to purchase a farm. By their master's will in 1747, the black Gibbs family was left 444 acres in Queen Anne's County, Maryland. However, only two members of the family remained in the county and still owned 50 acres each in 1783, while the others had sold their land and moved to Delaware. Even free blacks who had been provided for by their masters were drawn from Maryland by outside economic opportunities. The city of Norfolk, Virginia was a destination because its population and maritime enterprise offered exceptional urban possibilities.

Maryland planters now began to buy African slaves in the West Indies, from Bristol, London, Liverpool or New England slavers. Male slaves were more expensive than indentured servants, but they lasted a lifetime. Gradually, improvement in conditions on slave ships lowered the cost of slaves. Still, a single slave was far too expensive for the average Maryland tenant to afford – but this did not dampen the market for slaves as the wealthier planters bought more and more.

The plantation

Plantation slavery was not a monolithic institution the lives of slaves varied and they changed over time. In the century before the War for Independence, slave life expanded from a state of isolation to community. At first, the number of slaves imported from Africa had been small and overwhelmingly male as they toiled in the alien environment of a small rustic plantation. This changed by the 1700s as the numbers of native-born slaves grew, the gender ratio became more balanced, and on larger plantations they could interact to establish family and communal ties. Thus on the plantation a distinctive African American culture was ultimately created.

On Chesapeake plantations, African slaves lived in their quarters in groups of twenty or thirty, and this considerable size helped to ensure the persistence of African cultural traditions. The overseers saw to it that life was tedious and physically demanding.[4] From sunrise to sunset, they raised cash crops of tobacco, corn and wheat, and tended livestock and the master's kitchen garden as well as their own patches. Some fished and worked as watermen, while women performed menial tasks such as cooking, cleaning, sewing and washing. Some slaves resisted their bondage by refusing to work and running away.

In the plantation, each quarter consisted of a grouping of several slave houses. Plantations did not have the individual log cabins that we see in the movies that portray the slave quarter. Usually, slaves were housed in flimsy pole or wood frame barracks-like structures, which forced slaves to live together, regardless of their families. The presence of numerous pits under the floor for food and personal storage reflects the lack of family relationships within these structures. In the plantation main house, no room was set aside for domestics, leaving them to find shelter in a detached kitchen or stable.[5]

For field hands, the plantation workday lasted from dawn until sunset, with the exception of Sundays, Christmas, Easter, Michaelmas and Court days. Women and children joined men in the fields. Coupled with their grueling work schedules, few slaves had adequate shelter, clothing and nutrition to help them combat disease. Meals were usually limited to Indian corn and a bit of salt to form hominy.

Slaves were restricted to the plantation of their master and could not travel without their master's permission. Still, masters had trained male slaves in trades such as carpentry, cabinetmaking, masonry and mechanics. These slaves could be hired out by their master and even were permitted to earn money for themselves. Hiring out his slaves for these crafts or even field work allowed a master to gain extra income when his slaves were idle or his crops had failed.

Slaves as status symbols

Among the earliest visuals of slaves, we find two Maryland portraits of young male slaves and their equally young masters. One is of Henry Darnall III by Justus Engelhart Kuhn, *c.* 1710, the other of Charles Calvert by John Hesselius in 1761. The portraits were meant to be of the masters with the slaves in a subservient position to the side. The presence of the slave defines the paintings as being from the New World, while the ostentatious display of wealth in clothing and surroundings show the success of the slave-supported plantation. The paintings celebrate the practice of slaves being given to young masters to grow up with them, forming a bond of mutual support. Still, the slave in the Darnall portrait has a silver collar, a typical expression of New World slavery. He is holding a dead bird, which presumably Darnell had killed with the bow and arrow in his hands. It may appear that house domestics like these boys had an easier lot than those in the field; however, 'fieldwork had a beginning and ending each day, but in the plantation house, slaves were always at the beck and call and under the watchful eye of a master'.[6] (See Back Cover)

Free blacks of mixed blood

The only pre-War for Independence enumeration of Southern free blacks was in Maryland and it showed that free blacks were largely mixed bloods. In the words of a historian, 'the free negro caste was not only light-skinned but getting lighter.'[7] The census of 1755 counted about 1,800 Negro freemen, 80 per cent of whom were mixed bloods. Maryland masters had freed the sons and daughters of these unions so that free blacks comprised about 4 per cent of the colony's black population, but less than 2 per cent of its free population. It is unlikely that the free population of other Southern colonies could match these figures, so that it seems the free black population in the eighteenth-century South was declining.

Slavery in the mainland North

North of the Mason-Dixon Line, dividing Pennsylvania from Maryland, slaves were fewer and not concentrated in large numbers on plantations. Instead, slaves were dispersed among households, the norm being only one or two slaves per household. In New England in 1774, Rhode Island had the most slaves, with Newport having one to four blacks in 28 per cent of its households, while in Providence they appeared in only 17 per cent of households.[8] In New York, where some estates were as large as plantations, the labor force was chiefly white tenants. Slavery was thus limited to households, rather than plantations. In New York City in 1703, 37 per cent of the households had one to four slaves, while in two Hudson Valley counties, 21 per cent of its households had that number. By 1775, exceptionally outside of New York City, a quarter of western Long Island and 20 per cent of Staten Island were black.

Slavery's presence in the Hudson Valley spanned the river to Albany and even further north. In 1698, slaves represented only 1 per cent of Albany County's population, but by 1756 they were above 15 per cent, a figure allowing them to surpass New York City as the county with the greatest number of slaves. It was in rural areas outside of Albany that they were most numerous. By the 1740s, two Schuyler family properties, one immediately north of Albany at

Schuyler Flatts and the other on the borderland at Saratoga, numbered their slaves in figures ranging from seven to sixty-five. A seasonal rhythm in the slaves' work existed; in summer, the kitchen was moved from the house and a temporary wooden hut constructed, where slaves lived and gathered until the weather became cold. Producing the wheat staple required a ballooning of field hands during spring planting and late summer harvesting. The exposed location of Saratoga would invite French Canadian raiders to attack it and carry off slaves to be sold in Montreal. The eventual heir of the Saratoga estate would be Philip Schuyler, a major general in the Continental Army during the War for Independence.

Jamaica

In contrast, Britain's largest Caribbean sugar island was Jamaica, made up in the eighteenth century of extensive plantations worked by slaves, with the Jamaica Assembly dominated by the planters and a governor, who had minimal support from London. Jamaica's slave plantations dated from the 1680s and lasted into the nineteenth century. The triangular trade pattern made islands like Jamaica and the mainland colonies economically interdependent, a condition that was only severed after the War for Independence. The planter society that dominated Caribbean life was durable, even if its ideals were not accepted in Britain or many mainland colonies. These planters did side with Britain in the War for Independence, but their loyalty still proved to be out of step with British abolition.

With a population of 210,000 in 1776, Jamaica was Britain's fifth largest American colony, after Virginia, Maryland, Pennsylvania and Massachusetts.[9] It had most of the British institutions of the mainland: common law, a representative assembly, a militia, the Anglican Church divided into the parishes. These institutions worked similarly to those of the mainland Southern colonies. The assembly steadily rose to power at the expense of the royal governor. It was the great planters who controlled the assembly as well as the courts and parish vestries. They excluded the vast majority of the population in slaves from suffrage and due process because they felt the slaves were too brutish to be governed by English laws. They curtailed the militia because it interfered with sugar production, becoming dependent on Royal Navy and British army for defense. Dominating the vestries, they prevented the Anglican clergy in Jamaica or Britain from Christianizing or educating their slaves. Thus, Jamaica was extremely stratified between rich and poor as wealthy planters dominated a society of black bondmen.

Bermuda

A unique household slavery appeared in the midst of the Atlantic Ocean, in the British islands of Bermuda. They were engaged in trade from Europe, the West Indies, the North American mainland and Africa. Here it is argued 'the patterns of slaveholding and ways of making a living were unlike those of any other English colony'.[10] Before the War for Independence, the amount of land was so scarce that it had been impossible to establish a plantation economy and the population had risen to only 11,000. The acreage covered by one of its nine parishes was often less than that of a typical Virginia or South Carolina plantation. Still in the 1700s, the slave population rose modestly from 38 per cent of the population to 47 per cent. This was not the result of the importation of slaves, but rather the fact in the words of a governor, 'The blacks breed much'. Here was a healthy condition among slaves that would only later be reached first by the Chesapeake colonies and then others on the mainland.

A majority of Bermuda's black and white males were mariners or in related enterprises like shipbuilding. Censuses counted the rare category of 'Males absent at sea'. As many as one-third of white males were gone for months at a time, partially explaining the lower fertility rate of white women. Black males were often absent at sea and their disregard for the mores of white marriage meant that they had many partners. With the small population, white men had to take slave women as wives. Thus, Bermuda had a stable, but mixed, society of whites, blacks, mulattos, Indians and mustees. Distinctively, it was a largely maritime rather than agricultural community, where seafaring slaves were numerous.

Plantation mariners

Maritime opportunities for slaves are important because they show potential for them to be ultimately involved in the Royal Navy's wartime commitments. While the Bermuda situation was exceptional, conditions in the Chesapeake did eventually offer slaves a chance to develop maritime skills. 'The natives of the Chesapeake tidewater were part landsmen and part watermen, a combination that is not surprising in a region composed of alternative strips of land and water.'[11] In the seventeenth century, few whites claimed to be mariners in the Chesapeake because of a lack of trade, competition from the Northern colonies for sailors, and the conviction that tobacco planting was a surer way to prosperity. However, the crews of small sloops in the rivers were often made up of slaves or a few free blacks. With opportunities expanding for employment outside of a plantation's field work, a new segment of black society emerged that was a source of the earliest watermen.

As the number of slaves on the plantations grew, some slaves manned craft which were no larger than a dugout canoe. In the 1700s, the appearance of ferries and packets also increased the demand for them. Hired scows operated between Norfolk and nearby Portsmouth requiring the hiring of blacks to run them.

What the masters did not realize was that in West Africa, even as the slave emerged, natives were adept swimmers, divers, canoe makers and canoeists.[12] They had lived along riverbanks, near lakes, or close to the ocean and became proficient in maritime skills, while even incorporating water into spiritual understandings of the world. Transported to the Americas, Africans carried with them these skills and cultural values. They did not need the skills of Amerindians to build canoes. The aquatic abilities of slaves of African descent was no accident.

Chesapeake plantation mariners were different from those in the larger port cities of Boston, New York and Philadelphia, where black mariners were attracted as they offered opportunities for freedom.[13] The few Chesapeake places where mariners resided, such as Portsmouth, Annapolis, Chestertown and Oxford, were too small for the incidents of an urban crowd. It also meant that most blacks were slaves, so that the plantations' requirements rather than those of the towns drove the need for mariners and watermen in the South.

Still from the planters' standpoint, 'The mobility and worldliness of sailors were for the most part corrosive of bound labor.'[14] Slaves ran away to ships and captains were pleased to have skilled watermen and asked no questions. Although they constituted only 2 per cent of the plantation workforce, they made up a quarter of the non-field runaways advertised in Virginia and South Carolina newspapers. In 1771, Sam, a mulatto sailor in the Chesapeake, ran off after distributing stolen broadcloth to the crew 'in order to bribe them to secrecy'; his master felt that 'some person in want of hands might be induced to engage him'.

Black watermen in South Carolina's Low Country plantations contrasted with those in the Chesapeake. Segregation between blacks and whites was stronger, so that all-slave crews predominated on ships, while the densely populated black countryside gave slaves more autonomy. Planters tried to prevent intercourse between their plantation slaves and boat slaves. Slave trader and rice planter Henry Laurens warned his overseer at Mepkin Plantation on the Cooper River, 'Don't let the boat Negros amongst the Plantation Negros,' as he viewed his boat slaves as a potentially disruptive influence on other slaves.[15] In 1767, South Carolinians objected to Charleston's comptroller of customs issuing permits to boat slaves as, 'several of which are to common Negro slaves' and are creating 'a Shelter for illicit traffick'. When the War for Independence began, Carolina's planters would urge draconian punishments against disaffected black watermen, especially those who were harbor pilots.

Chapter 3

Fear of Slave Insurrection

In the eighteenth century, insurrections by armed slaves happened throughout the British colonies. In the mainland colonies, it has been contended, 'white fears about potential slave rebelliousness assumed near-hysterical proportions'.[1] These rebellions were brutally put down by whites, but, in fact, most of those in the mainland colonies were less intense when compared to the situation in Jamaica. Throughout the mainland colonies, the authorities firmed up their control over slaves by drafting slave codes to prevent insurrections. These slave insurrections were the early signs of discontent with the planters' plantation regime, just as the Boston Tea party and the *Gaspee* Affair foretold the movement for independence. When the War for Independence came, the planters in the Southern colonies would be as concerned with slave gatherings causing upheaval as the political ideals of 'no taxation without representation'.

Actually, slave insurrections happened in some Northern mainland colonies as readily as in the South. New York experienced supposedly black plots to burn the city in 1702, 1712 and 1741.[2] In 1712, twenty slaves set fire to a building and then ambushed the whites who came to extinguish it, killing nine of them with knives, axes and guns. Investigation led to seventy slaves being taken into custody and twenty-five, including women and Indian slaves, were convicted. Only thirteen were hanged, three were publicly burned at the stake, one was starved to death in chains, and one was broken on the wheel. Six others committed suicide to escape the prescribed torture.

In March–April 1741, white New Yorkers again panicked with the burning of Fort George, including Lieutenant Governor George Clarke's mansion, Admiral Sir Peter Warren's house, and two storehouses. Recalling the uprising of 1712, it appeared to whites that the slaves wanted to kill them and take over the city. Sixty-six confessions were extracted from terrified slaves and eighteen slaves and four whites were sentenced to be tortured and hanged; thirteen slaves were condemned to be burned at the stake and another seventy were transported to the West Indies, the usual means of ridding New York of unruly slaves.

South Carolina and Georgia

Not to be outdone by New York, South Carolina experienced the Stono Revolt of 1739, which was less of conspiracy and more of an uprising against their masters, culminating in a bloody skirmish.[3] The slaves escaped from their plantations and marched towards freedom in Spanish St Augustine, Florida, with which South Carolina was now at war. Eventually the marauding slaves numbered nearly 100, who confiscated arms, ravaged houses and killed twenty-four

white family members. In a short confrontation, South Carolina militia fired a volley at the slaves, wounding many and then knifed at least forty, cutting off their heads and displaying them at every mile post. Some slaves escaped into the woods or returned to their plantations, but about thirty more were shot, hanged or gibbeted alive.

Major incidents like Stono were uncommon in eighteenth-century South Carolina. Still, for several years after the Stono outbreak, the safety of the white minority and the viability of their plantation system hung in the balance. In the year following Stono, a conspiracy originated between the Ashley and Cooper Rivers, when between 150 and 200 slaves gathered in defiance.[4] They lacked arms and rather than heading toward Georgia, they aimed to enter Charleston and break open a store house of arms. Their numbers gave them confidence, but unfortunately it was also their undoing as one of their number warned the authorities and was rewarded with a new wardrobe and cash. Sixty-seven slaves were brought to trial and as many as fifty hanged to serve as an example. Slaves continued to escape from their plantations and survived because they were inaccessible to militia or slave patrols.

Not until the 1760s did these incidents lead to temporary runaway communities developing in South Carolina and Georgia. The governor of Georgia wrote to his counterpart in South Carolina about a group of forty escaped slaves that had existed 'for some time past' in the Savannah River swamp on the South Carolina side, who 'have frequently in the night time come over on this side & killed Cattle and Robbed Several of the plantations on the South Bank of the River'. A party of militia eventually found the slaves and after a short skirmish came upon their camp, described as 'a Square consisting of four Houses 17 feet long & 14 wide ... the kettles were upon the fire boiling rice & about 15 bushels of rough Rice, Blankets Potts Pails Shoes Axes & many other Tools'.[5] This camp was destroyed but most of the slaves escaped into the swamp and regrouped at a different location.

Actually, these runaway communities should be considered impermanent because the slaves regarded them as a temporary expedient. The runaways saw their escape as a means to obtain better conditions with their master or to look for a new master altogether. Masters were able to lure runaways back, treating them as only misguided truants, willing to negotiate to get them back, rather than punish them.[6] At this stage, the key point is that these runaways remained slaves and were willing go back to their home plantation if they were better treated.

Maryland and Virginia

In colonial Maryland and Virginia, small-scale rebellions of runaway slaves were also commonplace. During King George's War in 1746, runaways showed exceptional ingenuity, as they began with no arms and were not sailors, but still were able to cause havoc on the Atlantic Eastern Shore. Here five runaway slaves had escaped from Pennsylvania and roamed the Atlantic coast of Worcester and Accomack Counties.[7] They arrived at Sinepuxent Inlet in a rowboat with only a single broken scythe for a weapon. They seized a sloop, where a crewman testified they spoke 'good English'. Without mariner skills, they ran the sloop aground and rather than trying to free it, they seized another vessel. They eluded a sheriff's posse and moved south in Chincoteague Bay. On the way, they captured a New England vessel, which they proposed to use for an escape to sea with the help of its crew members. When the New England captives were sent to obtain water for the voyage, they alerted the countryside and several canoes of armed men descended on the runaways. Surrounded, they put up a fierce defense and only when their ammunition was gone did they jump overboard. Four were taken, while one drowned, and the survivors were placed in Accomack Jail, where they ultimately faced execution.

Most runaways actually did not go far and were soon caught.[8] The lack of towns meant that they could not melt into an urban population. Usually, they attempted to survive in an area with which they were familiar, where they might find support from their own relatives or friends. This was often in marginal areas of marsh and swamp along the rivers or in the islands, where they might eke out a living. In the face of this hardship, some chose to return to their masters, even though they lost their freedom and faced severe punishment.

Slave codes

To prevent slave insurrections, colonial legislatures drafted and passed slave codes, which were meant to discourage slaves from dangerous activities like gathering, being familiar with arms, running away, or pursuing watermen activities. It is evident that the codes were a reaction to the slaves' actions and in this sense, they had a part in making them.

Both Virginia and South Carolina passed laws 1723 and 1722 respectively, restricting slaves' access to firearms, but exemptions did allow at least one slave to carry a gun for a hunting party. Slaves were also able to carry their masters' arms to or from a militia muster. While laws for the private arming of slaves remained on the books in South Carolina, after 1715, in practice slaves were never armed. The chief reason for failure to exercise these arming laws 'was the overwhelming coercive powers available to individual masters and the white community in general'.[9] White supremacy was a more effective authority than any law to prevent blacks from arming.

Maryland's slave code focused on the prevention of all aspects of slave meetings and conspiring. The 1751 law was aimed at stopping 'the tumultuous Meeting and other Irregularities of Negroes and other Slaves'.[10] It stated that slaves who raised insurrection or poisoned whites, raped white women, or burned houses or storehouses, upon conviction were subject to death without benefit of clergy. Masters would be compensated for slaves condemned to death, while any person killing a fugitive slave was immune from prosecution and again the master was to be compensated. The law also discouraged whites from inciting slaves to run away. Those who caused a slave to leave his master were subject to repay the master or suffer a year in prison. The Maryland Assembly's planters wanted this law to snuff out the possibility of white cooperation with blacks.

In Virginia, the priority of preventing slave insurrection was demonstrated during the Seven Years' War. The House of Burgesses' planters would be inspired to allocate 55 per cent of their 1756 appropriation to the militia in charge of internal security and the control of slaves, while the remainder went to its Virginia Regiment, commanded by George Washington, crucially charged with defending the entire frontier against the French.[11] A year later, 200 of Washington's men were taken and sent to help garrison Charleston, South Carolina, from the possibility of slave insurrections, as South Carolina's provincial companies had been sent to the frontier. Clearly, preventing slave insurrection was far more important than defending the frontier.

FEAR OF SLAVE INSURRECTION

In reaction to the Stono Rebellion, South Carolina passed the Negro Act of 1740 to prevent an insurrection from taking place again. The act directly related to the event. It offered rewards from the public treasury to those (including Indians) who apprehended blacks south of the Savannah River (Georgia) and brought them in alive. For the Indians, special dispensation existed 'for every scalp of a grown negro slave with the two ears taken'.[12] Many of the articles required conviction of a slave before sentencing, but this failed to be enforced with the Stono insurrectionists, so the legislature now declared that every act done to suppress the Stono revolt was lawful forever.

The act asserted the right to search slaves for arms and ammunition; that it was unlawful for slaves to have firearms or offensive weapons; and that slaves involved in insurrection if convicted were punishable by death. Low Country planters feared their plantations would become harbors for fugitive slaves because often no white person resided there, establishing a plantation made up exclusively of slaves. Fines were imposed on masters until they sent someone to take change of the plantation. Finally, slaves were forbidden to 'keep any boat, pettiaguer, or canoe' for their own use because they could receive or conceal stolen goods and 'plot and confederate together, and form conspiracies dangerous to peace and safety'. The act was to be enforced by Charleston's constables, night watch and slave patrol, while in rural areas, by mounted patrols to hunt runaways. When the War for Independence commenced, this act was still in force.

The Southern slave codes were enforced by slave patrols, especially in wartime.[13] Originally taken from the colonial militia at musters, slave patrollers were set apart so that the militia could focus on outside threats from the Spanish, French or Indians, while the patrollers could focus on internal threat of a slave insurrection. They received pay in Virginia and became exempt from militia musters, advantages that critics claimed depleted the militia. Uniquely in Charleston, South Carolina the patrols grew from the town watch. They were composed of respectable middling members of society, often mounted and armed with whips and guns, exerting racial control nocturnally. In practice, they were separate from the militia, constables and sheriffs. Slave patrollers would be asked to perform enhanced duties when the War for Independence came.

Slave codes were not limited to the South. In reaction to New York's slave insurrections, the province passed three slave codes in 1702, 1712 and 1730, the last entitled 'An Act for more effectual preventing and punishing the Conspiracy of Negro and other slaves'.[14] This act of 1730 was necessary because the previous slave codes had become unwieldly and it was necessary to make them simpler. The new act aimed at curtailing the ability of slaves to move or gather, and prevented alcoholic drinking, which was thought to make them destructive. New York City also passed 'A Law for Punishing Slaves who shall Ride Disorderly through the streets'.[15] Its Common Council was specifically concerned to prevent slaves from absenting themselves from their master's house, holding a meeting of more than three slaves, gambling and going about after sunset without a lantern or lighted candle.

British authorities were shocked at the severity of the codes' punishments for blacks. Queen Anne overruled a New Jersey Act modeled on New York's 1702 slave code, because 'the punishment to be inflicted on the Negros is such as never was allowed by or known in the Laws of this Kingdom'.[16] In 1712, New York's Governor Robert Hunter apologized to the Lords of Trade for the ferocity of its act.

The harshness of the written codes did not necessarily reflect their actual use. Historian Eugene Genovese has affirmed: 'The slaveholders did not intend to enforce their severe legislation strictly and considered it a device to be reserved for periods of disquiet and especially for periods of rumored insurrectionary plots.'[17] While this perspective has a measure of truth, it depends upon considerations. We have seen that enforcement of slave codes varied as to whether it was done by slave patrols, a local court, jury, municipal government or state authority. Actually, many slaves accused of breaking these laws never appeared before courts, justice being administered by their masters, proud to do the whipping themselves. Slaves used their hostility to obtain better conditions from their master if they returned to the plantation. More certain is that the severity of the punishment was higher for convicted slaves than for whites involved in the codes. Furthermore, as Genovese himself contends, in time of stress like war such an explanation does not hold, so that the War for Independence is an exception to this rule.

The colonial legislature's planters built these slave codes around a genuine fear of uncontrollable blacks rather than a concern for the loss of life and property in an insurrection. While made in reaction to earlier insurrections, the codes would be dusted off during the War for Independence and used with a renewed intensity.

Jamaica's Maroons

West Indies slave uprisings were as common as those on the mainland, but they were bloodier and not as easily put down because whites were a small minority within a vast population of black slaves. In Jamaica, a major slave insurrection had begun in 1728 and ended in a compromise a decade later.[18] It concerned slaves who had run away from their Spanish masters, and were still independent when the British took over the island from Spain in 1655. The runaways had fled to the mountainous areas, where it was difficult for their owners to

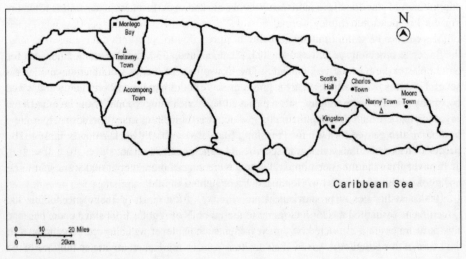

The Jamaica of the Maroons.

catch them in the bush, and they formed their own independent Maroon communities of free black men and women.

As the Jamaican planters imported more slaves from Africa to work in Jamaica's sugar plantations, rebellion by slaves increased. New slaves disappeared and ended up in the mountainous Maroon communities. These Maroon communities increased and, as they were seen by the planters as a constant threat, the Jamaican government decided to put an end to their existence. The First Maroon War was a government campaign that made the Maroons more determined to fight than ever, under the leadership of Cudjoe. By 1732, the Maroons were so successful that Admiral Charles Stewart predicted the entire island 'would be in the possession of the Negros'.[19] Seven years later, after much bloodshed, the government and the Maroons made peace. Freedom of the Maroons was recognized and land was given to them. They were to govern themselves, acting as a buffer between the British planters and their slaves. In return they would support the planters against foreign invasion and would help capture slaves that ran away from plantations and return them to their masters. It was hoped that free black Maroons could live in peace with the planters.

After twenty years of relative calm under these treaties, another rebellion occurred in 1760 between the government and the Maroons. It broke out in April at a plantation in the northern parish of St Mary.[20] These Maroons comprised upwards of 100 Africans from the Gold Coast, newly imported, and their leader was a Coromanti man known as Tacky. The speed of the initial assault enabled the blacks to overpower British forces at Fort Haldane and Port Maria, where they obtained arms and ammunition. They moved to overrun the Heywood's Hall and Esher plantations. By dawn the following morning, hundreds strong, they had fought their way inland, capturing estates and killing white settlers where they found them.

Two days later, the government received news of the destruction and it dispatched detachments from the 74th West India Regiment and from the 49th, together with three companies of black Maroons from Nanny Town, Crawford Town and Scotts Hall. Under the terms of their previous treaty, these Maroons were obliged to assist the British in the suppression of slave uprisings and the recapture of runaways. In addition to rewards for every slave killed or captured, they were also paid 7 pence and 1 half-penny per day, while their officers received 2 shillings and 6 pence.

Tacky's campaign spurred uprisings on estates in the parishes of Westmoreland, St John, St Thomas in the East, Clarendon and St Dorothy's.[21] These revolts would not be quelled for several months. Meanwhile, Tacky's forces took to the mountains, where they were joined by runaways who had previously been enslaved on French Guadeloupe. These men had been involved in an armed uprising there and had acquired skill in military operations. Despite a number of strategic victories, however, the slaves were eventually tracked down and killed by parties of Maroons. Tacky was reportedly shot by their sharpshooters.

For their part in the rebellion, 400 rebels were executed and about 600 were sent to be enslaved workers in the Bay of Honduras. The suppression of the uprisings cost an estimated £15,000, and the loss of property stood at £100,000. As a result of Tacky's Rebellion, the government petitioned the king to increase the number of regular troops in Jamaica as 'the forces in this island … were with great difficulty capable of reducing the rebellions'.[22] It was further proposed that, given their leading role in revolts, a provincial bill should be passed to impose prohibitions on the number of enslaved Coromanti people entering Jamaica.

However, the great demand for Gold Coast slave labor meant that no legislation along these lines was ever enacted.

Although some historians have attempted to find Maroon communities in South Carolina and Georgia like those in Jamaica, recent research has concluded that runaways in these states never reached the independence from whites achieved by the Jamaican Maroon communities.[23] In the mainland colonies, Maroonage would not appear until after the War for Independence and would never be as substantial.

While none of these slave rebellions succeeded fully enough to alter the nature of the plantation system, the combined effects were nevertheless clearly felt. The substantial black populations, through persistent and varied resistance to the enforcement of the slave system, brought colonies closer to the edge of upheaval than is realized. In the process, the slaves inspired a concerted counterattack from their anxious and outnumbered masters. The social equilibrium which emerged in the generation before the War for Independence was based upon a heightened degree of white repression and a reduced amount of black autonomy.

Chapter 4

Fear of Blacks becoming Christians

Plantation masters had argued that slavery was justified because slaves were not Christians but rather African heathens. This argument soon backfired as in the 1700s motivated clergy began to convert slaves to Protestant Christianity.[1] Still, planters influenced Anglican clergy and court judges to deny that baptism made a slave free. Among slaves, however, the impression that baptism could do this remained and in Britain, baptism initiated by blacks themselves became widespread, helping them to assimilate into society. Most planters saw the pious interests of their slaves as a source of discord which could fuel the feared insurrections.

In contrast in Britain, heads of a household with a strong sense of religion felt obligated to see their servants baptized and it was the custom for households to pray together every day. For the Anglican sacrament of baptism it was the godparents or sponsors who would announce to the priest the name of the person to be christened. Thus, baptism of older blacks was an opportunity to change one's name from a slave designation to a fully English name, a practice that supported one's achieved freedom. In court, a baptized black's testimony was given greater weight than one who was not, since it was assumed that those baptized were familiar with the Christian principles that were the bulwark of society.

Several forms of Methodism appeared in Britain and the colonies, which helped to assimilate blacks through practice of the sacraments of baptism and marriage. Selina, the Countess of Huntingdon, defined Methodist baptism in these terms:

> Baptism is a sacrament of the New Testament ordained by Jesus Christ, not only for the solemn admission of the party baptized into the visible church, but also to be unto him a sign and seal of the covenant of grace, to be continued in the church until the end of the world; which is rightly administered by pouring or sprinkling water upon the person, in the name of the Father, Son, and Holy Ghost.[2]

Along with baptism, marriage was also an important religious sacrament that helped black immigrants to put down roots in Britain. As many black migrants had come to the country after fighting in the military, men far outnumbered women. Among urban working-class communities, mixed marriages, between black men and white women, became common, particularly after 1750.

Also by the mid-eighteenth century, English evangelists like George Whitefield and the Countess of Huntingdon had educated and ordained black preachers such as David Margrett and John Marrant and sent them to the colonies. These preachers assumed that conditions in the colonies were as in Britain and that the fate of all blacks was to be free. Plantation masters saw it differently and actively sought to prevent these missionaries from preaching to and baptizing their slaves.

Christianizing the colonies

Anglican clergy and Methodist itinerants in the colonies found the task of Christianizing slaves formidable. The average parish was vast compared to those in England; churches were few and tiny, unable to support most Anglican clergy, so they needed outside support of the English Society for the Propagation of the Gospel in Foreign Parts or the charity Queen Anne's Bounty. The Society provided compensation for most Anglican priests, who made reports directly to them. Periodically, the Society sent letters to all their missionaries, including one in 1725 asking them to be more diligent in instructing and baptizing the slaves in their parish. At St George's parish on the upper Ashley River near Charleston, South Carolina, one of their missionaries Rev. Francis Varnod succeeded in having thirty slaves out of eighty parishioners attending his services.[3] However, this was rare; he was only able to do it by gaining the support of his parish's leading slaveholder. Most slave masters were obstacles to such success, believing that black converts would think they were free and cause rebellion.

The Anglican Church focused on promoting Christianity in the mainland colonies. The Society for the Propagation of the Gospel in Foreign Parts (SPGFP) had been founded in 1701 and three years earlier Oxford-educated Rev. Thomas Bray had established the Society for the Promoting of Christian Knowledge. They aimed to work overseas, irradiating ignorance of the Christian religion.[4] Libraries were established for the use of clergy and their parishioners, and books were shipped across the Atlantic. This was a remarkably far-sighted example of ecumenical cooperation. The societies continued to work closely with churches of different denominations, whilst retaining a special relationship with churches within the Anglican fold. Bray visited Maryland and took a great interest in colonial missions, especially among the slaves and Indians, writing and preaching vigorously against slavery and the oppression of Indians.

On account of the immensity of the task, the focus of SPGFP and SPCK never got much further than the building of churches and establishment of Indian missions. It was left to Bray to come up with a third volunteer organization in 1724, the Associates of Dr Bray, with a mandate to educate slaves in the British North American colonies. After briefly merging with a group intent on founding a convict colony in Georgia, the Associates concentrated on founding schools in the colonies. Ultimately, schools were established in Philadelphia, New York, Newport, and in Virginia at Williamsburg and Fredericksburg. The schools were not always a complete success and most closed by 1777 on account of the war, but the one in Philadelphia had Benjamin Franklin as a patron and actually reopened after the war. The Williamsburg school was supported by the William and Mary College. These schools provided one of the very few educational opportunities for black youth.

By 1760, Rev. John Todd, Anglican pastor of three Hanover County Churches, Virginia, claimed 'The poor slaves are now commonly engaged in Learning to read.' He claimed that while the Sabbath was once devoted to 'frolicking' it was now a time of learning to read at home or praying together. From 1746 to 1768, Rev. Thomas Bacon served as provincial rector of White Marsh Church and others in Maryland, baptizing, teaching and observing slaves. In his sermons, he urged slaves to be obedient to their masters and overseers:

> subject to them in all Things, and do whatever they order you to do, unless it should be some wicked Thing which you knew that GOD hath forbidden, in which Case you are to refuse, but in no other ... For your head Master, Almighty GOD, is looking on you.[5]

Thus, while obedience was emphasized it was qualified.

In places without plantation slavery like New York, Christianity had a mixed reception. In 1699, when William III offered 'A Bill for the Conversion of Indians and Negros', it had failed to win the necessary votes in the New York Assembly. Five years later, however, a Huguenot Elias Neau sought to open a school for education and conversion of neglected slaves and gained the support of the SPGFP and, locally, Trinity Church.[6] It began modestly with between fifteen and twenty-five students, who were usually baptized. Then came the 1712 slave revolt in which several of the insurrectionists turned out to be Neau's converts. He denied that he taught rebellion and Governor Robert Hunter supported him sending his own slaves to Neau's school, which survived the accusations. Neau died in 1722 and the school continued to be controversial, causing the Bishop of London to assure New York's slave masters that it taught only obedience to them.

The Great Awakening

There the question of Christianizing slaves rested until 1740, when a movement came from Britain that decisively marked the beginning of Emancipation Revolution in the effort to convert blacks to Christianity. Charismatic English evangelist George Whitefield visited New York, among other places in the colonies. His emotional and participatory approach to preaching drew vast audiences, including black men and women.

Whitefield was born in Gloucester, Gloucestershire, where he preached his first sermon, having been ordained a deacon of the Church of England in 1736. Earlier he had attended Oxford University where he met the Wesley brothers, John and Charles, in meetings of the Holy Club and when they left for America, he took over their duties, a role which would continue. He began to preach in the open to miners at Kingswood near Bristol and he enjoyed it so much that he decided to concentrate on evangelism, leaving the Wesleys' mainstream Methodism. Three churches were established in England in his name – one in Penn Street, Bristol, and two in London, in Moorfields and in Tottenham Court Road – all three of which became known as 'Whitefield's Tabernacle'.

Surprisingly, Whitefield was actually a plantation owner of slaves and would be instrumental in reintroducing slavery to Georgia. Yet in New York, Whitefield claimed that masters treated their dogs better than their slaves and he wondered why slaves 'have not more frequently rose up in arms against their owners'.[7] He argued that slaves' condition before God was the same as their masters: 'Blacks are just as much and no more conceived and born in sin, as white men are; and both ... are naturally capable of the same improvement.' Whitefield did not attack the institution of slavery, only its misuse. His visit to New York was followed by the slave conspiracy of 1741, in which the authorities were thankful in that only one of the convicted slave conspirators had been baptized. He was the most educated and pious of the conspirators, but this only served to intensify slaveholders' fears of Christian-led slave rebellion.

James Gronniosaw

Caught up in Whitefield's evangelism was black freeman James Gronniosaw. Born around 1710 into a royal family in what is now eastern Nigeria, he accompanied an African merchant to the Gold Coast where he was sold to European slave traders, who carried him on the Middle Passage to Barbados.[8] From there he was taken to New York City, where a wealthy Dutch Reformed clergyman and friend of George Whitefield, Theodorus Frelinghuysen, bought him, taught him to read and converted him to Christianity. After Gronniosaw heard the preaching of Whitefield and read the work of John Bunyan, he enjoyed a spiritual rebirth in 1747. Later, Frelinghuysen granted him his freedom and gave him £10.

During the Seven Years' War, Gronniosaw accumulated debts in New York and was forced to serve on a privateer and then as Royal Navy sailor and finally as a soldier at the capture of Havana. Ignoring his prize money, he contrived to go to England by escorting Spanish prisoners to Spain, where they were exchanged for British prisoners, who he escorted to Portsmouth. There, typically, his landlady swindled him out of his money. In London, Whitefield found him housing and paid for his expenses. After being baptized, he was married to Betty, a widowed white weaver. Because of economic depression after the war, the couple found it difficult to make a living in London and they became dependent upon Quaker charity. They both worked at Kidderminster in silk, where the religious environment was enhanced when the Countess of Huntingdon established a chapel.

Gronniosaw was disappointed that England was not a Christian utopia, but his biography, published in 1772, was paid for by and dedicated to the countess. As he was illiterate, his account was probably dictated to her. He concluded, 'As pilgrims ... we are traveling through our many difficulties towards our heavenly home, and waiting patiently for his gracious call ... to bring us to the everlasting glories of the world to come.'[9] Sales from his biography were meant to help him financially, although he died a year later. Certainly, he had continued to believe in Whitefield's and the countess's Christian messages.

Wesleyan Methodism

In Britain and the colonies, the early Methodist message was circulated through the organized spread of scriptures and applied by persuasive preaching and literature. The Methodist organization had emerged from experience in the American colonies in 1736, when the Wesley brothers were sent to Georgia – John by the SPGFP while Charles was named Secretary of Indian affairs. Arriving on the Savannah River, John first preached at Tybee Island. The Georgia colony did not allow slavery at the time, although it was legal and widely practiced in nearby South Carolina. When the Wesley brothers traveled to Charleston in July and August 1736 so that Charles could return to England, his journal recorded graphic descriptions of the torture and murder of slaves. He refers to a Charleston dancing master who whipped a young enslaved woman almost to death and then poured hot sealing wax on her bare skin. Charles went on to criticize a colonial government that essentially allowed slave owners to murder their slaves. There was a financial penalty for doing so, but the murderer could have it cut in half by simply admitting to the crime. Charles' incredulity at a system that allowed such a thing is expressed by his shocked comment: 'This I can look upon as no other than a public act to indemnify murder.'[10]

Three years later, John Wesley sent his first missionaries to the American colonies, where they found Methodist preachers already there, from Philip Embury in New York to Captain Thomas Webb, known as a most eloquent speaker. Anglican parsons such as Charles Inglis, Society for the Preservation of the Gospel missionary to Dover, Delaware, had become protégés of the evangelist George Whitefield. Inglis told his new parishioners at New York's Trinity Church that 'I glory in being a Methodist.'[11] He had acted like a Methodist, known for his evangelism while he was an itinerant preacher in Delaware.

The experience of the Wesleys with South Carolina's institution of slavery stayed with them. By 1774, John Wesley published his treatise *Thoughts upon Slavery*, where he criticized slavery as contrary to both Christian gospel and natural law. His appeal was based on the idea that every human being is deserving of basic freedom. He wrote, 'Liberty is the right of every human creature, as soon as he breathes the vital air; and no human law can deprive him of that right which he derives from the law of nature.'[12] His ultimate appeal is specifically Christian in character. He takes aim at both the institution of slavery and the transatlantic slave trade that facilitated it. He includes separate sections addressed to ship captains, slave-trading merchants, and planters, appealing to each to consider fundamental questions of justice and mercy in what they are doing. In late February 1791, just days before his death, Wesley wrote a letter to William Wilberforce in which he urged him to keep up the fight against slavery.

The Countess and the treatment of slaves

After forty years of financing Methodist chapels throughout Britain, the Countess of Huntingdon bought Spa Fields Chapel in London, which led the Established Church in 1779 to present her with the ultimatum: 'Close your chapels or get out of the Church of England!'[13] She at first used her legal right as a widowed peeress to appoint her own chaplains. Three years later, however, she and others left the Church and in 1783, at Spa Fields Chapel, held the first ordination of the countess's Connexion. John Wesley followed her example by ordaining his own Methodist preachers a year later.

Two black preachers had attended the countess's Trevecca College in Wales. Established in 1768 as a center of Calvinist Methodism, it turned out evangelists to preach to unchurched Britons and heathens in its colonies. Baptism of blacks on both sides of the Atlantic lead to spiritual development of black preachers, who attracted followings. Blacks were provided with their own Christian hope of freedom, which they believed was supported all the way to the monarch as head of the Church. It was no accident that George Whitefield had spoken at the college's inaugural sermon and the countess would become his patron. She oversaw the college, attracted pupils and supported ministers and also attracted financial support from wealthy London merchants like John Thornton. In the colonies, the planters accused her of encouraging slave revolts. Most notable of her missionaries was David Margrett, who, while he claimed to have been a runaway slave, was a proud product of Britain's black community, concentrated in London.

Margrett and Marrant

We know little of Margrett until 1767, when he was converted by Whitefield to Calvinist Anglicanism. Six years later, Margrett dazzled the countess with his preaching to blacks and whites and at a request for an 'African student', she sent him in 1774 to teach Christianity to her slaves at Bethesda Orphanage outside of Savannah, Georgia.[14] His ship the *Mermaid* landed first at Charleston, where he preached in open areas, including to slaves, whom he compared to Israelites, and was forced to leave immediately as such evangelism was feared by the planters. He asserted he came 'from a better Country than this, I mean old England' and he spoke fearlessly because he believed God would protect him and he claimed to be a second Moses, who would lead slaves from their bondage.

Moving on to Bethesda, Margrett's preaching caused consternation, for while he had been instructed only to Christianize, not to manumit slaves, he asserted that none of his color could be slaves. Word arrived that a party was coming from Charleston to silence him and prevent a slave insurrection. It was with relief to Bethesda's overseers that the countess agreed to have him return to England, where he arrived in late June 1775, having avoided bloodshed in the colonies. Margrett's willingness to speak out publicly against the institution of slavery as the War for Independence was emerging, introduced these Southern cities to the growing English evangelistic movement, which the planters could not tolerate. As an American observer who dealt with Margrett put it, in England, blacks 'get totally spoiled and ruined, both in body and soul, through a mistaken kind of compassion because they are black'.[15]

Another of the countess's Methodist students was John Marrant, who while born free in 1755 and nurtured in the colonies, served in the Royal Navy for almost seven years and finally was a preacher near one of her chapels. Marrant was a freeman born in New York but raised by his mother in St Augustine, Florida, Georgia and the Charleston area, where he obtained an education.[16] Against his mother's wishes, who wanted him to follow a trade, he learned to play the violin and French horn. In Charleston, at the age of 13, he heard George Whitefield preach and felt he pointed his finger at him, causing a spiritual rebirth, leading him to walk to the solace of the Carolina wilderness, where he lived among the Cherokees. Upon his return, saintly Marrant converted about thirty slaves to Christianity in a plantation outside of Charleston, incurring much white opposition. Early in the War for Independence, Marrant was impressed into the Royal Navy as a musician on the *Scorpion* and he claimed he saw action in 1780 at the siege of Charleston and a year later off the Dogger Bank against the Dutch on the 84-gun *Princess Amelia*, where he was wounded. To recuperate he was hospitalized at a navy facility for three and a half months and then served on a warship in the West Indies. Upon his return, he was hospitalized in Plymouth, where a doctor felt his injuries were serious enough for him to be discharged from the navy.

After his discharge, Marrant worked for three years for a London cotton merchant. More concerned for his soul, like Margrett he attended the countess's Trevecca College and became one of her preachers. When his brother, who had been transported to Nova Scotia after the War for Independence, sent him a letter describing the need there for Christian knowledge, Marrant determined to go as a missionary. The countess had him ordained as a minister in May 1785. His anti-slavery message would be more muted than that of Margrett, stirring up less opposition. He returned to England in 1789 and continued his ministry at a chapel in Islington, London, until his death in 1791, at which time he was buried in the churchyard. As a free American black, he had spent the war in the Royal Navy, which had cared for him after being seriously wounded, leading to time in England where his early spiritual inclination was fulfilled as one of the countess's preachers.

While serving as the chief Huntingdonian itinerant in Nova Scotia, Marrant met Cato Perkins, who would become a leading black evangelist. Marrant had him ordained in 1786 as an itinerant, choosing him to lead the Nova Scotia Huntingdonians when he left. Forty-seven-year-old Perkins had been John Perkins's slave in Charleston, South Carolina.[17] In 1778, he ran away from a plantation and was emancipated by the British during the Siege of Charleston, returning with the Clinton expedition to New York, where he worked as a carpenter. He is listed in the Book of Negroes and he was evacuated to Birchtown, Nova Scotia in 1783.

Anglicanism and the treatment of slaves

Along with Methodism, the Anglican Church played a more muted, but nevertheless important role in the early effort for the better treatment of slaves. Whitefield had gone throughout the colonies to encourage existing Anglican priests to Christianize slaves. In Maryland, vestries were particularly upset when Anglican parsons interfered with their slaves, attempting to convert them. For the parsons, conversion was difficult because slaves often understood English only imperfectly or were widely scattered at different plantations. Still, in 1724, Richard Sewell, rector of Shrewsbury parish, Cecil County, reported that he baptized ten slaves. From 1716 to 1745, Thomas Bacon, rector of St Peter's parish, Talbot County, purposely improved the religious instruction of slaves, showing the Anglican clergy's concern for them, despite the opposition of their masters.[18]

The Anglican Church appeared to be a unified force in both Britain and its colonies. In fact, it was undergoing considerable intellectual ferment and social change.[19] Despite its favored position, Anglicans were coming to view the Church as merely Britain's largest Christian denomination, emphasizing it as an umbrella for a wide range of Protestant beliefs. Effort was made to cultivate a practical piety, a disciplined will and openness to divine love.

This perspective is found in Beilby Porteus, who would eventually become Bishop of London. Though not willing to be a full-fledged evangelist, Porteus had a concern for slavery in the colonies which started early, as his parents were Virginian planters whose financial reverses had caused them to return to England in 1720. He was born at York in 1731, where he went to school, before starting at Cambridge. He graduated in 1752 and tutored until he was ordained. Ten years later, he was appointed domestic chaplain to Thomas Secker, Archbishop of Canterbury. Seven years later, he was chaplain to George III and as the War for Independence began, he was appointed Bishop of Chester.

Porteus took a keen interest in the affairs of the SPGFP. At the end of the war in February 1783, he was invited to preach the Society's Anniversary Sermon in which he outlined new objectives for the society. The audience consisted of forty members of the society, including eleven Anglican bishops. He criticized the Church's role in ignoring the plight of the 350 slaves on the society's Codrington Plantations in Barbados and he recommended the conditions of slaves be improved. These convictions were advanced in a sermon published the same year as 'The Civilization, Improvement and Conversion of the Negroe Slaves in the British West-India Islands Recommended'. He argued that the Church had a duty to convert the slaves to Christianity on its own plantations. Moreover, he asserted that humane treatment of slaves should be immediately enforced, regardless of whether they were likely to be emancipated or not.[20]

After Porteus made public the plight of slaves, he began to work on a Plan for the Effectual Conversion of the Slaves of the Codrington Estate, which he presented to the society in 1784. To his dismay, it was turned down by the bishops, the society showing the complacency of some Anglican leadership, who would still not accept responsibility for the welfare of their own slaves. This would not be an end to his effort.

The Great Awakening continues

George Whitefield died during his seventh evangelizing trip to America in 1760 and 17-year-old slave Phillis Wheatley was moved ten years later to pen an elegy for him, directed to his patron the Countess of Huntingdon. It read:

> Great Countess! We Americans revere
> We mourn with thee, that Tomb obscurely placed
> In which thy chaplain undisturbed doth rest
> His lonely tabernacle, sees no more
> A Whitefield landing on the British Shore [21]

In 1770, Wheatley would become the first published woman born in Africa who had been taken to Boston, Massachusetts aboard a slave ship, where she was purchased by John and Susanna Wheatley. Still a slave and unable to find a publisher for her collected poems in Boston, she went to England three years later and found one for her poems addressed to George III and Lord Dartmouth, Secretary of State for the Colonies, presumably thanking them for their part in repealing the acts opposed by the colonial legislatures. She lived for a while with John Thornton, the wealthy merchant and supporter of the Countess, and would be shown the sites of London by Granville Sharp. When she was asked to return to Boston to care for Susanna, she was promised freedom by the Wheatleys 'at the desire of my friends in England'. In Boston, she exchanged poems in a magazine with a soon-to-be-appointed lieutenant from Admiral Samuel Graves' squadron, John Rochfort. She offered a 'Crown of glory' to him and the Royal Navy. While she was able to marry, she died in poverty in Boston at the age of 31. The choice of Whitefield as her first subject shows the immense regard for him by blacks and whites in the British colonies.

The effect of the Great Awakening and the British effort to Christianize American slaves had its limits. The idea of the abolition of the slave trade or of slavery itself was not yet clear to white evangelicals. As a keen observer of the Emancipation Revolution has put it, 'The main thrust of eighteenth-century revivalism ended with the missionary, not the abolitionist.'[22] However, the missionaries created a black Christian leadership, which would be crucial to their cause during the War for Independence. Blacks who were able to read the Bible or to learn of it orally found that it inspired evangelism, giving them a blueprint for the future. To them, it outlined the path to freedom, providing them with the moral confidence that they deserved in God's kingdom.

PART 2

BRITAIN AS THE PROMISED LAND

Chapter 5

A Free Environment

The condition of British blacks differed greatly from those in the British colonies. Blacks found that the British Isles offered an environment which was more conducive to their freedom than in the colonies. They appeared in England when slaves were brought there by their masters and then ran away to be legally free. Many of these runaways were drawn to the sailor towns on the River Thames, east of London.[1] While British ports attracted black seamen, the actual number of British blacks remained very small compared to the colonies. Total figures for Britain's eighteenth-century black population can only be estimated, but a range of 3,000 to 5,000 – less than 1 per cent of Britain's population – seems probable. One could travel throughout the British Isles without seeing a black person, with the exception of London, so their numbers were never threatening. Even in London, blacks represented only 1 to 3 per cent of the population, while in contrast in New York City, they constituted almost 15 per cent.

In the past, white slavery had been a much greater reality in Britain than black slavery. As recently as the 1600s, the capture of British men and women and their sale into white slavery had happened along Britain's coasts. The Sale Rovers occupied Lundy Island in the Bristol Channel, a pirate nest that sent British captives to be sold in Algiers.[2] Efforts to ransom them constantly fell short and most spent the rest of their lives as chattels in North Africa. This experience heightened British hostility against any form of slavery.

British material culture demonstrates the employment of young black males as servants, for they appeared in this guise in paintings of aristocratic and middle-class family groups.[3] As early as the mid-seventeenth century, they were painted as well-dressed boys, reflecting the family's ties to mercantile success and the empire of trade. The images confirm that talented black boys were taken from American or West Indies plantations to England to become servants, cabin boys, or trained as artisans. This is demonstrated in a portrait by Johann Zoffany of Sir William Young's family in England, for he obtained his wealth as a sugar planter and lieutenant governor of both Dominica and Tobago. A black youth, John Brook, is steadying Young's boys on horseback and probably had accompanied Young to England from one of his plantations. Many West Indies' planters sent their illegitimate mulatto offspring to Britain to be educated and possibly integrated into white society. Their status in Britain was unclear, as while many were free, in the eyes of their masters they remained slaves. So many were servants that in 1773 the *London Chronicle* proposed to restrict blacks as servants to appease suffering white servants who could not find a position. Still, many blacks did not live in the aristocratic and wealthy surroundings found in the paintings.

Black Runaways

When, in 1719, Alexander King, surgeon of HMS *Rye Galley*, was about to leave Britain for the West Indies, William Jacobs, his black slave, ran away, afraid of the possibility he would be sold there.[4] Young black males like him, many of them children, were described in British advertisements for runaways. From their perspective, they had been taken from their families by their master, whom they had accompanied to Britain or had been sent by their master to Britain to be an apprentice. At first, they missed their family in what to them was an alien environment, but gradually, as they were baptized, obtained a surname of their own, increased in skill, and became used to freedom of movement, they decided to never return to the plantation, where they faced being a field hand. Despite a master's advertising his desire for his slave's return, it was relatively easy for slaves to escape their master's oversight in Britain, where slavery was not legally recognized. Masters had no recourse to the courts as in the colonies, their only possibility was these advertisements. This was different from runaways in the colonies, whose profile was older, more often women, and when captured they faced re-enslavement, hard field labor or in rare cases execution.

Black Mariners

Although the majority of the blacks would have been in domestic service, some were able to live more independently and escape, receiving wages aboard vessels engaged in American trade. When captains wanted to employ men of African origin, they first looked for them in a port's docks. Blacks found their skills as mariners mattered more than their color. They came to Britain on ships as free sailors or soldiers, chosen by captains and merchants, being discharged at ports at the end of a voyage. The close links of transatlantic slavery to certain British ports did mean that black sailors found the reassuring presence there of other black people. London led in the number of slave voyages until the mid-eighteenth century, when Liverpool took over. Blacks usually came as single males, lacking spouses, without their family connections in America or Africa – clearly a disadvantage in starting over. Black sailors rarely had the opportunity to marry; thus, their companionship was limited to their shipmates, who on land were prone to be boisterous.

During the War for Independence, at the peak of recruiting, perhaps 5,000 to 6,000 blacks served in the Royal Navy.[5] At 5 per cent, the percentage of black sailors in the navy was higher than the percentage of blacks living in London, though still well below that of New York.

Some blacks were willing to give up the comfortable but monotonous life of servant to seek adventure in the Royal Navy. This was the fate of Jamaican-born slave Francis Barber (alias Quashey) who was brought as a 7-year-old to London by his master, sugar plantation owner Colonel Richard Bathurst.[6] His plantation had failed and he been forced to sell over 100 slaves, although Quashey was one of four he held back and the only one he brought to England. Quashey was either a very bright house slave or Bathurst's own son, from a liaison with a slave woman, a common occurrence in Jamaica. Still a slave, he became the unpaid servant of Bathurst and his son, who had him baptized with the name Francis Barber and educated him at an inexpensive school far from London. Their wealth gone, the Bathursts seemed to be embarrassed by Barber because they could not afford to keep him. He remained with Bathurst's son, who sought a place for him as a servant in the household of his friend,

Samuel Johnson, who was not yet the renowned literary figure. Johnson took him in and in 1754, Bathurst's will gave Barber his freedom and £12. Barber might have remained with Johnson, who treated him indulgently, but he was now free and after a few quiet years as a servant, he left to join the Royal Navy, a career which will be detailed in a later chapter.

Barber must have experienced the advantages of black British mariners. Wills in Britain show that sailors received wages and prize money from which they obtained sums and possessions that they could bequeath, something not possible in the Americas.

London's East End Mariners and Merchants

While Barber lived in the city of London, many black mariners and runaways were drawn to east London's River Thames, which came to have the greatest concentration of black mariner population in England. On the north side of the river were Whitechapel, Wapping, Stepney, Shadwell and Lime House parishes, while on the south side were Southwark, Rotherhithe, Deptford and Greenwich.[7] In these East End communities, blacks were drawn by maritime employment, options for integration into British society, and a legal environment that made their re-enslavement almost impossible.

On the northern bank of the river, Shadwell was a perfect environment for mariners and colonial merchants. It contained four major ropewalks and dozens of cooperages, breweries and sugar refineries.[8] From its New Crane Stairs to Bell Wharf Stairs were clustered industries, providing the supplies and services needed by the thousands of ships, schooners and colliers finding their way to the Pool of London or preparing to sail to North America, the Caribbean, the Mediterranean, Africa or the Far East. Along this waterfront were numerous taverns that attracted seamen from more countries than anywhere else in Britain.

Shadwell's family connections spanned the Atlantic. Thomas Jefferson's mother, Jane Randolph Jefferson, was born in Shadwell in 1720, the eldest daughter of Virginia-born Isham Randolph, mariner and merchant, who lived at the Shakespeare Rope Walk. Seven years later, as a child, she immigrated to Virginia.[9] While the Randolphs were planters in Virginia, Isham's residence in Shadwell from 1717 to 1725 was driven by colonial trade. This sailors' section of the river was not ideal for bringing up Jane. It reflected Isham's role as ship master and merchant, rather than the family's Virginia aspirations as planters. When Jane grew up, she married Peter Jefferson in 1739. Two years later, he moved his family westward to Shadwell plantation, named for his wife's birthplace, and it was here that the future president Thomas Jefferson was born.

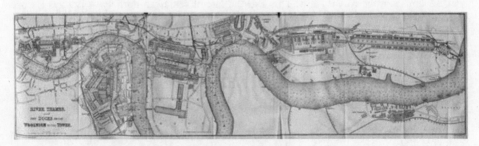

River Thames with the Docks from Woolwich to the Tower, 1882.

Sailor town lifestyle

On the Thames, above and between Deptford, were more sailor towns. On land, sailors were often restless and liable for disturbances. Many sailors of Irish, Portuguese, East Indian, Greek, Spanish, and African origin lived in temporary lodgings. They might enter into long- or short-term relationships with women in more than one port, punctuated by the fact that they might be absent for weeks or months at a time. In September 1763, an item appeared in the Annual Register describing an East End riot when:

> Four disorderly women being sent to Bridewell [workhouse], a parcel of sailors assembled in Rosemary-lane, with an intent to rescue them; upon which a file of musketeers was sent for from the Tower, and the sailors continuing obstinate in their purpose, the soldiers fired, when four were killed, and many mortally wounded, who died in a few days in hospital.[10]

What caused this bloodshed was that the women sent to the Bridewell workhouse had been arrested for prostitution. They were probably arrested for soliciting at 'disorderly houses' (brothels) around Wapping, Shadwell or Stepney, frequented by sailors who lodged there. The Seven Years' War had just ended, so there was a sudden influx of discharged sailors from the navy in the East End. It was a time of instability, with them massing, sometimes on account of unemployment, often leading to unrest and riot. The loyalty of Thames' sailors to the womenfolk was volatile and contradictory, with violence by sailors against women constant, and outbursts of male misogyny against brothels not infrequent. However, the September 1763 incident indicates an element of solidarity existed between the sailors and the disorderly women. This was the type of riot that was most likely to involve sailors.

Deptford

Among the numerous Thames' commercial docks were two important naval installations which attracted blacks: the Deptford Dockyard and next to it, the Victualing Yard.[11] Deptford's original Tudor dockyard had possessed one of two working docks on the Thames, which soon become too narrow, shallow and heavily used to be an attractive anchorage for the growing size of the navy's ships. Thus Deptford concentrated on building smaller warships and its role as headquarters of the naval transport service. The Board's transports and storeships were hired from the extensive Thames' merchant marine.

Deptford was now a small city of its own, rising to a population exceeding 18,000. Unlike the rest of London, where brick housing had become the norm to prevent the spread of fire, Deptford houses were of wooden frame construction. This reflected the vast quantities of imported lumber for its navy and private dockyards. How much of this lumber passed out from the naval yard illegally in the form of chips is an open question. Private shipbuilding yards appeared after 1739, when Royal Navy dockyards found themselves unable to meet the wartime fleet's pressing need for more ships. By 1783, William Barnard had formed a partnership with William Dudman and Henry Adams leasing 9 acres at Deptford for a new shipbuilding yard, later known as Grove Street. From 1780 to 1790, the Barnard yards completed forty-two vessels: twenty-nine for East India Company and thirteen for the Royal Navy.

As Deptford's role as a naval dockyard declined, the facilities of its Victualling Yard rose. Proximity to London's food markets made it convenient for victualling and it serviced the requirements not only of its own dockyard but those of Woolwich, Sheerness and Chatham. The Victualling Yard had emerged next to the dockyard in 1673, when Dennis Gauden, Surveyor General of Victuals, began to transfer operations from London's Tower Hill eastward to Deptford.[12] A Red House of brick was leased for naval victualling and in 1743 the Victualling Board, supported by the Admiralty, acquired its lease – intending to establish its main depot there. Plans were drawn up for a redevelopment of an 11-acre site to consolidate facilities for the purchase, production, packing and dispatching of foodstuffs, beverages and other victualling supplies in a single location. It would maintain naval stores, clothing, food, tobacco and rum. From October to April, the butchers slaughtered livestock that were driven from the Smithfield meat market across the river and down the Old Kent Road. Foods, including butter and cheese, were salted and pickled in cask, to preserve the products most liable to spoilage. Decayed food had to be condemned by a panel of ship's officers, in order for the ship's purser to receive credit for it. Most food was preserved long enough to create a healthy diet for ships' companies.

Employment opportunities were thus broader than in the dockyards, as food processing required specific skills. The slaughtering of livestock, its salting and preservation and placement in casks, were procedures that blacks acquired on plantations. During the War for Independence, the demand for foodstuffs by the navy in American waters and the British army on land was extraordinary. Black New Yorker Benjamin Whitecliff chose to settle there after he was discharged from the Royal Navy in 1783.[13] Three years later, the Deptford Victualling Yard expanded its layout, scale and complexity. As a result, the Navy Board centered its baking, slaughtering, curing and storing facilities at Deptford, creating even more jobs.

East End Churches

The old parish church of St Paul's, Shadwell, traditionally known as the Church of Sea Captains, had been rebuilt in 1669. As many as seventy-five sea captains were buried at the church and famous Captain James Cook worshipped there; his eldest son was baptized there in 1763. The trades around it included roperies, timber yards, sail makers, coopers, breweries and a flouting market. A path, which terminated at the Whitby public house, led from the church to the river. Methodism's John Wesley was attracted to preach at St Paul's.

Efforts to find blacks in London have concentrated on using parish church records to provide data on baptisms, marriages and burials. This has led to lower estimates of the number of blacks in London than once was claimed and confirmed the lack of a cohesive 'black community'.[14] However, black males did appear in all of the sailor towns' parish records and are often identified as mariners, although their appearance in the parish records are inconsistent because as sailors they were often on a voyage and unable to attend church.

Modifying the sailor towns' boisterous life style were Anglican and Dissenting Churches, which offered blacks a measure of stability by being open to them in dispensing the sacraments. Baptisms and marriages were religious rituals that helped black and white immigrants to settle and put down roots in Britain. As many black migrants had come to the country after service as sailors, men far outnumbered women. Among urban working-class communities, mixed marriages, between black men and white women, were not uncommon, especially in the latter half of the century. These marriages needed church approval.

Anglican parish churches dispensed East End respectability in various forms. The New Churches in London Act of 1711 had established a commission to erect fifty new churches in areas of population growth and rising Dissent, including the sailor town parishes.[15] Six of the twelve churches actually built were designed by Nicholas Hawksmoor, who produced imposing edifices, towering over working- and mariner-class homes, signifying the open presence of the Anglican Church.

St George's-in-the-East Church at Wapping was completed in 1729. Around the parish, trades grew for ship-rigging and rope-making, of which the names of streets are a reminder, for Cable Street was once the length of the standard cable measure: 600 feet. By 1780, there were 300 houses near the church; by 1800, the church administered an average of 500–600 baptisms and 400–600 burials a year. The parish extended down to the river.

Certain East End parish churches like Stepney's Holy Trinity Minories was noted for being able to conduct irregular marriages, as the church was not under the jurisdiction of a bishop.[16] Parish ministers married many blacks because it confirmed their freedom. Blacks who wished to be married, however, did not want the delay caused by the traditional practice of waiting three weeks after the announcement of banns, as the publicity might allow a former master to find them. Stepney also was a center of Dissenting Churches that avoided the traditional banns anyway. The Independent meeting house was on Bull Lane; the Presbyterians were represented on Broad Street; and the Quakers had a meeting house in Gracechurch Street.

Baptism remained crucial to blacks coming to Britain because it safeguarded their freedom and made them more acceptable to British society. Prior to 1770, few blacks were baptized at St George's-in-the East, Stepney, but in the 1780s the numbers increased dramatically to sixty-nine. This was because the rector, Reverend Herbert Mayo, aggressively converted and baptized blacks. Fittingly, he would be a member of the Committee for the Abolition of Slavery and contributed to the appeal for the Sierra Leone project to settle London blacks in Africa. In 1802, his obituary asserted:

> He was particularly kind to the negroes and uninstructed men of color; who, employed generally on board of ship, occasionally resided in his parish, which is full of sea-faring people. I suppose no clergyman in England ever baptized so many black men and Mulattoes; nor did he at any time baptize them without much previous preparation; that the inward and spiritual grace might accompany the outward and visible form of baptism. The attachment of these poor people to him was very great. Several of them never came into the port of London, without waiting upon him, by way of testifying the respect in which they held him.[17]

Mayo did his job well, serving not just his parish blacks, but those from all of the East End sailor towns.

The East End absorbs black Loyalists

In the aftermath of the War for Independence, black Loyalists went to British ports, seeking compensation for their wartime services, basking in their new-found freedom. In London, analysis of Parish Baptismal Registers shows that few blacks were born in Britain, most being immigrants from North America or the West Indies.[18] About half the immigrants came from Virginia and South Carolina, especially from Charleston, while Jamaica and Barbados were the origin of about a third of the black population. Further analysis of the parish registers from 1783 to 1787 shows that 144 of the 166 blacks were located in the East End parishes.

Registers also confirm an unfettered mixing of the races. As noted, the vast majority of migrants to Britain were males and over half of them could only find white women to marry. Their wives' network of family and friends helpfully drew them into the mainstream of society. This was the case of James Gronniosaw and his Betty, who married for love and shared religion.

Britain never experienced American integration and segregation, only outright assimilation. When in 1786, numbers of London black families were recruited to colonize Sierra Leone, abolitionist Granville Sharp confirmed that they consisted of some who had been officers' servants or Loyalists, but most were 'seamen, that have served in the Royal Navy, in the last war, or as rangers with the army in the American Woods, who deserved a generous requital'.[19]

Chapter 6

British Law, Benevolence and Religious Toleration

By the time of the War for Independence, many planters in the West Indies and American mainland came to see Britain as a dangerous place, where their valuable slaves were likely to be freed. The planters' ability to retain and recover their slaves was threatened by English Common Law. Additionally, a benevolence movement was expanding among British merchants, Royal Navy officers, churchmen and literary figures, which made them sympathetic to the plight of blacks who wished to be free. Religious toleration also advanced under the umbrella of the Anglican Church, emphasizing the need for a renewed spread of Christianity to the lower orders, including blacks.

Somerset Case

The Somerset Case in 1772 was a landmark in English constitutional and legal history. When the slave James Somerset set foot in England with his Massachusetts' master, Charles Steuart, he was baptized and ran away from him. His freedom was short-lived, for he was recaptured by Steuart, who now wanted to force him on ship to be sold as a slave in Jamaica. Somerset would get lawyers and they would ask, 'In England, where freedom is the grand object of the laws, and dispensed to the meanest individual, shall the laws of an infant colony, Virginia, or of a barbarous nation, Africa, prevail?'[1] Presiding in the court, Lord Chief Justice Mansfield felt his ruling was not meant to establish a legal precedent, yet he stated that a slave could not be removed from England to be sold, implying that the law found slavery illegal in England. The ruling meant that slave masters in England could no longer control their slaves by threatening to send them back to be sold in the American plantations.

The *Morning Chronicle* and the *Middlesex Journal* reported that several blacks were in court to hear the delivery of the Somerset judgement. After the judgement, the *London Packet* affirmed that 200 blacks had gathered at a Westminster public house to celebrate the decision. Knowledge of the Somerset Case, if not its details, spread to American blacks, urging them to pursue freedom from bondage. 'Word of that decision had slipped out in the debates in the House of Burgess and reverberated through the grogshops, back alleys, and forest retreats where blacks congregated.'[2] In 1774, Virginia runaway Bacchus aimed to flee to Britain, 'from the knowledge he has of the late determination of Somerset's Case', an idea his master noted that was too prevalent among his slaves. None of this was acceptable to American planters.

The Somerset Case would set a precedent for legal cases that followed. In May 1773, the Prerogative Court in London in *Cay vs. Crighton*, found that when a 'Negro' was not reported in an inventory of goods and chattels it was because 'Negros' had been declared free and not property and therefore could not be part of a personal estate. Upon contention, the judge further ruled that Somerset had closed the matter and thus a challenge was invalid. Later, in *Williams vs. Brown*, a slave escaped his master in Grenada and made his way to London and foolishly agreed to be a seaman on a merchant ship going back to Grenada. Upon landing his former master reclaimed him and he escaped only after he agreed to serve the captain of the ship for three years at wages. Back in London, he was able to sue for higher wages and while he lost his case, Justice Mansfield declared that he was 'as free as anyone of us while in England'.[3]

In 1779, Justice Mansfield heard the case of Amissa, a freeman who had been taken on the Gold Coast as a crew member on Liverpool slaver, *Britannia*, commanded by Captain Benjamin Hughes. When the vessel reached Jamaica, Hughes ignored Amissa's status and sold him as a slave, while covering up the transgression by claiming he had died on the voyage. On the Gold Coast, Amissa's family met another mariner who affirmed that he had seen him in Jamaica, so the family complained to the Company of Merchants Trading in Africa, asking that he be repatriated. The company sent another captain to search for him and he was found and carried to England. Captain Hughes was brought to trial and the jury awarded £500 against him. Amissa went back to his family in the Gold Coast and the local company officials explained how they had obtained justice for him.

Jamaica's influence

It has been contended that Mansfield's personal experience with British blacks from Jamaica had affected his decisions.[4] A young mulatto woman, Dido Elizabeth Belle, lived in his household, she being the illegitimate child of his nephew, Royal Navy captain Sir John Lindsay. His story shows how navy officers could have two families: one in Jamaica and another in Britain. Lindsay was born into an aristocratic Scottish family in 1737. By his nineteenth birthday he was a lieutenant on the fireship *Pluto*, serving in the following year under Admiral Edward Hawke. For the rest of the Seven Years' War, he would be captain of the frigate *Trent* in the West Indies, serving at the capture of Havana in 1762. When he returned to England he was awarded a knighthood, became an MP for Aberdeen, and in 1768 married Mary Milner.

While his union with Mary had no legitimate children, in Jamaica Lindsay had previously fathered, with different free mulatto or black women, at least five illegitimate daughters and sons. He arranged for slave Maria Belle to be brought to London, where Dido was born in 1761. Three years later, Maria Belle moved to Pensacola, Florida, joining Lindsay, as he was commander of the Pensacola Naval Squadron and owned a house in the naval yard. They returned to England and after time with her mother, Lindsay took Dido to be cared for by Lord Mansfield and in 1765 she was baptized. She was reared at Mansfield's Kenwood estate outside of London and educated by him, living in the household under his protection for the next thirty years. With the exception of one child who died young, the fate of Lindsay's other illegitimate children is unknown. Certainly, this is a commentary on white Royal Navy officers' extramarital sexual affairs with Jamaica's black women. It shows the dilemma of mixed-race children from the West Indies, for their mother's color made them slaves by birth, while their father's heritage gave them freedom. Their place was determined by the amount of acceptance they received from their British relatives like Lord Mansfield.[5]

Lindsay's actions also introduced the Caribbean absenteeism of owners, which was prevalent in all West Indies estates, where the owner rarely stayed long term on the plantation. Most wanted to gain a fortune quickly from the cultivation of sugar, but the low life expectancy in the tropics led them to retire to the more suitable conditions of Britain as soon as they had made a fortune. This is how they came to bring their mulatto offspring to Britain. By 1800, it was attorneys, managers and overseers who ran most Caribbean plantations.

Benevolence

British concern for blacks was not only moved by the law but also by the charitable inclinations that were driving its middle classes, including the officers and associates of the Royal Navy. For those who prospered, Christianity demanded that they redeem their souls through acts to uplift their less fortunate brethren. This ethic had medieval religious basis and thus had been applied in maritime communities for some time.

For example, Newcastle's River Tyne keelmen were a close-knit, colorful river community that worked in large, shallow boats (keels), carrying coal from the river's banks to waiting collier ships. As early as 1697, the keelmen formed a 'friendly society for the maintenance of the poor of their fraternity'.[6] Concerned for their well-being, in 1701 the keelmen gathered contributions for their Keelmen's Hospital, a cloister of fifty chambers around a grassed courtyard, for sick and aged keelmen and for widows and children of deceased keelmen, or for those who were ill or destitute. In 1729, about 200 keelmen formed themselves into a benefit society to regulate the hospital and keep it in repair. Support for the Hospital was raised by a levy of 2d a tide on the keelmen themselves. The Hospital became an early site for John Wesley's preaching in the 1740s and they appointed his brother Charles to be their chaplain.

Benevolence is seen in London, where Jonas Hanway became the personification of Christian charity. He remained an Anglican, with only a taint of evangelism, for after hearing Whitefield preach, he was disappointed that the man 'should demean himself like an inhabitant of Bedlam'.[7] Rational, fervent and sincere, Hanway wanted to express emotion through his zeal for charity. He was also firmly anti-slavery and in London he would relieve the distress of its poor blacks.

Jonas Hanway's baptism had been registered in Portsmouth on August 2, 1712. His father Thomas, an agent victualler, lived comfortably with his family in St George's Square. Hanway's mother already had two children by an earlier marriage, and a further daughter and three sons (including Jonas) arrived with the second marriage. Sadly, Hanway's father died after a fall from a horse in 1714, and with the loss of his income, the family had to move to rural Hampshire, where Jonas attended a small school.

At age 16, Hanway went to London to live with his uncle in Oxford Street, where he began training in accounting and business skills, equipping himself for a career as a merchant. From 1729, Hanway was sent to and worked at the English Factory in Lisbon, Portugal. It was a business center, due to the volume of British shipping using Lisbon's port and its role as the center for Portugal's empire. While gaining business experience, he was also influenced by Lisbon's tradition of philanthropy, focusing on the care and nurture of the young. Next Jonas joined the Russia Company and from St Petersburg he volunteered for a journey to Persia. His trip was eventful as he was held captive more than once. It would cause him to write the first of many publications, *An Historical Account of the British Trade over the Caspian Sea*. On his return to London, Hanway continued to promote the Russia Company, working from St John's Coffee House near the Royal Exchange. He would never marry.

In 1762, he was appointed a Commissioner for Victualling, the Navy Board charging him with the bakehouse and mills section. This duty brought him to Portsmouth dockyard on occasion, where his office was over the Square Tower in the High Street.[8] He built a slaughterhouse next to it and converted an old pier into a 'Beef Stage', to serve the fleet moored at Spithead. He held this office until the end of the War for Independence.

His work as a commissioner faded as he sought to improve the living conditions and opportunities for poor boys. He first emphasized the plight of 'Climbing Boys', young chimney sweep apprentices, and the lives of poor children at large. He urged that poor people should wash at least once a week and change their clothes every eight to ten days. By 1757, he was a governor of the Foundling Hospital, a position which would be upgraded to vice president.

Marine society

Young boys could make up 10 to 20 per cent of a Royal Navy ship's crew, a majority of them being servants, the rest being on the way to becoming midshipmen.[9] They were being nurtured up to the sea life, much like apprentices on land to their master craftsmen. Some on merchant ships were liable to desert and were regarded as a great nuisance, but they were still accepted because of the shortage of crew members.

Hanway's benevolence would affect the Royal Navy's recruiting of young volunteers. In 1756, he founded the Marine Society to encourage men and boys to join the Royal Navy before they were swept up by the impress. The organization was founded at the King's Arms Tavern by Hanway, merchant compatriots like Phillis Wheatley's John Thornton and navy officers like his brother Thomas. At first, their chief interest was providing clothing for older landsmen recruits, as clean clothing was felt to combat typhus. This effort next led to recruitment of boys for the navy. This was not easy because the recruiting undermined traditional poor laws, apprenticeship laws, and laws against vagabonds and rogues. Moreover, local authorities saw his effort as a means of dumping unwanted boys on the Society. Some boys must have been coerced by these authorities, while others were coaxed by the Society. The lure of the sea and the lifestyle of a sailor must also have encouraged boys to join.

The Marine Society's overriding concern was to provide boys with an opportunity in the navy. As the boys were for the most part from non-seafaring families, the Society increased the naval recruitment pool by several thousand. It also contributed to the health of the boys through its typhus prevention measures, such as regular bathing and changing into clean clothes. The Society would stand by its boys even after they were delivered to their ships, especially if their masters proved to be brutal or they were wounded in action.

Going to sea as a ship's boy during the Seven Years' War was dangerous, as a high casualty rate existed among the boys, yet if the youth managed to survive, as a sailor he had a faster route to economic independence than most land-based apprenticeships available to poor children.[10] The sea service offered two advantages for these children: it could be a disciplined institution where authorities or relatives sent a destitute or troublesome boy, or for the impoverished or non-conformist youth, the sea could be an escape from his misery or from a society where he was unable to conform. The Society not only recruited, but its goals were also meant to relieve London's youth unemployment, misbehavior and crime.

Some boys must have been black. Provision for blacks appear in the Society's regulations, allowing for equipping them, although they were required to be over 18 years of age – much older than the usual white boy. The Society advertised that it would clothe boys who came from beyond Britain, so long as they were living in Britain. Many of those blacks enrolled were already officers' servants.

Thomas Hanway

Throughout his charitable efforts, Jonas had the support of his younger brother Thomas, a Royal Navy officer. Born in 1715, he was the youngest of the Hanways, whom Jonas would have to look after. At 14, Thomas joined the navy and nine years later he passed his lieutenant's exams.[11] Rising to captain he served on various ships during the War of Austrian Succession, helping to crush the Jacobite Rebellion in 1745, by capturing a French ship loaded with stores and troops for the Stuart cause. Two years later, he was at the Battle of Cape Finisterre in northwest Spain. In this action, fourteen navy warships under Admiral George Anson attacked a thirty-ship French convoy commanded by Admiral de la Jonquière. The French attempted to protect their merchant ships by integrating their warships with them. In a five-hour battle, Anson captured six warships and seven merchantmen. Thomas gained considerable prize money and with his marriage to Ann Howe he became rich.

With the war over, Thomas was based on shore at Plymouth Dockyard until the Seven Years' War commenced in 1756. He was able to join Jonas in becoming a founding member of the Marine Society. In its first year, he placed a tenth of the boys attracted in the society, many of them from Hampstead.[12] Two years later, he was involved in a raid on St Malo, France and then he was named commander-in-chief at Cork, Ireland with the duty there of raising men for the fleet. In 1761, he was a commissioner of Chatham Naval Yard, a sign that a recent illness had limited him to shore-based duties. He served there for ten years and returned to London to be Comptroller of Victualling Accounts. He stayed with Jonas during this transition, but died soon after at his brother's house. Thomas clearly provided Jonas with a direct link to the Royal Navy.

Religious toleration

After the intense religious conflict of the English Civil War, the British environment came to offer a measure of religious toleration which was favorable to blacks. As noted, the Anglican Church legally endorsed an unprecedented level of religious diversity. Anglicans were coming to view their established church as merely Britain's largest Christian denomination, emphasizing it as an umbrella for a wide range of Protestant beliefs. The effort had begun with the Toleration Act of 1688, passed by Parliament in the aftermath of the Glorious Revolution. The act allowed for freedom of worship to Protestants who dissented from the Anglican Church, such as Baptists, Congregationalists or English Presbyterians. Dissenters were allowed their own places of worship and their own schoolteachers, as long as they accepted oaths of allegiance. It did continue some existing social and political disabilities for Dissenters, including their exclusion from holding political offices or positions in the universities. Preachers who dissented had to be licensed. These restrictions, however, would encourage further efforts by Dissenters in 1772, 1774 and 1779 to campaign to modify the act's terms. Typically, the act was amended in 1779 by substituting 'a belief in Scripture' for the previous belief in the Thirty-Nine Articles of Anglican churches.[13]

Part of the reason for this toleration was the already noted rise of Methodism. In the mid-1700s, Methodism evolved as a reform within this Anglican Church, emphasizing the ritual, prayer and communion of the Anglicans.[14] It went beyond Anglicanism, however, drawing from an emphasis on faith and conversion and adopting the behavioral rules of Quakers. Methodists discovered the primitive Christianity of the Bible, not only in simplicity, but in missionary zeal. Its roots were in the creation of societies and clubs within Anglicanism for reform and especially for missionary efforts in both Britain and its colonies.

John Wesley, the founder and guiding light of Methodism needs more explanation. He was born in 1703 in Epworth, Lincolnshire, the son of Reverend Samuel Wesley, a Dissenting minister turned Anglican. John's formative years were under the influence of his pious mother, Susana Wesley, who was also the daughter of a Dissenting minister.[15] Like her husband, she had returned to Anglicanism, but their dissenting experience gave them a more open perspective than usual. With this background, Wesley had his Methodist itinerants practice a similar compromise in that they did not apply the sacraments, leaving these duties for ordained Anglican divines. Not until after the War for Independence did Methodists separate themselves from the Anglican Church.

Dissenters

By the eighteenth century, 'Rational Dissenters' were actually Anglicans who believed that any state religion impinged on the freedom of conscience. They opposed the hierarchical structure of the Anglican Church and the financial ties between it and the government. They based their opinions on the Bible and on reason rather than on appeals to tradition and authority. They rejected doctrines of Original Sin or the Trinity, arguing that they were irrational. They believed that Christianity could be dissected and evaluated using the newly emerging discipline of science, and that a stronger belief in God would be the result.

In London's East End at Stepney, John Wesley found many Dissenters, separatists and independents. Originally, Stepney had been a village on the outskirts of the city, centered around the Church of St Dunstan's. Samuel Brewer took over its ministry in 1746, when the congregation had dwindled, and effectively increased attendance, leaving a very successful church at his death in 1796. An important independent, he was still friendly with Anglican clergy and belonged to the group of clergymen clustered around the evangelist George Whitefield, his particular friend. Brewer welcomed Rev. Samson Occom, a Mohegan Indian converted in the Great Awakening, and Nathaniel Whitaker, a Presbyterian minister, when they arrived in London in 1765 for a three-year effort to raise money for an Indian charity school in Connecticut. Occom called Brewer 'a warm Servant of Jesus Christ', and was allowed to preach at his meeting several times, the audiences making generous collections for his Indian Charity School.[16] Brewer was part of a group that met weekly to advise Occom and Whitaker, sending letters of introduction and recommendations to the leaders of surrounding churches in an effort to support their cause.

This new toleration included Catholics. By 1760, when young Catholic Charles Carroll of Maryland had finished eleven years of Jesuit education in France, he was not sure of what to expect when he continued his education England.[17] To his surprise, he found that the Hanover monarchs had let anti-Catholic legislation lapse and he spent his time without anxiety reading English law. Eventually, he would be the only Catholic to sign the Declaration of Independence.

Muslims

The new religious toleration even spread to Muslims. Ayuba Suleiman Diallo was born into a family of Muslim imams in West Africa in 1701. In 1731, while on a trading mission to the River Gambia to sell two black slaves to the British ship *Arabella*, Diallo was kidnapped, sold into slavery, and transported to Maryland where he was made to work on a tobacco plantation. Unfit for the task, Diallo escaped, was caught and imprisoned but permitted to write a letter to his father that came to the attention of James Oglethorpe, Deputy Governor of the Royal African Company and soon to be founder of Georgia.[18]

Oglethorpe was so moved by the letter that he arranged for Diallo's purchase and passage to England, where he arrived in London in 1733. Recognized as a deeply pious and educated man, Diallo mixed with high and intellectual society and was bought out of slavery by public subscription. His portrait was painted that same year by William Hoare, an accomplished artist, who painted many members of Georgian high society. Hoare's painting depicts Diallo as a man of intelligence, character and compassion, at a time when there was a new interest in Islamic culture and faith in Britain, a reflection of more tolerant values.

Freed from slavery, arrangements were made for Diallo's desired return to Africa – a rarity for victims of slavery. Returning to his home, Diallo learned that during his absence his father had died, the country had been ravaged by war and his wife had remarried. Despite his own life having been blighted by slavery, Diallo resumed his own slave-trading activities. He was certainly not the ideal that future abolitionists would look to.

The law, benevolence and religious toleration brought together Britain's merchant and naval leadership in private efforts, which would provide the background for abolitionism. None of these leaders was as yet an abolitionist in the sense of supporting the eradication of the slave trade or slavery itself, but this climate would make a future opportunity possible.

PART 3

OPPORTUNITIES IN THE ROYAL NAVY

Chapter 7

Navy Recruiting on
Land and Sea

At the beginning of the War for Independence, Ignatius Sancho, former slave orphan, now literate freeman running a family grocery in London, sent a letter to *The General Advertiser* meant to be seen by the Admiralty, concerning the raising of 20,000 seamen on a remarkable twelve-day notice. He concluded that his plan would rescue the navy 'from the scandalous censure of man-stealing and from the ingratitude ... of letting their preservers perish in time of peace!'[1] Here he identified the two chief problems in manning that the navy faced: the notorious impress and the cut back in naval employment in peacetime.

Peacetime

The manning issue Sancho wrote about derived from the fact that the Royal Navy was largely demobilized during peace. The officers spent these years ashore forgetting their profession, while the sailors dispersed to employment in merchant ships. The government failed to regulate the seafaring labor market, the exception being the Newfoundland fisheries, which it regarded as the true 'nurseries of seamen'.[2] At the approach of war, no time existed to train an experienced sailor and the supply depended on those employed in the merchant fleet. In June 1775, it was decided to increase the navy's manpower from 18,000 to 28,000, exclusively for use in North America. As war evolved, the figure would rise to more than 100,000 and the locations would become Atlantic-wide. Within such extensive figures, the most crucial element was the number of experienced sailors.

The situation of mariners in peacetime is demonstrated by a riot which took place in Liverpool in August 1775, before the outbreak of the War for Independence had become apparent. In this port, 3,000 underemployed mariners existed and rebelled against an effort by Liverpool merchants to reduce their wages. It began as sailors finished rigging the Guineaman *Derby* and demanded payment at the going rate of 30s per month.[3] The owners, however, offered them only 20s, as they took advantage of the underemployment situation. In protest, the men returned to the *Derby* and demolished the rigging and began to do the same to other ships in the harbor. The ringleaders were seized and sent to the Water Street tower prison, but it was attacked by a large mob and the inmates released. The rioters then marched to the port and derigged all the ships which were ready to sail. Under a red flag, they surrounded the city's Town Hall and Exchange, where they met the mayor and it appeared that the merchants had agreed to their terms.

The sailors celebrated, but it was short lived as they learned that the merchants had hired 300 men at 10s per day to apprehend those who had led the protest. By accident the constables fired upon them at the Town Hall, killing seven and wounding forty. Having broken into shops and armed themselves, the sailors returned to the Town Hall the next day, planted six cannon seized from the docked ships, then blasted away at the structure that was the symbol of the merchant oligarchy. From there they visited the houses of various merchants, destroying their records or forcing contributions from them. The riot was eventually quelled by a troop of Manchester Light Horse and fourteen of the ringleaders were tried in Lancaster, although all were discharged on agreeing to enlist in 'his Majesty's ships destined for America' – a gesture towards the new war effort. In time of peace, mariners in crowded ports without work were liable to riot over wages, causing city fathers and merchants to reap a whirlwind of hostility against their governing bodies.

Wartime

During war, conditions differed as sailors found full employment and could readily look for the best wages. Royal Navy crews were made up of impressed sailors who were experienced seamen, while volunteers were a mixed lot, some with experience, but many landsmen. We have seen as many as 20 per cent of crews were boys, apprentices as young as 6 or 8, from all levels of society, who were in training to be future seamen. The crews came from all over the British Isles and often included Cretians, Danes, Italians, Portuguese, Swedes, Hanoverians and Americans from every colony.

One source of mariners in ports were dealers called crimps, who enticed seamen from their ships and sold them to the ship that offered the highest bid.[4] Crimps were free enterprise operators who took advantage of mariners in ports, where they spent their advances, wages or prize money. Crimps were men or women who kept taverns or lodging houses, encouraging every sort of dissipation so that seamen would spend themselves into debt and ultimately be offered a choice of debtors' prison or placement on the ship, which provided the crimp with the most lucrative return. Despite their unsavory reputation, merchants and the Royal Navy were often forced to deal with them.

Volunteers

In wartime, volunteers made up half to two-thirds of those manning navy ships.[5] Even landsmen were lured by bounties from their local communities, for although they were untrained and inexperienced, they had the potential to make a deck sailor. They also had the option of choosing their own ship. The poorer and remoter parts of Britain were ideal recruiting grounds for volunteers. Since navy pay remained the same from 1653 to 1797, it was only an attraction for the poor. Instead, volunteers were lured by a captain who had reputation for fairness or a ship known for taking prizes. Officers appointed to command a ship would go to their home districts to attract recruits. Some actually led their tenantry to join, much as had been done by lords in the Middle Ages. One other source of willing volunteers were prisoners of war and debtors' prisoners, although criminals were not accepted. The notorious Impressment Service was actually responsible for collecting these volunteers, along with its other duties.

Black Sailors

The careers of sailors are difficult to follow because they pursued several employment opportunities, for which their motives are not always clear. Unlike black servants, the black sailor in British or American ports, usually without a master, would search for the ideal ship's crew, after the enjoyment of life in a port. In wartime, he might volunteer for the Royal Navy or for the British merchant marine, or even serve on a privateer. During the War for Independence, the navy hired private ships as transports, where a man could be employed by British merchants. He could also limit himself to local waters as a pilot, fisherman, keelman or waterman.[6]

Serving in the Royal Navy during the Seven Years' War, Brinton Hammon was the black author of the first British slave narrative in 1760.[7] It is unclear whether he was literate; therefore, it is possible he dictated his story. Hammon was originally from Massachusetts, but in 1747 as a slave, he left his master John Winslow with his permission and sailed from Plymouth, Massachusetts to the West Indies to obtain logwood. On the return, his vessel was caught on a reef off the Florida Coast, where Indians murdered the entire crew except for Hammon, who was rescued by a Spanish ship from St Augustine. Its captain made a deal with the Indians, giving them $10 for Hammon and persuading them to desist from killing any others.

Hammon was sent to Havana, Cuba where he lived as a slave with the governor, but when pressed on Havana's streets, he refused to serve in the Spanish Navy. After two failed attempts to escape, Hammon finally succeeded in being taken by the lieutenant's barge to the Royal Navy's 18-gun sloop *Beaver*, which sailed to Jamaica, after the governor's failed attempts to get him back. From Jamaica, he sailed in a merchant ship convoy to The Downs roadstead, southeastern England. Now regarded by the navy as a freeman sailor, he served on the 50-gun *Arcenceil* and then the 90-gun *Sandwich*. At Chatham Dockyard in May 1759, he joined the crew of the 74-gun *Hercules*, which was attacked by a larger French warship, in which seventy of his fellow crew members were killed and Hammon wounded. He was discharged from the *Hercules* because his disabled arm rendered him incapable of service. After being paid his wages, he was put into Greenwich Hospital where he soon recovered. After this, he sailed as the cook on the *Captain Martyn*, from which he was discharged in October. During his time in the navy, he did not have an officer as a master, hence he was completely on his own.

Like many sailors exposed to the attractions of London he soon dissipated his wages and caught a fever which required a six-week convalescence. After recovery, he could find nothing better than signing up for a slaver voyage to Guinea. Before it left for Africa, however, Hammon heard of Captain Watt's sailing to Boston, Massachusetts and he enquired as to whether he needed a cook. He did and Hammon abandoned the slaver, instead working to prepare the ship to sail to Boston. To his astonishment and joy, he found that his old master, who had become General John Winslow, was to be a passenger on the Boston-bound vessel. They were reunited, Winslow having thought Hammon was dead. Thus, Hammon seemingly gave up freedom to return to slavery with his old master – a decision out of sorts with virtually every other slave narrative. His final sentiments were a Christian acceptance of his fate:

How Great Things the Lord hath done for me; I would call upon all men, and say, O magnify the Lord with me, and let us exalt his name together! O that Men would Praise the Lord for His Goodness, and for his Wonderful Works to the Children of Men![8]

Blacks join the Royal Navy

By the end of the eighteenth century, the constant turnover of personnel made the Royal Navy the world's largest employer of free black labor. Since crews were usually incomplete, blacks, like Briton Hammon, who were passengers on ships often found immediate employment as they learned the ropes. Blacks' knowledge of their local marine environments made them ideal on smaller and more maneuverable warships. They were especially present in the crews of navy galleys. In 1776, Captain Andrew Hamond regarded galleys so crucial to control of Chesapeake Bay that he designed and constructed a 'Row Gondola Carrying 5 Swivels on each Side and a Six pounder in her head and another in her Stern', in which blacks successfully confronted rebel shore forces.[9]

Francis Barber volunteers

As noted, Frances Barber had been freed by his Jamaican master in 1754 and was living comfortably in London as a servant in the household of Samuel Johnson. However, in 1758, as the Seven Years' War raged, Barber ran away from his employer and joined the Royal Navy.[10] Earlier, he had sailed from Jamaica to England, served as a landsman aboard various navy ships, receiving regular pay and good reports and acquiring a taste for tobacco. While Barber freely volunteered, Johnson missed his servant a good deal, and to get him back falsely claimed that he had been impressed. Johnson sent letters to the Admiralty, resulting in Barber being discharged on October 22, 1760. Barber reluctantly returned to Johnson to be his servant.

Johnson was an early abolitionist, so why had Barber left? He never clearly set down his motives, which lead us to compare his life as a servant with that of the navy. He did not fit in well with other servants in Johnson's household, who were older than his 16 years and not black. While experienced mariners thought the navy pay low, it was far higher than what Barber received from Johnson. As a writer, Johnson's ability to pay was sporadic, while navy security in food, pay and healthcare was relatively consistent. As the number of blacks in the navy was estimated at 6 to 8 per cent, he was more likely to find companionship there than on the streets of London.

Benjamin Whitecuff volunteers

Another black navy sailor was Benjamin Whitecuff. He was a free black, born on Long Island, New York. During the War for Independence, he served Sir Henry Clinton as a courier in the waters around New York City but was caught and condemned by the rebels to death and sent to Boston to be hanged. Somehow, he escaped, but later his ship was taken by a rebel privateer, which again attempted to take him to Boston. On the way, a Liverpool privateer, the brig *Eagle*, captured the rebel privateer, freeing Whitecuff.[11] The privateer carried him to the West Indies' island of Tortola and from there he sailed to England. He volunteered for the Royal Navy brig *St Philips Castle*, which sailed to the Mediterranean in February 1782, where he joined renowned Captain Roger Curtis, participating in the defenses of Mahon, Menorca and Gibraltar. When the Gibraltar siege ended in 1783, Whitecuff was discharged and he settled in Deptford, where he was baptized and soon afterwards married Sarah. He had prize money and wages due him, a naval pension of £4 a year and the Claims Commission awarded him £10 for his services and the loss of his Long Island farm.

Robert Wedderburn volunteers

Jamaican mulatto Robert Wedderburn volunteered for the Royal Navy on the island at the age of 16.[12] France had joined the War for Independence in 1778 and Wedderburn sailed in a navy ship, typically complaining about the monotonous diet and use of flogging to maintain discipline. After a year, he arrived in Britain and left the navy and settled down in St Giles, London, a diverse parish inhabited by many free blacks, Jews, Indian sailors and Irish immigrants. Having acquired the skill in the navy, Wedderburn found employment as a journeyman tailor. He had pride in his craft because of the economic independence it afforded him, although he was not above being involved in occasional petty theft.

Wedderburn's earlier roots show how far he had come. He was born in 1762 in Kingston, Jamaica, the illegitimate son of James Wedderburn of Scotland and an African-born slave and his housekeeper, Rosanna. A doctor and plantation owner, James had restored the family's fortunes, which had been lost when they sided with the Pretender in 1745, and had been forced to migrate to Jamaica. Having used Rosanna, Wedderburn sold her back to her previous owner, Lady Douglas, when she was five months pregnant with Robert. Lady Douglas had agreed that Robert be free at birth and she became his godmother, allowing Robert to claim to be a freeman. However, to his father, James, Robert was just one of his five illegitimate mixed-race children.

Robert grew up in Kingston's urban environment under the care of his maternal grandmother, known as 'Talkee/Talky Amy', a slave who traded smuggled goods for her master and for other merchants on commission. At the age of 11, he saw his 70-year-old grandmother flogged within an inch of her life, accused of witchcraft. In later years, when Robert was living in Britain, his father's legitimate son and heir, Andrew Colville, defended his father when details of his escapades appeared in the British press. He denied his father's paternity of Robert and claimed that Rosanna was both promiscuous and unable to control her temper. It made sense that Robert was bitter over such accusations, as he continued to emphasize the white relations of his father and the British background he had acquired.

Impressment

Beyond these volunteer experiences, blacks were also pressed into the Royal Navy. Recruiting by impressment was the age-old right of the Crown to gain the labor of seafarers. Its role has been overemphasized because it could be abusive, with tales of men being physically forced to serve. In fact, impressment was restricted in numerous ways, including the prohibition that ships' boys could not be impressed. While impressment was often condemned by civil authorities, no one cared to replace it. Thus, 'the haphazard tyranny of the press gang reflected the weakness of the government and the inability to impose any regulated system on the labour market for seafarers'.[13]

Impressment in Britain

Revamped during the Seven Years' War, the impress service involved a lieutenant and a gang of six seamen seeking sailors that lived in a seaport or district. They only sought existing sailors taken on shore and thus in wartime, their effort contributed only about half of the necessary recruits – though they were the best seamen. Young black Olaudah Equiano was twice exposed to the impress in England, the first time at the Nore – the fleet gathering place at the mouth of the Thames – and the second at an inn by Westminster Bridge. As an experienced seaman, he hid when a press boat came aboard his ship at the Nore and he was saved somehow by the mate. In the second incident, Equiano actually worked with his master, a navy lieutenant, who led the press gang lodged at Westminster, impressing seamen from local taverns.[14]

When at peace, the press was scarcely needed to fill the navy's reduced ranks. Most recruits who were pressed and kept, ultimately stayed in the navy. Negotiations with the impress service were common and guilds that represented maritime workers made arrangements to meet impressment quotas, so that impressment was restricted by local agreements. The established Company of Watermen and Lightermen of the River Thames were regarded as a reserve for the Royal Navy and developed relationships with the London Impress Service. During the English Civil War, their watermen had been free from impressment, while the company negotiated higher rates of pay from the navy.[15] After this, the London Impress still sought watermen as they were qualified seamen. The press took watermen apprentices first because they were younger and felt to be more easily adapted to a shipboard existence. These press gangs were actually headed by members of the company in addition to marines and seamen from a ship, acting as a naval shore force. The press sought not only watermen, but deserters, escaped prisoners of war and returning sailors on leave. A few were impressed as punishment because they sold grog to the sick or concealed deserters.

London's sailor towns were a favorite place for the press service to operate at an inn or pub. Stepney had become a popular place of residence for seamen and retired naval officers. Speculative developers built housing there, which included some short rows of terraced houses, a groundbreaking innovation at that time.[16] Most London-registered ships sailed from docks in Stepney parish, which at the time took in much of East End's riverside. Here the press could be more certain of obtaining the desired seamen rather than landsmen. Along the Thames, the service operated from road blocks, but the law was clear that they could not just take any male, especially if they were inexperienced landsmen.

Liverpool was an impress special case because of its dominance of the slave trade and its lack of a Royal Navy facility.[17] Here no cooperation with the impress service existed. In fact, the city fathers and its sailors were bitterly opposed to even a search for volunteers and the mayor asserted that he would throw the press officers in prison before they could establish a press in his city. It was by no means unusual for Liverpool's sailors to attack the impress headquarters. During the War for Independence, Liverpool's corporation offered bounties to recruits and later increased them to 10 guineas for seamen and 5 for landsmen. The substantial bounties were meant to offset the need for impressment.

Impressment in the colonies

Colonial impressment was necessary for the convoys that plied the Atlantic. Anxiety existed between the need to protect trade by the colonial governments and the Royal Navy's inability during war to provide enough ships and seamen. In the Chesapeake, the threat of mariners' desertion was a problem, so that Maryland prohibited them from going ashore without leave. They were allowed very limited credit at taverns and could not cross a ferry or travel overland without permission from their captain.

During the Seven Years' War, Governor Horatio Sharpe of Maryland found that seamen were hard to come by. Most trade with Britain was not carried in colonial vessels, but in British merchant ships, whose seamen did not remain in Chesapeake Bay, but were lured to Northern colonial ports' lucrative privateering. Sharpe regularly faced Chesapeake tobacco vessels failing to sail 'for want of hands'.[18] As an expedient, he took Royal Navy sailors to fill the gaps in these tobacco ships' crews. Then to make up for the lost hands, the navy ship was empowered by the governor to conduct an impressment to replace the lost crew members. Thus, governors granted requests for presses, as long as they met prohibitions such as not pressing men from ship's crews with fewer than a dozen members. In this way, the press was recognized as a legal means of replenishing Royal Navy crews. Unfortunately, some navy commanders were too desperate for sailors to bother obtaining local credentials to carry out impressment.

Impressment in the colonies became a regulated and well-established practice. When in 1767, the navy's Captain Jeremiah Morgan of the sloop *Hornet* attempted a night-time impress in Norfolk to obtain sailors, town authorities, including the mayor, calmly confronted him and forced him to leave empty handed.[19] In this case, the rioters were the Royal Navy pressmen, not sailors. In New York, the local magistrates organized New York militia to serve as press gangs in recruiting sailors for the hired transports that plied between the city and the British Isles. The press was an accepted necessity to ensure sailors for maritime trade.

The Navy Press at sea

In the colonies, obstacles existed for the Royal Navy press to fully operate on shore, but at sea the press was more effective. Those pressed at sea were more likely to be skilled seamen than those taken on land. In September 1775, operating in Chesapeake Bay, the navy sloop *Otter*, under Captain Matthew Squire, made impressment a routine part of inspecting inward-bound ships. Squire stopped a ship coming from Maryland's Eastern Shore carrying a man identified as 'raising men to fight against the king'.[20] To punish and make use of him, Squire 'Prest him to raise men for the Otter'. A week later, Squire confronted two merchant vessels, one bound for Bristol, the other for Glasgow, with cargos of rum, sugar, coffee and beeswax. While the cargos were tempting, what Squire really wanted was seamen, so he impressed one man from each ship's crew. The *Otter*'s press would take only a few experienced mariners from ships it encountered, so as not cripple the ship's ability to continue its voyage. If this method was too slow, crews could be pressed from captured prizes. In 1776, the navy's Captain Andrew Hamond impressed the entire crew of the private schooner *Betsey*, while the schooner itself was returned to its owner's care.

After their arrival in Chesapeake Bay and the Delaware River, Hamond, Squire and other Royal Navy captains used the press chiefly to man their tenders and smaller galleys and barges. The advantage of pressing by tender was that the officers and men taken stepped directly into their new positions, without the usual distribution delays.

When in 1776, the Dunmore-Hamond fleet became the refuge of Loyalists, a lack of seamen existed, which justified the press. This situation was exacerbated by the need for crews in tenders that supported the larger warships.[21] When aggressive Matthew Squire of the *Otter* outfitted his second tender, Hamond was not pleased because he felt the *Otter* was too small to have more than one tender. This rivalry over crews for tenders continued when Virginia's Governor Dunmore created additional crew shortages by purchasing five more ships to serve as his tenders. Technically, these new commissions were Loyalist privateers serving under Dunmore as Admiral of the Virginia Navy. Dunmore's need for crew members and outfitting these new ships could not be filled by Hamond, forcing Dunmore to go to the Maryland and Virginia Eastern Shore to recruit new crews.

Interpreting the impress

Some historians make it seem that shore-based impressment was the only way the Royal Navy recruited and that the press's activities were a very cause of the rebellion that led to the War for Independence. To them impressment was an abuse that Atlantic sailors struggled against. These historians claim that this hostility 'first took shape among the buccaneers of America'.[22] Thus pirates and sailors are linked in protest in the early eighteenth century and then to the violence against taxation of the 1760s and 1770s.

However, assertions about impressment of sailors as a cause of the War for Independence stop cold as the war commences because all sides were forced to use the impress more extensively than before. In Massachusetts in 1779, not only sailors, but ships' cargos of pork, beef, flour and bread would be impressed to feed a growing fleet. It is also admitted by these historians that sailors 'were read out of the settlement at the [war's] end'.[23] While dissident mariners may have rioted before the Revolution, their motives were a matter of employment conditions, not 'no taxation without representation'. Mariners were not predisposed by the impress to support the rebel cause. In fact, as late as October 1783, Philadelphia seamen, blacks and 'loyalist leather-aprons' tore down the Stars and Stripes from Captain Stewart's vessel and triumphantly carried them through the streets.

Chapter 8

Advantages for Blacks in the Royal Navy

Some interpretations make it seem that the Royal Navy was a prison camp in which the conditions were so harsh that mariners tried to avoid serving there at all costs. This judgement emphasizes the use of the lash for discipline on ships and the impress's violence in recruiting sailors. Certainly, both of these activities may have been painful to sailors, but they must be judged by the standards of the eighteenth century, not the twenty-first. As we have seen with the impress, the supposedly arbitrary seizing of any males to become sailors, turns out to be a process of restrictions and negotiation meant to routinely provide for sailors in wartime.

As to the lash, it was universally used to punish and discipline people of all ages, whose passion, it was felt, had got the better of them. The whip was a recommended means in New England to break the obstinate will of children, apprentices and servants. Even radical reformer Robert Wedderburn, who had been flogged in the Royal Navy, when he called for a ban on flogging made an exception of those under 14, for children deserved to be flogged because it was essential to their upbringing.[1]

Maritime employment

If we return to the details of Ignatius Sancho's letter for the Admiralty, we see the attitude of a middling black Methodist father looking to provide his seven children with a secure future in the maritime field. He proposed that seamen should be enrolled and provided with a small stipend for life, which they could apply for as needed. Each sailor was to identify himself with a certificate signed by his ship's captain. In each port, a house of refuge was to be established for the sailor's sons, at the age of 6, to be taught navigation and school subjects to prepare them to be placed on aboard a navy ship at the age of 15. An option would exist for those inclined to shipbuilding in a navy yard. After ten years of faithful service the sons would be enrolled on the pension books. Funding could be taken from the notorious Irish list. This would affect Sancho's two sons, but he had five daughters, who he suggested could be employed in the fisheries, which opened 'many doors of useful employment for both sexes'.[2] To our knowledge, Sancho had never been in the navy, but he saw maritime employment as an opportunity for his children.

Blacks who joined a Royal Navy ship saw their condition differently than whites. As a historian has noted, 'a black sailor had one special qualification: … he was not likely to find conditions intolerable and jump ship.' Blacks found the navy to be a refuge from oppression, not just because it offered them freedom, but because the navy provided them with more security than parsimonious merchant vessels. The navy offered them abundant food, healthcare, religious services and even the possibility of a pension. Some black sailors

58

actually participated in its press gangs. 'To anyone bred on a plantation, this must have been a refreshing world of relative equality.'[3]

Food and Clothes

On each navy ship, the purser had to keep good accounts of food supplies because he was responsible for the entire value of the stores issued in England by the Victualling Board. His records covered every officer and man of the ship's company for each day, but he was only paid when food was actually consumed.[4] The purser also issued clothes, which he had obtained from a clothing contractor. He could act as private merchant, selling items not provided by the navy, such as tobacco. He worked closely with the cooper, monitoring the number of casks in the hold that the cooper maintained. He shared the responsibility for the mess book with the cooper, recording the consumption of food in the different messes onboard.

In England, the Victualling Board was second only to the Navy Board in size, for it maintained victualling yards and stores at several navy dockyards, most notably at Deptford.[5] The diet planned by the Board may have been monotonous, but it consistently provided enough calories for hard work and was one of the attractions of the navy. The inclusion of fresh vegetables and meat had, by the Seven Years' War, much reduced the incidence of scurvy onboard. The crew's high-calorie diet was far superior to that of ordinary men ashore or among sailors on merchant vessels. In a week, the official crewman's diet included 7lb of bread, 7 gallons of beer, 4lb of beef, 2lb of salted pork, 2 pints of peas, 3 pints of oatmeal, 6oz of butter and 12oz of cheese. One hot meal per day was the usual expectation.

Surgeons

At the beginning of the eighteenth century, care for infirm sailors on land was provided in rooms rented from landladies, who agreed to feed and care for their patients. While cheap, the system did not work; the ladies failed to meet their requirements and, in fact, they were encouraged to become crimps, selling those who recovered to a merchantman. It was impossible for doctors to treat such scattered facilities, and contagious diseases spread rapidly.

This changed at mid-century when the first naval hospitals were created at Haslar near Portsmouth and Stonehouse near Plymouth, under the direction of the Sick and Hurt Board. The board provided these hospitals with the latest drugs and medical equipment and salaried medical staff, who were forbidden to have a private practice. Upon arrival, patients were stripped, their clothes burnt, themselves washed in tubs of hot water with soap, and put into a clean nightshirt – which was regularly changed. A series of diets were available for different conditions. Sea officers regularly inspected the hospitals.

Naval hospitals were not limited to the British Isles. During the War for Independence in Nova Scotia, healthcare in Halifax's civilian, military, naval and prisoner hospitals would improve, enhanced by the arrival of numerous Loyalist surgeons. In the case of Halifax's naval hospital, Captain Andrew Hamond found it to be a disgrace.[6] It was located in a deteriorating commercial warehouse, built on piles over the water, with scarcely a roof or floors to it. He prepared for a new building by finding a 3-acre site on the harbor north of the naval yard, away from the town and the naval burial yard. With the support of the Sick and Hurt Board, bids were called for in December 1781 and John Loader, the yard's master shipwright, was placed in charge of the construction. Funded by the Navy Board, the new facility eventually cost almost £8,000, and when opened at Christmas 1782, it accommodated 200 patients in four wards. The staff consisted of a surgeon, a purveyor, a dispenser who acted as assistant surgeon, nurses for every ten to twelve patients, a matron, cook and porter, and two laborers. Its first physician was the Rhode Island Loyalist John Halliburton.

Chaplains

While the position of chaplain had legally been defined by the Admiralty, it was not filled except in the larger warships.[7] The chaplain was an inactive landsman among busy seamen. He visited the sick and performed many burial sermons and in battle, he assisted the surgeon. However, few chaplains were in priest's orders so that they could not administer the sacraments to their crews. A chaplain's spiritual role on a ship depended upon the strength of his piety and even more on the support of his captain. At least they were available on many navy ships, while merchant ships did not carry them.

Provision for disabilities and retirement

The navy offered its seamen a measure of retirement security. Dating from 1588, the Chatham Chest was an actual iron chest holding charitable funds, located at the Chatham Dockyard. The funds were raised by a shilling deduction from each seaman's pay and designated for pensions for disabled sailors or their widows.

Another retirement possibility was as a pensioner at the Royal Hospital at Greenwich. A project initiated by Queen Mary II, wife of William III, the hospital dated from October 1694 and would take fifty-five years to complete. The structure involved Britain's leading architects, Sir Christopher Wren and his assistant Nicholas Hawksmoor, who gave their services free of charge. The governorship of the complex came to be considered a plum that admirals sought as an alternative to sea service. The Hospital served for, 'the relief and support of seamen serving onboard ships … belonging to the Royal Navy who by reason of their age, wounds or other disabilities shall be incapable of further service'.[8] It was underwritten by a welfare deduction of 6d a month from seamen's wages and after 1696 a further 6d was added. By 1752, 1,400 pensioners were present and by 1779 they numbered 2,350.

Overlooking the Thames, the hospital provided free bed, board and medical care to disabled navy sailors who met qualifications of age, injury or sickness. Not just disabled seamen, but their wives, children and widows could apply for hospital funds. From 1710, seamen in the merchant service were included, and four years later seamen injured while engaging pirates were added. Pensioners were divided between those who lived in the hospital and those who lived out in Greenwich, a preference for those who were married. The diet was similar to that on board ship, consisting of beef, mutton, cheese and bread.

Typically, since race is almost never mentioned in British documents, the hospital's records do not indicate race, but before 1763, as many as twenty-seven pensioners were from Africa or America and may have been black.[9] Brinton Hammon has been noted as a black navy seaman who recovered at the Naval Hospital. He is documented serving on several warships in the Seven Years' War, resulting in wounds which disabled his arm, so that he was treated and recovered at the Naval Hospital. It appears he had no officers' patronage.

Officers' patronage

Naval patronage was different from that of the army, allowing successful commanders to choose subordinate officers who would reflect credit on them and secure them further victories, prize money and profit.[10] Those commanders who chose to support blacks' or mulattoes' advancement as officers, were in practice creating a precedent. This is reflected in the case of mulatto waterman John Perkins's service. His career in the Royal Navy, taking a number of ships and prisoners from the enemy in the Caribbean, would gain the recognition and patronage of admirals at the highest level.

Perkins was probably born in the parish of Clarendon, Kingston, Jamaica around 1750, the son of an enslaved woman.[11] He probably was a slave, but occasionally a mixed-race son of a prominent white man was acknowledged by his father and given an education to prepare him for a clerical or administrative career and this is a possibility with Perkins. As a mulatto child, he was sent to Kingston and Port Royal where he became a slave servant to a ship's carpenter, William Young, who took him into naval service. In 1759, he joined the *Grenado*, a bomb vessel, as Young's servant, along with a white boy, John Middleton.

In Jamaica, ship's boys were often black. Perkins and Middleton remained with Young when he transferred to the larger *Boreas* on March 7, 1760. Perkins was not the only black boy aboard; the muster book records five other black servants who joined at the same time and they were joined by two more, both of them captain's servants. On the *Boreas*, Perkins was present at two crucial events: the capture of Martinique in 1762 and then the siege and capture of Havana later that year.

Thus began a naval career spanning almost half a century, from the Seven Years' War and War for Independence, to the French Revolutionary and Napoleonic Wars. After the Seven Years' War, Perkins left Young's service and began work as a pilot. He became sufficiently adept to secure employment in the navy ship *Achilles*. On December 9, 1771 he had the misfortune to run the ship ashore coming into Port Royal. He was blamed for the incident, for as Admiral George Rodney remembered, it had been caused 'thro' the unskillfulness of the pilot'. Perkins was court martialed two weeks later and found guilty, so that thereafter he was rendered incapable of serving as pilot in any navy ships. The verdict was enforced and he had to return to life as a civilian pilot, but as his knowledge of the seas around Jamaica had increased, his expertise allowed him to ignore the court's ruling.

As the War for Independence commenced, Perkins re-emerged in late November 1775 in the Admiralty's muster books as one of six pilots on the 50-gun *Antelope*, then Rear Admiral Clark Gayton's flagship on the Jamaica station.[12] Three years later, he left the navy to secure his first command on a privateer schooner, the 10-gun *Punch*, although he continued to provide intelligence to the navy. As a privateer, he took over 300 prizes, particularly from French shipping off the coast of Saint Dominque and Spanish shipping into Havana. This was the beginning of his fortune, accumulated despite the color of his skin.

In October 1781, Admiral Sir Peter Parker returned Perkins to the navy as a lieutenant in the schooner *Endeavour*, making him one of the few mixed-race commissioned officers in the Royal Navy. In this role, he first came to the attention of the British public through a series of newspaper reports about his exploits. They included in 1782, the *Endeavour*, which as it sailed towards Port Royal with two prizes in tow, although 'surrounded by French ships'. Perkins escaped from them 'by dint of good sailing'.[13] In these reports, Perkins was represented as an accomplished navy officer, ignoring the fact he was a mulatto.

The prisoners on his prizes reported the mustering of French and Spanish ships of the line for an assault on Jamaica. When the enemy sailed in April 1782, Admiral Rodney's fleet intercepted and defeated them at the famous Battle of the Saints. Despite his earlier misgivings of Perkins as a pilot, Rodney was now so impressed with him that in July he promoted him to master and commander of the *Endeavour* for his 'behavior in taking the French sloop with so many Officers on board her, and by your many services to His Majesty and the Publick'.[14] The *Endeavour* was re-established as a sloop of war, its armament increased to fourteen guns and it became renowned for its sailing superiority. Rodney hoped Perkins would 'have an opportunity of exerting yourself in the Service of your King & Country with as much applause now you are her Captain, as when you was only her Lieutenant and Commander'. Perkins was again sent on a series of cruises off Saint Dominque to reconnoiter French forces.

However, Perkins' promotion was disallowed by the Admiralty and he was demoted back to the rank of lieutenant and the guns he ordered were removed. This had more to do with Rodney's relationship with the Admiralty than Perkins' record. In Britain, a new government headed by the Marquis of Rockingham had replaced the North ministry and the new First Lord, Augustus Keppel, had dismissed Rodney while he was sailing in the West Indies. A ship was sent out with the dismissal, but when word of Rodney's victory at the Saints arrived, the British public was so congratulatory that the new ministry was forced to offer Rodney insincere praise.

At the end of the War for Independence, the *Endeavour* was decommissioned and sold off and Perkins like most officers was placed on half-pay. He spent time in Jamaica, but traveled to Britain first in 1784 and then two years later. On neither occasion did he enjoy the experience: 'I could not bear it,' he wrote, 'I felt the cold to such affect that I was obliged to quit England in the month of October, and I believe it would have been the death of me had I not left.'[15] His lifestyle did not exactly fit into British society as by this time he had had nine children with three different women, only one of whom was probably his wife.

In his early life, when Perkins was technically a slave, his mixed-race status allowed him to pass for white, thus his skin color was not a determining factor in his career. His early experience as a carpenter's servant and ship's boy gave him a start on a career in the Royal Navy. Race was not an issue with the admirals he served under. On the basis of his achievements, he received the patronage of Sir Peter Parker and George Rodney. Jamaica's Governor Archibald Campbell concluded in a letter that:

> By the gallant exertions of [Perkins] some hundred vessels were taken, burnt, or destroyed, and above three thousand men added to the list of prisoners of war in favour of Britain; in short, the character and conduct of Captain Perkins were not less admired by his superior officers in Jamaica, than respected by those of the enemy.[16]

His prize money arising from his captures allowed him to buy an estate in Jamaica, ironically employing slave labor. His career shows that the Royal Navy offered opportunities for blacks to become officers.

Chapter 9

Protecting Free Seamen

Royal Navy captains succeeded in recruiting by developing a reputation as good officers to serve under, not just among mariners, but also among young officers. The captain was in a position to nurture the numerous boys and sailors who sought a position on his ship.[1] He would have to advance their careers, get them wages and prize money, and protect them when they were in harm's way. In turn, when they matured they would enhance the captain's influence throughout the maritime world. This dependent relationship between the captain, his officers and his crew was fostered by the fact that when at sea they had to work together in order to survive weather, sickness and war. In this way, sailors became dependent on their mates for survival, whether black or white.

Crew solidarity is visually seen in a painting of an incident which happened in 1749, portraying a heroic act of rescuing a crew member in the face of a shark attack.[2] The painting shows an incident when 14-year-old sailor Brook Watson dived into Havana Harbor for a swim, a shark sank its teeth into his leg, pulling him under, severing his right foot. His mates in a skiff, one of them black, rescued him. The leg had to be amputated at the knee and ever after Watson would have a peg leg. The English-born youth would go on as a successful London merchant and MP, becoming Lord Mayor of London, chairman of Lloyd's, and commissary general of Britain's forces. Watson probably commissioned the artist John Singleton Copley and upon Watson's death, he bequeathed the painting to Christ's Hospital, London, a boys' school for the poor, in the hope it would provide 'a most useful Lesson to Youth'. This gesture, worthy of Jonas Hanway, implied that in the unpredictable life at sea, an important source of protection would be a sailor's crew mates. The inclusion of the black sailor shows that they were now commonplace in ships' crews. (See Front Cover)

Flogging actually had a role in creating further crew solidarity. It was no accident that when a sailor was flogged it was before the entire ship's company. All sailors were subject to it, little room existed for favoritism. The courts and the navy prescribed the number of public lashes depending on the crime, while in the privacy of the home or plantation no legal restraint existed.

The navy disregards masters' claims

Slaves who served in Royal Navy crews were regarded by the Admiralty as too skilled to lose and were protected if their former masters came after them. Since the Admiralty controlled a seaman's wages they tried to make certain that a seaman's wages went to him rather than his slave master. In 1758, when a former slave, now a navy seaman, was discovered and arrested by his former master, the Admiralty contended, 'the laws of this country admit no badges of slavery' and instructed its admiral to prevent any future attempt to re-enslave a king's mariner.[3] This was fourteen years before the Somerset Case, which asserted similar principles in British courts.

The Royal Navy had not yet reached the point where it attacked the institution of slavery, but it preferred not to recognize the status of slaves on its ships. A few blacks did remain slaves as they served a navy officer on ship, who could claim their pay and prize money. Aboard a navy ship, however, the presence of slaves had to be hidden under false names as the Admiralty saw each ship as a microcosm of conditions in Britain. When in battle, they believed it was necessary to have the confidence of the entire ship's company working together, not the situation of a slave ship.

Olaudah Equiano and Michael Pascal

During the Seven Years' War, navy ships that sailed in American waters had slaves to their crews. Details exists on the relationship between black navy seaman Olaudah Equiano and his sometime master, Lieutenant Michael Pascal. The latter was a navy lieutenant from 1745 and Equiano's owner from 1754 to 1763. They are an example of the intertwined careers of a slave and his master in the Royal Navy.[4]

Their relationship began in the summer of 1754, when Equiano's existing master, a Virginia tobacco planter named Mr Campbell, received Pascal as a guest and business partner, selling him tobacco. Nine-year-old Equiano made quite an impression on Pascal, who subsequently purchased him from Campbell for £30–40. From there, Pascal took him to Britain with the intent of 'gifting' him to his cousins, the two Guerin sisters of Greenwich. During the voyage, Pascal named him Gustavus Vassa, after King Gustav Vasa, the Swedish hero who freed his nation from Danish rule.[5] At this point, Equiano had been renamed numerous times and he preferred to use his African name. Until the very end of their relationship, Equiano appears to have respected Pascal as a master who was willing to give him freedom of movement, while at the same time still regarding him as a slave.

Equiano and Pascal arrived in Falmouth, Cornwall at the end of 1754, as conflict with France again appeared. Equiano's career in the navy now began as Pascal's servant and a ship's boy. He would be a seaman on several navy vessels, from at least his ninth until his seventeenth birthday. He was in training, commenting, 'I had been learning many of the manoeuvers of the ship during our cruise; and I was several times made to fire the guns.'[6]

In a warship, gunpowder was kept below and boys (powder monkeys) brought it up in spark-proof containers in small amounts, only enough to fire a single gun, as too much exposed powder was liable to explode. On April 14, 1759, Equiano's ship sailed for Gibraltar where it joined Admiral Boscawen's fleet for the Battle of Lagos Bay. Equiano describes his participation from the midst of the gun deck. He brought powder to the aftermost gun and 'witnessed the dreadful fate of many of my companions', who 'were dashed to pieces'.[7]

The navy became Equiano's home, where he was assimilated into the ship's company. He was a friend of the boys onboard, as witnessed by his first bloody nose. This came about when boys were called on the quarterdeck and paired to fight: 'This was the first time I fought with a white boy' and 'it made me fight more desperately'.[8] The captain and ship's company encouraged him to continue participating. As to his education, one Daniel Queen, the captain's servant, taught him to shave and dress hair, and to read and explain the Bible, so that he was styled 'the black Christian'. Queen made Equiano feel that 'when our ship was paid off, as I was free as himself or any other man on board, he would instruct me … on how I might gain a good livelihood'. This was not necessarily what his master thought.

Unlike many British institutions, the social divisions of naval officers like Pascal were not class based. Some rose through the ranks of seamen and masters to gain their position, while others were admitted as officers despite humble origins. To be commissioned a lieutenant, candidates had to be at least 20 years old, have passed formal examinations in navigation and mathematics, and have served at least six years at sea. Further promotion to commander and then captain was through merit, bravery or patronage. Patronage allowed successful commanders to pick their protégés. As professionals, they chose subordinates who would reflect credit on them, and secure them further victories, prize money and profit. The timing also had to be right, for few could expect to be promoted or even hold a command during peace, when the navy was drastically reduced.

Pascal's career as a Royal Navy officer is documented, but it lacks the detail found in Equiano's autobiography.[9] Pascal was a descendant of the Huguenots and from 1736 to 1742 he served on a merchant ship. In the War of Austrian Succession, he became a naval lieutenant, but after the war ended, in mid-1751, he was put on half-pay. Pascal's family was not wealthy and he failed to have the patronage, which would have tided him over during the peace, when commissions were hard to come by. Unable to make ends meet, he requested and got leave from the Admiralty to go to Virginia with a merchantman for ten months. He had become captain of the *Industrious Bee*, a trading vessel based out of Guernsey in the English Channel. In late January 1752, he set sail from the mouth of the River Thames for Virginia. He spent the next years engaged in colonial trade and this is when he met Equiano. While his merchant service may have been lucrative, it obstructed his further promotion in the navy.

As the Royal Navy's need for officers increased with the Seven Years' War, Pascal again was able to serve. He would be promoted several times and received a number of different commissions. In June of 1755, he was a second or third lieutenant of the *Roebuck*, a 40-gun vessel, on which Equiano also served. The ship was used to transport troops, moving soldiers from garrisons in Scotland. Both the *Roebuck* and *Preston* – a ship that first lieutenant Pascal would command in January 1757 – participated in the blockade of Le Havre from the English Channel. After a promotion to first lieutenant of the *Roebuck*, he was re-assigned to the *Royal George*, the largest ship in the navy. Equiano accompanied him, which took them to both sides of the Atlantic. On January 1758, Pascal was on the *Namur*, a ship commanded by the famous Admiral Edward Boscawen.[10] It was his flagship at the siege of Louisbourg in 1758 and after its fall, Pascal served as its third lieutenant.

Equiano recounts that Pascal was wounded in this action, although he recovered quickly. Due to his heroism, Pascal was appointed 'master and commander' of the *Aetna*, which he took to England.[11] There, while technically a slave, Equiano enjoyed freedom of movement as his master was absent from the ship regularly, attending to business in Portsmouth, Greenwich and Gosport. Equiano renewed his friendship with the Guerin sisters and at his request they arranged to have him baptized at St Margaret's Church, Westminster. He also got along with

Pascal's mistress, as she entrusted him with the care and sale of her property. He showed skill in such dealings, which would ensure his future ability to purchase his freedom.

On April 12, 1761, Equiano and Pascal boarded the *Aetna*, which participated in the capture of the French island of Belle-Isle. Pascal delivered various war materials to the troops who were set to take the citadel. The ship was then sent to Basque Road, where Commodore Sir Thomas Stanhope's squadron blockaded the French in the port of Rochefort. The *Aetna* remained at this port until the summer of 1762 when it was sent back to Portsmouth. While Equiano received promotions as a seaman, his increased pay and prize money went to his master Pascal.

Pascal must have hidden Equiano's presence from his ship's records. Still, while a slave on a Royal Navy ship, Equiano had enjoyed the unfettered movement of a freeman and he accumulated some money, even though his master was entitled to his prize money. Now baptized, with the end of the war in sight, Equiano had begun to dream of a new life as a free man in London.[12] However, upon Equiano's arrival at Deptford dockyard on December 10, 1762, despite his demonstrated loyalty to Pascal, his master took him and sold him to merchant Captain James Doran to be taken to the West Indies. This was before the Somerset Case which would have ruled on the illegality of Pascal's action. While Pascal respected Equiano's intelligence, he evidently could not afford to be magnanimous as he needed the proceeds from selling him as a slave. Pascal's sale of him disturbed Equiano for the rest of his life.

Pascal's domestic situation was complicated. He never married, taking a mistress like many young sailors.[13] Equiano may have been a victim of this situation, as he blamed Pascal's cruelty on his second mistress, who lodged on the *Aetna*. Unlike the previous mistress, she was resentful of Equiano, believing that he was serving Pascal's first mistress, whom she regarded as a rival.

Pascal's career in the navy continued. He was sent to Portugal to aid its navy. At the end of the Seven Years' War, he and two other experienced commanders, Joseph Norwood and Thomas Lee, were made post-captains. He was made commander of the *Dispatch* in 1764 and a full captain as a result. This was his last promotion.

Meanwhile, Doran took Equiano to the sugar island of Montserrat, where he sold him to a Quaker merchant, Robert King, who while reluctant to part with such a talented slave, allowed him to save to purchase his freedom. Equiano worked hard in the sugar seasons as he 'rowed the boat, and slaved at the oars'. King manumitted him on July 11, 1766. While continuing to work for King, even after he had purchased his freedom, he found himself discriminated against in the mainland colonies as if he were still a slave.[14] While visiting Savannah, he got into a fight with a slave who injured him severely. To add insult to injury, the slave's master attempted to have him flogged and jailed, forcing him to go into hiding. Later in Savannah, Equiano was threatened by whites who claimed he was a runaway slave. Such incidents made him feel that he could only be truly free on a Royal Navy ship or in the British Isles. Despite his respect for King, he decided to return to the safety of England, as he continued to face the threat of being re-enslaved.

Having seen the Guerin sisters on his return to England, Equiano made contact with Pascal in 1767, claiming that his former master owed him prize money for capture of the *Temaire*, *Modeste* and *Centaur*, but it was useless as Pascal asserted slave master's rights. As a freeman, Equiano was able to assist the naturalist Dr Charles Irving in a 1773 Royal Navy exploratory voyage towards the North Pole led by Captain Constantine Phipps.[15] In England, Equiano never faced re-enslavement and made many friends, ultimately identifying himself as an abolitionist in his later autobiography.

By the mid-eighteenth century, the Admiralty had become committed to protecting slaves on its ships from their former masters. As most of Britain's blacks were free and Christian, protected by English Common Law, the word of black mariners became accepted by Admiralty courts in cases and in one case, two white men were hanged on the evidence of a black man.[16] Still, naval officers like Pascal held slaves on their ships as servants and while they might treat them as freemen, they reserved their hold over them, especially if they got into financial difficulty. Slaves who became free still faced abuse if they sailed in the colonies, where there was always a chance of their being re-enslaved. This was a lesson that Equiano would emphasize in his account of his life.

Chapter 10

Other Related Employment

The Royal Navy offered opportunities for blacks who did not want to be navy sailors. They could serve as pilots, in the Navy Board's shipyards, or as marines. During wartime, the navy hired merchant ships to carry men and supplies across the Atlantic in convoys, so this was also an option. These opportunities were constricted by long-standing employment conditions, which affected both blacks and whites.

Couriers

We will see how crucial couriers were in the early years of the war as governors sought to retain their authority in New York and Charleston. The role was dangerous because if one was captured, he was considered by the rebels to be a spy and likely to be executed. During the Philadelphia Campaign in 1777, Dick, a free black, took refuge on Andrew Hamond's *Roebuck* in the Delaware River, who employed him with a pass as a courier.[1] By 1778 he was in New York and was now known as Richard Weaver and a year later he would get himself, his wife and children to England, where he made a claim to the Loyalist Commission, based on his service as a courier. In a later chapter, we will learn how he became a corporal of the London 'black poor'.

Pilots

In colonial Virginia, an attempt was made to regard pilots as professionals and the government licensed them. In nearby Maryland and Delaware, however, pilots were unregulated. Maryland's Calvert proprietors' efforts to license them failed because they did not prosecute unauthorized pilots. Anyone with a knowledge of local soundings and a compass could claim to be pilot. When the War for Independence began, the rebel authorities in Philadelphia feared that pilots in Sussex County, Delaware would guide the Royal Navy through its Delaware River defenses to the very gates of their city.

In July 1781, Trap, the property of Captain William Lyford, was employed as a pilot on board His Majesty's Armed Galley *Fire Fly* in the Savannah River under Lieutenant James Howe. He died after two months' service. The need for pilots was essential for navigation, especially in waters which abounded with treacherous shoals and shallows. Captains who felt they could navigate the Delaware River or Chesapeake Bay without a pilot, often found themselves grounded on a sand bar. The navy's attitude towards pilots was that they were 'troublesome, incompetent and very expensive', the very cause of 'frequent delays and inconveniences to the Service' – yet they could not be dispensed with.[2]

We have seen that in Jamaica John Perkins used his pilot's skills to advantage. Another example was the black Jackson family of Norfolk, Virginia, which included at least two pilots who were hired by the navy. James and his brother, London, were slaves as the war commenced and James must have runaway in response to Dunmore's Proclamation – which is explained in the next chapter.[3] James went with Dunmore to New York in 1783, where he met the navy's Captain Henry Mowat, who took him to Nova Scotia in *La Sophia*. London remained a slave in Norfolk after James left, but he would defect to Alexander Leslie's expedition into the Chesapeake late in 1780. He would travel from New York to Nova Scotia on the same ship as his brother.

Navy dockyards

Another possibility for blacks was as workers in the Royal Navy dockyards, which built, supplied and repaired ships. These dockyards were centers of production, working with raw materials such as hemp and timber to meet specifications for rope production or wood construction. They were administered by the Navy Board, which supervised the hundreds of workers at each dockyard who split their time between manufacturing materials and building or refitting ships. Together, they formed the onshore naval establishment, the result of the burgeoning and increasingly efficient British state.

Five main dockyards existed in Britain: Portsmouth in the south, Plymouth in the west, Deptford and Woolwich along the River Thames to the east of London, and also to the east, Chatham on the River Medway. Chatham employed the county of Kent's largest workforce of more than 1,000. The officers and men in the yard included blockmakers, caulkers, pitch-heaters, blacksmiths, joiners and carpenters, sail makers, riggers, ropemakers and bricklayers, as well as clerks and laborers.[4] The hours were long, in winter from 6 a.m. to 6 p.m., and the wages were low, compared to what could be earned in a commercial yard. The advantages of dockyard employment, however, offset the low wages. Once an artisan or laborer had been employed, it was unlikely he would be dismissed, and from the 1760s a limited pension plan existed. In fact, jobs were monopolized by extended families and friends, who rigorously trained their sons in the skills needed in the dockyard to ensure that outsiders would not be competitive.

Overseas dockyards or careening yards such as English Harbor in Antigua and Halifax in Nova Scotia also had jobs. However, free blacks failed to obtain more than a few positions in North American yards. These yards were limited to the permanent one at Halifax and the temporaries at New York's Turtle Bay (1776–1783), Newport (1776–1779) and Charleston (1780–1782).[5] In the latter city, as in the Caribbean, it was slaves who performed most dockyard duties, while in Halifax, British families dominated employment, much as they did in England. Skilled shipwrights whether white or black were not common in the western Atlantic, thus Halifax had to import them from England.

Looking at New York's Turtle Bay, it becomes clear that black and white newcomers were not welcomed by existing dockyard workers. Located on the East River, during the war the yard employed an average of 244 workers, a bit more than Halifax.[6] It had been established by Admiral Richard Howe in September 1776, using seamen and ships' carpenters from the *Eagle* and then civilian carpenters from the city. Conditions like those in Halifax existed as New York's white families monopolized the jobs and attempted to prevent newcomers from obtaining them. New York artisans had long used municipal laws to keep newcomers out of their craft trades. In 1763, New York ship carpenters refused to work on transports unless their mayor limited licenses for this work to city residents. Twenty-one years later, ships' carpenters complained that competitors from outside the city were 'hurtful'. Whites and blacks in the continuous Loyalist influx were prevented from holding maritime jobs, let alone those at the yards. While the British military in New York were able to hire blacks to serve as seamen, they were unable to break the control of the city's existing artisan families over dockyard jobs. Moreover, private yards offered better pay. It was amazing that a few free blacks were employed at its dockyard.

Caribbean dockyard slavery

The Royal Navy's Caribbean dockyards found it impossible to wean themselves from using slaves. Preparing for the War of Jenkin's Ear, Port Royal in Jamaica and English Harbor in Antigua were the navy's principal Caribbean dockyards.[7] They were largely constructed by black slaves, white labor being almost impossible to find. When it came to manning the yards, slaves were also crucial because they were seasoned to the climate, which was debilitating for ships' mariners, making them unable to participate in careening their vessels. During war, the use of seamen for any work in the yards was discouraged because they were always in short supply for the ships.

Two distinct groups of slaves were used in the dockyards: hired slaves from the planters and those purchased by the navy, regarded as 'his majesty's Negros'.[8] Each had their advantages and drawbacks. The hired slaves could be employed for a project and then let go, but the planters' charges for their slaves were often exorbitant, especially if they were skilled. In contrast, those owned by the navy were well treated in terms of food and encouragement to form families, building a sense of loyalty to the navy. However, they existed on the books in peacetime, when they were not always needed. While it seems to be a contradiction in terms, the navy's slavery could be an opportunity for Caribbean blacks.

The navy's slaves were not just any slaves, as Admiral Charles Stewart, Commander of the Jamaica Station, outlined in 1729 at Port Royal. He was proposing a new careening yard at Port Antonio, which turned out to be short-lived because Jamaica could only support two dockyards. Moreover, Port Antonio was isolated from trade, its only strategic importance being to overawe the rebellious Maroons. In the effort to establish it, Stewart outlined an ideal use of slaves in existing yards. He felt a careening yard should have thirty 'choice Negros'; the next slave ship should bring fifteen to twenty Paupau or Calamentee blacks to be purchased as 'the properest and most serviceable in the island'; and the remainder should be seasoned boys and men.[9] The boys would be apprenticed to master caulkers, carpenters, or naval officers to learn a trade and the black caulkers who trained them would be paid.

Stewart was also willing to provide for the slaves' comfort and self-sufficiency. Ground was to be set aside for them as a kitchen garden and they were allowed to fish. Moreover, beef or pork for each man was provided weekly and rum as well. Finally, to prevent them from 'straggling', women would be allowed amongst them, inevitably resulting in families.

The proposal got to the Navy Board, which a year later added its input in a report to the Admiralty. The purchase of the slaves was readily approved, even though it was said that the king had never purchased slaves before. The Navy Board was most concerned about the boys' apprenticeships, wanting them to be the same as in British dockyards.[10] They would last for four years and the craftsmen would receive increasing remuneration for the boys' instruction.

Stewart was pleased with the approval, but he had difficulty in meeting his proposal's deadlines and he delayed buying slaves. Part of the problem was the proposed Port Antonio base, for he felt skilled slaves would not leave the existing Port Royal yard as they were married and would run away from Port Antonio to return to their wives. New slaves would also not do because they would have to recover from their Middle Passage, taking time to be seasoned and trained. The Admiralty, however, had turned down Stewart's proposal to purchase a few blacks from a slave ship – which he hoped to do because he had great respect for slaves who came from Calamentee. He still proposed that they could be put under officers on ships to learn to caulk and then returned to the yard.

Unfortunately, the planning for Port Antonio ended as it never became a viable dockyard, especially as the Maroon rebellion undermined its security. By 1749, all the artificers and laborers there had been drawn to Port Royal, including the 'king's blacks – men, women and children', as the Navy Board proposed to the Admiralty that Port Antonio be broken up.[11]

We can still learn from what was proposed and partially carried out in the 1730s and 1740s for Port Antonio. Aspects of its establishment were demonstrated when the king's slaves moved to Port Royal. In 1749, Admiral Charles Knowles was faced with a shortage of caulkers at Port Royal, so he ordered that eleven caulkers (including the king's negro caulkers) be kept on shore and not allowed to disappear into ships' crews. While eventually reducing the overall numbers because of peace, the king's slaves were retained, including those brought up as shipwrights and caulkers or wishing to be instructed in the trades. The black apprenticeship effort had worked and black families had appeared. Clearly slaves and their families were attracted to the yards at a time when others were running away to join the Maroons. Throughout the correspondence, the word 'Negro' instead of slave was used, even though it was obvious the navy was buying and maintaining slaves in the name of the crown.[12] The conditions described by Stewart for developing a dockyard labor force were certainly not those of Jamaica's plantation slavery.

Elsewhere at English Harbor, Antigua, three sources of slave labor existed. For one, some were hired from the planters; secondly, king's Negros appeared in 1744 as Knowles commented he had 'the opportunity of making a cheap purchase out of the prizes [of] twelve negroes for his Majesty's use, which I have directed to be trained up under artificers of the yard as caulkers and carpenters'.[13] Pay lists show that the training took place, although these slaves, including women, were also used to unload naval stores. The third source was the Governor and Antigua Assembly that offered 130 slaves to work on extensions to the careening wharf. The navy's dockyard Caribbean slavery appears to have been family based and was not at all comparable to plantation slavery.

Civil Branches

Blacks had opportunities to be employed by the British military in many capacities that did not require combat. Most runaway black men and women were skilled as plantation field hands or farmers. This did not necessarily disqualify them for military service. As noted, British officers in Bermuda, Halifax or Yorktown commented that blacks were far better than soldiers at building fortifications.[14] Ordnance units that developed during the Charleston siege offered them further opportunities, which transitioned easily into shipboard service as they were skilled servicing and firing guns. They also qualified to serve as navy cooks as well as victualling positions at Deptford or similar navy facilities.

While not directly related to the navy, the Civil Branches supported the entire military effort and were recruited from local black and white Loyalists but were expected to accompany the army wherever needed. The terms of enlistment were looser and the pay better than that of a soldier, making service attractive to refugees with families to support. They transported by land and water food, fuel and baggage; provided forage for the horses; repaired roads and bridges; built and maintained fortifications and barracks; issued and stored provisions; maintained and issued arms and ammunition; and established supply magazines. The branches included departments for Barrack Master Generals, Commissary Generals, Engineers, Quarter Master Generals, Wagon Master Generals and Royal Artillery. The size of the various branches depended upon the local and seasonal need. The numbers at New York swelled dramatically as the war progressed and the city filled with unemployed, homeless refugees from the countryside.

Marines

Another possibility for blacks was to serve in the marines. Musket men had long been hired for ships during war and sometimes companies of infantry were drafted for the purpose. As the Seven Years' War began, the Admiralty created His Majesty's Marine Forces with their own officers an official part of all its crews, except for the smallest ships.[15] They were able to impress under the Recruitment Act as they wanted landsmen, not sailors. They would make up 11 per cent of the navy's personnel in peacetime, and a quarter of its strength in wartime, based at Chatham, Sheerness, Woolwich, Plymouth and Portsmouth. The marines were not regarded as seamen, did not climb the riggings or stand watch, although they were expected to help with heavy work such as raising the anchor. They were at their best in conflict between ships, lining the quarter deck and forecastle, firing into the enemy ship to create casualties. They were meant to prevent an enemy from boarding, or lead the boarding of an enemy ship. They also were able to land and carry on the raids, in which blacks often participated, and some of their officers commanded companies of blacks.

After the War for Independence, the arming of blacks by the British became accepted policy throughout the British Empire. With the slave trade abolished by Parliament in 1807, British military officers openly experimented with recruiting blacks to serve in their forces. Rear Admiral Sir Alexander Cochrane raised marines while in command of the Leeward Islands station.[16] In 1810, he organized Marie Galante's free blacks into the Corps of Colonial Marines, which was enlarged with fugitive slaves from Guadeloupe. The Corps was paid from Marie Galante revenues, clothed from Royal Navy stores and commanded by Royal Marine officers.

Merchant vessels

Shipping needs during war encouraged a rise in the number of merchantmen and their crews to supply the military. The war effort in the rebellious colonies led to the Navy Board hiring merchant vessels that sailed in convoys under the protection of the Royal Navy. An alternative investment in privateers by merchants also expanded the need for experienced sailors. In wartime, however, traditional trades, including the slave trade, declined because they were considered too risky, especially as enemy privateers threatened them.

The composition of merchant crews was as diverse as those of the Royal Navy. Blacks appeared from diverging sources, from African natives to free American mulattoes. They not only served as sailors, but as servants, cooks, interpreters and pilots. As with navy ships, the abilities of a merchant ship's captain were crucial in welding the crew together to complete a voyage, regardless of race. As noted, it became necessary to employ Africans on slavers, so as to communicate with and control the cargo of slaves.[17] The rest of the crew accepted these Africans as coworkers and the black crewmen were willing to turn their backs on the slaves, even helping to put down onboard slave uprisings.

PART 4

EMANCIPATION COMMENCES

Chapter 11

Dunmore Sets the Bar for
Slave Emancipation

During the War for Independence, attitudes towards black people would favorably coalesce, initially promoted by evangelists, but also brought about by the British military's belief that they were doing the right thing in raising blacks to sustain their authority. The earliest to do this was Virginia's Governor, John Murray, Earl of Dunmore and his activities mark the beginning of the Emancipation Revolution.

Virginia's Governor Dunmore

From June 1775 to August 1776, Dunmore was the first to bring white and black Loyalists together in Chesapeake Bay. He offered freedom to slaves and a blockading Royal Navy squadron would play an overlooked role in supporting this. His early effort would produce what the planters called an insurrection of slaves that was to remain active for the entire war.

In August 1775, a clergyman told Dunmore, 'the captains of the men of war, and mariners, have been tampering with our Negroes … enticing them to cut their masters' throats while they are asleep.'[1] It had been a slave delegation that came first to Dunmore, giving him the idea that slaves would fight for the king in order to gain their freedom. Earlier in May, he had secretly written that he wished 'to arm all of my own Nigros [*sic*] and receive all others that will come to me whom I shall declare free'. When he was forced to flee from Williamsburg, they came with him. He also had the support of three small Royal Navy ships, the *Otter*, *Mercury* and *Kingfisher*, whose tenders were 'chiefly manned with runaway Negros'. Merchant ships joined them at Norfolk, forming a fleet that sailed the Chesapeake as the king's government on water.

His Proclamation of November 7, 1775 encouraged able-bodied male slaves to leave their masters. The proclamation also included white servants. Dunmore felt 'the lower Class of People', if an army were sent, 'would immediately join [him], even many of those, I am satisfied, that now appear in arms against us would willingly change sides'.[2] At the beginning of 1776, Dunmore had a fleet in Chesapeake Bay – that would be his base for the next eight months – attracting 1,000 whites, even more runaway slaves, and ultimately more navy ships, including Captain Andrew Hamond's 44-gun *Roebuck*.

At Christmas 1775, Admiral Graves had sent Hamond with a squadron to blockade the Delaware Capes. Hamond had met Dunmore three years earlier, when his ship the *Arethusa* was repaired at Andrew Sprowle's Gosport, Virginia shipyard. Early in 1776, Dunmore would ask for help from Hamond's navy squadron and he responded by arriving in the Chesapeake, although he could only remain a matter of weeks before returning to his commitment at the Delaware blockade.

Dunmore greeted him by reporting from his fleet: 'The tenders are every day bringing in vessels from the New England colonies, sent here for grain and flour; if we can but prevent them from being supplied with that most essential article of life, thousands of them must inevitably perish or return to their duty.'[3] Thus Dunmore felt he was preventing Chesapeake trade and contributing to economic difficulties in New England, which was the cockpit of the rebellion.

Hamond took command of the Royal Navy ships in Virginia. He joined the *Kingfisher* on the Elizabeth River and found 'the *Liverpool* and *Otter*, several transport vessels, and a great many others, with the inhabitants of Norfolk before it was burnt, under the protection of the ships, and his Excellency the Earl of Dunmore'.[4] After arming his prizes as raiders and manning them with soldiers from the 14th Regiment, Hamond sent them to seize a French vessel and then to the James River, where they took cattle, ships and ammunition. He ordered Captain Matthew Squire's *Otter* to make a raid towards Annapolis to take foodstuffs and tobacco, loaning it a lieutenant and forty men. Reports of the *Roebuck*'s activities led Congress to cancel plans to send a fleet against Dunmore, and Continental Commodore Esek Hopkins ignored Congress's orders and avoided entering the Chesapeake, instead taking his squadron to the Bahamas. Still, in late March, Hamond informed Dunmore that he had to follow his original orders and go back to the Delaware Capes, to which the governor protested so much that Hamond consented to leave the *Liverpool* and *Otter* with him. Later when the *Fowey* arrived from Halifax, he sent her to Dunmore, 'as I find [rebel General Charles] Lee is getting into his neighbourhood'.[5]

Unlike Hamond, a few Royal Navy officers were not supportive of Dunmore's emancipation. When Captain John McCartney of the *Mercury* refused to harbor runaway slaves, Dunmore wrote to Admiral Samuel Graves, commander of the North American Station, of McCartney's attitude, claiming he had been 'fraternizing with the rebels'. Supporting Dunmore, Graves had McCartney arrested and removed from the command of *Mercury*.[6] The navy accepted Dunmore's policies towards slaves.

The *Roebuck*'s return

In May 1776, the *Roebuck* again responded to Dunmore, returning to the Chesapeake, moving from the Delaware Capes to join him. In the bay at Hampton Roads, Hamond reorganized his ships and rest of Dunmore's fleet so that they could operate together. According to one estimate, on board were 155 escaped blacks, 88 of them belonging to the Ethiopian Regiment, 45 women and 4 children. An additional eighteen free blacks were also present. Hamond referred to the fleet as a 'Floating Town', which included vessels utilized for a blacksmith's shop, hospital care, a prison and stores. He had 'sails dried, and exercised the ship's company at great guns and small arms'; he sent his barge and cutter to assist in bringing ships from Norfolk, many of which were 'without rigging or furniture'.[7] He would be forced to destroy a few vessels which he judged unseaworthy.

Raiding by the fleet's tenders and craft spread British influence in the Chesapeake. As governor general and vice admiral of Virginia, Dunmore issued letters of marque to encourage a force of privateers and coastal craft. From Somerset County, Maryland, it was reported that Loyalists were gathering along the Pocomoke Sound to carry their cattle to barter with the fleet. Five fleet tenders had landed men on Hoopers Island and carried away sixty cattle and two men. A warship and several tenders were on the Nanticoke River threatening to take the wheat crop that was ready for harvest. Fear of the fleet spread along the Nanticoke as far north as the Broad Creek settlement in Delaware.

Yet, Hamond was apprehensive. He 'found Lord Dunmore and his Fleet in so much danger from the enemy … [and] I found myself under the necessity of attempting to move them before the enemy began their attack'.[8] He decided to leave Hampton Roads for Gwynn's Island, at the mouth of Virginia's Piankatank River, where fresh water, an excellent harbor, a quantity of stock and Loyalists existed. Before leaving, ever concerned to maintain the blockade, he dispatched Squire's *Otter* and its tender to cruise at the Virginia Capes for two weeks, preventing vessels from entering and leaving the bay, except for a provision ship coming to Dunmore from the West Indies.

In late May, the fleet of the *Roebuck*, *Fowey*, the returned *Otter* and about ninety sail headed for Gwynn's Island. He described the fleet as having 'valuable cargoes', but 'without seamen, which I was obliged to supply out of the Kings Ships'.[9] With the *Otter* serving as the rear guard, the fleet maneuvered to confuse the rebels and was able to make Gwynn's 'without the loss of a single vessel, except those we destroyed for want of materials to navigate them with'. At this time, Hamond rescued Lieutenant John Orde and his crew, who had been sent ahead to scout the island but had fallen into enemy hands. Hamond first landed his marines to help with Dunmore's sickly people and then he fortified Gwynn's to serve as a base. By May 30, he had reported to Captain Henry Bellew on the *Liverpool*, which he had left on watch at the Delaware Capes, that 'they talk of opening a market on [Gwynn's Island] for provisions, should that be the case, I hope we shall be able to send you something'. Another source claimed the *Liverpool* was 'well supplied with stock by the [Loyalists] at Indian River, the frigate having all her coops and sheep pens full; that four or five of those [Loyalists] were on board at the time [he] was there'. The *Liverpool* was able to send Hamond a Spanish snow bound for Philadelphia as a prize, with 1,000 hard dollars on board.

At the beginning of June, Hamond helped Dunmore outfit a tender, ordering Captain George Montague of the *Fowey* to supply it with precious ordnance, leads, muskets, pikes, cartridge boxes and belts, powder horns and two swords with belts. To boost morale at Gwynn's, Hamond celebrated the king's Birthday on June 4 with a salute of twenty-one guns fired from the *Fowey* and as many tenders as possible. Six days later, Hamond ordered the *Liverpool* to leave Cape Henlopen and come to Gwynn's 'in order to recruit your Ship's company'.[10] In July, Captain Squire had the *Otter* hove down at Gwynn's and its worm-eaten bottom resheathed.

Dunmore had purchased five small vessels to serve as tenders. 'Hearing … that there were a number of well affected subjects to His Majesty, on the Eastern Shore of Maryland', he sent 'three of the tenders there to bring off as many as were willing to come'.[11] As a result, the tenders brought in sixty recruits to Dunmore. They were placed in the newly formed black Ethiopian Regiment and the Queen's Own Loyal Virginians. While they would be inoculated for smallpox, Hamond observed 'the Negro troops' were 'recruited with six or eight fresh men every day, yet mortality among them was so great, that they did not now amount to above 150 effective men'.

The governor continued to use his tenders, harassing the rebels by 'constantly moving about, and making descents upon different parts of the coast; in order to supply the [Gwynn's] Island with stock' and take several rebel vessels.[12] Hamond reported that in Maryland's Eastern Shore a great majority of the people there and the lower Counties of the Delaware were taking up arms in favor of the king.

With Dunmore and Hamond sailing about the bay, fear existed among the planters on Virginia's Eastern Shore that he would soon annex Accomack and Northampton Counties. The Northampton Committee of Safety described their situation as desperate because:

> Our slaves numerous being more than double the number of whites; our militia not exceeding four hundred men, our people with few arms and less ammunition ... if Lord Dunmore was to demand our persons, ... the people around us would deliver us up rather than be exposed to the fury of his soldiers and our slaves.[13]

In February 1776, thirteen runaway slaves had seized a schooner in Northampton County to go to Dunmore. They were overtaken by a rebel whale boat, returned and placed under guard. Still, Dunmore's proclamation would induce 200 Eastern Shore slaves, including women and children, to run away and join him.

On June 29, by no means for the last time, the *Roebuck* was stuck on a sandbar near Wind Mill Point. Returning from Annapolis, the *Fowey* joined other craft in helping to free it and when the high tide allowed it to be pulled off the bar, it was undamaged. Three days later, the *Fowey* gathered several tenders at Tangier Sound to distribute weapons on Maryland's Eastern Shore. In five more days, the *Fowey* returned to Gwynn's with 100 volunteers for the army, cattle and food stuffs. Those disaffected, who had led in the recruitment, sought commissions from Dunmore as captains of their respective companies. In early July, Hamond ordered Lieutenant John Wright of the *Otter*'s tender *Fincastle* and the *Lady Susanna* tender commanded by Loyalist Bridger Goodrich to proceed up the Rappahannock River and destroy rebel galleys and 'to annoy the enemy by every means in your power'.[14]

In moving to Gwynn's Island, Hamond had overlooked the fact the island was close to the mainland. Its water supply soon became inadequate and with smallpox raging among the black troops, he feared it would spread to his crews. Hamond began to plan the evacuation of Gwynn's. He also realized that a majority of the more than 100 fleet vessels contained Loyalist non-combatants, who would be useless against a rebel attack. He complained that his ships had to guard these civilian craft and that the non-combatants were a drain on the fleet's limited water and food resources. He recommended that they be sent to St Augustine, New York or England. Dunmore was reluctant to force them to leave as he considered them to be allies and fellow exiles, who could attract further Loyalists. On July 9, however, the rebels began bombarding Gwynn's from a shore battery that was closest to the island. Dunmore's flagship was hit and he was slightly wounded. It was assumed that the bombardment was preparation for an outright attack on Gwynn's.

Dunmore's opposition was neutralized by the rebel attack; Hamond and Governor Eden of Maryland, who had joined him on Gwynn's, decided that the island would have to be evacuated. Although many of the smaller vessels had not filled their water casks and lacked crews, Hamond brought the fleet together. With the navy ships shepherding them, the fleet sailed northward to nearby St George's Island at the mouth of the Potomac River. On July 15 they landed at St George's, which Hamond described as 'about two miles long, has an excellent harbour on the east side of it, and a small haven on the north, sufficiently open at one end for small vessels to turn into it'.[15] Hamond had constructed a row galley at Gwynn's especially meant to confront rebel shore forces, which he put to use to protect the landing. It appeared at daybreak and in the evening, pounding the Maryland militia so that they contemplated withdrawing inland as the militia's Captain Razin Beall had been dangerously wounded. A study of similar galleys used by the British in the Carolinas and Georgia claims that the number of blacks in galley crews was much higher than their presence on larger navy ships, reflecting their skill in rowing these more maneuverable vessels.

Still, St George's also proved to be too close to the mainland. Supplies of fresh water and wood there proved to be inadequate. The *Roebuck* led a foray 100 miles up the Potomac to fill empty water casks and harass the rebels. Eastern Shore watermen participated in the Potomac venture. On July 23, *Roebuck*'s fleet was again shadowed by Maryland militia. Then 'with the assistance of the *Roebuck*'s Mariners, Volunteers, Blacks and Whites, [mustering] one hundred and Eight Men, [they] landed, under Cover of two small Tenders, and a [newly built] Row Galley … in which Captn Hamond had put a Six pounder'.[16] This diverse body forced the militia to flee and hide, burning William Brent's plantation and filling all water casks. This accomplished, Hamond returned to St George's.

Fleet dispersed

While the *Roebuck* was on the Potomac, the *Fowey* was the only protection for the fleet at St George's. Taking advantage of the situation, the Maryland navy's 20-gun *Defence*, which had previously threatened the *Otter*, came with two tenders up the river to attack the *Fowey*, and when the *Defence* appeared, a battery at Cherryfield Point was to support it. To resist the rebels, the *Fowey* rigged springs to allow it to turn more reliably rather than depend on the wind. Just as the confrontation was about to happen, the *Roebuck* appeared and the *Defence* and her tenders fled, retreating to the safety of Baltimore. At the end of July, Hamond sent the *Otter* with its tender to cruise off the Virginia Capes to renew the blockade, noting, 'the great number of familys inhabiting Vessels, ill provided with all Sorts of materials, that have ever since the destroying of the Town of Norfolk put themselves under the protection of His Majesty's Ships'. Hamond asked Squire to be prepared to escort the fleet's private craft to St Augustine and then return to the Virginia Capes.[17]

By August, Hamond judged the fleet lacked seamen and soldiers, so that 'remaining within the capes without power of acting against the rebels … only tends to bring disgrace on his Majesty's Arms'. He also admitted to 'being myself most heartily tired of carrying on a sort of Piratical War, which tended in no degree to benefit his Majesty's service'.[18] His words reflected his weariness in providing food, water, manpower and protection for a fleet of almost 100 sail, which required him to carry out continuous raids.

Having secured water for the fleet, Hamond decided to leave the Chesapeake. The fleet's last anchorage was off Tangier Island. With the blockade still in effect, the *Susannah*, a Rhode Island sloop, was taken. It turned out to be richly laden with rum, cider, cheese, shoes, soap and chocolate, which Hamond distributed among various ships in preparation for their journeys.

The fleet was dispersed in several directions. On August 5, fifty ships under protection of the *Otter* were sent to St Augustine, Florida and Bermuda. The next day, seven sail headed for England, under the protection of the *Fowey*, which after some distance was to return and cruise off the Virginia Capes. Maryland's Governor Eden was a passenger on one of them. Hamond was forced to destroy at least twenty un-seaworthy vessels.

On August 7, Hamond and Dunmore left the Chesapeake with twenty-five vessels sailing to New York. Besides the *Roebuck*, they included five transports, two vessels laden with rum, sugars and dry goods, and five small tenders and pilot boats. Hamond, however, was still concerned to maintain the blockade at the Virginia Capes. He ordered Captain Montague of the *Fowey* and its tender the *Pembroke* to remain on the station until joined by the *Otter*, when the *Pembroke* was to be sent to New York with their news. On August 13, the fleet arrived off Sandy Hook. Hamond concluded, 'Thus ended my Command to the Southward.'[19]

Blacks evacuated to freedom in New York

Overall, 3,000 to 5,000 black men, women and children had fled to Dunmore. Dunmore's runaways came from Norfolk and Portsmouth, the neighboring counties of Nansemond, Princess Anne and Isle of Wight, and the lower Eastern Shore.[20] Among the free blacks were the Weeks family of Norfolk, whose head would serve as a laborer with the British army. Black families joined Weeks from different owners so that for the first time his black family was united. On board were seamen Moses Stephens, Mathew Tucker, George Mills, John King and Edward Jackson, and Joseph Harris, the Hampton pilot. Not all slaves found freedom in the fleet, the ships that carried the eighty-seven black men, women and children of Loyalist Colonel John Willoughby were there for safekeeping, not freedom.

A substantial portion of the crews of Dunmore's Loyalist tenders and privateers would be black.[21] They included black runaways, freemen, and some slaves still under their Loyalist master's direction. The Loyalist Goodrich family had both slave and free blacks in their privateer crews. In April 1776, the twenty-four-man crew of Bridger Goodrich's tender was comprised mostly of slaves, and later when his *Lady Susanna* was captured, there were eight black crew members. Three or four blacks made up a part of the *Lilly*'s small crew when John Goodrich Sr was taken. While prejudice certainly remained among white Loyalist mariners, the captain of the sloop *Fincastle*, Robert Stewart, and his brother would ultimately free their slave crew members.

In Virginia, many slaves assumed that if they were baptized, they were set free – at least in the eyes of God. Seeing the experience in Biblical terms, black Methodists escaped to Governor Dunmore's fleet, sailing in the Chesapeake with him between December 1775 and May 1776. One of these was Moses Wilkinson, born a slave about 1746 in Nansemond County, where his master was Mills Wilkinson, a Suffolk merchant. Moses absconded from Wilkinson and became a self-appointed and charismatic Wesleyan Methodist preacher, who survived smallpox but was blind and lame as a result of the disease. Moses followed the precedent of his Old Testament namesake by leading his followers to Dunmore's freedom. On August 5, when Dunmore left Chesapeake Bay and sailed to New York, he took Wilkinson

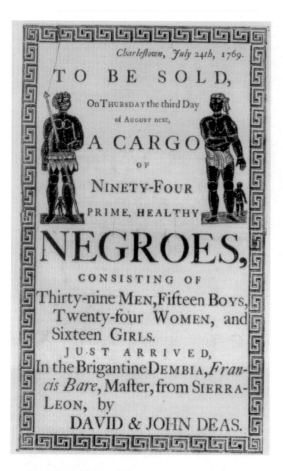

Left: *Advertisement for slave sale, Charleston, July 24, 1769.*

Below: *The Old Plantation in the South Carolina Lowcountry, by John Rose, c. 1785-95, Abbey Aldrich Rockefeller Art Museum, Williamsburg, Va.*

Right: *1761 Portrait of 5-year-old Charles Calvert's enslaved companion by John Hesselius, Baltimore Museum of Art, Baltimore, Md.*

Below: *1890s photo of single and duplex quarters, Brome House, St. Mary's City, Md.*

PACIFICATION with the MAROON NEGROES.

Drawn from the life by Agostino Brunias. From an original painting in the possession of Sir Wm Young Bart FRS.

Left: *Painting, The Pacification with the Maroon Negros, Jamaica, by Agostino Brunias, c. 1796.*

Below: *The Revd. Mr. [George] Whitefield preaching at Leeds, 1749, engraving on paper.*

Jn° MARRANT, *Who Preached among the Methodists in England, &c.*
Published by D. Boulter, Yarmouth 1795.

Above left: *Selina Hastings,
Countess of Huntingdon,
c. 1770, National Portrait
Gallery, London.*

Above right: *John Marrant,
Who Preached among the
Methodists in England,
published by D. Boulter,
Yarmouth, 1795.*

Right: *Phillis Wheatley,
Negro Servant to Mr. John
Wheatley of Boston, London,
Sept. 1773.*

PHILLIS WHEATLEY NEGRO SERVANT to Mr JOHN WHEATLEY, of BOSTON.

Reverend Freeborn Garrettson, aged 73, New York Public library, 1881.

Rt. Revd. Beilby Porteus, Bishop of London, by Henry Hopper Meyer, engraved by Fisher, Son & Co., London, 1833.

Detail of Family of Sir William Young, by Johann Zoffany, c. 1766–9, Walker Art Gallery, Liverpool.

Above left: *William Hoare's 1733 portrait of Ayuba Suleiman Diallo is the earliest British oil painting of a freed slave – and the first portrait to honor an African subject and Muslim as an individual and equal. National Portrait Gallery, London, loaned by Qatar Museum Authority.*

Above right: *Olaudah Equiano, frontispiece, first published March 1789.*

Left: *Ignatius Sancho by Thomas Gainsborough, 1768, the National Gallery of Canada, Ottawa.*

Chapter 12

Planters Fear their Slaves will oppose the Rebellion

In April 1775, British troops and colonial militia clashed at Lexington and Concord in Massachusetts. In the following months, Congress would negotiate with George III and send an expedition to conquer Canada. By March 1776, British troops would evacuate Boston, Massachusetts. This military activity, however, was not what concerned the newly formed governments in the South. There the planters struggled with existing problems that involved their slaves. They feared they were losing control of them and that they might join the British in opposing the rebellion.

Late Australian historian Rhys Isaac has outlined an existing opposition between gentry and evangelical cultures in Virginia, in which emerging slave religion played a part. This turmoil caused originally by the Great Awakening was there when the war came, upsetting the gentry's prevailing system of patriarchy. The antislavery preaching of some evangelists and the subversive practice of admitting black slaves into full church fellowship added to this cultural conflict. In a final desperate attempt to restore popular allegiance, the gentry would throw themselves into the cause of rebellion.[1]

Before the war, the gentry's power was based on control of the Anglican Church vestry, the court and the militia, establishing their dominant place in society. Church meetings were not wholly religious, as they served to reinforce colonial hierarchy by mixing the sacred and secular. Sunday mornings were an opportunity for the gentry to conduct business both before and after service. Card games, horse-racing, dances and other social activities encouraged competition, and created further hierarchy amongst men as they vied for wealth and prestige. In contrast, Methodists and Baptists were more concerned with a conversion experience, leading to an individual's salvation. They had little use for the old hierarchical ways and their message became popular amongst slaves. In many slave quarters, slaves came to have their own black preachers, who conveyed church discipline as modified by their communal conditions.

Attempts by the gentry to repress evangelists only further encouraged whites and blacks. The extemporaneous preaching style of uneducated Baptist and Methodist preachers was influential in the development of a rhetoric of slave freedom. Some of the more extreme revivalists had even questioned slavery and the conversion of slaves challenged traditional ways of life. These new sects also became popular with yeoman farmers, who found themselves excluded from the plantation economy.

While Isaac's perspective shows the planters' fear of evangelism undermining their control over slaves, it is not the entire story. Secular, economic and political conditions also enforced the gentry's overriding fear of a slave uprising – despite their efforts to outwardly ignore the possibility. As the Dunmore-Hamond fleet was sailing, in Congress at Philadelphia Thomas Jefferson's draft of the Declaration of Independence was being revised and the most controversial parts expunged, so that when approved on July 4, 1776 it did not address black slavery.[2] Yet the topic could not be ignored by the leaders of the independence movement. Virginia's delegation presumably represented the mainland colonies' largest black population, most of it enslaved, and with Maryland, it totaled nearly 300,000 persons. While the Chesapeake had more slaves, South Carolina's Low Country had the highest density of them. As slaves were so numerous in many colonies and were said to be restless in 1775, the fear of slave uprising remained endemic among Southern planters.

Fear of Slaves in the Chesapeake

Along with the evangelist threat, Chesapeake plantation masters found that slaves trained as mariners and watermen had experienced freedom. They had seen that 'ship captains and white watermen as the worst offenders against their fugitive slave code'.[3] Ship captains, who needed to fill their crews, widely accepted blacks who were or wished to be mariners. Going aboard a ship to work, allowed runaway slaves to pose as freemen. 'Shorthanded captains choose not to inquire about the background of willing hands.' Captains favored their use, not only because they were skilled, but because of the possibilities in their use: a captain could reward the runaway by making him a crewman, but if the fugitive was uncooperative he could sell him as a slave at the nearest port.

By the time of the War for Independence, slaves could command ships, putting their stamp on a voyage. In March 1775, the schooner *Liberty* left Hungars Creek on the Virginia Shore bound for the James River with valuable cargo of 133 gallons of rum and 200 pounds of coffee. The *Liberty*'s crew consisted of five watermen slaves, one of them, Stephen, serving as the trusted ship's master.[4] Around work opportunities, free blacks joined free mulattoes, indentured whites, surviving Indians, and their own slave kin, creating a mixed society of watermen.

Unwittingly, the planters had been a cause of black independence. They had trained slaves as skilled watermen, sailors and pilots, some already gravitating to merchant ships' companies. They had a hand in encouraging blacks to be watermen. Their plantations were located near waterways and needed watercraft manned by slaves to support their plantation tobacco and wheat economies. They favored the use of slaves for rowing and navigating their vessels, for the skills to maintain their ships, and for enterprises like shipbuilding, where they worked as carpenters, caulkers, sailmakers and blockmakers. As they already had an investment in slave labor, they sought to train their slaves to be familiar with fish nets and ships' carpentry. Slaves skilled as coopers were in demand to prepare ships' cargos. These activities made blacks into watermen, knowledgeable of navigating the bays and rivers. As a result, about one quarter of Virginia's runaway slaves were watermen or mariners.

Runaways

The War for Independence would cause the number of runaways to surge as never before and this situation remained the planters' chief concern. Apparently, it would also change the motives of runaway slaves.[5] Planters felt their runaways had a more militant nature, rather than previously when their attitude had been described as 'artful'. Virginia planters also thought their runaways wished to escape to another colony, wanting to get away from the place where they were bred. Chesapeake runaways now focused on freedom, escaping to northern Maryland or states above, where the institution of slavery was weaker. Former places of residence, where relatives existed, remained important destinations. Their kinfolk provided slaves with a route and prolonged place to stay.

In April 1775, six respectable gentlemen asked Maryland's Governor Eden for arms and ammunition to prevent an 'attempt ... by slaves and servants for their liberty'.[6] While at first Eden felt they were exaggerating the threat, after consultation he agreed to 'deliver up arms and ammunition to be employed to keep the servants and negros in order'. Eden's caution contrasted with Dunmore's exuberance to arm runaway slaves.

In July 1775, Maryland's future governor, Thomas Johnson, warned that Eastern Shore planters 'reluctantly leave their own neighborhoods unhappily full of Negros who might, it is likely, on any misfortune to our militia become very dangerous'.[7] In August, three Dorchester County slaves, who had killed a white man in an unsuccessful bid for freedom, were executed – typically by having their right hands cut off and then being hanged. A Dorchester County grand jury was summoned to investigate the evidence of insurrectionist plots involving whites and blacks. The County Committee of Inspection reported, 'The malicious and imprudent speeches among the lower classes of whites have induced [slaves] to believe that their freedom depended on the success of the king's troops. We cannot therefore be too vigilant nor too rigorous with those who promote and encourage this disposition in our slaves.' Thus, already Dorchester's planters linked poorer whites and blacks together as disaffected to the rebellion.

When the war came, the planters felt runaway activity increased as Royal Navy ships in the Chesapeake accepted them. In September 1775, friction developed between a Royal Navy ship's black crew members and newly formed rebel committees. One of the *Otter*'s tenders, the *Liberty*, was caught in storm and ran aground on the Norfolk River. Captain Matthew Squire and Joseph Harris, his black pilot – who was 'well acquainted with the many creeks on the Eastern Shore, at York, James River, and Nansemond'– successfully canoed from the stranded tender to the *Otter* in Norfolk.[8] However, rebel militia stripped the abandoned tender clean and burned it. Squire demanded the return of the tender and its stores from the Elizabeth County Committee, which replied that tender had been manned by runaway slaves like Harris, whose masters wanted them restored or compensated for, before anything from the tender was returned.

The Virginia Gazette claimed that Squire, in reprisal, had seized three passage boats with their slaves, which 'boats and negros it is likely, he intends taking into the king's service, to send out a-pirating for hogs, fowls, etc.'.[9] Ultimately, the committee would argue that the *Otter*'s tender was privately owned and 'not on his majesty's service', an unfounded distinction as Royal Navy captains often purchased local craft as their tenders, manning them with existing black mariners. The *Liberty* incident showed that the planters in the new Virginia government were determined to prevent runaway slaves from joining the Royal Navy.

The situation would continue until 1777, when slaves were able to conspire on their own, without Royal Navy support. In Virginia's Essex County, slaves were tried for 'being present at an unlawful meeting ... and recruiting men to be employed for purposes unknown and training them to arms and instructing them in Military Discipline'.[10] They wanted military training to oppose the planters' local militia and to be ready to support British ships when they next appeared. Toney, the slave of Loyalist James Garnett, was a leader in the conspiracy covering several plantations, which Virginia authorities would nip in the bud.

Ultimately, planter fear would cause them to retaliate against black Loyalist property. Free blacks, who held modest property, were especially targets. In Accomack County, Virginia, free black Shadrack Furman had welcomed British troops and offered provisions to the Gayton-Leslie expedition from New York in October 1780.[11] Although this expedition remained only briefly, another, headed by Commodore Thomas Symonds and Benedict Arnold, arrived at the end of the year. Two days later, rebel militia burned Furman's home and flogged and beat him to within an inch of his life, causing him to be blind. He escaped on board Captain Robertson's Loyalist privateer then lying at Tangier Island, which took him to Portsmouth, Virginia where despite his blindness, he became a member of Captain Frazier's Department of Pioneers. There he helped to identify Caleb Tigel and a man called Rose as rebel spies. When Portsmouth was evacuated, he and his wife were taken to New York and later went to Nova Scotia.

Fear of Slaves in South Carolina

In the winter of 1765, Charleston slaves had actually joined the Sons of Liberty's protest against the Stamp Act, but their interest was not welcomed. The blacks 'crying out Liberty' caused suspicion, rather than acceptance of them.[12] This was compounded late in 1774, when the familiar David Margrett landed in Charleston. He preached to slaves, speaking openly because he believed God would protect him, claiming to be a second Moses, ready to lead slaves from their bondage. After he reached Savannah, word came that a party was coming from Charleston to silence him.

South Carolina's planters were reluctant to join the independence movement as their attention focused on the possibility of a slave uprising. As their representative to the Continental Congress put it, the state could not contribute to the war effort 'by reason of the great proportion of citizens necessary to remain at home to prevent insurrection among the Negros, and to prevent the desertion of them to the enemy'.[13] They felt they had to intimidate their slaves, so that they would be unable to take advantage of the crisis.

At the end of 1775, the planters sought to make an example of a successful black freeman and licensed pilot Thomas Jeremiah, who could navigate the notorious sand bar at the entrance to Charleston's harbor. He was accused of conspiring, when he commented that if Royal Navy ships came to Charleston, he would 'pilot them safely up'. He was respected among the city's black population and actually owned slaves. Evidence for the charge was lacking, but his position as a propertied Loyalist encouraged the planters to circumvent a trial and Governor William Campbell's efforts to prove his innocence. They hanged Jeremiah, burning his body to prevent burial of his remains. Clearly, Charleston's planters continued to be paranoid over the possibility of a slave insurrection.

Charleston slaves would continue to make their way to the coast and seek refuge aboard British warships, while others fled overland to British East Florida. They would also join

British sailors in night-time raids along the South Carolina coast. Laying in Charleston Harbor were the Royal Navy's *Tamar* and *Cherokee* that became magnets for fleeing slaves, joining Governor Campbell and his family on board.[14]

By the end of 1775, 500 fugitive slaves were camped on Sullivan's Island within Charleston's harbor, awaiting opportunities to board Royal Navy vessels.[15] The island's lazaretto and quarantine station, dated from 1707, created to serve as a gathering compound for African captives, who had survived the Middle Passage. As they were being prepared for sale, slaves escaped and inhabited the less-developed portions of the island, and were further augmented by runaways. When the War for Independence began, those runaways on Sullivan's Island cooperated with, and had the support of, the navy ships docked there.

The planters could not tolerate black defiance of white authority. On December 9, General William Moultrie ordered Major Charles Cotesworth Pinckney to take 150 militia and in a surprise night attack, capture the island's refugees. While this attempt failed, a second one succeeded in which the rebel troops were disguised as Indians. Reinforced by fifty-four Catawba Indians, they struck before dawn and killed an estimated fifty blacks. Several more were captured, along with a few British sailors. Only twenty slaves escaped, being saved by navy warships. The Charleston Council of Safety expressed satisfaction with the operation, declaring that it would 'serve to humble our Negroes in general'.[16] Thus, the first bloody action of the war in Charleston was between white and black Carolinians – nothing like the situation at Lexington and Concord!

The planters now centered their rebellion on preventing the Royal Navy's acceptance of their runaway slaves. On behalf of the Council of Safety, wealthy plantation owner Henry Laurens told navy Captain John Tollemache that he could no longer obtain supplies in Charleston because he was 'habouring and protecting negros, who fly from their masters to Sullivan's Island'. The planters also accused him of holding fugitive slaves on his warship *Scorpion*. He replied that the blacks 'came as free men, and demanded protection', and he refused to return them to their masters.[17] When the *Scorpion* left Charleston with 'the best pilot in this harbour', the planters claimed the pilot was taken illegally and that the navy ship had between thirty and forty slaves on board. The ship's blacks may have included the familiar John Marrant.

Clearly, slaves ardently desired freedom and saw the Royal Navy ships as agents of freedom, rescuing them from the risks they faced in Charleston. On January 6, 1776, the *Cherokee* and *Tamar* sailed away for New York with Governor Campbell's family and many runaway slaves. These last included Isaac Anderson, an Angola-born slave, who would eventually migrate to Nova Scotia.

Another was free black Scipio Handley, who would serve the British throughout the war. He was the son of a free black woman, who sold gingerbread and cakes in the Charleston markets.[18] As a young man, he followed his mother to the markets, selling fish and fruit. Prohibitions discouraged them, for slaves were not allowed to keep a boat and black fishermen were regarded as disorderly and prone to escaping. In 1775, he was caught carrying messages for the embattled Governor Campbell on the *Cherokee*. It was rumored without substance that Campbell had brought arms to inspire a slave uprising against the rebellious planters.

As Handley had been assisting the governor, the fears of Carolina planters about British connivance with their slaves was confirmed. Thus, he had to be made an example of and sentenced to death. While awaiting execution in the Charleston jail, a file was smuggled to him 'by the hand of a friend' to sever his iron manacles.[19] He jumped two stories from his cell window and escaped to Sullivan's Island, which was still under the protection of navy warships. On Sullivan's Island he joined the refugees sheltering in flimsy huts thrown together from found materials. By the time the island was first attacked by Pinckney, he had gone to New York with Campbell.

In New York, Handley would join the Royal Navy and he sailed to Barbados, where he remained until on hearing that the British had recaptured Savannah, Georgia, he returned to the mainland. He arrived as Savannah came under siege by the French under the Compte de Grasse and the Americans under Benjamin Lincoln. He described that Savannah:

> was very bare of troops all that was in it were Employed both White & Black,
> in order to Endeavour to keep them [the enemy] off, as if they had succeeded
> in their attempt they would have had no mercy on many, as they had often
> threatened his life if ever he should be caught for quitting Charlestown.[20]

During the six-week siege, Handley was employed in Savannah's armory distributing grapeshot to the redoubts and batteries. While doing so, at four in the morning, he was struck in the right leg by a musket ball. Initially, the surgeons feared the limb would need to be amputated, but the wound remained infection-free. Though healed, it remained painful, 'at times was so very great that he is Obliged to keep his Bed for two or three days and therefore rendered entirely unfit for service'.[21] Handley would be evacuated from Savannah in 1783 and would make his way to London, where he claimed compensation from the Board of Loyalist commissioners. We do not know if the claim was granted or what became of him, but it was evident that he had served Governor Campbell from the very beginning of the war.

The planters sought to make an example of free blacks like Handley, expressing vigilance and vindictiveness toward them. The prevention of the loss of their valuable property in slaves would be the highest priority of South Carolina's and the Chesapeake's rebellious planters. This was in contrast to Congress's concern to ignore the problem of slavery and develop a Continental army and navy to carry on war against Britain.

Chapter 13

British Military Policy towards Slaves

No less a rebel icon than Tom Paine claimed that British commander General William Howe 'expects [Loyalists] will all take up arms, and flock to his standard, with muskets on their shoulders. Your opinions are of no use to him, unless you support him personally, for 'tis soldiers, and not [Loyalists] that he wants.'[1] Following Paine, it has become commonplace among historians to claim that the policies of the British military towards blacks were based not on their promise of freedom as much on the immediate need for manpower in the navy and army. British officers are thus seen as totally self-serving without any understanding of black concerns.

The Ministry

In America, the overall command of the military fell to the general who commanded the army, relegating the admirals of the Royal Navy to the role of handmaiden to the army's needs. Beyond this, Lord North's ministry did not direct or interfere in policy concerning slaves, merely ratifying the local decisions of its officers. Lord Dartmouth, the Secretary of State for the Colonies at the commencement of the war, was a supporter of the Countess of Huntingdon and when she was ill in 1767 he was considered to be her possible successor. While an evangelist, he did not carry his religious views into politics, and even opposed the chartering of the charity college in New Hampshire for Indians that today bears his name.

Two changes in strategy emanating from the ministry's Lord George Germain did indirectly affect blacks in America. Neither went into effect until 1779; the first emphasized the need to expand Loyalist support, including that of blacks, by organizing and arming them, the second – the 'Southern Strategy' – refocused the war on the colonies where plantation slavery was most extensive.

As seen, Governor Dunmore had set the early example of emancipating blacks to win the war. Such a policy existed only as long as he was in Virginia and it was not quite an official policy of freedom for blacks who served the British. His policy would re-emerge as Generals William Howe, George Clinton and finally Guy Carleton set conditions for black service for their entire command, affecting the navy.

The Howes' pacification

Despite reference to it by black runaways, the brothers William and Richard Howe, respectively commanders of the army and navy, never made a proclamation that specifically concerned blacks. Both did issue proclamations that encouraged Loyalists to defect or that offered pardons to rebels that would put down their arms and become peaceful. Off Massachusetts Bay in June 1776, Richard Howe proclaimed:

> that due consideration shall be had to the meritorious services of all persons who shall aid and assist in restoring the publick tranquillity in the said Colonies, or in any part or parts thereof; that pardons shall be granted, dutiful representations received, and every suitable encouragement given, for promoting such measures as shall be conducive to the establishment of legal government and peace.[2]

Richard had been named commander of the North American Station, so the brothers worked together on military objectives and reconciliation with the colonies. Richard had accompanied him invading the Chesapeake in the summer of 1777, where he witnessed blacks attempting to join his ships. He actually had previous experience with the slave trade in Sierra Leone, where he captained the *Glory* and settled a dispute between Dutch and British merchants. Howe was not an expressive man, however, and it is not known what he thought about his West African experience.[3]

Both Howes had always supported reconciliation and William's interest in establishing Loyalist regiments was to strengthen support for the British cause, not simply to fulfill a need for manpower.

Quantitative analysis of New York's *Book of Negros* supports the contention that it was Howe who actually brought more blacks into the ranks of the army than Dunmore or Clinton.[4] This was the result of a flurry of activity from August 1777 in which Howe emancipated blacks who joined his brother's ships in the Chesapeake or supported his capture and occupation of Philadelphia. Mainly from New Jersey, Maryland and Virginia, slave and free blacks flocked to the city, allowing Howe to create several Loyalist units. These included black and white recruits for the Maryland Loyalist battalion, which came by sail or land from Somerset County's Dames Quarter, the Nanticoke Valley, Deal Island in the Chesapeake, and Delaware's Sussex County. By May 1778, the battalion, numbering 336 – close to its authorized strength – was ready for action in Philadelphia and a month later they participated in the evacuation of British army to New York.

In late August 1777, near Head of Elk, William Howe tried to win over the peaceable inhabitants of Pennsylvania, Delaware and Maryland. He offered a pardon to residents who had taken up arms against the king if they would voluntarily surrender themselves to the king's troops. It was a tempting offer, especially for the disaffected among the militia being gathered to oppose him. He also extended protection to those 'not guilty of having assumed legislative or judicial authority', having 'acted illegally in subordinate stations' and having 'been induced to leave their dwellings, provided such persons do forthwith return, and remain peaceably at their usual places of abode'.[5] In terms of the rebel military, Howe offered 'a free and general pardon to all officers and privates, as shall voluntarily come and surrender themselves to any detachment of His Majesty's forces'. While this was British pacification at its best, it offered nothing specifically for blacks. Still, with the evacuation of New York in 1783, when certificates of freedom were issued by General Samuel Birch to blacks, Howe's proclamations were mentioned along with those of Clinton as a reason for black recognition.

Clinton accepts black families and raiding

After William Howe, Sir Henry Clinton became commander-in-chief. Previously, in 1776 at Cape Fear, he had shown 'tenderness and humanity' in providing runaway blacks with provisions and clothing so that they would become Black Pioneers. He also had an understanding of the needs of black refugees in the New York area while he was in command there.

By 1779, raiding activities were now expected and approved by the British military at the highest levels. British commanders were encouraged to work with Loyalists to destroy the rebels' ability to carry on war. On June 7, 1779, the Commandant of New York, David Jones, announced that 'All Negros that fly from the Enemy's Country are free', warning that no person could claim them and those who tried to sell them would be severely prosecuted.[6] Unlike Dunmore no distinction appeared between men and women, a policy which in practice had been going on for years.

Clinton followed Jones a few weeks later with the Philipsburg Proclamation, also addressed to all 'Negros' rather than just slaves. It 'most strictly forbid any Person to sell or claim Right over any Negroe, the property of a Rebel, who may take Refuge with any part' of the British forces.[7] Although Clinton's meaning has been questioned, it appears the proclamation applied to black males, women and children and even the incapacitated – all were no longer required to do combat service in order to be free. The only possibility of blacks being sold into slavery was limited to those taken while serving in the rebel military. Wherever British lines or ships appeared, no ambiguity now existed as to freedom for black families for the proclamation did not aim to raise black military units. As a result, considerable numbers of black women and children came to New York.

Clinton was able to put his policies towards blacks into effect in the New York area. In 1780, on New York's waterways, irregular black and white Loyalists contributed to the continuing war. Following orders from Lord Germain to increase his use of Loyalists, Clinton created the Board of Associated Loyalists and approved instructions to encourage privateers to attack rebel property. They read that Loyalist raiders should be provided with appropriate shipping, 'not commanded by the King's officers … to be manned by themselves, and that their mariners shall not be impressed into any other service'. It also said that Loyalists 'may … form conjunct expeditions, in any quarter, with such [privateers], as may … be for the future under one general direction and regulation'.[8] Here was authority for Loyalist privateers to organize raiding parties on their own initiative.

Elsewhere, in August 1781, General Charles Cornwallis blandly assured Virginia's Governor Thomas Nelson that masters could search for their slaves within the British lines and 'take them if [the now freemen] were willing to go with him'.[9] When Cornwallis surrendered, the Board of Associated Loyalists was agitated by failures in the surrender terms, although they affected only Cornwallis's surrendered army. Clinton soothed them by issuing an order to the army to treat them equally to the King's troops and not to allow any distinction or discrimination. Clearly, this included the black Loyalists.

Clinton also proposed post-war resettlement of freed blacks on lands forfeited by the rebels. Freemen and women who swore allegiance to the crown could expect to receive the same benefits as white Loyalists: land, provisions and rights. In supporting these activities,

Clinton became highly respected by blacks serving in the military. On New Year's Day 1781, members of the Black Pioneers sent him this greeting:

> We some of your Excellency's old Company of Black Pioneers, beg leave to Address your Excellency wishing you a happy new Year and the greatest Success in all your Public and Private undertakings and assure your Excellency that we remain.[10]

With the war over, Clinton retired to England, where he continued to offer a helping hand to blacks he had served with. In London, he provided veteran Thomas Peters with introductions to Granville Sharp, William Wilberforce and the Clarkson brothers. After this, Sharp would encourage Peters to approach Clinton for continued anti-slavery support.[11]

PART 5

THE BRITISH MILITARY VIES FOR BLACK SUPPORT

Chapter 14

To Disappear on a Privateer

For the British state, privateers were a cheap method by which during war it could supplement its naval force. While known for taking lucrative prizes, for blacks privateers offered anonymity, which they found useful in preventing their re-enslavement. Less regulated than the Royal Navy, privateers offered short service for the duration of a voyage, so that blacks had time to pursue other interests. Unlike pirates, however, they were licensed by the state. For merchants they were an alternative investment during war, which supplemented their traditional trading practices. As an investment enterprise, black slaves were considered to be more appropriate for privateers than free blacks.

No privateer ever seemed to have its full complement, thus competition for experienced seamen both white and black was fierce.[1] In the race to recruit black seamen, it is assumed privateers' prize money was more extensive than in the Royal Navy because the privateer focused only on obtaining prizes, while the navy ships had limited time for such diversions. A black seaman who served on a privateer could hope that a string of valuable prizes would be taken. Yet, danger for black mariners existed if their ship was taken by an enemy privateer, since as prizes they were liable again to be sold into slavery.

During the War for Independence, Lord Germain supported privateering because it not only did damage to enemy shipping, it also encouraged desertion from the Continental forces. It was hoped that rebel privateer crews would also desert, causing their ships to be unable to sail through lack of crews.

Privateer possibilities

Economic adversity forced many free blacks to join a privateer. Ukawsaw (James) Gronniosaw was an exceptionally literate and Christian black, who during the Seven Years' War was forced to find work on a privateer. Previously a slave in Barbados, he had become a freeman in New York. However, Gronniosaw had fallen into debt to a friend of his former master, who threatened to have him sold back into slavery unless he agreed to pay him back by joining a privateer and earning prize money.[2] He joined a privateer as cook to raid the Caribbean. The ship took five French merchantmen near Hispaniola and with three other British privateers, attacked a convoy of thirty-six ships and took a third of them. He survived the fighting in contrast to many of his mates.

When Gronniosaw returned to New York and the captain distributed the prize money, his former master's friend took it all and even a hogshead of sugar that was Gronniosaw's property, though his debt obligation was far less. While his captain stood up for him, Gronniosaw decided that it was wisest not to pursue the matter further. Done with his privateering, he found he could not support his family in New York, so he decided to enlist in the 28th Regiment of Infantry, which served in Barbados, and then in Admiral George Pocock's fleet that captured Martinique in 1762, and finally at the siege of Havana. He had become wiser about the value of prize money to a black sailor.

Black refugees in New York privateers

In North America, New York was the most consistent origin of Loyalist privateers. Its merchants had become experienced as privateers during the Seven Years' War, obtaining letters of marque and purchasing shares in privateering ventures. The city would be occupied by the British from its conquest by the Howes in 1776 until the very end of the war and it became a magnet for Loyalist refugees. It was the seat of an Admiralty court to clear prizes and its careening yard and maritime enterprises supported privateers. Robert Bayard, descendant of a Huguenot family and judge of the New York Admiralty Court, authorized privateers broadly:

> to attack, surprise, seize and take all ships and vessels, goods, wares and merchandises, chattels and effects whatever, belonging to the inhabitants of the said colonies now in rebellion, and all ships and vessels with their cargos, apparel and furniture, belonging to our subjects in Great Britain and Ireland, which shall be found of from the said colonies.[3]

In the early years of the war, New York's merchant community claimed to have suffered a lost opportunity because Parliament's Prohibitory of Trade Act restricted privateering. These restrictions were gradually whittled away by Sir Henry Clinton and Parliament, allowing New York privateers to go to Delaware Bay to support Sussex County Loyalists.

In 1778, the new commander of the New York naval station, Rear Admiral James Gambier, was praised for his support of privateers. It was said his 'astonishing exertion to the private ships of war' and 'the success of the enterprisers … seems indeed to have given a hard blow to the rebellion'.[4] By then, New York as well as Staten Island and Perth Amboy, New Jersey were centers for Loyalist privateering.

New York Governor William Tryon sought permission to issue commissions and letters of marque for privateers, as he could charge a fee for issuing them. From March 1777, he licensed 185 privateers and five months later he was given the authority to provide more. Even the ministry's Peace Commissioners authorized an expansion of privateering to meet the French challenge on the high seas. By 1779, Tryon was promising generous bounties for 'seamen, ship carpenters and other landsmen' to man privateers.[5] Between August 1778 and April 1779, 121 privateers were fitted out in New York to challenge the rebels. As a result, the number of ships' libels taken by privateers at New York's Vice Admiralty Court rose to two-thirds of the total, the remainder belonging to the Royal Navy.

In New York on February 6, 1779, four blacks in their twenties deserted from the Virginia Company of blacks, employed by the Royal Artillery as laborers. The *Royal Gazette* stated, 'It is believed they are gone on board some of the Privateers, or concealed for that purpose.'[6] Evidently the rewards of a privateer had seduced them.

Three months later, Sir George Collier's expedition to Chesapeake Bay contained many New York privateers. When Collier returned from the Chesapeake to New York, however, he found that his seamen were deserting to privateers because of lucrative bounties. To make up for this competition, New York City merchants were willing to donate ships to the Royal Navy. Still, crews would remain more difficult to come by than ships. In 1780, regulars of the 82nd Regiment were lured to a privateer because they were offered a share in the prizes.[7] As a result, inspections were put into effect to prevent regulars and Royal Navy sailors from joining privateer crews.

A few months after Collier's expedition, the New York privateer *Irish Hero* came into the Chesapeake on its own, but while chasing prizes it ran aground on the Northampton coast and the crew set her afire. The plucky captain and some of the crew set out in a longboat and eventually made it back to New York. At the same time, the privateer *Charlotte* arrived in New York with the captured prize *Success*, taken off the Virginia Capes. The overall take of this New York privateer was estimated by Tryon at £600,000 and a list of prizes published in *Rivington's Gazette* show that many came from the Chesapeake. New York owners of privateers, such as John Watts, John Armory and Theophilact Bache, and captains like William Bayard's son, Samuel, profited from the goods taken by the privateers and sold in New York.

Actually, many rebel merchant cargos ended up in British-held New York rather than their supposed destination, usually the West Indies. The diversion of rebel cargos to New York was the result of a captain deciding he could do better with the British. In 1780, Captain James Anderson, a former lieutenant in the Maryland navy, cleared Baltimore with a destination of the West Indies. However, once out of the bay, Anderson headed his ship for New York, sold his cargo there, and returned to the Chesapeake as a Loyalist privateer. Similarly, Captain John Stump, an assistant to supply Commissioner Henry Hollingsworth, procured flour and sailed out of the bay. He pretended that his flour had been captured en route to Boston, but actually he went to New York, where he sold the flour to the British army. Once this illicit trade was discovered, captains had to become Loyalist privateers to protect themselves from retaliation.

Some New York privateers favored slaves over free blacks. Most of these were letters of Marque because merchant ships' voyages centered on trade, making privateering only incidental. Slaves of these merchants found it difficult to desert as their master knew all about them. Additionally, a slave's share of prize money went to his master, so that his presence on a ship was an incentive for a master or investor.

The Royal Navy had a long history of restricting – if not outright opposition to – privateering because it lured sailors from their ships. In 1776, Admiral Richard Howe feared it would deprive the navy of seamen. Two years later, an advertisement from New York's *Royal Gazette* noted that five seamen had deserted from the *Persus* and a reward was offered to informers upon 'any masters of owners or privateers who have inveighed, concealed, or any ways entertained the above [sailors]'.[8]

Goodrich family

During the war, the Loyalist Goodrich family of Portsmouth, Virginia had slave and free blacks in their privateer and tender crews. In April 1776 the twenty-four-man crew of Bridger Goodrich's tender was comprised mostly of slaves, and later when his *Lady Susan* was captured, it had eight black crew members.[9] When John Goodrich Sr. was taken by rebels, three or four blacks were part of his *Lilly*'s crew. While some Loyalist captains still saw slaves as property, the captain of the privateer sloop *Fincastle*, Robert Stewart, with his brother, would ultimately free their slaves who had served as crew members.

While using blacks in the crews, Loyalists were especially jealous of retaining their slaves. The Goodrichs had feared that Dunmore's proclamation might encourage a slave rebellion. In February 1776, when John Goodrich Sr. requested return of his escaped slave on board a navy sloop in the Chesapeake, Captain Hamond had him sent to Goodrich.

By the summer of 1777, Bartlet, William and Bridger Goodrich were reunited in New York and joined Willie and Robert Shedden to form Shedden & Goodrich, a company dedicated to privateering and supply of the British. Bridger Goodrich bought a fine Bermuda sloop and refitted her as a privateer, using slaves in her crew. While most of the family operated their privateers from New York, he used Bermuda as a base. On his initial voyage, he took five prizes – two of which belonged to Bermudians – which he brought back to that island, upsetting some Bermuda merchants who favored neutrality. Henry Tucker, formerly of Somerset County Maryland, had continued to trade with the rebels and he formed an association to boycott Bridger's privateering.[10] In 1779, Bridger's fleet of Bermuda privateers blockaded the Chesapeake and took prizes at Fox Island. Back in Bermuda, he blatantly became engaged to Elizabeth Tucker, a kinswoman of Henry Tucker, and his association's opposition to Bridger's privateering melted away.

Bermuda's seafaring slaves

Bridger found that Bermudian slaves in his crews were exceptional because of conditions in their island. In 1748, George Whitefield visited Bermuda and felt that its Anglican clergy had a 'knowing' commitment to participate in church and community life. A substantial number of both whites and blacks had been churched by them. From 1755 to 1772, Reverend Alexander Richardson of St Peters Church kept meticulous count of the 1,118 whites and 1,535 blacks he baptized.[11] By mid-century, black children were attending school and plans called for an exclusively black school. Bermuda never had laws that forbade slaves to be baptized or to be taught to read or write. These conditions were a result of Bermuda's slave mariners, who would become a resource for privateers.

The war had disrupted Bermuda's traditional reliance upon trade with the rebellious North American colonies. Gradually, Bermuda's economy would be reconstituted with new demands for ships, fortifications and British garrisons, which required labor and food supplies. Using the proceeds of privateers like those of Bridger, prize goods were sold to the beefed-up British military, so that the economy, like that of Halifax, became dependent on the expanding British military establishment.[12]

Bridger found an economy built around shipping rather than the Chesapeake's plantations, which offered unique maritime opportunities for blacks. Male slaves were in demand as highly skilled shipwrights and sailors. Merchants put unusual trust in their slave sailors and slaves were even permitted their own private ventures as merchant-mariners. Slaves were valued, skilled, acculturated and literate, presided over by a loose, easygoing system of control.

Slaveholders of ordinary means, as well as the affluent, recognized and approved of slave marriages, often named slave children for themselves or for members of their families. They usually bequeathed slaves to relatives, avoided breaking up slave families, sometimes manumitted individuals, and almost never sold them. It helped that slaves were barred from testimony in court, encouraging their participation in evasive smuggling.

Rather than saving to purchase freedom, Bermudian slave sailors invested in creature comforts, directly converting their labor into improving their quality of life. With ready money and opportunities to shop in a wide range of overseas markets, they purchased items for themselves and imported considerable quantities on to the island. They took pride in their appearance and spent money on personal adornments, especially at weddings, funerals and festivals. Despite the reforming efforts of the Bermudian Assembly, numerous clandestine public houses served rum and bibby at sites where slave sailors could relax after months at sea. As slaves working in Bermuda were commonly paid wages, sailors would have found ready customers for their private ventures in the island's slave community, making them conduits for the flow of material goods, tailored to the tastes of black Bermudians.

Bermudian privateering with slaves

Privateering had a long history in Bermuda. During the War of Jenkins' Ear, the first venture was the sloop *Popple*, named after Alured Popple, Bermuda's governor. It was commanded by Captain Samuel Spofferth, who had married into the Trott family. Near Curacao, he captured a Spanish ship with a cargo of merchandise, including 8,000 pieces of eight. He brought the ship and its cargo back to Bermuda.[13] By June 1740, Bermuda had sent out more than twice as many privateers as any mainland colony and by the end of the war, a sizeable fleet of Bermudian privateers existed. Well-known Bermuda family names like Outerbridge, Perinchief, Tucker, Dickinson, Wilkinson, Harvey, Darrell, Lightbourn, Dill, Frewen and Butterfield were involved as owners, captains or sailors.

Cedar timbers and sloop rigs made Bermudian privateer ships superior carriers, but slave crews made them profitable. This edge was particularly advantageous in war, when the wages demanded by merchant seamen on privateers skyrocketed to reflect the increased risks they ran and the labor shortages caused by Royal Navy impressment. In contrast, Bermuda's merchant marine benefited from a stable wage structure because slave sailors could not strike for higher pay. During war, Bermudians kept their fleet fully employed in the intercolonial carrying trade, enhancing their profits by charging freight rates higher than peacetime, but still lower than those of their competitors, while maintaining static operating expenses. Usually, these veteran crews of Bermuda's weatherly sloops outsailed their enemies.

As noted in the war, British authorities had delayed in approving privateering and during the lull some Bermudians continued to trade with the Americans with whom they had family ties. Governor George Bruere calculated that since 1775 over 1,000 craft had reached American purchasers by way of Dutch St Eustatius. Some Bermudian merchants were heavily involved in moving merchandise bought in St Eustatius and Martinique to the mainland by a variety of stratagems, using false papers to avoid the Royal Navy or British and Loyalist privateers.[14] This was the situation that Bridger found and successfully dismantled, while Admiral George Rodney would take St Eustatius and clear it of illicit traders.

As Bermuda's privateers were manned by black slaves, the men were likely to be sold when captured. It happened in 1780 when a British privateer out of Bermuda was taken by an American letter of marque from Philadelphia and the black Bermudian slave sailors who made up the privateer's crew were sold. An American sailor from the privateer deserted to the

American crew and bragged that his fifty former slave shipmates were sold for a 'hefty price' in the Havana slave market, while he remained free.

In another case of May 1782, the *Regulator*, a 20-gun Bermuda-built privateer was captured by the American frigate *Dean* and taken to Boston. Typically, seventy of the seventy-five crew members were black slaves, Captain George Kidd and his four officers being the only whites. Rather than the usual selling of slaves at auction, the Massachusetts' prize court offered the slaves a choice of freedom in Boston or a return to slavery in Bermuda. To the shock of the court, all of the blacks chose to return home to Bermuda as prisoners of war under a flag of truce. Most of them were placed on the *Duxbury*, an American truce ship sailing from Boston, but mistrusting their captors the disciplined slaves seized the ship to the cry 'Huzzah for Bermuda'.[15] They set a course for home and arrived in Bermuda on June 24. At the Admiralty Court, the *Duxbury* was condemned as their prize. The rest followed. Sadly, one died, but the other sixty-nine were reunited in Bermuda. The island held an unusual attraction for its slaves because it promoted residential and familial stability among them, which in turn bound master and slave together.

Privateering from Charleston and St Augustine

Privateering at British-occupied Charleston from 1780 to 1782 contrasted with Bermuda. At first, to dispose of captured prizes, the Vice Admiralty Court in Savannah sent a representative to Charleston to take depositions on captured vessels and send them to the court to be tried. Crucially, in October 1781, Charleston's own Vice Admiralty Court reopened, acting independently of the military authorities.[16]

This was just in time, as several privateering raids originated in Charleston in the following year. To the south, Beaufort, half the size of Charleston, but better protected by the Outer Banks, dominated shipping in Port Royal Sound. In March 1782, Major Andrew Deveaux, son of a Beaufort Loyalist planter, planned the attack on his home town.[17] Three Loyalist privateers, the *Peacock*, *Rose* and *Retaliation*, left Charleston for the Carolina coast to take prizes and capture public stores believed to be in Beaufort. On April 4, the privateer squadron entered Beaufort Harbor without identifying itself and seized the pilots and townspeople who went out to greet them. The next day, Loyalist militia rowed ashore under Major Isaac Stuart and occupied Beaufort, driving off local militia gathered by planter Lieutenant Colonel John Easton. The privateers spent the next five days plundering the town and vessels in the harbor, and skirmishing with local militiamen, who increased in numbers as they came from neighboring communities. Having spiked the cannon in the town battery, the Loyalists returned to their ships but remained in the harbor, where they were able to take an incoming sloop. The town sent two fire rafts against them, but they failed to do damage and an exchange of prisoners (whalers, townspeople, slaves) was negotiated. On April 17, the privateers returned to Charleston's Vice Admiralty Court with their prizes. Charleston would remain a base for Loyalist privateers for the rest of the war.

In nearby St Augustine, black slaves were in the crews of privateers that took slaves from prizes and disposed of them as slaves. Mary Port Macklin describes in her journal how after living in Charleston, when the war broke out, she came to St Augustine. She and her husband Jack had emigrated from England to Charleston in 1775, where they operated an eatery until they refused to take an oath of fidelity to the rebels. Her husband was thrown into jail and all their property seized and sold. Eight months later they were sent as Loyalists first to Savannah and then to St Augustine. When they arrived in St Augustine, they had no money or work, so her husband 'took the command of the Privateer named *Polley*'.[18] On his first privateering voyage, which was destined for St Eustatius, his share of the prize included three negro lads, Primes, Jems and Pollichor, whom he took with him on his later privateering voyages. His second prize included the enslaved couple named Robert and Nancy. They became Mary's slaves when John went on his third privateering voyage. John continued this career, leaving Mary in St Augustine. Thus, as a privateer from St. Augustine, his prizes included captive blacks who were treated as both free and slaves.

Privateers have drawbacks

To free blacks, the prevalence of slaves on privateers made them nervous because opportunities existed to re-enslave them. For black mariners the possibility of their privateer being captured by rebel privateers was a nightmare. The American Prize Courts assumed that black mariners were property to be sold as slaves, not prisoners. Planters were interested in their decisions because they might involve having their runaways returned or be able to purchase prize blacks to replace their runaways. The courts released only those blacks who were too old or incapacitated. Of course, many privateers did not bother with the courts, but simply sold black mariners as prize goods at the nearest port. Careful study of this has led a historian to conclude that blacks 'viewed American ships, and not British, ships as coercive tools of tyrannical power'.[19]

On land, black mariners could easily melt into the inns and pubs that catered for sailors, but when they rioted they faced the same consequences as whites. Privateer crews in ports could cause trouble. In Liverpool, England the crews of privateers could become dangerous in the streets and commit outrages. Late in 1778, Mayor William Pole of Liverpool wrote: 'Great complaints have been made to me, as your chief magistrate, that numbers of engaged and entered on the several privateers ... frequently assemble themselves and go armed in a riotous and unlawful manner through the town ... Otherwise, I shall be under the most disagreeable necessity of calling to my assistance ... the military stationed here.'[20] While the threat remained, the crowds subsided. On land, black mariners could easily melt into the inns and pubs that catered to sailors, but when they rioted they faced the same consequences as whites.

Overall, serving on a privateer was a mixed blessing for free blacks. As seen, life in the Royal Navy was more secure for a seaman's livelihood did not depend on circumstance and even if his ship was lost or he were taken prisoner, a sailor still was compensated. Crews of private warships received no wages and most privateers deducted the cost of their food and medical care from their prize money. Privateer ships were built for speed; thus they were usually smaller and overcrowded, conditions that spread vermin.[21] To free blacks, the prevalence of slaves on privateers made them nervous because numerous opportunities existed to re-enslave them. Only in exceptional Bermuda did slaves seem to be satisfied in serving in a privateer crew. As seen, life in the Royal Navy was more secure as a seaman's livelihood did not depend on circumstance, for even if his ship was lost or he were taken prisoner, a sailor still was compensated.

Chapter 15

Loyalist Provincial Units

Loyalist commitment was most enduring if an individual agreed to do military service. When questioned by Parliament on the quality of Loyalists soldiers, Joseph Galloway, the Philadelphia Loyalist, responded that 'as soon as they are disciplined, they make very good soldiers'.[1] The earliest efforts to raise Loyalist troops were locally inspired, creating partisan groups in opposition to rebel militia. Blacks served among whites in these provincial regiments and sometimes they were recruited for specifically black units such as Dunmore's Ethiopian Regiment.

While the provincial units were land based, it was not unusual for recruits to have also served in the Royal Navy or in privateers. The case of New York's John Thompson shows that blacks moved from provincial units to the navy. Thompson's story begins in the New York area before it was taken by the Howes in 1776.[2] Governor William Tryon and his secretary, Edmund Fanning, maintained royal government in two warships moored in New York harbor. They used black couriers like Thompson to communicate with the Loyalist Mayor David Mathews in the city. Born free on Long Island, Thompson was the servant of Fanning and in June he was caught in the act of carrying messages. He had been betrayed by deserting sailors so that he was jailed by the rebels. During the Howe brothers' attack on New York, Thompson was able to break his chains and escape with ten other blacks to the British on Staten Island. He was recruited into Fanning's Loyalist regiment, the King's American Regiment or Associated Refugees. After serving much of the war in this unit, in 1781, perhaps at Charleston, South Carolina, he chose to serve on the Royal Navy ship *Warwick*, from which he was discharged three years later at Portsmouth, England, as the war had ended. With Fanning's support, he applied jointly to the Loyalist Claims Commission and received some compensation. Ultimately, he and his wife would go to Sierra Leone in Africa.

Blacks in provincial units

Provincial units like Fanning's Loyalist regiment were raised by a designated officer, who was wealthy enough with a reputation for leadership to attract recruits for the regiment. A designated number of men was set for the unit and it was thought to be ready when that number was approached. This recruiting caused rivalry between provincial units to meet the manpower goal. Famed Robert Rogers recruited his Queen's American Rangers by underhanded methods, ultimately forcing the authorities to remove him and thirty of his officers.[3] As a result, in March 1777 the newly designated Inspector General of Provincial Forces, Alexander Innes, felt reform of provincial units was needed through the expulsion from the ranks, not only of 'Sailors', but of 'Negroes, Mullatoes, and Indians'. When it came to these units, sailors were viewed as 'improper persons', who would serve better on ships. Of those Innes discharged, at least forty-five were specifically provided to the Royal Navy. As for blacks, Innes's zeal for this reform soon waned and his effort was limited to this attempt to improve conditions in the Queen's American Rangers.

A number of blacks had enlisted in 1776 in Brigadier General Oliver DeLancey's Corps raised at New York. When, in early November, a party of 1st Battalion under Captain Jacob Smith was captured near Setauket, Long Island, of the twenty-three captured, half were black. Three years later, DeLancey's son Stephen commanded a battalion which was transported as part of Archibald Campbell's expedition that captured Savanah, Georgia, where blacks would be even more numerous. The DeLanceys were a powerful New York family who had the resources to raise this provincial corps.

Prince of Wales American Regiment

The loyalty of blacks in raising and serving in provincial regiments is exemplified by Governor Monforte Browne's black servant, freeman Samuel Burke. He was a native of Charleston, South Carolina, but had migrated to Clare, Ireland in 1774 and then met Browne in England. He 'entered into his service' and traveled with Browne to the Bahamas, where he and his master were taken prisoner by Esek Hopkins' Continental squadron.[4] Governor Browne was held in captivity in Connecticut and then exchanged to live in New York and raise the Prince of Wales American Regiment. Burke was at his side assisting in recruiting the regiment as he 'could speak the Irish tongue'. While in New York, Burke married Hannah a 'free Dutch mulatto Woman' by whom he acquired a house and garden in the city. These, however, were soon appropriated as barracks and his wife was turned out of doors. Undaunted, Burke and his wife continued to serve Browne, taking part in the Danbury expedition where Burke was 'badly wounded'. He left the regiment following the Siege of Rhode Island, but he continued to be attached the unit.

Burke and his wife were involved in the capture of Charleston in 1780. In fighting outside of Charleston at Hanging Rock with General Sumter's irregulars, Burke was so severely wounded he was almost given up for dead. The Prince of Wales American Regiment would never recover from its losses in this defeat. Burke's fighting days over, in August 1783 he was evacuated to England. In London, he sought help from the government with testimonials from both Fanning and Browne. He received £20 and went on to a job in an artificial flower garden.

Black Pioneers

Among the almost exclusively black units were the Black Pioneers, who were personally raised by Henry Clinton at different times for various campaigns. While the non-commissioned officers in the units were to be black, the commissioned officers were white. The main task of a pioneer was to provide engineering duties in camp and combat. These included clearing ground for camps, removing defense obstructions and digging necessaries. The unit initially consisted of forty to seventy-one escaped slaves from the Carolinas and Georgia who Clinton continued a keen interest in.[5] They had been recruited during his ill-fated 1776 expedition to Cape Fear, North Carolina and then Charleston.

The unit would be commanded by Lieutenant George Martin of the Royal Marines, with the provincial rank of captain, with Robert Campbell as lieutenant and Thomas Oldfield as ensign. Clinton instructed Martin to treat his men with respect and decency and to be sure they were adequately clothed and well fed. Most importantly, Clinton promised them emancipation at the end of the war. Clinton brought the company northward, so that they would participate in 1776 in the capture of New York City. They would also serve in Rhode Island, Philadelphia and Charleston.

In December 1776, Clinton was given the task of taking Newport, Rhode Island, choosing the Black Pioneers as the only provincial unit to accompany him. After its capture, they remained in Newport until Clinton was given overall command in New York; he recalled them to the city and then sent them to Philadelphia to join the occupation army. While at Newport, New York and Philadelphia, the company recruited many runaways, but never grew in size beyond 50–60 men, the new recruits barely keeping up with losses to disease.

Before the Pioneers sailed to Philadelphia, they were given a new commanding officer, a North Carolina Loyalist Allan Stewart. He was a veteran of the Seven Years' War, coming to America as the war commenced. During the occupation of Philadelphia, the unit was ordered to 'Attend the Scavangers, Assist in Cleaning the Streets & Removing all Newsiances being threwn into the Streets'.[6] In June 1778, the company marched with Clinton's army from Philadelphia to return to New York. Among those who joined it in New York were Stephen Blucke and Murphy Steel, who will be prominent in a later chapter.

During the Siege of Savannah in 1779, two additional companies of Black Pioneers were raised. One company was commanded by Captain Angus Campbell of the South Carolina Royalists and Captain Hartwel Pantecost, while the other was led by Captain John McKenzie of the British Legion. They were armed and actively involved in skirmishing at McGillivray's Plantation in the Georgia interior. A year later, 200 Pioneers accompanied Clinton at the Siege of Charleston. They met another corps of Black Pioneers, which had been raised in Savannah in 1779. During the occupation of Charleston, they served under Lieutenant Colonel James Moncrief as part of the Engineers and Ordnance Departments.

After the capture of Charleston, Clinton returned to New York, taking Captain Stewart's company with him. It remained in New York for the remainder of the war. In addition to their normal duties, occasionally the men were allotted out as servants, cooks and tradesmen to high-ranking British officers. The Pioneers would be among the last Loyalists to be evacuated from New York City in 1783. They went to Nova Scotia, where many ultimately received free land grants.

Occasionally, even Black Pioneers were faced with the danger of being re-enslaved, if their former master could prove to be a needy Loyalist. In New York in November 1778, Daniel Manson of Charleston claimed to have suffered 'the wreck of a very good fortune from his attachment to the government'.[7] He gained the ear of the notorious Inspector General Alexander Innes, who requested that Clinton be told that Manson had found one of his former slaves in the Pioneers and wanted him restored. Manson claimed, 'The fellow loves his master and would wish to go to him.' The result of the request is not known, but to support such a claim, the Loyalist master needed evidence of both hardship in his service of the crown as well as the slave's disposition towards him.

Thomas Peters

Thanks to his restless activities, extensive knowledge exists of one of the Pioneers' non-commissioned officers, freeman Thomas Peters. In 1760, at the age of 22, Peters was captured by African slave traders and carried in a slaver to French Louisiana. He was sold and put to work in the sugar cane fields, although he was rebellious, running away three times. Viewed as a trouble maker, he was sold to British colonists and then to another master, William Campbell, in the port of Wilmington, North Carolina on the Cape Fear River. The port offered slaves opportunities not found on plantations, as maritime sawyers, caulkers, tar burners, stevedores, carters and carpenters. Here, slaves were hired out by their masters and even allowed to keep their own lodgings, although a ten o'clock curfew was imposed to prevent them from 'uncurbed liberty at night'.[8] Peters became a millwright and found his wife, Sally; a daughter Clairy was born in 1771.

As war clouds gathered in 1775, the British commander at the fort at the mouth of the Cape Fear River offered protection to slaves who would 'elope from their masters'. Slaves began to run away, although Peters waited until March 1776, when Sir Henry Clinton's expedition arrived. Lieutenant George Martin began to organize escaped slaves like Peters into a Black Pioneer company to dominate the river. Peters would go with the company to New York and for the rest of the war he served under Martin in the Black Pioneers and Guides. He was with the British forces that occupied Philadelphia in 1777 and was twice wounded in subsequent action, for which he and his friend Murphy Steel were raised to the rank of sergeant. We will pick up his further life in New York in Chapter 18.

Carolina Black Corps

Clinton's proclamation of 1779 had led to the formation of the Carolina Black Corps in South Carolina. With the evacuation of Charleston pending in late 1782, British commanders pondered the fate of black soldiers under their command. A need for a black pioneer corps on the West Indian island of St Lucia encouraged Guy Carleton to order the formation of the Carolina Black Corps.[9] It was raised in Charleston from among those slaves promised freedom by the British, who chose the option of enlistment for service in the West Indies. They would be paid at a rate of 8d per day. In December 1782, 264 free black troops from South Carolina, under the command of Captain William Mackrill, arrived at St Lucia, where they were organized into the Carolina Black Corps. The unit served on St Lucia until the end of the war, when it was transferred to the island of Grenada.

Surviving the war, the Carolina Black Corps continued as a provincial unit paid and supplied by the British government. It was the first black regiment to become part of the West Indian peacetime defense establishment.[10] Although the regiment was used mainly for labor and fatigue duties, at least one company of the corps was organized as armed dragoons and tracked Maroons and runaway slaves in Jamaica. After fifteen years of service, surviving elements of the Carolina Black Corps were enlisted into the First West India Regiment in 1798.

Local Corps

Some units served as notably as the Provincials, but were not on the establishment list. These volunteer local corps were raised by a governor of a province, were often paid, served for a fixed period of time and wore uniforms. They operated primarily within the province where they were raised. Since these units were not raised by order of the army commander in chief, they were not considered Provincials or liable for service outside their province. Dunmore's Ethiopian Regiment is the best example of a local black unit as it was formed early in the war, before official policy toward Provincials had been adopted.

As a black unit, the Ethiopian Regiment created hostility from the planters, who saw it as a ploy to steal their valuable slaves. The Virginia General Convention replied to Dunmore's proclamation by branding his offer of freedom as a blow to the foundations of Virginia's plantation society. It announced that all 'negro or other slaves' in insurrection 'shall suffer death, and be excluded all benefit of clergy'. Virginia's slaveholding planters would respond to Dunmore's black regiment by abandoning the royal government and deciding to support independence.

In early 1776, a rebel editor, Alexander Purdie of the *Virginia Gazette,* made fun of the idea of black soldiers, using racial stereotypes to criticize the prowess of the Ethiopian Regiment, claiming:

> To perform the military exercise, and comply with their native warlike genius, instead of the drowsy drum and fife, [they] will be gratified with the use of the sprightly and enlivening barrafoo an instrument peculiary adapted to the martial tune of *Hunger Niger, parch'd corn*, and which from thence forward is to be styled – the Black Bird March.[11]

The barrafoo was a West African gourd-resonated xylophone, a type of struck idiophone, which would be impossible to march with. The raising of black Provincial and local units left the planters with few choices as to which side to support in the war.

Chapter 16

Effective Irregulars

Another option for blacks was to join a group of irregular raiders, technically refugees and associators, usually including white Loyalists, but sometimes an exclusively 'black brigade'. These units were often commissioned by the commander in chief, but could also be established by the commander of a garrison or a governor. They served without pay and usually without uniforms. They were expected to earn their pay and food by woodcutting, by procuring supplies for the British or by plundering the enemy. While mostly land-based in origin, irregular activities required the skills of watermen and their craft to carry out stealthy forays. Sometimes they freed slaves, who became part of their operation. They fell outside the bounds of military discipline. They had much to lose if captured since they had no formal protection as prisoners. Here we will look at raiding in the New York and Charleston areas and then in the Chesapeake, where the British lacked a continuous base of operations.

Raiding in the New York area

During the British occupation of New York, black freemen were involved in raiding. To sustain Loyalist raids from New York, a series of British blockhouses were erected on the New Jersey side of the Hudson and at Sandy Hook, garrisoned by Loyalists, many of them free blacks. The posts served as warehouses, collecting points for livestock and firewood for the city, as well as intelligence gathering, which threatened Washington's army and its supporting militia.

Most noted of these black raiders was former slave 'Colonel Tye' (Titus Cornelius), who as the war commenced was described as a runaway 'about 22 years of age, not very black, near 6 feet high'.[1] Hearing of Dunmore's emancipation, he had joined him and when Dunmore sailed to New York, he returned with him, going back to his native New Jersey. From Sandy Hook, he led his Black Brigade of former slaves and white servants on night-time raids of rebel militia leaders' houses. Efforts to stop him failed, especially in July 1780, when Anthony Wayne's Continentals were driven back with heavy losses from the Bull's Ferry blockhouse. Unfortunately, in September, when he attempted to capture Captain Joshua Huddy of the Monmouth County militia, Colonel Tye was wounded and ultimately died of lockjaw. His followers included Stephen Blucke, whom we will see involved in the black settlement of Nova Scotia.

In July 1779, Clinton's Commissary of Captured Cattle employed three cattle rangers, each leading a party of ten mounted blacks. They were to provide fresh meat equitably among New York's competing military units. Two years later, Clinton authorized William Luce, New

Jersey Loyalist, to create a raiding force 'for his Majesty's Service. One Company of Able Bodied Men, to be employed in Whale Boats & other Armed Vessels'.[2] They were to receive the same pay as Marines on armed vessels and be clothed and armed as provincial forces. In 1782, they grew from 80 to 125 men, raiding by water against rebel strongholds. On January 8, 1782 they joined about 300 British regulars in attacking rebel whaleboats at New Brunswick, New Jersey.

Board of Associated Loyalists

From January 1781, the Board of Associated Loyalists provided an aggressive platform for irregulars in carrying on the war. The Board aimed to employ refugee subjects within the British lines by annoying the seacoasts of the revolted provinces. With their history, many Loyalists joined for revenge and to confiscate goods as partial compensation for their own losses.

A foray was authorized by the Board in New York, targeting Toms River, New Jersey as a nest of rebel privateers and the site of valuable salt works.[3] On March 23, 1782 the Armed Boat Company, joined by forty Associated Loyalists, attacked the Toms River blockhouse. Several were killed and wounded on each side, but the Loyalists took the blockhouse and the bulk of the rebel garrison. Among the captives was Captain Huddy, who ultimately was hung by other Loyalists, making the incident a cause célèbre to the rebels. In June, forty whites and forty blacks of the Armed Boat Company landed at Forked River, New Jersey and burned homes and the salt works. A year later, the company numbered seventy at the East River Boat Yard and at Fort Kniphausen on the Hudson, formerly Fort Washington.

Raiding from Charleston

During Charleston's occupation, cavalry officer Banastre Tarleton described how 'Upon the approach of any detachment of the King's troops, all negros, men, women, and children ... thought themselves absolved from all respect to their American masters, and entirely released from servitude. Influenced by this idea, they quitted the plantations and followed the army.'[4] These followers would become raiders.

The runaway slaves of rebel masters who reached Charleston were considered public property. Their fate was administered by John Cruden, in charge of sequestered rebel estates from September 1780. He seized over 100 estates that held more than 5,000 slaves. The slaves would produce food on the plantations for the Charleston garrison and when they were not needed, they were taken into Charleston for military projects. Cruden tried to make the estates profitable, but many lacked an overseer and were ruined by raiding from both sides. It became difficult to bring supplies from them after the British withdrew into the city in September 1781.

Cruden would make two proposals for using Charleston blacks in defense of the city. The first of January 1782 was stimulated by the arrival of Lord Dunmore who still felt success in the South was dependent on using blacks to support the crown. Cruden and Dunmore proposed to Clinton an overly ambitious plan to raise 10,000 blacks, who were felt to be superior to white soldiers as they were adapted to fatigue and climate of the region.[5] The non-commissioned officers' ranks would be filled by blacks, although whites remained in the top commands. An enlistment bonus would encourage them, followed by a promise of freedom for loyal service.

A month later, the goals of Cruden's second plan were more realistic. He sought to use his black public refugees for raids in the coastal rivers and inlets. His plan was to raise a corps of 700 independent mariners, much as the Board of Associated Loyalists had done in New York. They were to come from the refugees, including 'determined Negros', and serve on 'vessels properly calculated for entering the inlets on the coast, and the men occasionally land and take post for such time as might be necessary to destroy these places … that have become a receptacle for privateers and trading vessels'.[6] Personally, Cruden asked for neither rank nor pay. He sent the plan to Charleston's commander Colonel Nisbet Balfour, who felt he lacked the power to initiate it, so Cruden sent the request to Clinton. Apparently, it went no further, Clinton must have felt he had too much on his plate to consider it.

Near the end of the war in 1782, black dragoons were noted by Whig officers as actively raiding around Charleston. At Wadboo plantation, Brigadier General Francis Marion's much superior force beat off an attack made by about 100 South Carolina cavalry and militia, including 'some Coloured Dragoons'.[7] They flew the standard of Tarleton's British Legion. Earlier, the legion had left Carolina with Cornwallis when he moved to Virginia, but doubtless this was a holdover. Although black dragoons may have been part of a Black Pioneer group or local militia, their origin is unclear.

Targeting Chesapeake plantations

Chesapeake Bay was dotted with plantations which had prospered by exporting corn and wheat to the West Indies as well as tobacco to Europe. By the mid-eighteenth century, the great planters who held the plantations had separated themselves from the rest of society. Plantations were not only economic engines, they were visual demonstrations of the wealth and prestige of a planter family. They sought to make their plantations centers of refinement and gentility that set them apart from the lower orders. They constructed elegant mansion houses and expanded the number of outbuildings to cover their growing enterprises. In the War for Independence, rebel plantations became targets because they were hubs of production, now sending their bounty to the Northern bay depot at Head of Elk or Petersburg, Virginia, both Continental army bases.

Slaves were the plantation's labor force and access to the Chesapeake made it relatively easy for them to run away. As they were familiar with the waterways, runaway slaves would attack their masters' plantations in conjunction with white Loyalists or privateers, freeing the residing slaves.[8] Blacks were identified among those attacking plantations, usually living nearby or having returned from British-occupied New York. Early in 1776 at Dames Quarter, Maryland's Eastern Shore, wealthy planter William Roberts was roused from his bed at night, had his hands and feet tied, and was taken captive, while his slaves were freed. The leader of the Loyalist band was John Wallace, whose family had been in Dames Quarter for generations. He saw Roberts as an obstacle in making Dames Quarter into a Loyalist enclave.

By 1779, Continental Major John Cropper was on leave to visit his Bowmen's Folly plantation on the Virginia Shore when it was attacked by Loyalists in the night. He escaped in his night clothes, while his wife Peggy with her infant daughter were removed by the insurgents to an outbuilding and a train of powder was laid to blow up his house.[9] He was able to save the house, but the enemy had broken up his furniture and crockery, besides defacing the house, and thirty slaves were gone. On April 24, he and Peggy finally returned to Bowman's Folly to live, the state galley *Diligence* under Captain Watson having arrived at Metompkin to protect them. The nocturnal affair had greatly upset Peggy and the loss of his slaves had ruined Cropper's immediate prospects for making his plantation profitable. This attack would force Cropper to resign from the Continental army in August 1779 and turn his compete attention to the defense of his property in Accomack County.

On September 24, 1780, two or three Loyalist barges came up the Nanticoke River to Vienna, Maryland and destroyed several ships in the yard, including the brig owned by Captain Robert Dashiell, cousin of County Lieutenants George and Joseph, and seized public arms and slaves. Greatly outnumbered by the defenders, a Loyalist force of just twelve whites and twenty-one blacks occupied Vienna for two days. It was reported, 'A number of negros are gone on board them', and after the raiders had left it was feared, 'all the negros [in the vicinity would] run to them'.[10] On their return down the Nanticoke, they destroyed the nearby plantation of the Henry family and took two slaves.

Loyalist waterman Joseph Whaland would be a notorious raider of the Chesapeake and Delaware coasts. A mulatto, Lazarus, served with him and a slave, Caesar, acted as pilot on his tender. Whaland's *Rover* was captained by a 'mulatoo, named George, six feet high' when it captured Captain John Greenwood's schooner.[11] In 1781, Whaland, John McMullen, and Jonathan Robinson frequently acted in concert, employing black slaves as crewmen, whom they freed during their attacks. A year later, John Harmanson of Northampton, the Virginia Shore, complained, 'The barges have become very thick. I have suffered much by them. Have lost some of my best negros. Two of them taken out of my kitchen in the dead of night.' It is unclear as to whether they were taken by the raiders or ran away on their own.

In April 1781, Colonel George Corbin, County Lieutenant of Accomack, identified a conspiracy of slaves 'who had prepared themselves with [rounded metal disks] as instruments of death and had marked [on] them their devoted victims'.[12] This plan was discovered by the master of a slave engaged in the plot and the ringleaders were hanged. In the summer, barges chiefly manned by Accomack blacks repeatedly landed and fired on inhabitants, seizing goods, 'even to the cloths on their backs'. And 'several inhabitants of this county living near the water have been lately accosted and their houses burnt to ashes'.

Virginia militia Major Levin Joynes claimed, 'These [blacks] were really dangerous to an individual singled out for their vengeance whose property lay exposed.'[13] In July 1781 at Pungoteague Creek in Accomack, a Loyalist privateer under Captain Robinson came from a successful foray at Wallops Island with 4 barges, landing 100 men, 'a large number of them blacks'. After they were discovered, militia arrived to skirmish with them and one black was killed as they returned to their barges. They left for Watts Island, after which they traveled north and eluded any pursuers. Taking two days to gather 150 militia, George Corbin organized a pursuit, which, despite a five-day effort by the militia, could not find them. The ability of waterborne raiders to escape before the militia could be gathered was a problem that rebel authorities needed to solve.

These raids would influence the Virginia Assembly when they discussed the possible manumission of slaves. In June 1782, the representatives from Virginia's Eastern Shore were not impressed by proposed laws in the Assembly to encourage manumission. While admitting the political promise of universal liberty and the religious obligation to emancipate blacks, Accomack County petitioners identified blacks as consistently opposing the War for Independence. They argued against manumission:

> Because from the great number of Negroes which have joined the enemy
> from this county, the great damage such have done under sanction of British
> Government, the great number of relations and acquaintances they still have
> among us, and from the [refuge that] the houses of such manumitted negroes
> would probably afford them and other outlying slaves.[14]

To the Accomack gentry, slaves did not deserve manumission as they had consistently supported the British during the war.

As late as December 1782, rebel authorities struggled with the issue of how to protect their plantations. Jonas Belote, of the Accomack County militia, was lured by bounties to volunteer to be part of a picked force. Belote's duty was specifically to prevent 'the landings of ... the tories and the plunder of the negros who kept a regular intercourse with the [British]'.[15] His patrol was to follow Loyalist vessels along the Chesapeake coast and prevent them from landing. The militia would remain on their farms until his force called them out, thus the usual delay in opposing the enemy would be reduced. This force was not only to protect plantations but to prevent slaves from joining British privateers. Belote marched to Wachapreague to take a Loyalist vessel that was seizing tobacco and provisions from a warehouse; two weeks later, he moved to Pungoteague Creek to prevent Loyalists from taking more provisions. As late as this, blacks were still part of raiding parties that freed slaves along the Chesapeake coast.

Chapter 17

Blacks in British Savannah and Charleston

The next two chapters involve case studies of the blacks in three mainland cities occupied by the British military: Savannah, Charleston and New York. The British occupations of the three ports offer an opportunity to see the detailed interaction between the British and their black compatriots.

Savannah and Charleston were among the chief centers of the mainland South's plantation slavery and deserve to be treated together. Before the war, in the two cities, few blacks were free and those that were free were usually mulattos, the product of unions between whites and blacks. While some mulattos were the result of the proverbial intercourse between a wealthy white master and his female slave, a majority of them were the result of unions between indentured white men and black women servants. By the end of the war, this situation would be much different.

Again, the fear of slave uprising was the primary consideration of Southern planters when the War for Independence broke out. After France entered the war in 1778, the greater British presence in the South gave slaves more opportunities than before to run away from their masters and join British forces as free men and women. The British military seemed to be more sympathetic to the plight of slaves than the needs of their masters. Even Loyalist slave owners in Savannah and Charleston would be caught between their attachment to the crown and the retention of their valuable slaves, so that they regarded the British offers of freedom with suspicion.[1]

Savannah

A long-standing outside influence was the escape route for black runaways from Savannah to the haven of St Augustine, Florida. Until it was ceded to the British in 1763, Spanish governors in St Augustine had offered freedom to refugee slaves if they would become Catholics. In the Stono Revolt, St Augustine was the destination for the rebellious slaves. During the War for Independence, Governor Patrick Tonyn of East Florida maintained a refugee policy, which caused the black population to quadruple, while the white population increased only modestly.[2] Most of the slaves were concentrated in newly built plantations that surrounded the city. In 1781, Tonyn asked for slaves to work on the city's defenses and armed slaves, paying the slaveholders in the outer districts for each slave's working day.

The city also had a small number of free blacks, who made a living by selling produce, fish, game and crafts in the public market or by practicing as ironsmiths, butchers and masons.

After Savannah was taken by the British in 1779, New York's Provincial Lieutenant Colonel Stephen DeLancey was shocked during the occupation when he experienced the nastiness towards slaves of Savannah's 'Negro Driving' overseers. He felt blacks 'are inhumanly treated, are two-thirds naked, and are very disgusting to the eye'; he could not get used 'to the great cruelty made use of to the poor ignorant wretches'.[3] Evidently this contrasted with the treatment received by blacks in his provincial unit.

DeLancey was in Savannah because Sir Henry Clinton had sent 3,000 Germans and provincials to Georgia to capture the city. Commanded by Lieutenant Colonel Archibald Campbell and protected by a squadron under Admiral Hyde Parker, it was the first step in the Southern strategy that took the war to Georgia as it was believed that white and black Loyalism was stronger there. The British arrived in late December 1778 and were guided by a black pilot named Samson over the Savannah River bar and through the swamps by elderly slave Quamino Sally, surprising Savannah's rebel garrison. Simultaneously, from St Augustine, Brigadier Augustine Prevost crossed the St Marys River into Georgia. After token resistance, the rebel forces abandoned Savannah, leaving it to be occupied by both British armies.

Clinton wanted Savannah to be a secure post from which to invade the Carolinas. Campbell was charged with the occupation of city and the cultivation of Loyalist support. He showed a concern for the civilian population, making the occupation popular.[4] Inhabitants flocked to serve the British, 2,000 of them white and 5,000 enslaved or free blacks. As noted, he formed the company of Black Pioneers commanded by white South Carolina Loyalist Angus Campbell and a few Pioneers were also attached to the regulars. In the unfolding events, these numerous blacks would perform notable duties.

David George of Silver Bluff

Many of the 5,000 blacks came from plantations in Savannah's region and one of them has left an account of his life. It was meant to demonstrate that untutored slaves on their own could become evangelistic Christians as readily as those schooled in England. David George was born in 1743, far away on the Nottaway River in Essex County, Virginia, of parents who were brought from Africa and he noted disapprovingly that they had not the fear of God. As a plantation slave, his first work was fetching water and carding of cotton, and then he 'was sent into the field to cultivate corn and tobacco until he was nineteen years old'.[5] His master's name was Chapel – 'a very bad man to the Negroes'. George was whipped many times on his naked skin, often till the blood ran down over his waistband and his family members were treated even more harshly. He drank often, but did not steal, did not fear hell, and felt he was without Christian knowledge, though sometimes he attended Nottaway, the Anglican Church, about 8 miles away.

George's cruel usage by his master was the reason he ran away. He escaped from the plantation about midnight, walking all night, until he got over Roanoke River, and met white traveling people, who helped him on to Pedee River. He worked there two or three weeks, when 'A hue and cry' found him and his new master advised him to flee towards the distant Savannah River, which took several weeks. He worked there for two years, before his original master came after him again, forcing him to run to live among the Creek Indians. He resided in different villages and with an Indian trader for over four years, where he worked hard and felt he was treated kindly. Certainly, George was willing to travel great distances to be free, working his way to Georgia, finding refuge with Native Americans.

George ended up at Silver Bluff trading-post plantation, on the Savannah River, between Savannah and Augusta, where the owner George Galphin purchased him from his original master. Galphin was married, but also had children by mulatto and Indian mistresses. Preachers were infrequently allowed to visit Silver Bluff, 'lest they should furnish [the slaves] with too much knowledge'.[6] George had a great desire to pray with his fellow slaves, but was ashamed of his sins and went to a swamp to pour out his heart before the Lord. A Baptist preacher and former slave, George Liele, had preached in a corn field and George went and told him that the Grace of God had given him rest. Liele recommended that in the intervals between services he should engage in prayer with friends. Then George began to exhort in the Church and learned to sing from a book of hymns by Isaac Watts.

Liele was followed by Wait Palmer, who preached to a large congregation at Galphin's Mill. He was a powerful evangelistic speaker and as he was returning home, George told him how he was with God. Palmer came again and asked him to beg his master to let him preach to them and his master allowed Palmer to come frequently. Palmer designated Saturday evening to hear what the Lord had done for us and the next day George, his wife and others were baptized in the mill stream.

As war clouds gathered, Palmer was again forbidden to visit Silver Bluff, so he asked George to keep the congregation together. Although he felt he was unfit, George was appointed an Elder and received instruction from Palmer on how to conduct himself. He was not prepared for the duties, but he got a spelling book and attempted to read. His master had kept a white schoolmaster to teach the white children to read. George asked the children to teach him to read. Secretly, they gave him lessons and then corrected him. Finally, he was able to read the Bible so that he could understand the scriptures. He continued preaching at Silver Bluff and the church's attendance increased to thirty or more.

When Colonel Archibald Campbell's force surrounded Savannah in 1779, George Galphin fled from Silver Bluff, leaving his slaves to fend for themselves.[7] Acting as freemen, George and fifty slaves went out to greet Campbell and to claim his protection as black Loyalists. They moved into Savannah and George worked on the city's fortifications during the Franco-American siege of 1779, acting also as a food broker for the troops at a butcher's stall, as well as continuing to conduct religious services for blacks. His wife, Phillis, was hired to do laundry for British officers.

In Savannah, George was aided by his early mentor, George Liele, who deepened George's Christian convictions. After the siege, George lived in Savannah with his family for two years in a hut belonging to Lawyer Gibbons, while he also continued to keep his butcher's stall. He was issued a military pass which certified he was free and 'A good subject of King George'.[8] Eventually, friendly Major General James Paterson arranged for George and his family to go to Charleston to be evacuated.

Blacks and Whites defend Savannah

George experienced the siege of Savannah, which came about in 1779 when General Prevost reached the outskirts of Charleston but overplayed his hand as he lacked the resources to besiege the city and he was forced to retreat. During the crisis, South Carolina's Governor John Rutledge had painted a picture of chaos created by Prevost's invasion, requesting help from French Admiral d'Estaing in the West Indies. He decided to respond to the request as he still needed to demonstrate the valor of French arms by retaking Savannah.

By September 1, 1779, d'Estaing's fleet of 42 sail and 5,000 French troops arrived at the mouth of the Savannah River. His forces included black volunteers from Saint Dominque – an opportunity for blacks to meet blacks in battle. The French were to cooperate with a rebel army under General Benjamin Lincoln. D'Estaing hoped the isolated British garrison would be easy prey, warning Lincoln that his ships had been at sea for too long and badly needed refitting, so that he had only a narrow window in which to take Savannah.

In Savannah, the Royal Navy added two row galleys to its Savannah River force and Captain Hyde Parker (son of Admiral Hyde Parker) ordered twelve blacks – 'out of a number that had taken refuge on the King's ships'– to be borne on the ships' books as 'Ordinary Seamen'.[9] Those who had once been rebel slaves were now free. On land to prepare Savannah's defenses, Captain James Moncrief of the engineers had 300 blacks working constantly.

In the face of d'Estaing, the British abandoned Tybee Island and lighthouse to concentrate the defense of the Savannah above it. At first, the Royal Navy squadron was ordered to shadow the French fleet as it advanced up the Savannah River. Considering the odds, it seemed best to sacrifice the squadron for the defense of the city, and most vessels were sunk or burned. Responding to Prevost, their captains came ashore and brought their seamen (of whom thirty were black), marines and canon to support the town's batteries. Most of the batteries would be manned by sailors and marines; according to one analysis 19 per cent of them were black. The engineers' department now consisted of forty-one blacks and thirty-nine whites. Free black Scipio Hanley was employed in the armory, a waterman about whom we shall hear more later. Also, sailors on transports, privateers and merchant vessels volunteered to be assigned to posts. Thus, black mariners became an important segment of Savannah's onshore defense, bringing blacks and whites together.

With the river blocked, it took d'Estaing two weeks to move beyond the lighthouse and he was unable to get close enough to bombard the city. Captain James Moncrief, the commanding engineer, constructed an entrenched defensive line on the plains outside the town, using slave and free black labor. He secured the city's river front by throwing a boom across the river. British troops came in to defend the town from all over Georgia. At least 620 blacks were involved in erecting fortifications, as Black

Pioneers, volunteers or seamen. Uniquely, 250 black freemen were armed and formed into a battalion to serve as skirmishers. This black battalion would become a permanent part of the city's garrison.

Prevost's defense forced d' Estaing into a prolonged siege. At the beginning of the siege, a ball came through the roof of the stable where David George and his family lived and shattered it, which made him move to nearby Yamacrow where they sheltered under the floor of a house. D'Estaing was ill-prepared to establish land batteries, for his ship's cannon had to have their carriages modified for service on land and be manned by his sailors. He was finally able to erect batteries with tools loaned by Lincoln, and his sailors were able to bombard the town, ineffectively against the strong British lines, sheltering troops and gun crews. As scurvy had broken out, d' Estaing became desperate to end the siege and move his fleet, so he decided to launch a frontal attack on October 9 on the Spring Hill redoubt. However, a counterattack by marines and two companies of the 60th drove him back with the loss of 700 to 900 Frenchmen, killed, wounded or taken prisoner, without counting the rebels.

After the failure of the frontal attack, the besiegers lost heart as many French and rebel troops deserted to the British. On October 20, d'Estaing left his camp, retreating down the Savannah River to return to France. He was most concerned to save his fleet for another day, having momentarily brought French and American forces together. By the end of the year, he was back in Europe.

Afterwards, Colonel Alured Clarke praised the services of the blacks which were documented in certificates and reported:

> I have daily applications from the Masters of Negroes who left them under the sanction of Sir Henry Clinton's Proclamation, on that Subject. The arguments used by the masters are, that they have conformed, and become good subjects. Those of the Negroes; the Proclamation above mentioned, and most of them add, having served in the defense of Savannah, … and the apprehensions they are under of being treated with cruelty in consequence if they go back.[10]

Having weighed the claims of both sides, Clarke favored the service during the siege of the 200 black soldiers and 5,000 black workers.

Savannah's role in taking Charleston

On news of the Franco-American repulse at Savannah, Sir Henry Clinton was able to continue his Southern Strategy by preparing an expedition against Charleston, South Carolina. On the day after Christmas 1779, the Charleston-destined fleet, commanded by Admiral Mariott Arbuthnot, amounted to ninety-six ships, consisting of transports, supply ships, five ships of the line, and five frigates.[11] It was readied at Sandy Hook, but as they moved south, violent weather created confusion and ships actually returned to Sandy Hook on January 24. The fleet had to regroup at Savannah and replace much of its lost ordnance, before it sailed northwards towards Charleston. The troops were landed at Seabrook Island from February 17; they then moved closer to Charleston, positioning themselves on marshy James Island at one side of Charleston's harbor. They included white and black Georgia Loyalists raised in 1779 and sent to Charleston in December. The King's Negros raised in Savannah would also serve in the expedition.

Charleston's surrounding plantations

As noted, Charleston was built on a peninsula between the Ashley and Cooper Rivers, with the port on the Cooper River. To reach the port, ships had to cross an extensive inner harbor with occasional fortifications, the entrance to the harbor being obstructed by a bar. The rivers offered access to the immediate interior and along them were low country plantations, growing rice and indigo, cultivated by numerous slaves. These plantations required the continual import of slaves and it was no accident that over half the city's population was black.

Inside Charleston, the Continental army numbered over 5,000 white troops, commanded by General Benjamin Lincoln, while the civilian government was headed by Lieutenant Governor Christopher Gadsden. The city's fortifications had been improved through the requisition of slave labor from the surrounding plantations, but, unlike the British in Savannah, no freedom had been offered. In fact, a 1776 law remained in effect that slaves who joined the British would be punished by death. Gadsden would insist that Lincoln could not abandon the city by taking his army out of it in a strategic retreat.[12]

A high point for the navy during the siege was the capture of Fort Moultrie. After gaining control of the Ashley River, securing the Cooper River and port on the other side of the city became a priority for Clinton. It required action by the navy, when Arbuthnot felt he could move in the direction of the Cooper River. He preferred not to use Clinton's soldiers, who anyway were heavily involved in the siege. On May 4, Captains John Orde and Charles Hudson led 200 seamen and marines in ships' boats to Sullivan's Island. This detachment succeeded in passing the fort before daylight, unobserved by the rebels, and took possession of a redoubt on the east end of the island. After some negotiation, Fort Moultrie's commander surrendered his garrison of 117 Continentals and 100 militia without resistance. It contained forty-one guns, four mortars and supplies of powder and ammunition. Charleston's principal fortification was now in the hands of the Royal Navy.

Clinton continued the siege using several heavy guns loaned from Arbuthnot's fleet. He gained control of the Cooper River's upper reaches using his own troops and Charleston was completely cut off. Near the end of the siege, armed blacks appeared, having captured two rebel dragoons and eight horses, and a naval officer noted that 'our armed negros skirmish[ed] with the rebels the whole afternoon'.[13] After negotiation, Lincoln capitulated on May 12, 1780, surrendering the garrison and the remaining warships, the largest military concentration in the South. One naval historian has called the Charleston Campaign 'the biggest and most successful British amphibious operation ever mounted'.

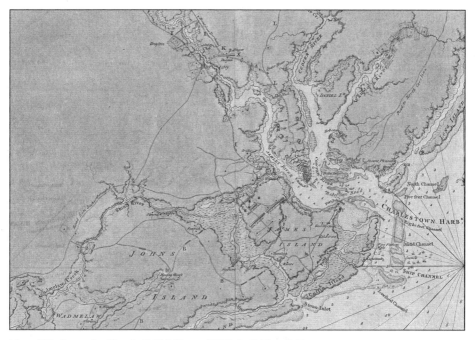

Map of Charleston detailing the British Siege of 1780, R. Philips, 1808.

Charleston's occupation

With the exception of New York, the British occupation of Charleston would be one of the longest and most successful, especially in contrast to the difficulties the British would face in the rest of South Carolina. The Clinton-Arbuthnot expedition had viewed Charleston principally as a naval base from which Carolina trade could be controlled. Lord Germain, however, had suggested that it should also be considered a base from which to encourage Loyalism and subdue the inland South.[14]

South Carolina's slave-based plantation economy would be interrupted by the occupation of Charleston. During the siege, British officers had encouraged large numbers of slaves from the surrounding plantations to join their forces. Most of these black refugees were former slaves of rebels on the surrounding plantations. They had runaway to Charleston and become the crucial portion of the city's labor force, but they remained strictly under military and municipal control. Only at the very end of the war would hundreds of Charleston's slaves be freed by the British.

Large numbers of black slaves, who had been promised their freedom by the British, would play an important role in the city. Familiar black sailor John Marrant witnessed Clinton's victory parade after the city fell and to Marrant's delight his old benefactor, the king of the Cherokee Indians, who had sheltered and protected him when he escaped to the Carolina wilderness, was in the parade. Marrant had not been the only runaway to seek British protection. Slave Cato Perkins had run to the British during the siege. He would return to New York with Clinton, where his skills as a carpenter were appreciated.

After the surrender, Clinton formulated a policy to handle the increasing number of slaves in Charleston. Runaways of Loyalist masters were to be returned to them, but with an important limitation that they were not to be punished by the master. In practice, Loyalist runaways were mixed in with those of the rebels and it was difficult to separate them, leaving the British military with little time to act as slave catchers.[15]

The process was much different for the runaway slaves of rebel masters, who were considered to be public property. In Charleston, they were fed and clothed by the military and performed various garrison duties, a system that was based on the slaves' free consent for which they were paid. At least 800 were serving in the military's engineering and ordnance departments, involved in strengthening the city's defenses and removing the sunken rebel hulks from the Cooper River to facilitate trade. Crucially, they were promised their freedom if they served well, but only at the end of the war.

In March 1781, 652 refugee slaves who had joined the garrison were serving as laborers, artificers, drivers and nurses. The Royal Navy's *Providence*, on duty in Charleston Harbor, put them to work as caulkers, carpenters and blacksmiths. Refugees were allowed to go home in the evening and received wages similar to those paid hired slaves before the war.[16]

Analysis of advertisements for runaways from 1780 to 1781 in the South Carolina *Royal Gazette* shows that a great number were thought to be with the army, but right behind them were those on board ships, while the fewest remained on plantations. This last is an indication that runaways could not find security in a plantation, even during the British occupation. The advertisements also show that runaways preferred to escape to Charleston instead of locations in the woods or swaps of the hinterland.[17]

Sailors and blacks

Charleston's port was regulated by government authorities. From July 1780, the Intendant General of Police and the superintendent of the port were given control over the city's trade. Initially, trade revived with the British Isles as well as locally with Savannah, Georgetown, South Carolina and St Augustine. Illicit trade between the city and the countryside also flourished as the rebels sought munitions to carry on the war and popular British manufactures. In return, food appeared to feed the city's expanded population which now included the British military as well as large numbers of white and black Loyalists. One practice not allowed was the export of slaves. Interested masters had to receive permission from the commandant. It appears, however, that Governor William Bull found that this ban on exportation was impossible to enforce. Some slave trade remained in occupied Charleston.

During the occupation, a Royal Navy careening yard was established in Charleston, known for its ample naval stores. Navy convoys carried supplies to Charleston, Savannah and St Augustine and the navy's protection of trade continued as rebel privateers increased in Carolina waters. Along with Captain James Gambier's *Raleigh*, the *Roebuck* now under Andrew Snape Douglas left Virginia and returned to occupied Charleston on November 21, 1780, where the two ships spent two months protecting the trade entering the city and patrolling its environs. At the end of the year, further assistance was requested as 'many vessels have been taken of great value within sight of the town'.[18] In February, additional protection came from two schooners, paid for by the contributions of Charleston merchants.

It was argued that cavorting with sailors made the public slaves bold and saucy, conduct upsetting many slaveholders. In February 1782, a social event 'the Ethiopian Ball' took place as British officers joined black women at a ball and supper in one of Charleston's most elegant houses. That rebel leaders considered it a shameless mixing of the sexes was a foregone conclusion. The organizers happened to be 'three Negro wenches', not the officers of the garrison, although they had agreed to participate. Certainly, they were defying the segregation of the races which was a hallmark of Charleston society. One historian has concluded, 'For a moment … slaves experienced a world turned upside down.'[19] After this, the Police Board decided it had to crack down on licenses for houses of public entertainment.

Blacks in Charleston's Loyalist companies

The question of arming slaves was often raised by British officers, especially John Cruden. However, Charleston was never seriously attacked by a combined Franco-American force as happened with Savannah. Clinton avoided making a major decision over arming slaves and actually passed the question on to his successor, Guy Carleton, who was far too involved in the overall evacuation to make a judgement.

Free blacks were not restricted. Estimates show that half of all South Carolina's free blacks resided in Charleston, but their numbers were small and it is difficult to identify them. They could have served in two Loyalist regiments, which included blacks when formed. The Charleston Volunteer Battalion was created to assist the city's garrison. It would be disbanded for the British evacuation of Charleston in December 1782.

The other Loyalist regiment appearing during the occupation was known as Montagu's Corps. It was made up from the prisoners captured from the Continental army, who had surrendered at Charleston and Camden, South Carolina.[20] In February 1781, Charles Greville, Lord Montagu, one of the last royal governors of South Carolina, went on board prison ships in Charleston harbor and recruited hundreds of rebel captives after promising they would not have to fight fellow Americans – only the Spanish. He commanded the regiment, which initially had 500 men. On August 10, 1781 the regiment was sent to Jamaica, where it saw combat and was praised by the authorities. On the basis of this success, Montagu went to New York harbor to recruit a second battalion of 100 men from the prison ships. After the war, many of Montagu's regiment went with him to Nova Scotia, where they were given land grants.

Black irregulars existed between the British and rebel lines, carrying on 'private war' against rebel slaveholders. In 1782, raiders were often comprised entirely of refugee slaves from the immediate countryside. 'Negro Dragoons' marauded at night in their local neighborhood, where a rebel master believed they had 'large conexions & as the surrounding plantations are peopled with large gangs of unruly Negros … whose masters are absent from them I cannot think myself safe a single night'.[21] This sounds much like conditions in Chesapeake Bay.

It has been argued that the British occupation and its aftermath created an unusual situation in regard to black freedom. We have seen British authorities in Charleston had to cope with an independence and familiarity not previously known in slaves. While South Carolina planters remained deeply committed to slavery, wartime conditions created slaves who 'enjoyed a larger degree of autonomy than anywhere else on Mainland North America'.[22]

Boston King is well treated by the British

For slave Boston King, British-occupied Charleston was a beacon of freedom. He was born about 1760, 28 miles from Charleston, on the plantation of Richard Waring. King was proudly the son of a literate mill cutter slave, originally from Africa, while his mother was a seamstress with knowledge of Native American herbal preparations. He waited on his master as a house slave until he was 16, when his master apprenticed him to a Charleston carpenter, who took a dislike to him and singled him out among his apprentices for a beating, until his master intervened and brought him back to the plantation. In his youth, King would have a remarkable dream, which would lead him to refrain from swearing and 'acknowledge that there was a God'.[23]

King sought a better life and left the plantation for British-occupied Charleston in 1780. Before reaching the city, however, he caught smallpox, forcing him to quarantine with other infected blacks away from a British army camp. He was brought 'the things I stood in need of' by a kind officer from DeLancey's brigade, which had come from Savannah. When marauding rebels came near the infected blacks, they avoided them fearing the pox, while British officers continued to support their recovery in a cottage near their hospital. Recovered, King became a servant to regular officer Captain Grey, but left him after a year for the post at Nelson's ferry, from which he was charged with carrying dispatches through the enemy lines into Charleston. He finally settled in occupied Charleston, where he joined the crew of a man of war (it may have been the *Raleigh* or *Roebuck*) probably as a ship's carpenter. She went to Chesapeake Bay and captured a prize and then took it to New York, where the account of King's career continues in the next chapter.

Chapter 18

Blacks in British New York

The case of Boston King continues as he arrived in New York. There he hoped to find work as a carpenter, but he was without the necessary tools and thus could not serve with the 'negro carpenters' in the engineers' department. He married Violet, a former slave from North Carolina, twelve years his senior. He returned to the sea by volunteering for a pilot boat, which was taken by an American whale boat and he was sent as a captive to New Brunswick, New Jersey. Here he was 'again reduced to slavery', even though he admitted his new rebel master treated him as well as could be expected.[1] With the aid of friends, however, he conspired to pass the rebel guards, wading and stealing a whale boat to get to the British on Staten Island, who provided him with a pass to freedom in occupied Manhattan.

In the city, Violet was inspired by the spiritual emotion of the familiar Daddy Moses. King was also uplifted and would ultimately become a Methodist preacher in Nova Scotia and England, where he received a Methodist education. By 1783, the evacuation of British troops from New York was being planned, and the Kings, along with most of their brethren, feared they would be re-enslaved if their former rebel masters came to New York. However, the Kings received a certificate of freedom from General Samuel Birch, 'which dispelled all our fears and filled us with gratitude'.[2]

A haven for blacks

New York had long been a haven for black people like the Kings. You will remember, New York had the largest number of slaves in the Northern colonies, so that when the city was taken in 1776, their treatment during the next seven years of British occupation is crucial to following the Emancipation Revolution. The city's region became the headquarters for the British army and navy as well as the center of Loyalist military units and privateering. Secured by the powerful British military, New York would be the most important place of asylum for blacks. At the end of the war, New York would be the base for the largest number of Loyalist migrants to other parts of the British Empire. It was the place that offered blacks a wide range of choices to alter their fate.

Even before New York City was taken by the British, the Dunmore-Hamond fleet arrived at Staten Island discharging its Loyalists, including 130 black families from the Chesapeake. This was the earliest of many Royal Navy ships to land runaway slaves who had been promised their freedom. The result was a growing number of newly free blacks to add to freemen already there. They were envied by most slaves who desired to become free. After 1776, the situation was recognized, as the number of newspaper advertisements for runaways increased dramatically.

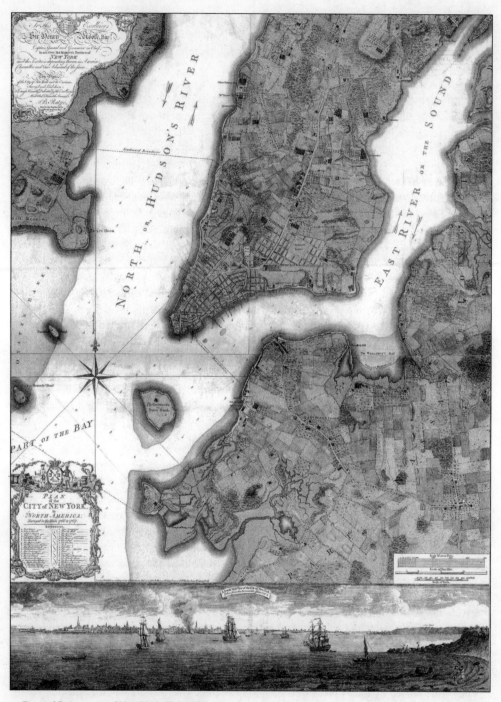

Bernard Ratzer map of New York City, 1770.

When Washington's army was driven out of the city in 1776, many rebel slave masters followed them, residing in the nearby Long Island–New Jersey area. Some were able to take their household slaves with them, others actually left them in the city to maintain and guard their property. Of male slaves still sold in the occupied city, most were young boys. Many slaveholders remained and thus became Loyalists and expected the British military to respect their property in slaves. In this perception they were mistaken.[3]

Ships in the harbor were an obvious choice for runaways. Eighteen-year-old black hairdresser Luke hired himself out to the officer of a ship. The military need for black sailors took precedence over the requests of Loyalist slave owners. While masters of vessels were warned not to hire runaways, they looked the other way in filling their crews, for once a slave made it to a ship, it was impossible for a former master to get his slave back.

It was in the New York area in June 1779 that Sir Henry Clinton announced his Philipsburg Proclamation, addressed to all 'Negros' rather than just slaves. It 'most strictly forbid any Person to sell or claim Right over any Negroe, the property of a Rebel, who may take Refuge with any part' of the British forces.[4] Clinton had deliberated over it and would enforce it. It allowed Loyalist masters to hire their slaves to the military, receiving compensation if the slave were killed.

In New York, Clinton also split his Commissary Department into three branches in which blacks were employed. The Commissary of Captures was meant to find and take captured moveable property to be used by the army. The purpose of the other two – the Commissaries of Captured Cattle and Captured Forage – were appropriate for black skills.[5] Free blacks worked under contract in these capacities, which could involve combat. In March 1780, the Quartermaster General's department provided the Commissary of Captures with 500 blankets and hats, as well as 35 Stroud cloths for jackets. They also employed blacks as gardeners at several locations to raise vegetables for the navy and army. Certainly, this service gave blacks far more choices than they had as slaves.

During the war, British authorities sought to protect refugee blacks from the efforts of their former masters to re-enslave them. When, in October 1779, a British soldier forced himself into a cart driven by a black, a Dr Baily intervened and apparently led the black to the safety of a house. The authorities, however, found his intervention suspicious as Baily had actually seized the man to sell him as his own property and he was jailed, while the black cartman remained free. Later, in July 1783, Deputy Judge Advocate Stephen Adye turned back Jacob Duryee's attempt to forcefully carry off Francis Griffin, a free black under British protection. Duryee argued his right to property wherever he could find it, to which Adye retorted that a 'general commanding an army in a hostile country possesses powers beyond what even His Majesty himself enjoys'![6] Duryee was ordered out of the British lines and fined 50 guineas.

Returning to New York newspaper advertisements, historians have scrutinized the efforts of New York's masters to recover their slaves, in which the majority of adverts were for men. Loyalist slaveholders would not receive much help from the British military to get runaways back. Clinton accepted the word of blacks over their masters, when it came to deciding as to whether the black wished to return to his master. Moreover, the British did not easily accept the claims of Loyalist masters for the return of their slaves. The authorities required documentation to prove a legal title before they would consider a slave being sold or returned to its claimed master. Advertisements to sell slaves now emphasized the legality of the ownership. The requiring of documentation had the effect of reducing the city's illicit slave trade.

Daddy Moses

Fulfilling Dunmore's offer of freedom in 1776, the crippled Daddy Moses and his followers had been carried by the Royal Navy to New York. There, Moses built his black congregation with his spellbinding renditions of Old Testament stories in the familiar form of call and response. He adapted the Wesleyan Methodist emphasis on oral communication and spontaneous religious response to create a religious expression that could coexist with older African infusions such as conjuring, divination and sorcery. A self-appointed preacher, his form of worship was tainted with 'enthusiasm', a term referring to extravagant emotional responses, speaking in tongues, visions, spirit-possessed delusions and trances. Completely illiterate, Moses appealed to visions to reveal the will of God and the way to eternal salvation, finding resonance with the African practice of ecstatic soul possession. A white visitor to one of his meetings was so affected by the intensity of his preaching that he 'felt frequently distressed for him, his feelings were so exquisite and he worked himself up to such a pitch that I was fearful something would happen to him'.[7] His ecstatic preaching had an electrifying effect on his listeners, who might at any time be seized by the spirit.

Not only Daddy Moses' followers, but on August 16, 1781, Black Pioneer non-commissioned officer Murphy Steel demonstrated that he had experienced voices:

> Murphy Steil [Steel] of the Black Pioneers Says, That about a fortnight ago at Noon, when he was in the Barracks of The Company in Water Street, he heard a Voice like a Man's (but saw no body) which called him by his name, and desired him to go and tell The Commander in Chief, Sir Henry Clinton, to send word to Genl. Washington That he must Surrender himself and his Troops to the King's Army, and that if he did not the wrath of God would fall upon them.
>
> That if General Washington did not Surrender, The Commr. In Chief was then to tell him, that he would raise all the Blacks in America to fight against him. The Voice also said that King George must be acquainted with the above.
>
> That the same Voice repeated the aforesaid Message to him several times afterwards and three days ago in Queen Street insisted that he should tell it to Sir Henry Clinton, upon which he answered that he was afraid to do it, as he did not see the Person that spoke.
>
> That the Voice then said that he must tell it, that he was not to see him for that he was the Lord, and that he must acquaint Sir Henry Clinton that it was the Lord that spoke this; and to tell Sir Henry also, that he and Lord Cornwallis was to put an end to this Rebellion, for that the Lord would be on their Side.[8]

Steel was testing the limits of his new-found freedom in New York. He would be urged often by this voice to action on the street and, ultimately, he believed it was the word of God. He used Christianity to publicly express God's commands in this letter to Sir Henry Clinton himself. With God supporting Steele and his newly freed black brothers, he felt the rebellion might yet be put down.

Crisis forces impressment

New York was the headquarters of the North American Station, the home of the largest navy fleet in the mainland. To man the fleet in time of emergency would require a city-wide press of volunteers and seamen. It was then the press was so well organized that many blacks chose to volunteer, rather than be swept along with it. Not just freemen, but the slaves of Loyalists might be pressed. Such a crisis would happen on at least three occasions, all in response to the appearance of French fleets.

The first crisis was in July 1778, when Admiral d'Estaing's French fleet arrived off Sandy Hook, threatening New York. Admiral Howe had no reinforcements from the Channel Fleet and he was forced to make do with New York resources, building his crews by pressing white and black volunteers from its transports and creating marines from the army by lot. Seamen were prohibited from enlisting in a provincial regiment. The merchants in New York's Chamber of Commerce agreed to supply recruits, to provide fire ships and to scout for Howe. D'Estaing came within a mile of Howe but dared not attack the shallows of Sandy Hook as they were unknown to him.[9] Howe outmaneuvered him and saved New York.

The next emergency occurred almost a year later, when the French fleet at Newport sailed under Chevalier Destouches destined for Chesapeake Bay. In his ships were troops commanded by Baron de Viomenil, who hoped to establish a French presence in Virginia. At the eastern end of Long Island, Admiral Arbuthnot now applied 'for a general press both afloat and ashore to raise seaman for the fleet' to prevent Destouches from entering Chesapeake Bay.[10] He wrote to Lord Germain that he would impress all New York's sailors for his fleet. He explained that the measure was only temporary and that he would 'revive the spirit of privateering' in the near future. Clinton feared that he would denude New York's naval defenses, but Arbuthnot was able to outsail Destouches, arriving outside of the Chesapeake Capes ahead of him. Despite maneuvering by both fleets at the entrance to the Chesapeake, Destouches ended up stuck outside the bay, thus his only option was to return to Newport, leaving the bay to Arbuthnot's fleet. For now, the Chesapeake belonged to the navy.

In October 1779, Arbuthnot now threatened to 'press man for man, out of privateers and merchant vessels' any sailor who had deserted a navy ship.[11] It did not happen, as by April 1780 privateers had become so important to the war effort that the navy's Commodore Francis Drake agreed that no sailors would be impressed from the city's privateers. This still left Drake to impress whites and blacks from regular army soldiers and members of the city's volunteer military companies. Jeby, a 35-year-old runaway, headed for the Hudson River to sign on a Royal Navy ship.

The last impress crisis, in October 1781, involved the return to New York of Admiral Thomas Graves's fleet from its indecisive confrontation with de Grasse at the Chesapeake Capes. Graves and Admiral Samuel Hood were reinforced with three ships arriving under Admiral Robert Digby. It took time to refit their damaged vessels and to impress for a relief fleet, which would consist of twenty-five ships. The city's Chamber of Commerce offered to raise volunteer white and black seamen and able-bodied landsmen with a bounty, and although they were to serve only for the duration of the relief, they would receive full navy health benefits, and for those on transports, navy pay above that of their existing compensation. To top it off, the new recruits were to be protected from future impresses. By this means, 240 were recruited.[12] The fleet sailed on October 19, but Cornwallis had surrendered at Yorktown the previous day. Hood blamed Graves because he failed to respond more rapidly. As the naval war had now shifted to the West Indies, Graves and Hood would pursue de Grasse there. It is evident that New York's merchants, especially in the Chamber of Commerce, were accepting the use of the impress in emergencies.

At the beginning of the war, few free blacks existed in Savannah, Charleston and New York; by the end of the conflict, free black men and women would be more numerous. In New York, freedom for blacks under British authority was readily available, if not in Charleston or Savannah, where slavery remained in place until the end of the war. Southern cities had different conditions to New York; half of their population was made of slaves, while New York's black population was at the most 15 per cent. Charleston's slave population came largely from the plantations that surrounded the city, while New York's had a more diverse origin, including runaways from South Carolina and the Chesapeake, who arrived on Royal Navy ships. In the occupation of Charleston, slaves who joined the garrison were paid their own wages to perform duties in the defenses and on navy ships, rather than the compensation going to their masters. This was certainly not the plantation slavery they had been born into, but it stopped short of being freedom until the war ended. The world of New York's free blacks was much broader as they wrote letters to British officers, petitioned the local government, helped those who had escaped their masters and were free to insult their former masters. This situation has led historians to speculate that because of its many black Loyalists, New York State was one of the last Northern states to pass a very gradual emancipation law in 1799.[13]

PART 6

THE GROWTH OF
BRITISH COMPASSION

Chapter 19

Evangelists and Anti-Slavery in the Royal Navy

It has been assumed that the eighteenth-century Royal Navy was a profoundly irreligious environment. Contemporary opinion held that sailors in general – being beyond the reach of conventional, parochial Anglicanism – were irretrievably immoral, profane and superstitious. John Wesley had preached among Newcastle's keelmen, because of 'So much drunkenness, cursing and swearing (even from the mouths of little children) [had never been] seen or heard before'.[1] Christian evangelist John Marrant noted that after almost seven years of service in the Royal Navy, 'a lamentable stupor crept over my spiritual vivacity, life and vigor; I got cold and dead.' Against this perception, before and during the War for Independence, evangelists appeared in the navy among its officers, who were determined to strengthen their crews by spreading their religious convictions to them. Some of them, through a renewed faith in the saving grace of God, would become abolitionists.

The state of religion before the war is exemplified by the Admiralty's 1731 Regulations and Instructions which provided for the presence of a ship's chaplain to minister to the crew, but the effort was regarded as feeble because the position was unattractive. Those few impoverished clerics who were prepared to brave the meagre pay and privations of shipboard life were frequently disregarded by the crew. One cleric claimed, 'I was fed, coaxed and stared at – if in my den, forgotten; if at large in every body's way; of no manner of use – and at best, endured.'[2] While daily prayer using the Anglican liturgy was prescribed in the Regulations, it was observed only sporadically at sea. There was a sense of the disparity between the confessional, pastoral ideal and the realities of life afloat.

Respect for chaplains

In the words of an historian, 'Protestantism was the foundation that made the invention of Great Britain possible.'[3] The navy was vital to Britain's religious self-identity for since the sixteenth century, Protestants had seen the fleet as a crucial bulwark against the Catholic powers of Europe. Protestantism and naval power retained popular resonance and thus it became a basis for evangelism in the navy. Given the appearance of evangelism among abolitionists, it should be no surprise that it also rose among navy officers, counteracting the previous lack of piety in naval culture. Respect for chaplains' preaching was crucial to this change.

Evangelism

Between 1775 and 1815, Christianity in general and evangelism in particular would become integral to naval life. The navy became an agency for evangelism, first through its officers and then reaching ordinary sailors through the distribution of Christian literature and off-duty gatherings for shared Bible reading and prayer. Beyond their convictions, officers saw religion as a means of combatting indiscipline and immorality among their crews. Crew problems were to be met by reversing the prevailing neglect of public worship. As the war continued, the British public came to view the Royal Navy as an instrument of moral policy because of the revival of religion among British tars.

In 1779, The Naval and Military Bible Society was formed by George Cussons and John Davies, lay Wesleyan Methodists, supported by John Thornton, the wealthy evangelist and founder with Hanway of the Marine Society. Its aim was 'For purchasing Bibles to be distributed among British Soldiers and Seamen of the Navy, to spread abroad (by the blessing of God) Christian knowledge and reformation of manners'.[4] They issued Bibles and Testaments directly to sailors and soldiers, both to Anglicans and Dissenters.

Growing literacy amongst common sailors, and their ability to write letters, disseminated evangelism to the men below deck. Olaudah Equiano was befriended by Daniel Queen who taught him to read the Bible, while his ship's clerk taught him to write. Evangelism crystallized because of the dynamism of a pious officers like Adam Duncan, James Saumarez and Edward Pellew, many of them the sons of clergy. To these officers, religion could not only be personal, rather it had to reflect a desire to evangelize servicemen, using every practical means at their disposal – including patronage, preferment and political clout – to convert the nation to heartfelt religion. These Anglican officers were called 'Blue Lights', while the crew was identified as psalm singers, because this activity was the essence of their devotions.[5]

This religious reform was marked by the growth of informal, Methodist-style prayer and Bible gatherings on board ship, a phenomenon that became relatively common. These religious gatherings often sprang up among a portion of the crew without officers' intervention, but they could not thrive without their approval. Whereas some commanders feared that Methodist-style groups might subvert distinctions of rank, others actively sought to encourage personal faith through setting up reading classes and establishing subscription libraries. Messmate groupings of like-minded believers even brought older seamen together with ships' boys.

Navy evangelists support abolition

The experiences of naval officers in the War for Independence fostered an unmatched flurry of comprehensive plans and essays, moving anti-slavery ideals into areas not previously thought possible. They envisioned what historian Christopher Brown called 'an empire without slaves', worked by free black men and women vested with certain rights and liberties enjoyed by British subjects.[6] More than just the abolition of the slave trade, they wished to abolish colonial slaveholding itself. They factored imperial interests into their proposals and were themselves active in rethinking colonial administration.

129

Andrew Burn's conversion

An experienced Marine officer, Andrew Burn wrote extensively on the value of a Christian life, some of it in the form of religious tracts which could reach the lower deck. His publication in 1789 of *Who Fares Best, the Christian or the Man of the World*, by its title shows what he felt was the fundamental question of his life. He also penned pamphlets against the slave trade, calling for a boycott of West Indian sugar. He wrote a detailed account of his conversion to Christianity, a path fraught with backsliding, typically caused by conditions in the navy. As an evangelist, he experienced a transition to abolitionism through his awareness of his personal sin combined with the saving grace of Christ's atonement, giving him the confidence to oppose the bondage of slavery. In this sense, his autobiography is similar to those black emancipation writers, who also emphasize their conversion experience as vital to obtaining their freedom.[7]

Burn had gone through a religious conversion which led him to be an anti-slavery advocate. Born in Dundee, Scotland in 1742, he was the son of a naval purser. During the Seven Years' War, his father took him on a Royal Navy ship to the North Sea and Jamaica as his assistant clerk. Not surprisingly he found shipboard life to be 'a place so unfavorable to the growth of religion', but this would not stop him. In 1761, through the influence of a family friend, he obtained a commission as lieutenant in the Chatham Division of the Marines. His mates noted, 'Our new messmate is as great a Methodist as Tomlinson,' a reference to Robert Tomlinson, an evangelist and fellow officer, who had been his shipmate.

With the Seven Years' War over he went on half-pay and to make ends meet he was forced to go to France as the tutor of a young gentleman. Here he read Enlightenment authors like Voltaire, Rousseau and Hume and found they lost sight of religion in their effort to support natural rights. Rejection of such allurements also included gambling and alcohol. A near-death experience aboard ship stiffened his religious resolve, but it was only after his brother died that he went through a harrowing conversion experience.

He returned to duty at Chatham dockyard, had a relapse of his faith, but regained it and determined to exercise it on shipboard. When the American colonies rebelled in 1776, he sailed on the *Milford*, carrying artificers to Halifax's careening yard and then to Boston to patrol New England waters. In 1779 he sailed with the East Indian fleet, which stopped at the Goree slave station, West Africa, finding it abandoned by the French. He would continue as a Marine and eventually in 1808 he became colonel commandant of the Woolwich division. Here was an officer whose renewed faith dominated his life.

James Ramsay's experience

Another budding abolitionist was Royal Navy surgeon and then chaplain James Ramsay. He was born at Fraserburgh, Aberdeenshire, the son of William Ramsay, ship's carpenter, and Margaret Ogilvie of Angus.[8] Apprenticed to a local surgeon and later educated at King's College, Aberdeen from 1750 to 1755, he obtained his MA degree and continued his surgical training in London under Dr George Macaulay.

Entering the navy in 1757, Ramsay served as surgeon aboard HMS *Arundel* in the West Indies, under the command of young Charles Middleton. The *Arundel* intercepted a British slave ship, the *Swift* of Bristol, which was in distress and no other surgeon save Ramsay would board the vessel, where he found over 100 slaves living in the most inhumane conditions. This scene of filth would have a lasting effect on him. While serving at sea he also fell and fractured his thigh bone, disqualifying him from future sea service and leaving him lame for the rest of his life. He planned to take a living as a clergyman in the West Indies so that he could devote himself to ministering to slaves.

In July 1761, Ramsay left the navy to take holy orders. Months later, he was ordained in the Anglican Church by the Bishop of London. As he wished to work among slaves on the Caribbean, he traveled to the island of St Kitts, where he was appointed to St John's, Capisterre and the following year to Christ Church, Nichola Town. While there, Ramsay married Rebecca Akers, the daughter of Edmund Akers, a St Kitts' plantation owner. They had one son and three daughters. Their son died young of smallpox, having caught the disease from his father, who had been volunteering on a ship with the disease on board and carried the infection home in his clothes.

Ramsay set out welcoming both black and white parishioners into his Capisterre church with the aim of converting the slaves to Christianity.[9] He was not only the pastor; he provided free medical service to the community's poor. When appointed surgeon to several plantations on the island, he was able to see first hand the conditions under which the slaves labored and what he considered the brutality of most plantation masters. He strongly criticized the cruel treatment and punishment meted out to the slaves and became convinced of the need to improve their conditions. Involved in local government, he was attacked by the planters, who resented his effort to improve their slaves' conditions. His letters to England illustrated these problems.

Ramsay left St Kitts in 1777, exhausted by the continuing conflict with the entrenched planters and merchants. He returned to Britain and briefly lived with his former commander, Charles Middleton, at Teston, Kent. He found Lady Middleton was even more involved in the campaign against the slave trade than her husband.

Renewed, Ramsay rejoined the navy in April 1778, accepting a position as chaplain in the West Indies with Admiral Samuel Barrington, Commander of the Leeward Islands Station, and became engaged in intelligence gathering for use against the French. He returned to Britain in 1780 at the suggestion of Middleton, serving as his personal secretary, with the intention of helping him to reform the Navy Board. He was installed as Vicar of Teston and Vicar of Nettlestead, Kent – these valuable livings being a gift from Middleton.

Ramsay viewed the leaders of the American rebellion as defenders of plantation slavery. In an inquiry published in 1784, he argued the British policy of salutary neglect had not only fostered independence but had caused the growth of a slave-owning planter aristocracy, whose views now dominated the rebellious legislatures. It was they who had established the slave codes to protect themselves, creating 'scenes of horror, oppression, inhuman murders, and unrelenting cruelty'.[10] He argued that Parliament needed to reassert its authority to bring about a gradual emancipation of slaves in the empire. In preparing the slaves to be free subjects, it would be necessary to teach them social responsibility by placing them on juries, and educating and Christianizing them. Masters needed to go to church with their slaves, as liberty and religion were inseparable. Ultimately, he argued that free labor was more productive than that of slaves and that it would be best for only freemen to work on plantations.

During the last years of the war, Ramsay worked on *An Essay on the Treatment and Conversion of African Slaves in the British Sugar Colonies*. In this he conferred at Barham Court with Beilby Porteus, soon to be Bishop of London, who used Ramsay's draft as he attempted to convince the SPGFP to improve the condition of their West Indies slaves. Porteus urged him to publish his essay in 1784. It was the first time that the British public read an anti-slavery work by a navy writer who had witnessed the suffering of the slaves on the West Indian plantations. In over 300 pages it urged the civilizing of slaves through the instruction in Christianity and recognition of their intellectual capabilities. The essay received overwhelming support from the critics, who ignored the West Indies lobby. Challenges by the plantation owners in England were slow to come, but, ultimately, they attempted to refute his allegations with vitriolic attacks on Ramsay's reputation and character.[11]

Now a leading abolitionist, Ramsay met with researcher Thomas Clarkson in 1786 and encouraged him in his tireless efforts to obtain first-hand evidence of the terrors of the trade, leading to the formation in London of the Society for the Abolition of the Slave Trade. On several occasions, Ramsay also met with William Pitt the Younger, the future prime minister, and his friend William Wilberforce.[12]

The Middletons at Barham Court

Based in Teston, Ramsay was draw into a group of influential Anglican politicians, philanthropists and churchmen. Hospitality for them was offered by Margaret and Charles Middleton at their Barham Court estate. Charles was the son of Scots, Robert Middleton and Helen Dundas. By this time, he had used his position as comptroller of the Navy Board to agitate for bureaucratic efficiency, which he felt would lead to moral improvement, especially for sailors. He combined ostentatious piety with unashamed careerism as he sought to influence the Admiralty. From the standpoint of evangelism and anti-slavery sentiment, his marriage in London to Margaret Gambier on December 12, 1761 was even more important than his naval career.[13]

Margaret Gambier Middleton would persuade Ramsay to publish accounts of the horrors of the slave trade. She was a pious and charitable Christian, instrumental in the movement to abolish the slave trade. She came from a naval family, the Scottish Gambiers. Born about 1740, she was the daughter of James Gambier, an attorney and warden of the Fleet Prison, and Mary (Mead) Gambier.[14] Her parents were descendants of Huguenot refugees and were evangelical Christians. As a teenager, her independent mind was evident in her refusal to marry her father's choice for a husband.

Instead, she married Charles Middleton then a mere post captain, who had commanded the *Emerald* in the West Indies during the Seven Years' War. It was a lucrative experience as he gained prize money from taking French ships. He had met Margaret fourteen years earlier, while a young lieutenant, but as her parents thought him unsuitable he had been forced to wait for her hand. Disinherited by her father for her intransigence, Margaret had moved to Barham Court to be close to her schoolmate, now recluse and lady bountiful, Elizabeth Bouverie, another Huguenot descendant. They shared views that attracted respectable evangelicals, especially women. Two years later, after service aboard the *Adventure*, Charles moved in at Barham Court with Margaret and Elizabeth and for the next twelve years they farmed Elizabeth's land, he having reverted to half-pay as the war was over. While he did not realize it, he would never go to sea again. This triumvirate proved inseparable and defended their evangelistic causes with zeal.

At Barham Court, 'Charles and Margaret shared a world-view where Christianity was central and its implications clear – evangelism, abolition of slavery, and moral reformation of society – and where high office gave singular opportunities for these goals to be attempted.'[15] Margaret was a central figure in the early abolition movement. She corresponded with Ramsay over a twenty-year period and supported his next important pamphlet, *An Inquiry into the Effects of Putting a Stop to the African Slave Trade and of granting Liberty to Slaves*, published in 1784. She urged her husband, a backbench MP for Rochester, to support the abolition of the slave trade in Parliament. Feeling inadequate to take up the issue in Parliament and knowing that it would be a long, hard battle, Charles suggested the young MP William Wilberforce as one who might be persuaded to support the cause and he was regularly invited to Barham. Wilberforce was introduced to Ramsay and Thomas Clarkson at Barham.

The Middletons had connections with similar devout Anglicans who shared their religious concerns, notably Admiral James Gambier, Margaret's nephew. They also were joined at Barham Court by poet evangelist, Hannah More, who told Margaret in correspondence that 'you have the first title to every prize on the whole slave subject'. In her poem, *The Slave Trade*, More would use Ramsay's story of the noble slave Quashi, who committed suicide rather than killing his master who was in his power.[16] Margaret became involved in the strategic planning behind the various anti-slavery bills put before Parliament. Bishop Beilby Porteus, William Wilberforce and the black emancipist Olaudah Equiano joined her circle in the 1780s to plan for an anti-slavery reform. Christian Ignatius Latrobe, a leading figure in the Evangelical Moravian Church, after spending four months at Barham Court in 1786, stated that the 'abolition of the slave trade was ... the work of a woman'. Unfortunately, she died in 1792 too soon to see the anti-slavery campaign to completion. That year the first Abolition Bill to end slavery failed; although it passed the Commons, it was rejected in the Lords.

Charles Middleton in the navy

Charles Middleton's role as a reformer at Barham complemented his concern to reform the Navy Board. A brilliant administrator, the navy was lucky to have Middleton. Yet he had major flaws: he was totally self-centered and unable to command the respect of his naval peers. Born in Leith in 1726, at the age of 12 Middleton probably served on a merchantman and at 15 he joined Captain Samuel Mead's 90-gun *Sandwich* as a captain's servant.[17] With the War of Austrian Succession, he sailed to the West Indies and returned there during the Seven Years' War, passing his lieutenant's exam and moving ultimately to captain of the 14-gun *Barbadoes*. While at sea in the West Indies, he began reading the service of Morning Prayer to his ship's company on Sundays, followed by a sermon. Only the watch was exempt from participation. Like his friend Porteus, he was no Methodist or enthusiast, remaining a staunch Anglican. However, this was the beginning of his evangelism, which we have seen fortified four years later when he married Margaret. He was a friend of Hanway, an original contributor to the publication of Equiano's *The Interesting Narrative*, and he would support the first expedition to settle Sierra Leone.

At the end of the War for Independence, much soul searching took place over the loss of the thirteen colonies and this included criticism of the Navy Board. Middleton defended the Board's handling of the war under his direction, including the letting of contracts to private yards. He affirmed 'that the manner in which contracts are made at present by the Board, by exciting a competition in the most ardent manner, and accepting of the lowest offer from any person who can offer sufficient security has totally put an end to [corruption]'.[18] In defending his administration, he felt that his handling of the Board needed no improvement.

Middleton's ambition led him to hope for a seat on the Admiralty, so that as comptroller of the Navy Board he could more effectively present his policies. He believed the comptroller should even play a role in selecting commanders-in-chief at sea, usually restricted to the Admiralty. As a reformer, Middleton focused on restricting the system of gratuities that supported members of the board from the commissioners down to the lowest clerk. Anything that involved paperwork required fees and the clerks, especially, earned far more from their fees than their salaries. Sometimes the fees verged on being bribes and thus Middleton saw them as a source of criminality.[19] He was well meaning in his objectives, but eliminating these practices was easier to plan than to put into effect. One of his most famous reforms, the coppering of all ship bottoms, proved on application to be only partially successful. Middleton spent years trying to reorganize the Navy Board, but when he resigned in 1790 his ideas had not been fulfilled and he was completely frustrated.

Ultimately, at the age of 79, Middleton was elevated to a peerage and his appointment in 1805 as First Lord of the Admiralty would give him the ability to briefly implement his reforms in full.[20] The resulting revision of the Regulations and Instructions bore his imprint, spelling out officers' responsibilities for the spiritual and general welfare of their men, as well as codifying the educational and pastoral roles of the chaplain for the first time. His manifesto emphasized the responsibility of the ship's captain for religion and good conduct on board his vessel, in conjunction with a sober, serious chaplain. In February 1806, Middleton resigned his position on the fall of William Pitt's government – thirty-two French sail of the line having been captured during his short term in office.

James Gambier

Naval officer James Gambier was the nephew of Charles Middleton, by Margaret's marriage to him. Gambier felt that religion could contribute to the management of seamen. He was born on October 13, 1756 at New Providence, the Bahamas, the younger son of John Gambier, the lieutenant governor of the Bahamas, and of his wife, Deborah Stiles, a Bermudian.[21] He was the nephew of Vice Admiral James Gambier and was brought up at Barham Court by his Aunt Margaret. In 1767, 11-year-old James was entered on to the books of his uncle James's 64-gun guard-ship *Yarmouth* at Chatham dockyard near Barham. Two years later, he went with him aboard the 50-gun *Salisbury*, as his uncle assumed control of the North American station. Twenty-four-year-old James served in the War for Independence as commander of the frigate *Raleigh* under Admiral Arbuthnot at the siege of Charleston, where he led a landing party, which took the Point Pleasant Battery and Sullivan's Island.

Eventually, James Gambier would be known as 'Dismal Jimmy' or 'Preaching Jemmy', for it was said that god-fearing officers profited under him. Seamen called him Blue Light for his sanctimonious tendencies and he required his men and officers to be exposed to evangelical messages, hymns and tracts. Rear Admiral Eliab Harvey referred to him as a canting and hypocritical Methodist and of practicing 'methodistical and Jesuitical conduct', implying that his religious demeanor covered an unworthy character. He refused to allow women to come aboard his ships unless they carried marriage certificates and given that few did, it was a harsh restraint on his men. Swearing was dealt with objectively, officers being heavily fined and seamen being obliged to parade up and down for hours with a 32lb shot harnessed in a collar on their shoulders. He showed how far a naval evangelist could go, the result of his Aunt Margaret's influence.

Rising evangelism in the Royal Navy was the result of officers becoming convinced that it improved the discipline and literacy of their crews. From this conviction, some would join the abolitionist movement, especially at Barham Court. Their reforms led to compassionate Christianity gaining wider presence among officers and ultimately crews. More permanently, their effort led to the establishment of organizations aimed at serving the lower deck, namely the Society for Promoting Christian Knowledge, the Naval & Military Bible Society and the Religious Tract Society, which offered Bibles, prayer books and tracts to the crew. The navy's Christian convictions would now be directed towards abolitionism.

Chapter 20

Accepting the Burden
of Black Families

The growing number of Loyalist non-combatants, including black families that had fled to them, was a concern that British officers had to shoulder as the war continued. When, in November 1781, Lieutenant General Alexander Leslie arrived in Charleston he took overall command of British forces there and in Savannah, East Florida and the Bahamas. In Charleston he faced the problem of 'the numbers of loyal inhabitants and of helpless refugees, with their women and children'.[1] The burden was very serious and he wanted Clinton to advise him on what he should allow the refugees. Three months later, Leslie wrote to Clinton:

> the people of the county are daily coming to us to seek protection which, though entailing a burden on ourselves, is not to be refused to them. I regret the heavy and increasing expense of provisions and money by this means, and by the militia now with us; but their misery and helpless situation justifies our attention to them.

Certainly, the presence of black families in ports like Charleston and military camps increased the cost of the war as they would have to be maintained, even though they were only incidentally involved in the military effort. Lord Germain in London was willing to accept in principle the obligation to blacks for their service in the war, allowing the resources of the British state to assume the burden of black families.

Enduring slave families

The development and perseverance of the slave family has been traced by historians. At the beginning of the eighteenth century, the possibility of forming slave families in the Low Country or the Chesapeake was constricted. This was chiefly because plantation masters did not recognize slave marriage or slave kinship in making economic decisions on the distribution of their slaves, which might involve sending family members hundreds of miles from each other.[2] Despite their masters' ambiguity, slave marriage increased throughout the century, largely through the efforts of the slaves themselves. In the Low Country, the continued increase of imported slaves on large plantations led to either two-parent or solitary households in the slave quarters. In contrast, the Chesapeake plantations were smaller and thus finding mates in them was more difficult, causing one-parent households to predominate. This meant that Chesapeake slaves had to find mates on nearby plantations and once married travel back and forth to have conjugal relations, one parent maintaining the children while the other was responsible for visiting. Since the slave codes discouraged mobility, it was necessary for the couples to gain their masters' permission to maintain their unions at a distance.

In both regions, slave kinship developed as families remained in their slave quarters long enough to be extended. A natural increase among slaves occurred in the Chesapeake before the War for Independence, well ahead of that in the Low Country. Chesapeake blacks may have had the one-parent household, but this was offset by their extended families living longer, including grandparents, siblings, in-laws, sons and daughters who resided within an area.[3] It has been noted that this condition made the slave trade in the Chesapeake unnecessary by the time of the war.

Some slave parents could help to sustain their families by passing on their skills to a younger generation. Black fathers who were plantation blacksmiths sought to have their sons work with them to be taught their father's skills. In some plantations, families monopolized a craft so that they were kept together as a workforce. Many female and male slaves were watermen, who were allowed to pursue endeavors after their work hours, on Sundays and during the night. An idea of their skills can be found in the work of Betsey Bailey, a slave who lived through the War for Independence and was the grandmother who nurtured young Frederick Douglas in Tuckahoe, Talbot County, Maryland. She was 'a capital hand at making nets used for catching shad and herring, and [Douglas had] known her to be in the water waist-deep, for hours involved in heavy seine-hauling'.[4] This is what she did when she was too old for field work.

Still, many masters continued to ignore families when they divided slaves by sale and bequest. Taking children from their mothers was common practice in masters' gifts and bequests, and masters could even dispose of children still in the womb.[5] Increasingly in the eighteenth century, the hiring of slaves had the effect of disrupting families. Rented slaves might have three or four different masters requiring that they reside in several locations. Ultimately, children would also be hired out. Despite these difficulties, by the time of the War for Independence, more than half the slaves in the Chesapeake and Low Country had formed families.

Before the war, most runaway slaves did not go far and were soon caught. It was kinship ties in the surrounding area that facilitated runaways to escape from their masters.[6] Usually, the runaways attempted to survive in a familiar area, where they might find support from their own relatives or friends. In the face of this hardship, many chose to return to their masters, even though they lost their freedom and faced severe punishment.

Early acceptance

During the war, this situation would change as slave families escaped to the British and could be taken great distances on ships. Royal Navy ships and transports took white and black Loyalists to British-held ports in Atlantic waters. They included women and their families who fled to British ships or within British lines. Overall by 1776, estimates claim that 3,000 to 5,000 black men, women and children fled to the Dunmore-Hamond fleet in the Chesapeake and then were dispersed to British territory. Black singles were married in occupied British ports like New York and would survive as families there. While many were freed, some would remain slaves until freed at the end of the war.

Early on, Loyalist military units' books carried the names of women as well as men. On May 21, 1776, the *Dunluce* of the Dunmore-Hamond Fleet carried fifty free black women of the Ethiopian Regiment to take possession of Gwyn's Island in the Chesapeake.[7] A few women were sent to the hospital brig or were servants or, more surprisingly, were designated as officers. They were recorded by the surnames of their owners, as most slaves had only a first name. Men comprised the majority of the regiment.

Black families are carried to New York

After the evacuation of Philadelphia in 1778, the new commander-in-chief, Sir Henry Clinton was asked by Lord North's ministry to recruit more Loyalists as the war had escalated and men had to be dispersed to confront the French in the West Indies, the English Channel, and even Africa and Asia.[8] The ministry felt that the insurrection in the Chesapeake of whites and blacks should be continued and promoted as far as the Carolinas and Georgia. The Royal Navy now had the go-ahead to openly support black Loyalists, regardless of the financial burden.

From 1778, British expeditions to the Chesapeake returned to New York with numerous black and white refugees. In the Chesapeake, Tangier Island remained the center of recruitment for transport to New York. Cato Ramsey, slave of Benjamin Ramsey of Cecil County, was able to get from there to New York by 1778 and served in the General Hospital Department.[9] Five years later, he had a family, a wife and 5-year-old son, also named Cato, appearing in the Book of Negros, compiled in New York in preparation for final evacuation.

In May 1779, when Sir George Collier's squadron returned to New York from a successful foray in Chesapeake, it carried 518 blacks, chiefly families, whom Clinton would welcome with his Philipsburg Proclamation. Crucially the Proclamation promised to 'strictly forbid any person to call or claim right over any Negro the property of a Rebel who may take refuge with any part of this army'.[10] Additionally, Collier carried ninety whites, many of them shipwrights. Of Collier's Chesapeake exploits, George III wrote in September 1779, 'It is rather remarkable that Sir G. Collier, with so scanty a force, should have been during the five weeks able to effect more objects against the rebels than the admirals that commanded such large fleets.' A year later, Dorchester County Lieutenant Joseph Dashiell commented, if the Loyalist ships 'stay on [Smith] Island all our negroes will run to them, & the Life of No Whig here will be safe'. Twenty of them had already gone.

Loyalist commanders at distant and exposed outposts from New York City, found they could not sustain Clinton's proclamation as Leslie did. At Oyster Bay on Long Island, Colonel John Graves Simcoe welcomed black recruits to fill the ranks of his regiment, but he had to stipulate that they not bring their wives.[11] Simcoe was a stickler for discipline and he felt the presence of wives undermined his regiment's readiness.

Late in 1783, naval inspection rolls for the evacuation ships in New York harbor, while not indicating family relationship, do give us enough information to identify at least 450 family groupings, three-quarters with children in them.[12] Nearly 1 in 4 of the 2,887 free or slave blacks were not yet 15 years old. Among those older, their origins included 60 West

Indians, and 123 men and 140 women, who were freeborn in the mainland colonies. Among the older males, the vast majority were from Virginia, followed by South Carolina and the New York-New Jersey area. Six out of seven of the older group had been slaves, but many were now free. About half had different surnames from their owner, showing they wanted to put their enslavement behind them.

The Price

As the war continued, the price of Loyalism to the British rose as non-combatant families were supported. Feeding sympathetic blacks, Loyalists, refugees and Indian allies became a costly burden for the British, something that Congress and the states could not possibly afford. Gradually, the cost added to the expenses of the navy's supply convoy system. At New York in 1781, the expected cost of feeding the Associated Loyalists and other refugees caused Clinton to ask for an additional 6,000 rations for the following year.[13]

By then, the navy supply system was not only feeding and caring for 44,000 troops in North America but also provincial regiments, disaffected auxiliaries, refugees, Indian allies and free blacks, numbering altogether over 28,000. Clearly, the number of victuallers necessary for the care of Loyalists was much greater than for the army alone. Despite close calls, the Navy Board was able to sustain the supply convoys.[14] Still, some questioned as to whether the valor of Loyalist mariners and black irregulars could offset this rising cost.

Chapter 21

Methodism Undermines the New Governments

By the time of the War for Independence, the most popular form of evangelism was the Anglican reform called Methodism. We have followed its rise as John Wesley and the Countess of Huntingdon established it in Britain and introduced it to the mainland colonies. More than any other form of evangelism, Methodism had the potential to create abolitionists. It profoundly influenced slave and free blacks as well as white sailors, serving as a moral justification for their conduct.

This Methodist Revolution would parallel and interrupt the War for Independence. In 1777, Continental General William Smallwood was ordered to head off disaffection on the Maryland Eastern Shore, as he had explained their principal motive was 'Religion'. Some were simply 'deluded' by it, but 'by far the greater number conceal their motives & make Religion a Cloak for their nefarious designs'.[1] Smallwood did not identify a denomination in his report, but his letters show that it was Methodism he most feared. His views reflected his traditional Anglicanism, for as a planter he served at least one term as a vestryman of Durham Parish, Charles County, Maryland.

Methodists ignored Smallwood's claims because they felt religious and moral reform was most important. Rebel planters found Methodists to be dangerous and readily accused them of being Loyalists, even though their revolution was spiritual, not political. Most Methodists were pacifists and uplifters of the downtrodden, while Congress and the states sought to create armies and navies. The Methodist Revolution appealed to the forgotten lower orders: the poor, blacks, women and watermen. Methodist preaching to slaves tampered with the gentry's absolute control over them. Methodist evangelism emphasized the spread of their message by a preaching fraternity, usually without education or ordination, independent of the existing parish system, a vestry or even a chapel.

Methodist itinerant preachers and their converts had to be defined by rebels as disaffected. Methodists shared attitudes with the Quakers, such as simplicity in dress and demeanor, pacifism, anti-oath taking, and anti-slavery sentiment. Yet, Methodists were a product of the broad Anglican umbrella, a new effort within that Church to reach constituencies that had been neglected. During the War for Independence, religious momentum was definitely with them.

Methodists supported the 'no taxation without representation' protest of the 1760s and at the end of the War for Independence were taking measures to create a Methodist Church in the new United States. In between, however, rebels associated Methodists with unbroken ties to the mother country.[2] Most of the preachers, like Francis Asbury, John Wesley's handpicked envoy to the colonies, retained their British citizenship and tried to avoid the independence movement, accepting shelter from Loyalists. Most British-born itinerants became Loyalists. Even if some itinerants came to favor independence, rebels like Smallwood quickly classified all Methodists as Loyalists in disguise.

Methodist message spreads

What caused Methodism to grow faster than other denominations was its extraordinary ability to sustain missionary organization and preaching drive. In its system of circuits and conferences, the Methodist Church would possess an unparalleled structure for expansion. As the instrument that guided Methodist believers from sin to salvation, missionary preaching and revivals were impossible to resist, both as listeners and as practitioners.[3] Here are some of the hallmarks of the Methodist message, which rebels found threatening.

Disruptive pacifism

Despite their origin, Methodist itinerants and their followers had differences with Anglican parsons and gentry. Pacifism was coupled with a refusal to take oaths of loyalty. From the rebel standpoint, anyone who refused to swear an oath to Congress was automatically considered an enemy, as no idea of a loyal opposition was tolerated. Rebels pointed out that itinerants like Freeborn Garrettson interfered with military recruitment. In 1776, the appearance of Garrettson interrupted a Caroline County, Maryland militia muster. Thirteen-year-old Ezekiel Cooper described how, 'When the hour of [an itinerant's] preaching came on, the captains [of militia] marched their company into the yard and grounded their arms under two large shade trees, and the people in general heard [the itinerant] very civilly and decently.'[4] What rebels viewed as a threat to militia discipline was seen by Cooper as an uplifting religious experience.

In September and October 1777, when Caroline County Loyalists assembled weapons in several militia storehouses, their defiance was blamed on Methodist preachers. Anglican vestryman and later Maryland Governor William Paca claimed, 'an insurrection of [Loyalists] on the borders of Queen Anne's and Caroline Counties was headed by some scoundrel Methodist preachers. A body of eighty, assembled in arms, were dispersed [and] the captain and chief Methodist preachers are among the captives.'[5] Their activities spilled over into Kent County, Delaware, where Methodists were accused of encouraging Loyalists, as it was claimed Methodist preachers were involved in arming them.

Caroline County continued to be center of Methodist disruption. In 1780, leading rebel Nathaniel Potter wrote to Governor Thomas Sim Lee:

> the spirit of Methodism reigns so much amongst us that few or no men will be raised for the war ... when there is any call for raising men, for their preachers to be continually attending their different posts ... I am ... persuaded is the greatest stroke the British ministry ever stuck amongst us.[6]

Potter expressed a link between the British ministry and the Methodist movement. His opinion was respected as he had been a delegate to the Maryland constitutional convention of 1776 and a supply commissioner in charge of purchasing pork for the Continental army in Caroline County. His brother Samuel, commander of the Caroline County militia, expressed similar sentiments. In Caroline, Methodist itinerants continued to interfere with the recruitment of rebel soldiers.

Itinerant preaching and revivals

No separation of church and state existed in Maryland or Virginia, so that their legislatures felt they had the authority to regulate Methodist preaching. In 1776, the Maryland General Assembly passed a law which imposed a modest fine for preaching without taking an oath of allegiance to the state. With the Howe brothers' invasion in October 1777, the Assembly passed a much more stringent Act for the Better Security of Government, which required any man who preached to take an oath of loyalty to the state. It was designed for Methodists and Quakers who refused to take oaths. The Maryland loyalty oath was unique because it required not only allegiance but also that one swear to bear arms.

In 1778, twenty Methodists were indicted for preaching and not taking the Maryland oath. When itinerant John Littlejohn refused to acknowledge the restrictions, he was nearly 'tarred & feathered by some of the better sort as they suppose they are'.[7] Hostility to itinerants would continue in Queen Anne's County after Freeborn Garrettson was attacked in 1778. In the northern part of the county, an itinerant was attacked, tumbling down a stairwell with his assailant. Another itinerant, Philip Gatch, was praying at the end of a service when an assailant seized his chair to use as a weapon, which Gatch held on to until the congregation came to his rescue. Most itinerants experienced violence as supposed Loyalists, even though they tried to be aloof from the political conflict. Despite the fact that Methodist itinerants were threatened and jailed for violating these acts, they continued to preach and develop a popular following.

Preaching to blacks

Methodists cultivated not only the white middle and lower orders but free blacks and slaves. Chesapeake society was not then as segregated as it became in the nineteenth century, but rather a place where black and white might pray together. The planters, however, regarded Methodist itinerants' speaking out against slavery as more dangerous than overt Loyalism. Mixing with blacks and advocating pacifism were seen as being more perilous to the social order than simply supporting the king. The Methodist reforms attracted the poorer elements of society, whom the vestries felt could be too easily persuaded to run away. Figures for membership in the Eastern Shore's Methodist congregations in the 1770s and 1780s show that almost one out of every three Methodists was black. In Cecil County, the Methodist membership was almost evenly split between whites and blacks. Even more striking was the recognition that the few Methodist planters who taught their slaves the Bible had nothing to fear from them – that, in the words of Phoebe, Charles Hynson's wife, Methodist slaveholders 'could leave every kind of food exposed and none [was] taken by' [their previously thieving slaves].[8]

Methodist itinerants expressed an evangelism that was welcomed by both blacks and whites. English itinerant Thomas Rankin had condemned the Continental Congress for claiming to fight for liberty when their members were keeping 'hundreds of thousands of blacks in cruel bondage'.[9] Because he spoke passionately about the sin of holding slaves, itinerant Robert Williams was unpopular with a white congregation in Norfolk, Virginia, which shouted him down whenever he tried to preach. Black Methodist converts like Daddy Moses and Mary Perth were drawn to Williams for the very reasons that white colonists felt anxiety. Among Governor Dunmore's recruits were a number of black Methodists, whose presence made it seem that Methodism supported him. By 1784, Methodists had joined Quakers in supporting the abolition of slavery.

Threat to the vestries

It was Methodists, not Quakers or Presbyterians, who would challenge the planters' control of the vestries. Middling and lower members of Anglican churches were tired of the vestry's aristocratic antics and remembered the legislature's mandatory tithes eating into their pocketbooks. They were not about to overthrow the vestries' domination, but they did seek to reform them, and it was here that the influence of Methodism emerged as a threat to the power of the slaveholding gentry. To the vestries, Methodists were Loyalists because of their evangelism.

The planter elite claimed that Methodists threatened their influence over vestries by appealing to the lower orders and competed with their republicanism in terms of popular culture. The Virginia gentry had long viewed themselves as model English gentlemen, opposing the threat of evangelism to their control over vestries. In Virginia, it has been said, 'evangelism began as a rejection and inversion of customary practices', while the independence movement 'initially tended towards a revitalization of ancient forms of community'.[10] The gentry viewed Methodism as an attack upon their position in society because Methodism emphasized an alternative to the exclusionary politics they had long practiced. With its call to missionary preaching, its enthusiastic revivals, and its growing religious societies, it was a danger to the existing vestry rules.

What upset the vestries and Anglican clergy most was the freewheeling practices of Methodist itinerant preachers, emphasizing on-the-spot conversion without tax or traditional theological obligations. The scorn of Methodist preachers for vanity made them natural opponents of the planters. The elite felt that Methodist outdoor spiritual meetings were contrary to their best interests and some sermons were regarded as seditious. Methodists retorted that they had been forced to make use of churchyards because Anglican vestries had shut them out, even though they scrupulously avoided preaching when Anglican services were scheduled. Besides, it was not a Methodist priority to build houses of worship, they preferred to meet their people out of doors.

The vestries wanted parsons to be educated men, properly ordained in England. Instead, Methodist itinerants, regardless of their education, emphasized their ability to reach a large and diverse audience. The Methodist spiritual ministry was more important than contemporary debate over independence or any form of politics. Methodist itinerants preached a gospel of faith, pacifism and equality of all men. In 1777, Joseph Cromwell, the first Methodist itinerant in Talbot County, was illiterate, unable to even write his own name. He was also described as rude, but he preached with an authority that few could match. His focus was on the spiritual revolution rather than worldly affairs. Francis Asbury, the future Methodist bishop, claimed, 'he is the only man I have heard in America with whose speaking I am never tired.'[11]

Freeborn Garrettson

Methodist itinerants carried the Wesleyan message. Of these, we know most about Freeborn Garrettson because in 1791 he published an account of his experience and travels and, forty-two years later, Nathan Bangs wrote Garrettson's biography based on it. He was born in 1752 into a wealthy Anglican slaveholding family, living near the mouth of the Susquehanna River, which flowed into Chesapeake Bay. In 1775, he went through an agonizing personal conversion to Methodism, signified by the manumission of his slaves. He was physically attacked for this act by a slaveholder. In response, Garrettson said his heart bled, 'for slaveholders, especially those who make a profession of religion'.[12] He held prayer meetings in his house, which were condemned by the local Anglican parson and vestry.

The English itinerant Martin Rodda offered him opportunities to become a Methodist itinerant, which he was not yet confident he could do. Finally, he was willing to be a substitute itinerant and traveled in Cecil, Queen Anne's and Caroline Counties bringing Wesley's message to all levels of society. He then was licensed as an itinerant by English itinerant Thomas Rankin. Garrettson was not only a man of deep piety but of gentility; he had a cultivated mind, with refined manners, and high social position, so that he could bring the Methodist message to the leading gentry if he chose.[13] Yet his desire was to reach the lowest levels of society.

Garrettson's first full-time itinerancy involved the Frederick Circuit in Maryland, then into Virginia, with the Fairfax and Brunswick Circuits, and finally into North Carolina. He again met with Rankin and participated in the Deer Creek, Virginia Conference in May 1777.[14] It was here he found a black boy whose power in prayer was exceptional. He did not cross the Chesapeake until May 30, 1778; by then Rankin and Rodda had returned to England and Francis Asbury, their new leader, was in hiding at White's plantation. While four itinerants had been appointed to travel to Somerset County, three of them soon disappeared and Asbury remained in hiding, leaving the full task of spreading Methodism to Garrettson. From 1778 to early 1781, he held Methodism together in the Chesapeake and Delaware areas, as Asbury continued in seclusion.

As he traveled, Garrettson formulated views on the War for Independence, which was taking place around him. A Marylander, he was not so attached to Britain as his mentors Rodda and Rankin. He opposed the war because it was 'contrary to my mind, and grievous to my conscience, to have any hand in shedding human blood'.[15] He argued that taking an oath violated the teachings of God, especially if it required the bearing of arms, which the Maryland Loyalty Oath required. To the rebels, the fact that Garrettson would not bear arms, automatically made him a Loyalist. His idea of perfect government came neither from Paine's natural rights nor Dickinson's British constitution, instead he followed the example of the primitive Christian church as interpreted by Wesley. Garrettson was a fearless revolutionary when spreading the Methodist message.

What upset the rebel authorities most about Garrettson was that magistrates were too intimidated by his threats to their souls, so that they feared to fully apply the law against him.

Moreover, when he was finally jailed in Cambridge, Maryland, he had influential friends among the planters, who could produce the exorbitant £20,000 bond for his release.[16] Many who provided for his safety were disaffected and Loyalists. His association with them, his refusal to take the state loyalty oaths, his opposition to the war, and his view that the only true sovereign was God, made him an enemy to Maryland's, Virginia's and Delaware's new governments.

Methodists spearheaded the Loyalist evangelical movement in the Chesapeake. They disliked the War for Independence because it disrupted what they felt was most important: religious and moral reform. They were pacifists and uplifters of the downtrodden, while Congress and the states sought to promote the war. Methodists were tied to Loyalism through their continued respect for John Wesley and their English-born itinerant preachers, as well as the wealthy disaffected supporters, who provided safe houses for their itinerants. Methodist evangelism appealed to the forgotten lower orders, blacks, women and watermen. Methodist preaching to slaves tampered with the planters' absolute control over them. The gentry found Methodists to be dangerous and readily accused them of being Loyalists, even though their revolution was spiritual, not political. By 1784, Garrettson, Daddy Moses, John Ball and Boston King would carry the Methodist message to Nova Scotia.

Right: *Thought to be
Francis Barber by Joshua
Reynolds, 1770s, Tate
Collection, London.*

Below left: *Quobna
Cungano, detail from
etching by Richard Cosway,
1784.*

Below right: *Robert
Wedderburn, son of the late
James Wedderburn Esq. of
Lavereste, frontispiece from*
The Horrors of Slavery,
1824.

Painting by William Windus, entitled Black Boy, *c. 1844. This poor boy is said to have crossed the Atlantic from the West Indies as a stowaway and been found by Windus on the steps of the Monument Hotel in Liverpool. Windus then employed him as an errand boy. This painting was put in the window of a frame-maker's shop. A sailor relative of the boy saw it, found the boy and took him back to his parents. Walker Art Gallery, Liverpool.*

Britannia seated at the foot of a statue of charity inscribed 'Marine Society', as a woman at left brings two poor children towards her, and members Jonas Hanway, John Thornton and William Hickes stand at right with another boy. After Edward Edwards, British Museum, London.

Above: *Caricature of Greenwich Pensioners, by John Thurston, late 1700s.*

Below: *Painting of Deptford Dockyard by Joseph Farington, c.1794, showing (left to right along the shore): - Officers' houses & offices - The double dry dock - Quadrangular Great Storehouse - A pair of shipbuilding slips - Wet dock (or basin) - Shipbuilding slip - Mast houses and mast pond - Boat house.*

Above left: *Detail from the Jovial Crew, Thomas Rowlandson, 1786. Black sailor wears a pink neckcloth, a brown short jacket with cloth covered buttons on his mariner's cuff, and a pair of trousers.*

Above right: *Granville Sharp, by G. Dance, frontispiece of Memoirs of Granville Sharp, 1820.*

Left: *A West Indies flower girl and two other free women of colour by Agostino Brunias, c. 1770*

Above: African Hospitality *is an anti-slavery print by engraver, John Raphael Smith, after a painting by his brother-in-law George Morland. The print was published in 1791 as a companion to another called* The Slave Trade. *The image depicts the kindness of Africans ministering to a shipwrecked European family, an abolitionist ideal. The National Museums of Liverpool.*

Right: *Lieutenant Rev. James Ramsay, by Carl Frederik von Breda, National Portrait Gallery, London.*

Above: *Barham Court, Teston, Kent.*

Left: *Admiral Charles Middleton, later Lord Barham, by Isaac Pocock.*

James Gambier, 1st Baron Gambier, by William Beechey, 1809, National Maritime Museum, Greenwich.

Portrait of John Clarkson, unknown painter.

Left: *Portrait of Captain Philip Beaver by John Opie, c. 1805.*

Below: *Bible-reading on board a British frigate c. 1830, Detail of painting by Augustus Earle, National Maritime Museum, Greenwich.*

PART 7

THE TURNING POINT: EVACUATION BECOMES MIGRATION

Chapter 22

American Slaveholders seek
return of their Slaves

Throughout the war, rebel plantation owners tried to get British authorities to return their runaway slaves.[1] The planters' efforts to deal with the British for their return, however, were thought by Congress and state authorities to expose them to the temptations of Loyalism. It was felt that in bargaining, the masters might be seduced into becoming Loyalists. State leaders forbade negotiations with ships' captains for the return of their slaves. Near the end of the war, however, Congress and George Washington were willing to negotiate with the British to get their slaves back.

It has to be remembered that slave patrols had been operating in Virginia since the war commenced and were seen by the planters as the best means of preventing runaway slaves. In Richmond County, on the Northern Neck, pay for slave patrollers rose throughout the war as an incentive for more rigorous patrols. In 1776, about one third of the county's expenditure for jobs was paid to nineteen men for patrolling.[2] By 1781, as the state was invaded, patrols were still the largest single item in the county's budget. Slaves taken by the patrols were jailed and not always returned to the masters; in Virginia they often ended up in the state lead mines. Despite the expenditure on local patrols, slaves would continue to escape.

Mary Willing Byrd is determined to get her slaves back

In the Chesapeake on December 30, 1780, Thomas Symonds' squadron arrived from New York in Hampton Roads, Virginia with General Benedict Arnold's army. It then moved up the James River in the direction of Richmond, foraging for or destroying the corn, pork and barrel staves produced by slaves at the river's plantations. Having captured Richmond on January 5, when Arnold advanced to and returned on the James, he docked at Westover, the plantation of Mary Willing Byrd. The widow of suspected Loyalist William Byrd III, she had been raised in Philadelphia and was the first cousin of Peggy Shippen, Arnold's wife. Arnold camped at Westover and may have briefly considered the possibility of plantation masters coming to Westover to reclaim their property in slaves. A message was directed to Governor Thomas Jefferson, who 'was not fond of encouraging an intercourse with the Enemy for the recovery of property', though he was willing to listen.[3] Arnold, however, could not dally, he had orders from Clinton requiring him to go to Portsmouth so he left Westover on January 10 and arrived nine days later at Portsmouth to initiate a base. Mary watched from Westover's windows as he left with forty-nine of her slaves. This was probably the last she would see of them or Arnold, although British forces, later under command of General William Phillips, would briefly anchor there on April 24.

One of Mary's key losses was the house slave Walter Harris. Known to her as Wat, he was married and had several children. Arnold took him as a guide on his visits to Westover and he later served with Cornwallis at Yorktown. He was among the few allowed to leave Yorktown on the Royal Navy's *Bonnetta*. After a year in New York he went to England; he would never return to Westover.

Mary had the responsibility for indebted Westover on her shoulders and she spent the rest of the war and beyond trying to get her slaves back. Her first effort was approved by the Continental commander Frederick William von Steuben in which Royal Navy Lieutenant Charles Hare came to Westover in the *Swift* under a flag of truce, bringing her a few gifts and news of his bid to find her slaves.

Washington had given von Steuben the impossible task of building an army by using only the available Virginia militia. Typical of the problems he faced was Major George Turberville, an attorney and militia officer from Epping, who on his own seized Hare and his vessel. Mary responded to Hare's seizure with a letter to von Steuben vouching for Hare and claiming he had 'no intentions that are not perfectly honorable'.[4] Mary explained that he had tried to bring her slaves back from Portsmouth, but once they knew they would be returned, the slaves 'hid themselves, and tho searched for, seven days, could not be found'. Certainly, this was consistent with Clinton's policy of not returning slaves to their masters if they did not want to go back.

After Mary posted her letter to von Steuben, Turberville and his militia showed up at Westover, intending to search the plantation and examine her private papers. Mary described how Turberville's men came in the middle of the night, 'to Westover, made prisoners of my whole family – Mr Meade, who conducted him to my Chamber, which he instantly entered, notwithstanding my two eldest daughters were a sleep in one bed, and myself in another … It was Liberty that Savages would have blushed at.'[5] Von Steuben sent an immediate rebuke to Turberville for taking the patrol to 'Mrs Byrd's House'. He ordered Turberville to have Hare and his vessel sent back, but it was disobeyed and 'Von Steuben's open letter in answer to Mr Hare [was delayed] by Mr Turberville'. When Mary contacted von Steuben, she also appealed to Governor Thomas Jefferson to intercede on her behalf and help restore her good name.

In spite of von Steuben's order, Turberville refused to let Hare or the *Swift* go. Instead, he appealed to militia Colonel James Innes asking him to go directly to Jefferson for a ruling on Hare and the *Swift*. Innes sent Jefferson a request for his opinion and an explanation to von Steuben and then dispatched Turberville to personally discuss the situation with Jefferson. Naturally, von Steuben sent a letter to Jefferson complaining that the state militia officers 'acted without my orders and reported their proceedings to government alone'.[6] Jefferson ultimately knew he had to support von Steuben, ordering Hare released, and Turberville was dismissed from the militia and returned home.

Mary was charged, however, with 'trading with the enemy'.[7] Her trial, scheduled to begin on March 15 before a special commission of *oyer* and *terminer* in the General Court, was postponed for a week, after which she went to Richmond to defend herself. This would have been the opportunity for the militia officers to present evidence supposedly extracted from their incursions at Westover. The trial was never held, however; the authorities were contritely silent and Mary righteously returned to Westover. The Virginia judiciary released the *Swift* back to von Steuben. Jefferson briefed the Marquis de Lafayette on the details, but the new Continental commander in Virginia declined to involve himself in such a messy controversy, leaving von Steuben free to send Hare back to Arnold at Portsmouth.

Within a month, facing economic difficulties, Mary began running advertisements in the *Virginia Gazette* to sell Westover.[8] Her attempt failed and when Lord Cornwallis arrived in Virginia and stayed at Westover, she tried again to use a private flag to recover her slaves, including Wat, who was now serving with Cornwallis as freeman Walter Harris. She kept up her contention that Arnold had promised to return her slaves, applying two years later to Guy Carleton in New York for their return, including Harris, who was now in New York. After the war ended, she sought compensation from London, but she was never rewarded. Here was a mistress who tried to deal with the British for the return of her slaves, a dangerous activity to local rebels, even if they could not find evidence of her Loyalism. On top of this she was a woman, an easy target for bullying militia.

Government discourages negotiations for return of slaves

Mary's difficulties in seeking the return of her slaves was not an isolated example. In April 1778, in the Chesapeake's Somerset County, planters petitioned George Dashiell, the county lieutenant, to go under flag of truce to British ships at Tangier Island and to enquire after slaves who had 'absented themselves from their master's service'.[9] Evidently, the planters felt they could separate the British military and naval commanders from the irregular raiding of Loyalist privateers and watermen. Neither Dashiell nor the Maryland Council would allow them to go. The Council explained that:

> We are sorry for the loss the gentlemen of your county have sustained by their Negroes going away, but we cannot conceive the enemy would restore them, unless their masters make concessions which no American ought to do. It is very unlikely that if a man avowed his principles to support the cause of America, that he would be so far favoured as to have his Negroes or any other property returned. We have had many applications similar to the present, but our impression of the impropriety of permitting our people to go to the enemy to solicit favors, is so strong that we have rejected every one and hope and expect, some method will be fallen on to indemnify them, without their being obliged to crouch to our enemies.[10]

In May 1782, the Virginia legislature finally ordered all holders of runaways to deliver them to their masters. If the master was unknown an advertisement would be placed in the *Virginia Gazette* seeking them. It proved ineffective, especially as during the Cornwallis campaign, many slaves had been taken by their allies, the French.

Continental generals hope to minimize black migration

Beyond the attitude of local government, Congress charged its Continental generals – watching the evacuations of British garrisons from 1782 – with preventing the migration of Loyalist civilians and former slaves. Washington at New York, Nathanael Greene at Charleston and Anthony Wayne at Savannah were hopeful they could reduce the exodus of slaves, whose loss would be an economic blow to the war-torn states. As it turned out, the three Continental armies they commanded were too weak to threaten the firmly entrenched British garrisons that greatly outnumbered them, and their role at best was to watch the British evacuate.

Shadowing the evacuation of Savannah, General Anthony Wayne of Pennsylvania tried to obstruct numerous evacuees by convincing Georgia Governor John Martin to offer Loyalist deserters the incentive of 200 acres of land, a cow and two breeding swine, as well as a pardon and protection.[11] The deserters were only required to join Wayne's force. Meanwhile, planters still sought to reclaim their runaway slaves.

Wayne had only 600 men, chiefly Virginia Continentals, around Savannah and while he often wrote to his Continental superior, Major General Nathaniel Greene of Rhode Island, for reinforcements, he was consistently turned down. The entire Southern Department numbered only 2,700 effectives and Greene replied that he had discontent among his ranks and ordered Wayne to join him near Charleston as soon as the British evacuation of Savannah was complete.

As Wayne watched Savannah's defenses, his men were suddenly attacked in the dark of the night from the rear. He thought it was the Savannah garrison circling behind him, but in fact it was 300 Creek warriors under the war chief Guristersigo, guided by blacks, who had come a distance from the back country. The Creek's allegiance to the crown was well known and Wayne found his horse shot from under him as he rallied his troops. Guristersigo was killed, but most of his warriors escaped. Wayne had to wait until after Savannah was evacuated to be able to march into the city and then he could stay only a few weeks, following his orders from Greene, arriving in South Carolina on August 9, 1782.[12]

Two destinations of Savannah's British migrants made Greene and Wayne uneasy. Many refugees went north to Charleston, causing Greene to assume them to be reinforcements to prolong British control of the city. Those Savannah refugees who went in the opposite direction to St Augustine, inspired Wayne to boast that if St Augustine were not evacuated, he would 'get possession of it before the Spaniards'.[13]

During Wayne's and Greene's watches, exiled South Carolina Governor John Rutledge had written to Francis Marion authorizing him to invoke the death penalty for blacks who supplied the British with provisions or intelligence. Greene had little control over Marion's irregulars. He ordered Wayne to restrain rebel plundering of Loyalists and the vicious bloodshed that been prevalent during the war in the back country. Greene feared that this bloodshed might compromise the evacuations and disturb the peaceful relations that now existed. News of Admiral Rodney's victory at the Saints over the French had to be ignored and Wayne saw his occupation of Georgia as depriving 'the British of a considerable tract of territory with which they expected to go to the European [negotiations], where the fate of America will ultimately be decided'.[14] However, he hoped the issue of black evacuees would not be settled at the European peace table.

While Wayne was watching Savannah in 1782, the state of Georgia awarded him two rice plantations on the Little Satilla River, near Savanah, totaling 1,300 acres. Both plantations – Richmond and Kew – had been confiscated from Loyalists and abandoned for several years as the state sought to get clear title. Although the buildings were mostly intact, the slaves had disappeared from the plantations. They now were needed to repair dikes and make various improvements to restore the property. If this happened, experienced rice masters told Wayne that the plantations could produce 800–1,000 barrels of high-grade rice, worth more than £3,000.

After the war, Wayne debated the idea of splitting his life between his holdings in Pennsylvania and Georgia, although his wife made it clear she would remain in the North. Finally, Wayne decided to mortgage his Pennsylvania property for about £5,000 and in 1785, he became a Georgia slaveholder, purchasing 47 slaves – 15 men, 11 women, 9 boys and 12 girls – and hired an overseer to direct them. The slaves cost £3,300, with about a third needed up front and the remainder paid in five annual installments.[15] He tried to make a go of his rice plantations in the 1780s, but he was inexperienced with rice cultivation and instead he sank deeper into debt. By 1791, his creditors had taken over his plantations. Ironically, the same happened to Nathanial Greene, who was awarded Mulberry Grove plantation by the state of Georgia near Wayne's plantations. After the war, Greene also worked hard to make a go of it, but died of sunstroke in 1786, deeply in debt. Managing gifted plantations had consumed both Northern generals.

Washington hopes to minimize black migration

In the New York area, Continental commander George Washington was the leading slaveholder to confront the British over the return of slaves. Guy Carleton would be the final British commander to turn away rebel or neutral masters who visited the city to reclaim their slaves. With the preliminaries of the peace now signed but not approved by Parliament, on May 6, 1783 Washington proposed he and Carleton meet to discuss the 'true intent and spirit' of Article VII of the preliminaries, which concerned the return of slaves.[16] He had been surprised to hear that a large number of blacks had already embarked, since his purpose was to negotiate the return of runaway slaves to their rebel masters. He personally felt this violated the spirit of the preliminaries, but he was ready to sit down and discuss how to prevent the further carrying away of blacks belonging to citizens of the republic.

Carleton answered quickly that it was impossible to tell when his evacuation would be completed but that he had already requested that Congress appoint inspectors to come to New York and help superintend the embarkations. Three were appointed, but they found Carleton's views unhelpful. They learned they could perform their duty, 'except in the case of negroes who had been declared free previous to [Carleton's] arrival: as [he] had no right to deprive them of that liberty [he] found them possessed of … ' and he would not 'prevent their going to any part of the world they thought proper'.[17] Had blacks been denied permission to embark, Carleton argued, they would simply have run away and it would have been impossible for former masters to find them. He was motivated by 'feelings of humanity as well as the honor and interest of the nation whom I serve'. Carleton later claimed that Article VII affected only blacks who came after the articles had been signed, that is after December 31, 1782 and involved only those outside of the British lines.

Carleton did allow Washington to appoint a three-man commission to report on infractions to rebel property including slaves. In June 1783, they came up with a test case, reporting to Carleton that former slave Thomas Francis was on board the *Fair American* about to sail for the West Indies. Escaping from his master, he had come within the British lines in November 1782, enlisting in the Jamaica Rangers. Their request went unanswered, showing where Carleton's sentiments continued to be and the commission was soon disbanded.

Those who stayed

In a few cases, blacks would decide to stay where they were, though not as slaves of their former masters but rather in their own free communities. A recent comprehensive analysis of Maroon communities concludes that while the war fostered many runaways, they were not Maroons, as they were inspired by the British, creating Loyalist communities in which blacks were integrated with, not separated from, whites. Maroon living conditions were difficult for most blacks, thus few were anxious to form all-black Maroon communities. One historian concludes, 'The maroon way of life was only for the resilient few and [the War for Independence] may not have made it much more alluring.'[18]

Maroon communities did exist in the Carolinas and Georgia after the war. Scarcely any black communities developed in isolation, without apparent white support. Maroon communities did exist in the Carolinas and Georgia after the war. Late in 1782, the Savannah evacuation left behind a body of armed blacks who called themselves the 'King of England's soldiers' and were well trained in military tactics, and had no intention of returning to bondage.[19] They still existed in October 1786 when a party of white militiamen clashed with their growing community living at or near Tybee Island, many having served with the British during the war. The attack resulted in the death and injury of several Maroons and the abandonment of this settlement. If caught, Maroon leaders were usually beheaded and those who escaped fled even further into the Georgia wilderness.

Another Maroon community was established in the 1780s on the swampy sides of the lower Savannah River at Belle-Isle, on the dividing line between Georgia and South Carolina. They had first gathered in the aftermath of the Siege of Savannah in 1779. Its leader was a slave named Sharper, in war Captain Cudjoe, perhaps named after the famous Jamaican Maroon. His second in command was another slave, Captain Lewis.[20] In March 1787, militia forces commanded by James Jackson burned this community, but the scattered Maroons built a second settlement on Bear Creek. To garner needed resources and provisions, Cudjoe and Lewis led parties in raiding nearby plantations. Colonel James Gunn, with a small force of South Carolina and Catawba militia, attacked the Bear Island community two months later. Many, including Captain Cudjoe and his wife Nancy, escaped. Captain Lewis was captured and taken to Savannah where he was tried and convicted of murder and robbery, and hanged, his severed head stuck on a pole. This renewed black opposition, without British support, was aimed at the planters, who had gone to war to retain their property in slaves.

Most rebel planters failed to get their runaway slaves back. This was despite a late effort by the Continental army and state governments to oppose their embarkation with the British. Black determination to retain their freedom caused the dislocation and economic stress the war would take on the United States.

Chapter 23

Royal Navy Transports
Carry Blacks Away

The British evacuation, which at first seemed a humiliating conclusion to the War for Independence, became a logistical feat for the Royal Navy, showing its ability to carry thousands of black and white Loyalists to widely dispersed parts of the British Empire. More crucially, it fulfilled the pledge of British officers to protect their black allies and see to it that they had place in an evacuating ship. Blacks rarely feared going on board a British ship because their preachers like Daddy Moses or David Margrett emphasized the Old Testament perspective that they were leaving bondage for freedom in a promised land. This process would continue, even after the peace was signed, making the evacuation the turning point of the Emancipation Revolution.

The evacuation has been treated as admission the British lost the War for Independence, a reason to rethink their priorities including participation in the slave trade, but this was not how the British saw the situation in the last two years of the war.[1] From the naval standpoint, the war was Atlantic-wide, not limited to the thirteen colonies. De Grasse's French fleet had left the Virginia Capes, so that the defense of the Chesapeake had fallen to the Maryland and Virginia navies. They faced the continued operations of Royal Navy ships, Loyalist privateers and irregular watermen barges frustrating their efforts to control the bay. Insurrection on the Chesapeake continued as late as March 1783. Meanwhile, Rodney's victory in the West Indies at the Battle of the Saints over de Grasse was seen as a restoration of the Royal Navy's superiority in the Atlantic Ocean.

The evacuation

By April 1782, an evacuation of the British North American garrisons seemed imminent, when the Navy Board's Charles Middleton sent the new First Lord August Keppel an estimate of the transports necessary for the task. Middleton believed that if New York and Charleston were evacuated simultaneously, 60,000 tons of shipping would be required for the troops alone – with 25,000 additional tons for ordnance, provisions and stores. No more than a third of this was on hand. Middleton felt that because of the possibility of continuing the war in the West Indies, New York should be evacuated first and Charleston later, as it was closer to the Indies. He would have New York's garrison removed by September.[2]

Middleton's proposal was too narrowly defined as he was chiefly concerned with returning troops to Europe. In fact, the effort would not just require the removal of garrisons but the migration of thousands of civilians. As white and black Loyalists often outnumbered the garrisons, they would make up a substantial portion of any embarkation. Military authorities agreed; they could not be abandoned, regardless of the demands on shipping. The civilians and even some garrisons were to be evacuated to various locations, where the goal was actually to resettle them. Thus, the evacuation became a migration to new homes in the British Empire, rather than a purely military operation. It would also dovetail into the beginning of Britain's abolitionist movement, which was to eventually end the slave trade in 1807.

Carleton's initiative

Freedom for slaves had become a policy formulated by the British military in America, from Dunmore to William Howe, to Henry Clinton, to Guy Carleton. The last would be the final advocate of the policy and its strongest supporter. Carleton had administrative experience as governor of Quebec, where he had introduced and seen passage of the Quebec Act, offering French Canadians religious and legal toleration. Yet he also had military talents, as Lord North explained in 1779, in that he was 'so much of a soldier, and so little of a politician, such a resolute, honest man, and such a faithful and dutiful subject, that ... he wishes to see him entrusted with a part of our defense in this critical moment'.[3] The problem in evaluating his motives has been that he was exceptionally secretive, ultimately having his wife destroy his personal papers.

Born in Northern Ireland in 1724, Carleton had been educated by his stepfather, Thomas Sketon, an Anglican clergyman.[4] He had risen in the army supported by James Wolfe, the conqueror of Quebec. In 1777, Carleton, as governor of Quebec, had asked to be relieved before Burgoyne left to invade Lake Champlain, but his replacement, Frederick Haldimand, did not arrive until March 1778. When Carleton returned to Britain, he found himself in much favor because he not been directly involved in the Saratoga campaign, which was blamed on Burgoyne and Lord Germain. While Carleton and Germain had long feuded, when called upon to testify as to the minister's strategy, Carleton remained strictly neutral in his commentary. Although inactive in England for almost five years, he gained the respect of many, including George III. When Germain resigned and the North government fell in early 1782, Carleton became the logical choice to carry the delicate matter of recognizing American independence and bringing an end to the war. He not only got along with the king but with the Marquis of Rockingham's brief government and with Shelburne. He was designated commander-in-chief to replace Sir Henry Clinton, who finally was able to return home.

Carleton arrived in New York on May 5, 1782 to carry out his duties as commander-in-chief. His instructions were both vague and expansive as Shelburne designated him a commissioner 'for restoring peace and granting pardon to the revolted provinces in America'.[5] Carleton relished the role of peacemaker, but it soon became evident that the ministry wished the revolted provinces to receive their independence. He thus shifted his emphasis to the evacuation, realizing that the effort would include thousands of civilians who would have to be transferred to various locations in the empire. He became aware that it was not only the cost of transport the government would have to pay, but also the planning and cost of settlement, from clothing to medicines, to farm tools, muskets and ammunition. The transports would not only carry the migrants but their personal beds, chairs, boxes, kitchen utensils and even livestock. He would be sensitive to the fact that some Loyalist military units wanted to settle together. He had no orders to organize or spend money, but Carleton would allocate over £8,000 to support refugees from New York province, while New Jersey received £4,000. London never objected to his effort.

In New York, Carleton would work harmoniously with the Royal Navy's commander Rear Admiral Robert Digby. They gathered transports and warships for evacuation of Savannah, Charleston and New York, although lack of transports meant the effort was spread over two years.

The war would continue during the evacuation. Washington and Maryland's Governor William Paca would beg Carleton in New York to bring an end to the enduring conflict. The states were broke and unable to continue the war. American hopes depended on diplomacy in Europe, as they were not capable of further military action at home. The Earl of Shelburne had worked with Benjamin Franklin to create a preliminary agreement at the end of 1782. However, Shelburne was ousted by Parliament as chief minister in mid-February 1783 over the unpopularity of the preliminaries. Carleton did not receive news of the preliminary articles from London until April 5, 1783, allowing him only then to declare an end to hostilities, to which Washington followed suit. Peace between Britain and the United States continued to be negotiated and was not signed until September 3, 1783 and official recognition of it would not reach America until 1784.

Carleton designated Savannah as the first place for removal as it did not require extensive naval support. On July 11, 1782, a minority of Loyalists left Savannah and moved to Tybee Island at the mouth of the Savannah River to await transports for New York, Charleston, St Augustine or Jamaica. In fact, many black and white Loyalists did not have to wait as they went by coastal barge or overland, southward to St Augustine or northward to Charleston.[6] Two-thirds of the garrison of 1,000 were Loyalist units, while the civilian exodus numbered over 5,000, more than a third of the entire Georgia population.

General Alexander Leslie was in charge of both Savannah's and Charleston's evacuations. In Charleston, blacks outnumbered whites because rebel estates around the city had been seized and their slaves liberated from their masters. Leslie wrote to Clinton on January 29, 1782 that the people of the country were daily coming into Charleston. They were also receiving Savannah's free blacks who had been evacuated over land and water to Charleston. British officers had adopted black families as servants, promising them their freedom, so that the obligation had to be kept. Blacks had also been promised freedom by previous commanders such as General Prevost, Lord Cornwallis and Lord Rawdon. In March, Major James Moncrief, chief of the engineers' department, wrote to Clinton about the numerous blacks attached to his department, praising them for their support and asking that their future be fixed before the evacuation. Eventually, he led the evacuation of 800 free blacks from the engineers' and ordnance departments.

Soon Leslie was responsible for feeding over 15,000 people in Charleston, which required foraging in the countryside, exposing the parties to armed clashes with Continentals and rebel militia. Late in 1782, navy sailors were employed in cutting wood at places like Dill's Bluff, where escorting troops were able to defeat the Continental troops that attacked them.

State governments faces former slaves migrating

South Carolina's Governor John Mathews ordered the 'swamp fox', Francis Marion, to apply the Negro slave code of 1740 to blacks taken in arms as they 'must be tried by the Negro Law; and if found guilty, executed'.[7] Marion was to terrorize and prevent as many blacks as possible from embarking in the navy transports leaving Charleston. This also became General Greene's military policy.

In August 1782, as Leslie was preparing to evacuate Charleston, Governor Mathews warned him that if South Carolina-owned slaves were carried away he would retaliate by making it impossible for British merchants to collect the debts owed them. Leslie responded by setting up a commission of four members, two from each side, the two rebels being allowed to reside in Charleston and to help return slaves to their previous owners. He agreed to return slaves to rebel masters, 'except such slaves as may have rendered themselves particularly obnoxious on account of their attachment and services to the British troops, and such as had specific promises of freedom'. The commission was implemented but was interrupted when Leslie sought the return of three captured British soldiers who had been taken by Greene's men while the commission was functioning. Governor Mathews promptly called back his two commissioners, so that the evacuation went on without the presence of rebel observers.

As a result, in November Leslie convened a board of British officers and Loyalists to examine black refugee claims. Outside of the State House, masters who acquired permission to enter the city were allowed to find and try to persuade slaves to return to their plantations. The majority of blacks insolently told the masters they were not going back. Moreover, the British board was inclined to accept black testimony as to the veracity of their freedom. This board also liberally awarded the status of freeman – as promised – to many South Carolina blacks.

Leslie asked Carleton how he should treat the blacks who were under Commissioner John Cruden, employed by the different departments and those in arms. Carleton replied that Leslie give former slaves who had been promised freedom and to those who feared the reprisal of a former master the opportunity to leave. They could not 'in justice be abandoned to the merciless resentment of their former masters'.[8] When evacuation came, Cruden decided that the slaves still on the sequestered estates would be returned to their owners, unless they were in danger of being punished by their former masters or had been promised their freedom. British policy came together in this way.

After the incident of the British soldiers being captured, Leslie found Greene to be conciliatory. Leslie began the evacuation in August 1782 and it continued until December 14. He remained willing to allow rebel masters to search the departing vessels for their slaves, but British naval commanders refused to let them search their ships. It was suggested that Leslie ask Admiral Digby in New York to order his commanders to comply. Leslie sent some evacuees to New York, although others sailed to Jamaica, England, St Augustine, Halifax and St Lucia. Cooperating with Digby, Andrew Hamond sent a convoy of twenty-five ships from Halifax to Charleston in late September and it returned in mid-November, bringing Charleston Loyalists to Nova Scotia.[9]

Overall from Charleston, 3,794 whites and 5,333 blacks went chiefly to Jamaica and St Augustine on 130 Royal Navy ships. Charleston would send Jamaica its largest number of emigrants. These included nearly 5,000 slaves and 200 free blacks. The latter were asked to register at church vestries and provide information about their emancipation. Black Pioneers had been recruited in Charleston and Savannah for work in Jamaica. While slaves were by far the majority in Jamaica, the free black communities numbered 4,000, concentrated in Kingston and Port Royal, where they could settle.

Among the black migrants to Jamaica was George Liele, the preacher who inspired David George. Liele was the first black Baptist in Georgia, and the first black Baptist churches in American resulted from his evangelism. He was born in Virginia in 1752 but lived much of his life as a slave in Georgia. He was converted and baptized by Matthew Moore, an ordained Baptist minister. When Liele felt the call to preach, he was encouraged by his master, Henry Sharp, Loyalist and Baptist deacon. Sharp also freed Liele. He was licensed as a probationer around 1773, and for two years he preached in the slave quarters of plantations surrounding Savannah, including the congregation formed at David George's Silver Bluff.[10]

After Sharp's death in battle in 1778, Liele made his way to British-occupied Savannah, where Sharp's heirs would have re-enslaved him but for the intervention of Loyalist Colonel Moses Kirkland. Over the next few years, he built a congregation of black Baptists, slave and free, including those led by David George. In 1784, Kirkland arranged for Liele and his family to be transported by the British to Jamaica. As he owed Kirkland money, Liele went as an indentured servant, a status which he soon shed in Jamaica, as the vestry and governor recognized him as a freeman.

Settling in Kingston, Liele formed a church on his own land. His church flourished, despite persecution from whites. By 1791, at Kingston he had publicly baptized in the sea – while at Spanish Town he had baptized in the river – altogether 400, mostly black, Jamaicans. For these public acts, he was charged with preaching sedition and was thrown in prison, but he was later acquitted of the charges. In exchange for a number of concessions, including inspection by authorities of every prayer and sermon, his ministry was tolerated, and he was allowed to preach to the poor and enslaved on plantations and in settlements. Liele also organized a free school for black children, taught by a black deacon. A few adult members of his congregation also learned to read, as all were keen to learn. They had begun a permanent brick meeting house, which was completed with the aid of England's Baptist Churches.

It is estimated that 14,000 migrants left Charleston. A majority were probably the enslaved of Loyalist masters who would continue a life of bondage in the new locales. Blacks, however, were given their freedom by the military for serving behind the British lines, or claimed freedom from their previous rebel masters, or were appropriated by the military. David George and his family were among the freed evacuated from Charleston to eventually settle in Nova Scotia. During the war, South Carolina would lose an estimated 25,000 slaves, one quarter of the pre-war population, chiefly from the evacuation, but also from casualties and dislocations during the war.

The day after the evacuation was completed, nineteen jovial British sailors remained to see 'the end of the frolic'.[11] They were escorted to their ships by Continental troops, who took the opportunity to congratulate Leslie on the manner in which he conducted the removal.

New York

In New York, by the summer of 1782, Carleton had started to focus on destinations like Nova Scotia. He wrote to Hamond that, as a beginning, 600 migrants were planning to go there and that each family needed a grant of several acres of land.[12] Meanwhile, in Halifax, Hamond had organized transports and escorts to be sent to New York for its evacuation, which would include at least 27,000 white and black Loyalists. Carleton and Digby did not wait for permission from London authorities to evacuate blacks and by April 1783, Carleton had sent the first free blacks to Nova Scotia.

In mid-August, Carleton received word from London to evacuate all of the city's military and Loyalists, a task carried on by transports and navy ships for the rest of the year. His Book of Negros records black evacuees from April to November 1783, covering 1,336 men, 914 women and 750 children who largely went to Nova Scotia, although some were destined for Quebec, the Bahamas and England. Two-thirds of them had originally come from Virginia, Georgia and the Carolinas, while the rest were from the middle colonies. Estimates show that 14 per cent of them were born free, or had been freed before they joined the British, or had bought their freedom earlier.[13]

In early June 1783 in New York, a fleet of transports carrying 1,500 Loyalists headed to Nova Scotia under Admiral Digby in the *Atalanta*. They arrived in Conway (renamed 'Digby' in 1787). He returned to New York in July and continued to direct the evacuation of blacks from the city. He ordered Lieutenant Philips of *L'Abondance* and Lieutenant Trounce of an armed storeship into the Hudson River to receive blacks from the transport agent Captain Henry Chads. After inspection, they were to proceed with them immediately to Port Roseway, Annapolis and St Johns, Nova Scotia.[14] On November 10, 1783, 103 members and their dependents of the Company of free negroes, attached to the civil branch of artillery, all of whom had proper certificates and passes, were allocated the bounty of blacks in other departments, which included clothes, money and a ration per diem.

On November 30, 1783, a few days after the official evacuation day of British forces from New York City, *L'Abondance* departed from Staten Island on its way to Port Mouton in Nova Scotia. On board was the Black Brigade, the last of the estimated 4,000 black refugees heading for a new life of freedom. The brigade was the remnant of the several regiments of escaped slaves and free blacks who fought for the British in Virginia, South Carolina and around New York City.

New York's final evacuation fleet left for Halifax on November 25, 1783. Altogether over 20,000 military and 30,000 civilians had left New York for the West Indies, St Augustine, Abaco in the Bahamas, as well as Nova Scotia. Ten days later, Carleton departed from Staten Island to return to England, where Lord North praised him for his 'act of justice'.[15]

Robert Digby in New York

Carleton's naval compatriot in the migration from New York had been Admiral Robert Digby, who had replaced Marriot Arbuthnot as commander of the North American Station. Arbuthnot had famously not got on with Sir Henry Clinton, as they struggled over objectives and the distribution of prize money between the army and navy. Digby would be more cooperative and he was named along with Carleton as a commissioner 'for restoring peace and granting pardon to the revolted provinces in America'.[16]

Carleton's naval partner was born on December 20, 1732, the third son of Edward Digby and his wife, Charlotte Fox, of the Irish noble house of Digby.[17] As a younger son, Robert had to make his own way and so he entered the Royal Navy as a boy of 12 or 13. In his personal life, he met Eleanor Jauncey, the widowed daughter of Andrew Elliott, the Loyalist who would become acting governor of New York, and they were married in 1776. His marriage, at the advanced age of 44, came as a surprise to his family. Even more surprising was the fact that Digby already had two illegitimate sons, one of whom, Robert Murray, entered the navy and rose to the rank of admiral.

By March 1779, Digby was a rear admiral, raising his flag aboard the *Namur* and then the *Prince George*, serving in the Channel Fleet until 1781, when he was appointed to the North American Station. He arrived to take up the post off Sandy Hook, on September 24. There he would find Admiral Thomas Graves, about to try to relieve Cornwallis for a second time and he courteously refused to assume command until Graves' expedition was over. Shortly afterwards, he shifted his flag from the *Prince George* to the *Lion*, in order that the former be given to Admiral Samuel Hood's fleet now going southward. Despite this gesture, he fell out with the difficult Hood, causing a letter war over the allocation of prize money. He could not bring himself to supplement Hood's scurvy-ridden ships with his own men, although he did give Hood four ships supposedly to save South Carolina, when in fact de Grasse's fleet was now in the West Indies.

Digby would be directly involved in the gathering of transports from locations far beyond New York. He was able to assemble the evacuation fleet for Charleston from the West Indies, St Augustine, Halifax and Quebec, as well as New York. As he found confusion, especially with the victualler transports, he directed that they be placed under the command of his agent for transports, Captain Henry Chads.

During the coming evacuation, to prevent efforts to re-enslave blacks by rebel masters, Carleton pressed Digby to appoint guard ships to protect the inhabitants. Instead, Digby recommended that Carleton pay attention to the shore as navy guard ships could not 'prevent boats landing in and about New York all hours of the night'.[18] Digby and Carleton found they could sympathize with the most vulnerable of the city's black community. In New York, blacks were free to write letters and petitions, help those who had escaped their masters, and even insult their former masters.

The unsung heroes of the evacuations were the transport mariners, many of whom were black. Samuel Kelly, a white sailor, who served on ships in New York's and St Augustine's evacuations, has left a record of their presence. As a teenager, he was employed in the mail packet and transport services. He befriended a 12-year-old black boy from Guinea who had been purchased as 'a livery servant' for the postmaster of Madeira.[19] Several times he was dispatched to find the boy, who had absconded to the shore to fulfill his craving for sugar. The culprit was flogged by the cook with tamarind twigs. While Kelly's ship was based in Charleston, a black stole a goat belonging to Commodore James Gambier and 'was stripped naked, his surface tarred over, and then rolled in Fowl's feathers', a Loyalist punishment that was a novelty in Charleston though commonplace in New England. Life on a packet or transport was not easy for young blacks, but it was no different from what Kelly experienced.

The last evacuation

Another evacuation actually took place after the Treaty of Paris was signed, involving Britain and Spain, not the United States. From 1784 to 1785, East Florida was evacuated from St Augustine and the St Mary's River by the British, as Spain had won the Floridas in the peace negotiations. However, the colony had absorbed 4,581 black and 2,998 white Loyalist refugees from South Carolina and Georgia, expanding its population from 4,000. This influx caused its evacuation to be often postponed. Several transports waiting in the St John's River actually employed a black named York to build and protect a refuge to keep their ships' fowls and hogs, which were constantly disappearing. While the Spanish Governor Manuel de Zespedes arrived in St Augustine in July 1784, it was not until November 1785 that British Governor Patrick Tryon left, as Loyalists sought to delay implementation of the treaty.[20] The refugees finally went to the Bahamas, Jamaica, Nova Scotia and Britain.

From St Augustine, the chief destination for evacuees was the Bahamas as result of an effort by its Loyalists. When Charleston was evacuated at the end of 1782, Colonel Andrew Deveaux and his irregulars went to St Augustine with other refugees. He had previously led privateers taking Beaufort and in St Augustine he became aware that a Spanish force had seized the nearby Bahama Islands. He financed an expedition to return them to the British fold. He fitted out 5 or 6 privateers with 65 men and was joined at Harbor Island, the Bahamas, by 170 more, making an armed force of 235 provincials, volunteers and blacks.[21] Nassau's Spanish garrison, under Don Antonio Claraco Sauz, consisted of 600 troops, 70 cannon and 6 galleys, certainly outnumbering the attackers. However, Deveaux blockaded the harbor, making it appear that his force was much larger and after a few well-directed shots, on April 18, 1783, Sauz surrendered without putting up a defense. Deveaux became temporary governor of the Bahamas and established a cotton plantation on Cat Island. In the Treaty of Paris, the Bahamas had been given to Britain, whose dominion over the islands would never again be challenged. This was the last naval action of the war.

PART 8

A NEW EMPIRE CONCEIVED WITHOUT SLAVES

Chapter 24

Continuing Black Migration to Britain and Africa

While it had never been the chief destination of black migrants, when the War for Independence ended, England and especially London attracted more black refugees than before. Black seamen were discharged in London and other English ports. By then, most British blacks were neither servants nor slaves in wealthy households, but rather living independently as free men and women. Most had difficulty in making ends meet and some joined the ranks of London's enduring poor. London's beggary was an accepted station in life for both the poor and those wealthy enough to offer charity to them.[1]

The immediate problem after the war was to find jobs for blacks so they could support themselves. This was not easy as black mariners found the navy and its supporting dockyards reduced for peacetime, cutting down on employment opportunities. As newcomers, blacks lacked the established family connections that secured apprenticeships and employment. Still, benevolent whites were out to help them.

It should not be assumed that all blacks in Britain were doomed to poverty, some had, or would, become successful members of the growing middle class. Equiano is an obvious example, but he was not alone. Nathaniel Wells, the biracial son of a plantation owner in St Kitts, became a justice of the peace, High Sheriff of Monmouthshire and deputy lieutenant of the county. Another is Caesar Picton, who used legacies from the family he served and his business sense to become rich.[2] How many blacks were able to raise themselves out of poverty has never been adequately studied, but certainly it was not impossible to become well off in Britain.

Loyalist claims

Some blacks came to Britain to make Loyalist claims for the loss of their property in the war while serving the British cause. Among them was freeman Shadrack Furman of Accomack County, Virginia's Eastern Shore. In January 1781, while in the act of destroying several Loyalists' properties, including his own, rebel troops mutilated Furman. He was lashed and tortured to the point that he was blinded and his leg was nearly severed. Besides being a freeman, his crime was that he had entertained and provisioned British troops.[3] Upon partial recovery, Furman was rescued by the privateer belonging to Messrs. Graham and Hodges then lying at Tangier Island, commanded by Captain Robertson, and taken to Portsmouth, where despite his crippling injuries, he joined Captain Frazier's Department of Pioneers. While this incident certainly fortified his Loyalism, his fraternizing with British troops was not unique. He was targeted by the rebels because he was free and held property, so that masters felt his example encouraged runaways. Later in London, he was able to petition the Commissioners and receive a modest pension of £8 annually, demonstrating that the commissioners would recognize documented service regardless of color.

The Loyalist Claims Commissioners would honor almost half of the forty-seven black men who completed petitions. These annual pensions would be up to £20, a sign of the esteem in which blacks were held.[4] Still, few blacks could document the loss of property demanded by the commissioners. Other rewards would be necessary to help Loyalist blacks find a place in the new empire.

Relief of the poor

As a result of being freed during the War for Independence, many free blacks and their families had migrated with high expectations of how their freedom would improve their lives. In England, they were able to petition and openly express their opinions. Their aspirations would fit neatly into the abolitionists' need to demonstrate that free blacks were capable of the same deeds as whites in the settlement of the empire. Long term, abolitionists believed that free labor would replace the slave economy of the West Indies.

The winter of January 1786 was harsh in London, resulting in the formation of a Committee for the Relief of the Black Poor under the leadership of the able Jonas Hanway. His crowning charitable achievement, Hanway would organize the committee at Batson's Coffee House. Its first object was simply to provide food, medical care and clothing for blacks, who were able apply at designated taverns and infirmaries.[5] It was financed by a private subscription whose contributors included Reverend Herbert Mayo and the politician William Pitt the Younger. The committee commenced distributing food each day at Whitechapel's White Raven and Yorkshire Stingo public houses. They would also offer small amounts of money to 1,943 London blacks to tide them over during the winter.

The use of East End public houses as relief centers supports the contention that many blacks were concentrated in the sailor towns that have been previously described. East End public houses offered mariners lodging, food and drink, where they could be entertained with diversions, from backgammon to singing. It is likely that blacks already frequented these public houses. Two communities had grown up around the White Raven, known together as Mile End, while the Stingo was on Lisson Green in Marylebone. Both public houses were kept open each day, where needy blacks could apply for broth, a piece of meat and a two-penny loaf.

The charity handed out there, however, was not a long-term solution to black poverty. Many were veterans of the War for Independence to whom gratitude was owed and in the face of poverty it was the benevolent committee that first suggested an opportunity for them to move to a place which might be better suited to their condition. Thus, the committee suspended its charitable efforts to debate the possibilities of black emigration to Nova Scotia or the Bahamas, the latter having the advantage of being warmer.[6] Other places like Sierra Leone would also have their advocates.

Debate on Destination

The Black Poor Committee debated where a free black colony should be placed. James Ramsay's writings favored Africa in order to replace the West Indies as a source of tropical products. The committee realized it needed to have input from the London poor themselves, so they established a representative organization. In May, they had divided interested blacks into companies under a corporal, who could write and give administrative accounts to the committee. After scrutiny as to qualifications, Hanway chose the first eight corporals, who were soon expanded until they reached twenty-five companies with about twenty-four members in each. The original corporals give an indication of the black leadership: four of them had been born in the mainland colonies, New Jersey, New York and Charleston, two had been born in Africa, one in Barbados and one was a lascar from Bengal. Five had come to England from various employment on ships and three had come on Royal Navy ships, serving as stewards or cooks. Only two could both read and write, though three others could read.[7] They soon represented the views of the black poor, although they had been appointed, not directly elected. To remedy this, the committee proposed that five deputies, who were charged to attend the committee meetings, be elected by the blacks themselves. Thus, the black poor would be represented at the highest level of the committee and it was the corporals and then deputies who made the final choice of their destination.

The Black Poor Committee was about to choose the Bahamas, when the black representatives intervened in favor of West Africa's Sierra Leone, which the committee felt was unhealthy and a conflicting base of the slave traders. It would ultimately bow to the blacks' wishes. Sympathy for them was found at all levels of the government, including the navy as they had experienced the support of Loyalist blacks during the war. The sailing of the blacks to Sierra Leone was to be overseen by Navy Board commissioners, whose comptroller was none other than Charles Middleton. Finally, two known abolitionists, Thomas Steele and George Rose, Treasury Board secretaries, were charged with the day-to-day support for the expedition. The government head, William Pitt, was also known to support the colony.

While the Black Poor Committee and the government had become convinced of Sierra Leone as the destination, Hanway found that the London blacks had to be coaxed into believing that it was the place for them. He met them first at the Yorkshire Stingo, where he handed out charitable allowances and sought their signatures to an agreement that they would volunteer for Sierra Leone. After repeating this effort, over 600 signed up. They were demanding, asking for an 'Instrument of Liberty', a document to prevent them from being re-enslaved, as well as mobile forges, tea and sugar, and most controversially arms, which eventually led the navy to provide 250 muskets and cutlasses.[8] Now Sierra Leone was designated as the 'Province of Freedom'.

Granville Sharp

Unfortunately Hanway died in 1786 and was buried in the crypt at St Mary's Church, Hanwell. In his place, Granville Sharp became the committee's undisputed leader and his motives, like those of Hanway, were humanitarian.[9] His sincere Christianity was coupled with a respect for English constitutional history, though not with the usual emphasis on the balanced constitution, but rather looking earlier to the Anglo-Saxon period, where Sharp saw government organized in terms of Frankpledge. It was this primitive form of government that Sharp felt would be best for the establishment of British colonies, which could be tested in Africa. His interest in reform was no accident, he also supported the representational reform of the Commons that was being promoted by Rev. Christopher Wyvill in the Yorkshire Association.

Sharp was born in 1735 in Durham into the Archdeacon of Northumberland's family, where he had eight older brothers and five younger sisters. With this High Church background, Sharp was not an evangelist, having religious convictions similar to those of Bishop Porteus. In fact, in 1779 he was involved in trying to get Anglican bishops to oppose the slave trade. The family also became famous for their musical outings on a barge in which Granville's bass voice was most admired. At 15 he was apprenticed to a linen draper, but this was not for him. He experienced the navy as a clerk for the Ordnance Office at the Tower of London. In 1765, he began his true vocation with legal challenges to the slave trade in the case of Jonathan Strong. He would quit the Ordnance to follow his charitable causes and depend upon the financial support of his brothers. His strength would emerge in organizing the campaign to establish the colony for London's black poor in Sierra Leone.

Late in the War for Independence, the slaveship *Zong* had sailed from the Guinea coast to Jamaica with about 440 slaves aboard. Sickness erupted among the slaves so that the captain realized that they would not fetch a good price and he claimed that the ship was short of water so that he no alternative but to toss 132 slaves overboard. The legal issue was divided: was it about the murder of fellow human beings or was it about a cargo of chattel property?[10] After some maneuvering, the owners of the *Zong* asked their insurance underwriters to reimburse them for their lost property. The underwriters refused the claim, acting like abolitionists, arguing the blacks had been murdered. The first trial of the case was in favor of the owners, but the underwriters would not give up and they appealed to Lord Mansfield of the King's Bench, the very judge who ruled in the Somerset Case a decade before. Mansfield concluded that the case deserved a reconsideration and ordered a new trial, but it appears it never happened.

Sharp attended the trial and was willing to pick up the pieces and use the *Zong* case to campaign against the slave trade. He chose to send his protest letters to the Admiralty because 'all murders committed on board British ships, belong properly to the Admiralty Department'. Sharp enclosed evidence that he felt would cause criminal prosecution of the murdering owners. He made his point, although as with the second trial of the *Zong*'s owners, there was no follow-up.

Sharp and his committee were now focused on the settlement at Sierra Leone as a chance to show that blacks could form a model community, based on guidelines from his Short Sketch of Temporary Regulations. His committee would combine commerce with Christianity, 'intertwined with the ethic of benevolence' to redeem Africa from the misery of the slave trade.[11] They hoped that blacks and whites would have a chance to start a new life in Sierra Leone. The government was persuaded to be generous, giving them provisions for Africa to last until the colony could support itself. Royal Navy warships would protect the expedition and settlement of the colony. After their first few months in Sierra Leone, Sharp would be the chief link between the black settlers and the England they had left.

Willing black settlers

The expedition would suffer from delays caused by the fact that while nearly 1,000 blacks had expressed interest in joining the colony, when it came to boarding a ship, the number fell to fewer than 300. Starting life anew in unknown Africa had to be measured against the existing kinship and religious networks blacks had developed in London. The final figure for those who came onboard was 344 blacks: 290 men, 43 women and 11 children, certainly only a small percentage of the London's black poor.[12] Also on board were 115 whites: 75 women, 31 men and 9 children, reflecting mixed-race couples or widows. A few were white artisans, who had been recruited by the committee as their skills would be valuable in to the new settlement. Among the blacks were Mary Byrd's former house slave Walter Harris and his family. Another ready to embark was John Thompson, Loyalist Claims applicant, who had been discharged from the Royal Navy at Portsmouth, and had married Ann and had their daughter baptized at St George's church, Shadwell. Another black family was that of discharged Royal Navy sailor Benjamin Whitecliff and his wife, Sarah, who were living in Deptford. Another family that had accepted was that of Richard Weaver, whose wife and daughter would go with him.

The figures show a socialization that had been going on in London's East End, namely the marriage of white women to black men. Such marriages were legal and unremarkable in Britain as witnessed the lives of James Gronniosaw, Quobna Cugoano and Olaudah Equiano. The committee showed no concern over this intermarriage, but the West India lobby did, ignoring their own philandering with slave women in the colonies.

Middleton's Navy Board had assumed that it was preparing transports and supplies for the 1,000 figure and thus it had accumulated excessive supply and transport. The surplus situation not only caused delay, but was bound to lead to controversy over what to do with the excess. The shortfall in participants demonstrated that the decision to migrate was completely in the hands of each black family – their emigration had not been forced by the committee, or the government, or the navy.[13]

Black support for the expedition

As a sign of respect for the abilities of blacks, Sharp had named aforementioned Olaudah Equiano to the committee, which designated him 'Commissary on the part of the Government'.[14] His wages were paid by Middleton's Navy Board, he would work from Deptford and he was to be a liaison with those blacks ready to sail on the ships. In this position, he reported directly to the navy commissioners, where he revealed the decline in the number of those going, accounting errors and the excess of supplies prepared for the expedition.

Sharp wanted Equiano to work with Joseph Irwin, who had been elected by the blacks as superintendent of the colony. Previously, Irwin had cooperated with Sharp to prevent the re-enslavement of blacks in England and gained the confidence of the embarking blacks. Irwin was to purchase the supplies for the voyage and settlement and give Equiano the government's surplus provisions, which then would go to the black poor remaining in London. Controversy developed between the two administrators as a result of the decline in the number of blacks who would sail. Equiano wanted the surplus maximized and given to him, while Irwin was not clear on the extent of the surplus because recruiting efforts continued, while those already onboard ships had to be fed during the delay as conditions deteriorated.

In addition to Equiano, the colony had the qualified support of London free black Quobna Cugoano. Born in Ghana and enslaved in Grenada, he had been brought to England by his master, where at age of 16 in 1773 he was baptized at St James's Church, Piccadilly as 'John Stuart'. Fittingly in 1787 his *Thoughts and Sentiments on the Evil and Wicked Traffic of the Slavery and Commerce of the Human Species* was published. In it, he thanked the gentlemen who had supported the London poor and he was grateful to the government for fitting the ships, clothes and provisions for the Sierra Leone expedition. He felt that in the committee's effort, 'humanity has made its appearance in a more honorable way of colonization, than any Christian nation have ever done before'.[15] This did not prevent him, however, from being critical of the delays in getting the expedition underway, as he was Equiano's friend. He was suspicious of the chosen location because it was slave-trading territory and he suggested that a treaty of agreement with the nearby African inhabitants be made even before the expedition embarked. Cugoano seems to have wanted to be directly involved in the colony, later suggesting that he might lead a second colonization attempt from Nova Scotia to settle Sierra Leone with free blacks.

Cugoano detailed the motives of the blacks who decided that Sierra Leone was not for them. While many blacks were previously brutally enslaved, as the result of the War for Independence they now had precious freedom in Britain. They were thankful for their new home and afraid of being ensnared again. Many felt they needed more assurances of security and safety in Sierra Leone. They were aware the colony was being established where forts existed to carry on the captivity and enslavement of Africans – a dangerous location.[16]

Some twenty-first-century historians have found 'racism' in the activities of the committee and government, claiming that black migrants participated in the Sierra Leone project against their will.[17] It was said the government simply wanted to get rid of blacks, who were a growing segment of London's poor. Scant evidence of this exists. For a start, the government wanted to find a way of rewarding, not expelling, Loyalist blacks. Racism is called into question by the committee's acceptance of intermarried black and white couples. Blacks, through their elected deputies, were involved in planning the expedition from the beginning and it was they who demanded firearms and chose Joseph Irwin as their expedition leader. While they may have been poor, the London blacks were fully independent to make a choice and that is why only a minority actually chose to embark. Even if the colony's success might prove illusive, the cooperation between blacks and whites in creating the expedition was exemplary, proving that loyal blacks could contribute to the settlement of a new part of the empire.

Thomas Thompson

Before the expedition sailed in March 1787, Royal Navy Captain Thomas Boulden Thompson was placed in charge of the squadron for protection of the transports. Equiano asked him to inspect the delayed ships and he found they lacked supplies and ordered them; he found the problems were not completely Irwin's fault, but equally Equiano's. He described commissary Equiano as 'turbulent and discontented, taking every means to actuate the minds of the Blacks to discord'.[18] Later, Granville Sharp himself expressed disapproval of Equiano's behavior. To quell the squabbling between Equiano and Irwin, Thompson suggested that one of them had to go. The committee chose Equiano, who promptly switched from promoting to deprecating the project.

Thompson would be responsible for carrying the settlers to Africa. Following a re-allocation of commands in January 1786, he had become commander of the 16-gun *Nautilus*. He brought the *Nautilus* into Portsmouth from the Guinea Coast to be fitted out. Despite his service in Guinea, Thompson admitted he never visited a slave ship 'as my disgust always got the better of my curiosity'.[19] Later, in 1799, he would marry Anne, eldest daughter of Robert Raikes, the Sunday school advocate, and she made him into a firm abolitionist. For now, he focused on feeding the ship-bound Sierra Leone migrants on stores obtained from Plymouth, which included not only bread and pork, but raisins and currants for the sake of health.

Thomas Thompson had entered the world on February 28, 1766 in Kent, the son of Richard Boulden and Sarah Rigden.[20] His maternal aunt was married to Commodore Edward Thompson, who adopted Thomas following the early death of his father, and whose surname Thomas took. Serving in the War for Independence in June 1778, young Thomas joined the 28-gun *Hyena*, commanded by his uncle, which went to the West Indies and a year later he returned home with a convoy. In August, the *Hyena* went to New York with a convoy, from where she sailed to Charlestown and then Barbados. When she returned to Falmouth in January 1782, Thomas decided to remain in the Leeward Islands, where he was commissioned a lieutenant, serving as commander of the 8-gun schooner *Berbice*, in which he captured a larger French privateer.

When the war ended, Thompson was aboard the 50-gun *Grampus* under the command of his uncle. Royal Navy patrols were already present on the West African coast to offer protection for British slavers against those of rival nations. The *Grampus* sailed for Africa's Guinea Coast early in 1784, as part of the navy's African Squadron, giving Thomas further experience in navigating the African coast. She returned to Portsmouth in July for a thorough refit and remained there for the best part of a year, awaiting return to the African coast in the autumn of 1785.

Having experience on the West African coast, Thompson was the logical choice to lead the Sierra Leone naval force. In April 1787, he commanded the *Nautilus* as it escorted the 461 migrants aboard three transports, the *Atlantic*, *Belisarius* and *Vernon*. They stopped at Tenerife to get cheap wine for his sailors, which when mixed with 'Peruvian Bark', produced quinine to prevent malaria. From there, they went to the Sierra Leone estuary where the 'Province of Freedom' would be established. Arriving at the estuary on May 10, Thompson landed, scaled a hill and set a Union Flag on a pole, claiming the territory for Britain. Immediately, he had to verify this ceremony by negotiating a treaty with local African kings, who were to recognize the 'purchase' of land for the colony.

Thompson was taking notes to write a 'Narrative of the Voyage of the Nautilus' for the Admiralty in which he would bend over backwards to objectively describe the conditions he found in Sierra Leone.[21] He noted the problem of establishing the colony in an existing slave-trading area and the lack of fresh water at its site. He would inform the Admiralty that fevers and fluxes had carried off numbers of the migrants who remained on the ships. Among them was Superintendent Irwin, so that Thompson became the only person, along with his sailors, who could provide leadership and prevent discord.

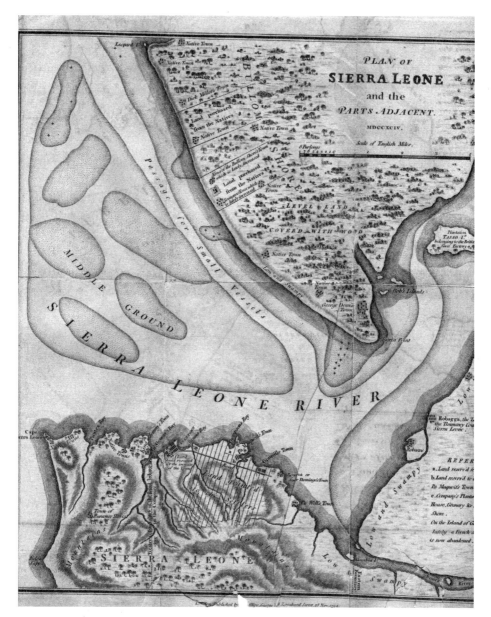

Plan of Sierra Leone and Parts Adjacent, 1794.

Thompson encouraged the ill and discontented blacks to land and build huts for protection against the rain, a place which collectively was dubbed Sharp Town. He established trade with the natives using beads for exchange. He invited African chiefs to visit and distributed presents among them. He would send out a surveyor for the proposed distribution of land

and he employed parties in cutting wood. He set his men to catch fish, not only for the ship's company, but also the black settlers. In this way, he attempted to stretch the provisions brought by the ships.

During his tenure, he found that a majority of blacks were not prepared for the ordeal of settling, though a substantial minority were industrious and if supported promised to do well. He was unable to persuade the settlers to work on the building of a house of worship or a house for the Anglican chaplain and missionary Patrick Fraser. By the end of the year, he concluded that Sharp Town was not going well because the settlers had been forced to live in 'anarchy' or had become dependent on the nearby slave traders.

Having competed his orders, Thompson departed for England in September 1788. By then, fewer than a third of the original migrants were left. Beyond their death from malaria and fevers, their location was not promising. The principal British slave-trading post in the Sierra Leone estuary was at Bance Island.[22] While the slave traders were naturally skeptical of Sharp Town, they needed workers for their factories and they looked to the Sharp Town leaders to support them when dealing with African monarchs like King Jimmy. While the black settlers realized the possibility of re-enslavement, many traded for goods with the slave traders and some took jobs with them to make ends meet, creating an uneasy relationship, which was exacerbated when settlers broke into and stole from the Bance Island store. The slave traders and the Sharp Town settlers would forge a relationship of necessity that was far from the ideals of Granville Sharp's committee.

Henry Savage

A year later, the Admiralty sent another Royal Navy ship to West Africa, the 28-gun *Pomona*, Captain Henry Savage commanding. Born in 1737, Savage had become a lieutenant in the Seven Years' War. His ship had not specifically been sent to support Sharp Town, instead it was to distribute copies of and enforce the Dolben regulations, which had been passed in Parliament to require improvement of the conditions under which slaves were transported from the slave factories.[23]

After anchoring in St George's Bay, Sierra Leone estuary in November 1789, Savage dispersed copies of the regulations but was unexpectedly beset by complaints from representatives of both the free settlers and the slavers, who looked to him to remedy their grievances. They complained the local King Jimmy had become a menace, violating the agreements he had made, attacking the free settlement and taking and selling slaves that were not his to sell. He needed to be reminded of his solemn promises and Savage decided he would have to do it.

Savage could not get Jimmy to appear onboard the *Pomona*, so he sent a party of sailors, including armed marines, four settlers and a slave trader, to find him.[24] Savage watched from the deck as the boats were beached and Lieutenant Wood and his companions disappeared into the trees. Then came the crack of musket fire, a sudden plume of flame behind the shoreline and smoke rising over the palms. Someone had fired into Jimmy's village and set a thatched roof on fire, which spread to the entire village. It was the dry season and it took only minutes for the entire compound to be reduced to charred sticks, certainly a diplomatic disaster.

Sailors and marines were seen running back in hasty confusion to the shore. Alarmed, Savage sent a second boat to pick them up. As the men were swinging their legs over the gunwales, a volley broke from the line of trees and a marine sergeant, the lieutenant of the relief boat, and a black settler were killed. Savage trained his guns on the shore, 'clearing' the bush. Over the next few days he repeated the exercise. In response, Jimmy's men shot at anyone attempting to land for water. A week later, overlord Naimbana's deputies came and ordered Jimmy to desist and for the moment he did so, albeit grudgingly. Savage insisted that a general palaver be held to settle the grievances peacefully. As his part of the bargain, however, he agreed to sail away with the *Pomona* before the palaver was held so as not to influence it.

Once the *Pomona* was gone, King Jimmy was free to impose his notion of justice and issued an ultimatum to the settlers to leave Sharp Town within three days. Then he burned their village to the ground. Only about eighty of the original colonists survived, although they were still stubbornly there in 1791, when renewed efforts were made to sustain the settlement.[25] Savage's expedition revealed the true conditions in the Sierra Leone estuary, as the settlers were attacked by local Africans and their survival depended upon cooperation with British slavers as much as the Royal Navy.

It had become evident to Granville Sharp that the London poor were not prepared to be African settlers and that the committee would have to look for help if the colony was to survive. Despite the Province of Freedom's failures, Sharp still sought to aid the surviving settlers. He asked Pitt for supplies and 'a stout sloop of war' from the Royal Navy.[26] Pitt, however, was silent. Abolitionist Alexander Falconbridge and his wife were sent to Sierra Leone on a slave ship and confirmed that thirty-six men and twenty women – six of them white – were all that remained. Falconbridge also noted that King Jimmy and the slave traders remained hostile and urged, 'for God's sake send me a ship of force.'

Sharp now sought to gather merchants to found a company, which after stiff opposition from the West Indies' planters and slavers, was incorporated by Parliament in May 1791 as the Sierra Leone Company. Middleton and Admiral George Young – earlier a promoter of a colony in New South Wales, Australia – represented the navy on this new board of directors. While not hostile to the new company, Pitt's government could not ignore the colony's difficulties and therefore they were no longer enthusiastic about African colonization. The government's interests were consumed in opposing the French Revolution. This meant that Royal Navy ships on routine missions were now the only government link to the colonizing effort.

The first Sierra Leone expedition was the result of a combination of imperial stewardship and the desire for an abolitionist testing ground in Africa. Unfortunately, the idealism of Equiano and Sharp – neither of whom would actually live in Sierra Leone – was challenged by the reality of African conditions. One is struck by the similar difficulties in the founding in the early 1600s of the original Jamestown colony which eventually became Virginia. Without the transport and appearance of Royal Navy ships, the African colony would have suffered even more. Despite failure, this is only the beginning of the Sierra Leone colony, as the continued effort shall be described in the next chapter.

Chapter 25

Counter Revolution

One of the accepted conditions of revolutions is that later in their development a conservative reaction to the most radical elements appears, in order to moderate the revolution's excesses. This effort to moderate was led by the conservative business element of the new Sierra Leone Company, who would attempt to turn the clock back, administering a colony that they aimed to make a commercial success. In this new phase of Sierra Leone colonization, it will be crucial to evaluate the cooperation between emigrating free blacks, the Royal Navy acting as the government's agent, and the businessmen on the new company's board of directors.

Despite this shift, free blacks would continue to be involved in the effort to settle Sierra Leone. This counter revolution would be initially supported by an influx of blacks from Nova Scotia to Sierra Leone. A vocal minority of these new settlers had not been happy in their previous homes and their complaints have gained historians' attention. Expressed in petitions and audiences, their discontent would be stimulated by their developing freedom and need for government resources to support their resettlement. The appearance of black leadership in these endeavors showed that blacks were equal to whites in their ability to endure the privation necessary to settle new territories. This was not, however, what the new Sierra Leone Company expected.

Nova Scotia

Looking at the two decades after the War for Independence, a majority of free and enslaved blacks would remain where the Royal Navy ships and its transports had landed them. Nova Scotia had been an important destination for black migrants. It has been seen by some as an icebox, where it was too cold for transplanted black and white Loyalists to make a living. In fact, the province had a maritime climate, not so different from that of the British Isles. Yes, snow was heavy in winter, but the surrounding Atlantic waters moderated the temperature, so that it was constant, rather one of fluctuating extremes. Nova Scotia did have an extensive coast, no place being far from the sea, which was abundant with fish and a trading corridor. Communities existed on the coast, from Annapolis Royal's rich agricultural area to Lunenburg, a trading center of German merchants. Both places were wealthy enough to have been raided by New England privateers near the end of the War for Independence.[1] True, the center of the colony was completely forested and undeveloped, but game was found there and wood was plentiful, ready to support a shipbuilding industry. Crucially from the standpoint of the blacks, no plantations or slave factories existed.

Halifax was Nova Scotia's chief city, port and navy careening yard. Its extensive harbor was the closest to Europe of any North American port. During the Seven Years' War, it had served as a naval counter to the French fortress of Louisbourg on Cape Breton Island, which was taken by the British and systematically razed. From then on, Halifax became popular with the Navy Board because of the 'convenient situation of His Majesty's yard … its utility for heaving down ships stationed in North America, and supplying them with stores, and the preservation of the wharfs, storehouses, and other works erected there in the course of the war'.[2] In October 1764, an Admiralty Court had opened in Halifax for the adjudication of prizes. By the 1780s, Halifax's careening yard would be capable of copper bottoming ships. Its location and facilities had made it an ideal place to disembark white and black Loyalist refugees.

Among the refugees were about 3,500 free blacks, who had been transported to Halifax and were then dispersed to places along the coast. They were a diverse lot, having been carried there from New York, Savannah, Charleston and St Augustine. Hundreds of Loyalist refugees in New York had joined the Port Roseway Associates to create a new settlement together in Nova Scotia. These Loyalists, with their families, servants and slaves, founded the community of Port Roseway, shortly renamed Shelburne. The free blacks there formed a separate enclave known as Birchtown, honoring the officer in New York who signed their passports.

Thomas Peters

Thomas Peters was one of the free blacks, with a stronger military background than most. When the provisional peace agreement was signed in November 1782, he and his wife, Sally, were in New York awaiting evacuation.[3] The ship from New York carrying the Peters and fellow soldier Murphy Steele and wife Mary would be a victim of the weather. It would be forced to Bermuda, not reaching Annapolis Royal, Nova Scotia until May 1784.

A sergeant in the Black Pioneers, Peters continued to be a leader of the black refugees who went to Annapolis County, settling with more than 200 former Black Pioneers in Brindley Town, near Digby. Although Loyalists were entitled to three years' worth of provisions to sustain themselves while establishing homes and farms, the Annapolis County blacks received only enough provisions to last eighty days and, unlike the whites, were required to work on the roads. Community life was established, but the settlers continued to lack a means of self-support. While the navy had got them to Nova Scotia, the administration for such an influx of Loyalists on land was lacking and the land-granting process too cumbersome to meet their immediate needs.

In August 1784, Peters and Steele petitioned Nova Scotia's Governor John Parr for Loyalist land grants.[4] In response, the government surveyor, Charles Morris Jr, was ordered the lay out 1-acre town plots for seventy-six black families at Brindley Town. When the blacks attempted to settle on larger farming plots, they were twice removed because of conflicting claims to the land. Without provisions or land sufficient for farming, they came to sustain themselves with kitchen gardens, fishing in the Bay of Fundy, and the assistance of their white neighbors and British charities.

Having failed to obtain the desired land in July 1785, Peters crossed to newly designated New Brunswick province, where on October 25 he petitioned Governor Thomas Carleton for farms for the Brindley blacks. He was told that his people would receive equal treatment with other Loyalists, but his petition was unsuccessful. By then, of the blacks, only about one-third in both provinces had actually received land.

After waiting for replies to five different petitions sent to colonial officials, in 1790, Peters determined to appeal directly to the government in London. He was given power of attorney by some blacks in Nova Scotia and New Brunswick to represent their case and by November 'at much trouble and risk', he had made his way to London.[5] There he met his former Black Pioneer commander George Martin, who introduced him to abolitionist Granville Sharp, who arranged for him to present his petition to the Secretary of State for the Home Department, Henry Dundas. Peters sent Dundas an outline of the blacks' general grievances, noting that the rights of free British subjects, such as the vote, trial by jury, and access to the courts, had been offered to them. He also gave a detailed account of their futile efforts to obtain land. Peters had been sent to procure 'some Establishment where [free blacks] may obtain a competent Settlement for themselves' and pointed out that although some blacks wished to remain in North America, others were 'ready and willing to go wherever the Wisdom of Government may think proper to provide for them as free Subjects of the British Empire'.

The possibility of Sierra Leone

In England, Granville Sharp had dropped his interest in Sierra Leone and became totally devoted to the abolitionist cause. The new Sierra Leone Company was now in charge and sought to continue the involvement of the British government as it had the resources to transport and resettle blacks. The government's principal agent in colonizing became the Royal Navy with its related Victualling Board and Navy Board.

In London, Peters took his complaints to the directors of the new Sierra Leone Company and they responded by offering him and his followers a home in Sierra Leone.[6] Peters quickly accepted their offer and the directors successfully negotiated with the government to pay the costs of transporting Nova Scotia blacks to Sierra Leone. The company decided to appoint a representative to join Peters in returning to Nova Scotia and recruiting black settlers. Their choice was Royal Navy Lieutenant John Clarkson, who volunteered for the task. Clarkson was told by the directors not to dwell on Peters' description of the ill-treatment of blacks. In the fall of 1791, the two men would travel to Nova Scotia's black communities to promote colonization in Sierra Leone.

John Clarkson

The brother of the abolitionist Thomas Clarkson, John Clarkson was the second son of Reverend John Clarkson, headmaster of Wisbech Grammar School in Cambridgeshire. He was born in the headmaster's house and, despite the early death of his father, continued to attend the school until 1777, when at the age of 12, he entered the Royal Navy as a 'young gentleman' on Captain Joshua Rowley's ship, the *Monarch*.[7] He served primarily in the Caribbean and observed the slave trade at first hand. By his eighteenth birthday, he had been on nine ships in five years, passed his lieutenant's exams at Port Royal and been commissioned. He witnessed Admiral Rodney's triumphal entry into Jamaica after the Battle of the Saints and in June, he sailed the sloop *Bloodhound* with dispatches and mail from Kingston to Spithead.

With the war over, John was relegated to half-pay and with Admiral Rowley retired, he failed to obtain a ship. He was competing with an estimated 1,200 half-pay lieutenants. While initially unmoved by the slavery he had witnessed in Jamaica, he now was exposed to his brother Thomas's passionate views on the immorality of slavery, especially during the *Zong* incident, and he decided to offer assistance to the abolition cause. He and Thomas supported the original Sierra Leone enterprise and in 1788 Sharp requested that free lots in the colony be reserved for them. For the renewed effort at Sierra Leone, John's combination of Royal Navy leadership and abolitionist sentiments seemed ideal. Thus, he would be appointed the Sierra Leone Company's representative in Africa and given a year's leave by the Admiralty to recruit blacks in Nova Scotia.

Nova Scotia's settled blacks

In Nova Scotia, it turned out that Thomas Peters had only the support of a minority of blacks, probably because he was not interested in the spiritual concerns that dominated the settlers' life. Experienced black and white preachers were bringing black Anglicans, Methodists and Baptists together. During the war, blacks had gathered around their preachers who led them in the evacuation and they continued their respect for them. A preacher's ability to dispense baptism and speaking ability gave them power over their gatherings. In contrast, the military organization of black males, after arrival in Nova Scotia, usually disappeared. A review of the leadership of the religious denominations is essential to understand Nova Scotia's free black settlers.

Stephen Blucke's majority

The Black Brigade, under Colonel Stephen Blucke, had arrived in Shelburne, Nova Scotia still organized in military companies. Born in 1752, Blucke was a literate mulatto from Barbados, typically the son of a black mother and a white father.[8] Coming to the mainland, he made his way to New Jersey, where he became acquainted with Stephen Skinner, who later in Nova Scotia would became his ally. Blucke joined the British in New York, where he married Margaret, a 30-something black woman, who had been born free in Mrs Coventry's New York household.

When, in 1780, black guerrilla leader Colonel Tye died, Blucke had been given the honorary rank of 'Colonel' and taken command of New York's Black Brigade. It was an elite group of guerillas within the Black Pioneers, who were definitely armed. At first, the Black Brigade raided independently, but later it fought with the Queen's Rangers, a Loyalist unit. The Black Brigade operated in Long Island, New York City and in Monmouth County, New Jersey. They targeted specific rebels who they would kill or kidnap. As with most in the brigade, Blucke's service is documented because he received a certificate of freedom before he left New York from General Samuel Birch.

In Nova Scotia, the brigade settled in Birchtown, northwest of Shelburne, with a population in 1784 of 1,521 free blacks. Blucke attended an Anglican church and taught in a school for black children, supported by the SPGFP. A successful farmer, fisherman and black militia commander, he became the leader of the Birchtown blacks. He organized them into work crews, which constructed the Annapolis road and performed other public works.

When John Clarkson came to Nova Scotia to gather blacks for his migration, Blucke and his wife entertained him at dinner and listened. However, Blucke became Birchtown's leader of the opposition to the Sierra Leone project. He organized a petition of black families, opposing the use of public funds to transport the blacks away from Nova Scotia.[9] His effort was successful in the sense that about two-thirds of Nova Scotia's free blacks would remain. Later, Blucke's reputation suffered as his enemies accused him of misappropriating funds and he died mysteriously in the woods in 1795.

John Marrant and Cato Perkins

You will remember that, after serving in the Royal Navy, John Marrant was confirmed by the Countess Selina of Huntingdon, who hosted his ordination in her chapel at Bath. Three months later, Marrant embarked on a three-year mission among the blacks, poor whites and Micmac Indians of southeastern Nova Scotia.[10] Birchtown, where Stephen Blucke resided, became the seat of his ministry. There he founded a church, appointed pastoral assistants, and organized a school for 100 local children. With no regular means of support beyond 10 guineas from the countess, Marrant struggled to sustain a church during his years in Nova Scotia. His Birchtown parishioners were so destitute that they could scarcely afford to maintain him and the ailing countess did not answer his requests for further support. Depleted by illness and devoid of funds, Marrant left Nova Scotia in January 1788. Two years later, the familiar Cato Perkins became the countess's chief pastor in Nova Scotia. He went to hear Clarkson's appeal in Birchtown and was persuaded by it, so that Perkins' entire congregation would agree to go to Sierra Leone, making up a quarter of the migrants.

John Ball, Daddy Moses, Freeborn Garrettson

In Loyalist Nova Scotia, the Wesleyan Methodists had an impressive list of preachers. When Clarkson called a meeting in Birchtown, rain forced the gathering into the Methodist chapel where Daddy Moses presided. Later, on hearing a sermon by Daddy Moses, Clarkson 'felt frequently distressed for him, his feelings were so exquisite and he worked himself up to such a pitch that I was fearful, something would happen to him – The Congregation appeared very attentive.'[11]

Moses had also made an early convert of John Ball, who preached very well throughout Nova Scotia, 'considering his colour and station'.[12] Clarkson appointed him leader of the Wesleyan Methodist contingent in the migration. He would remain Moses Wilkinson's deputy on the voyage to Sierra Leone.

When the new Methodist Episcopal authority was instituted in 1784 in Virginia and Maryland, Freeborn Garrettson's first assignment was Nova Scotia, as it was known to be the home of white and black Loyalist refugees. The Methodist establishment felt he was the right man for the task. When he arrived at Birchtown, he regulated the society and formed them into classes. He was the only preacher whose orders came from 'Mr Wesley'. Other Methodists were the Boston Kings, whose wife in conversion had been 'struck to the ground, and cried out for mercy', so that Garrettson comforted her.[13] Here was the ultimate Methodist itinerant at work, but he was called away from Nova Scotia in 1787, before the Sierra Leone effort.

David George

You will remember David George, the Baptist preacher in Georgia, who survived the siege of Savannah and got a passage to Nova Scotia. George came to Halifax and went from there to Shelburne to preach and baptize amongst the black settlers in Birchtown. George had opposition from the white population and it became much more hostile as white people joined his congregation.[14] When he baptized a white person, whites rioted, beat him with sticks and drove him away. When John Clarkson came, George befriended him and supported the migration to Sierra Leone. Clarkson named him leader of one of the three companies for the migration.

To stay or leave Nova Scotia

As a result of Peters' London charges, Nova Scotia's Governor John Parr had been ordered to make an inquiry into the Annapolis area's land problem. If Peters' description proved accurate, the blacks were to be located immediately on good land. Those who chose not to accept grants had a choice to either enlist in a black army unit to serve in the West Indies or remove to Sierra Leone.

Parr had appointed Alexander Howe and Job Bennet Clarke commissioners to investigate Peters' charges.[15] Though Dundas undoubtedly intended their investigation to include all the complaints Peters made, the commissioners chose to interpret their task as an examination only of Peters' landless situation. Having heard evidence from Peters and the officials involved in land distribution, they upheld Peters' description but concluded that the reason he had not obtained land was his 'hasty' departure for New Brunswick in 1785. The fact that blacks who had remained in Nova Scotia had received no land was ignored and no remedial action was suggested.

The Nova Scotia and New Brunswick governments appointed agents who publicized alternatives available to blacks, deliberately misconstruing the Sierra Leone Company's intentions. It was felt the exodus of even a minority of blacks for Africa would remove black consumers and deprive the provinces of useful laborers, so that they would remain thinly populated.

Clarkson

In the face of this opposition, Clarkson arrived in Nova Scotia in October and began recruiting in the black settlements of Halifax and Shelburne counties, sharing his activities with Peters.[16] In neighboring New Brunswick, Peters met with determined opposition from local whites, who did not wish to lose black labor or have his charges corroborated by mass emigration. False debts and indentures were fabricated, officials harassed Peters and his recruits by demanding proof of free status and it was claimed that Peters would receive a fee for every black he fooled into going to Africa as they would actually be sold into slavery.

Nevertheless, some blacks responded with enthusiasm to the offer of free land, racial equality and full British privileges in Sierra Leone. About 1,200 emigrants gathered in

Halifax, almost 500 of them from Peters' recruitment, making up perhaps a third of the free blacks in Nova Scotia. The migrants would include the familiar names from the War for Independence: Isaac Anderson, David George, Boston King, Cato Perkins, Nathanial Snowball, Harry Washington, Daddy Moses and Thomas Peters.[17]

As the initiator of the project and leader of nearly half the emigrants, Peters became unofficial second in command to Clarkson. Together they inspected the ships and made arrangements for the journey. To channel complaints from individuals, Clarkson appointed Peters along with the preachers David George and John Ball as superintendents over the emigrants. Peters expected special status and according to Clarkson he felt piqued at not having been given absolute charge of the emigration. He was less willing than the others to accept Clarkson's word as law and discord appeared between the two leaders. No major disruptions were caused, however, and on January 15, 1792 a fleet of fifteen ships left Halifax for West Africa.

Freetown

Arriving in Sierra Leone in early March, the black Loyalists immediately began clearing a site for their settlement, which they fittingly called Freetown.[18] Unfortunately, rations were short, the rainy season brought fever and death, and the expected distribution of land was delayed by sickness, the inexperience of the administration, and the interference of slave traders and the indigenous population. Instead of becoming free landed proprietors, the black Loyalists found themselves worse than in Nova Scotia as paid employees of the company. Their discontent was voiced at a meeting on April 7, when Peters was chosen to present their demands to Clarkson.

Unknown to Clarkson while he was recruiting in Nova Scotia, in London, the Sierra Leone Company had introduced a new constitution for the colony providing for a government made up of white officials appointed from London. Clarkson was surprised when he arrived in Sierra Leone to find he had been made governor, but it was evident his authority was subordinate to the decisions of the company. In addition to Clarkson, there were several white councilors appointed chiefly to further commercial interests, while no blacks, not even Thomas Peters, had a position. Given these constitutional requirements, Clarkson could only regard Peters' demands as an attempt to replace the company's government with one headed by himself. A sincere humanitarian and abolitionist, Clarkson was convinced that a successful Sierra Leone colony would benefit black people everywhere and that the disorder of Sharp's earlier colony had to be prevented or it would suffer the same fate. He assembled the entire population and addressing Peters, he announced that 'either one or other of us would be hanged upon that tree before the palaver was settled'.[19] When he challenged the black settlers to choose between himself and Peters, none moved to Peters' side.

With this confrontation behind him, Clarkson chose to accept Peters' explanation that he had only acted as spokesman for the settlers, but privately he was unsure of Peters' intentions and assigned spies to watch his movements. For his part, Peters continued to remind the people at Methodist meetings of the promises made to them, which had been delayed as the new colony suffered from high mortality that threatened its survival.

Furthermore, on May 1, Peters was accused of stealing from the trunk of a former comrade in the Black Pioneers, a settler who had died of fever. His defense – that he had simply recovered property owed to him – was not accepted, and he was sentenced to return the goods and receive a public reprimand. The humiliation shattered his credibility, which was not revived before he himself fell victim to fever in June. He died in dishonor, denied the respect of the people he had led to Africa.

In August 1792, symbolically the first public building in Freetown, Harmony Hall, was opened as the social center for the new town, a place where settlers congregated and local African kings were invited to dine. It provided unity between the remaining settlers of 1787 living in Granville Town with the new Nova Scotia settlers in Freetown. Clarkson set up a committee to facilitate the union.

While only a minority had attended Anglican churches in Nova Scotia, in Sierra Leone it would become the custom for all to go to Anglican services conducted by the company chaplain. As chaplains were often replaced, Clarkson himself took over the duty, sometimes reading from books of sermons, but when addressing a pressing concern, creating his own.[20] Attendance of blacks was considerable and was seen as the forum for the governor to meet with his black constituents. As in Nova Scotia, blacks were drawn to their religious leaders, representing the Wesleyan Methodist, the countess's Connexion, and the Baptist denominations. Not only were they offered opportunities for worship but the services had come to be political forums for black aspirations. Long term, they would establish a Protestant Sabbath tradition on the African West Coast.

The Company Directors

As governor, Clarkson had been charged with various duties by the directors, but from the first he found that the survival of the colony took precedent over their aspirations. The directors felt that the colony needed to carry on trade, moving to develop Africa's rich resources to replace the productivity of the West Indies.[21] To this end, they had required an initial quit rent of a shilling per acre to steadily rise to 4 per cent of a crop, but given the conditions of undeveloped land, Clarkson knew it was doomed to fail. When, after some land was distributed, blacks protested the quit rent, he soothed them by claiming it was not clear when it would be implemented. Another issue, which dated from their recruitment, was the directors' claim of control over the shoreline, where they wanted their own docks and warehouses constructed. This prime land was soon appropriated by the settlers, from whom Clarkson suggested the company could buy the sites back when the proposed facilities were actually built. The company also insisted on establishing its own plantation on an additional site that was best for sugar cultivation, for which Clarkson was to negotiate. He did not oppose the company's economic policies outright, but he immediately selected only those projects which would enhance the ability of the blacks to continue the settlement.

Clarkson's pressing realities were numerous. On the day that Peters died, 600 settlers were sick and 5 others expired. By September, 14 per cent of black population and two-thirds of the white population were dead, leaving only a little over 1,000 of the original Nova Scotia migrants. Before any effort at trade could be made, the population had to be made healthy and sheltered. He candidly wrote to a new councilor about the privations the Nova Scotia blacks faced:

> The people here have been deceived through life and have scarcely ever had
> a promise made that was performed; they have been removed from America

in the hopes of bettering their condition and of improving the black character, under the protecting laws of the British Constitution. A person likely to benefit here must be very circumspect ... he must bear with their ignorance, make any allowances for their change of situation, and must not be hasty with them always keeping in mind, that the success of the colony and the civilization of Africa will greatly depend upon the management of the Nova Scotians.[22]

Clarkson returns to England

Clarkson grew weary of the problems in Freetown and by the end of 1792 he decided to return to England for rest and recuperation so that he might return revived. The settlers were upset, but he pointed out he had not expected to be governor when he joined the project and he assured them that he would represent their interests directly in London. In England, while he was abundantly thanked for his efforts in private by the company's directors, no public recognition appeared. The directors found that he and his brother Thomas were too critical of their priorities and they accused the two of being inspired by the Jacobinism the French Revolution was spreading.

David George accompanied Clarkson on his return to England. George wanted to play a mediating role in keeping his black Baptists calm by appealing to the directors about abuses. He was delivering a petition to them signed by forty-nine settlers, including himself, Boston King and eight black women and widows. The petition recognized Clarkson's patience and love to 'men and women and children' in the community and requested that he be returned as their governor.[23] However, the directors saw George's request as insolence and they decided to gently ask Clarkson to resign, but when he refused, they dismissed him.

The company then made an effort to discredit Clarkson and he was never again officially involved in the settlement of Sierra Leone. Still, he kept in contact with the settlers, personally answering their requests and meeting with the likes of Boston King when he came to England. As late as 1794, Moses Wilkinson would beg Clarkson to return to Africa because he was 'our Only Friend'.[24]

After Clarkson

Henry Thornton – the son of wealthy John of the Countess and Marine Society – was now the Sierra Leone Company's leader, a banker and MP. He and his directors were most concerned with the economic success of the colony and less with the plight of the black settlers or respect for their rights. The old ideas of a quit rent and use of the waterfront by the company were revived, while the distribution of land outside of Freetown was stopped, to prevent the settlers from farming independently. Instead, the company sought to control the settlers' economic life by forcing them to sell their produce to the company and buy their necessities at the exorbitantly priced company store. The only way the settlers could earn income was to work for the company's low wages, leading to a system of debt peonage. White Anglican company administrators would also make fun of the evangelical enthusiasm found in the settlers' Methodist and Baptist services.

Clarkson's replacement as governor was Zachary Macaulay, 24 years old, an arrogant reformed drunkard, who had administrative talents but was without sympathy for the black settlers. Macaulay's chief qualification was a previous six years as an overseer on a slave plantation in the West Indies – an odd choice for a project overseen by abolitionists. His countenance was dour, accentuated by blindness in one eye and a right arm made useless by an accident. He arrived in Freetown in early January 1793 and attacked 'the reigning folly of Methodists of this place in accounting dreams, visions and the most ridiculous bodily sensations as incontestable proof of their acceptance with God and their being filled with the Holy Ghost'.[25] He disdained those inspired by Daddy Moses or the Countess of Huntingdon's Connexion, led by that 'reprobate' Cato Perkins. He tried to force unbending Anglicanism upon the settlers, but soon found that even David George's Baptists – whom he had cultivated – were hostile.

Macaulay's only bright spot was the dusting off of Sharp's original ideal of political participation, for which elections were held, including voting by women, who may have been the earliest to be enfranchised in British history.[26] The company did not mean the elected were to interfere with their overall control, rather their purview was limited to local affairs, such as keeping animals from roaming the streets. The appearance of politics, however, did stimulate opposition to the company's policies, leading to petitions and the election of representatives to carry their grievances to the company in London.

In 1796, Methodist preacher Cato Perkins and Isaac Anderson were chosen to carry a petition to Thornton and the directors. These two blacks had been enslaved in South Carolina, but ran to the British during the war. Anderson had joined Lord William Campbell and left for New York with him. In Sierra Leone, he would criticize the company's control over waterfront property. Recruited by Clarkson as both were carpenters, in Sierra Leone Perkins became involved in the black colonists' politics and organized Methodist missions to the native African population. His congregation would rebel against the company's requirements and he led a strike of fellow carpenters against them. While in England, he also took the opportunity to study with the countess's Connexion and contacted Clarkson, while Anderson worked as a servant.

Clarkson sought to get Perkins and Anderson's petition to Thornton, but they waited in vain until the directors told them to put their request in writing. They showed knowledge of the English constitution and asserted that they deserved 'a governor authorized by the King' and they felt they should have a voice in the choice of the person who would govern them. They would not accept the company's choices which, with the exception of Clarkson, had 'injured us'.[27] After an exchange of letters, they found they could not budge the directors. The representatives concluded that 'the manner you have treated us has been just the same as if we were Slaves'. They returned in frustration to Sierra Leone, Anderson being ready for action.

The black evangelists rebel

Detesting Macaulay, the black settlers began a policy of insult and disobedience, hoping they could drive him away. He identified the dissidents as being from the followers of Daddy Moses. He reported that Moses compared him to Pharaoh, but reminded his flock that his oppressive rule must be endured until 'God in his own good time would deliver Israel'.[28]

Throughout these difficulties, many of the settlers continued to write to Clarkson, who provided them with advice. The settlers remained faithful subjects of the king and hoped to seek redress when Royal Navy frigates called at Freetown. Early in 1798, a navy ship appeared and the captain was given a petition which explained their history as far back as

Nova Scotia, especially as to how in consequence of their 'good behavior in the last war' they had never been obligated to pay a quit rent for their land. The captain chose to give their petition to Macaulay, who found it dangerous enough to delay collection of the quit rent.

Still, Macaulay was under pressure from the company to collect the quit rent. He had drawn up new titles to the settlers' land which included the quit rent, but most refused to even pick them up or return them. He went ahead with a register of those who had not complied and designated their land as 'unallowcated'.[29] They included the most successful farmers like Isaac Anderson, Harry Washington and Nathaniel Wansey, who were producing rice, coffee, pepper and ginger, though not sugar. Actually, a majority of the settlers, though anxious to have the status of owning land, had never been interested in farming, instead they worked as artisans, sailors, stevedores, tradesmen and fishermen. Baptist leader David George actually had a license to run a tavern.

Macaulay had created an explosive situation. He, however, would leave Sierra Leone in 1799, although the company would still keep him as permanent secretary operating from England. His new duties included seeking a royal charter for the colony, so that the company could do away with elections, which reflected the settlers 'misguided' views, and establish a new and separate court system. This required the consent of Parliament, so that the appearance of this authority at Freetown was much delayed.

The counter revolution reached its peak in the summer of 1800. The new governor, Thomas Ludlam, faced an impossible task of governing, after the discord that Macaulay had created. When he attempted to influence their elections, settlers at Freetown decided to rebel against him and the company. They gathered their followers at Cato Perkins's Methodist pulpit on September 3 and renounced their allegiance to Ludlam.[30] Perkins and Daddy Moses were at the core of the rebellion and nearly all of the Huntingdonians supported it. The leaders actually hoped for a peaceful transfer of power. Ludlam was outnumbered, but at the crucial moment in late September the Royal Navy ship *Asia* appeared in the Freetown Harbor, delivering Jamaican Maroons sent by the company to save him.

After the arrival of the Maroons, they were too experienced in dealing with whites to immediately take on the rebellious black settlers.[31] The Maroon chiefs refused to sign the land grant agreement Ludlum presented and, like the settlers, they opposed a quit rent. They were not in any sense farmers. They persuaded Ludlam to try to prevent bloodshed by negotiating with the rebellious black leaders. Anderson was pleased by the terms Ludlam offered, but the governor would not wait and sent the Maroons to surprise Anderson's camp, killing two, while the rest escaped into the mountains.

Most of the rebels returned on their own and Ludlam had thirty-one men in his custody within a week, but he had not received the company's charter from England, so he had no authority to charge them. When it finally arrived, it did not allow for the charge of treason, although it did allow for charging the rebels with writing complaining letters and arming themselves against the government.

Two members of the Methodist congregation, Isaac Anderson and Frank Patrick, were executed by hanging. Anderson you will remember, along with Perkins, was treated rudely by the company in London, leading to more threatening letters against the directors. Forty of the most respected settlers, most of them Methodists, were sent into exile at other places along the African coast. Ludlam was in charge of this, although he did not enjoy the experience and left at the end of the year. While Daddy Moses himself was not among those exiled, his evangelical Methodism was never able to regain its pre-eminent position in the fractured community at Freetown. The Promised Land they expected was not to be realized. In England, William Wilberforce absurdly called the black rebels 'Jacobins as if they had been trained and educated in Paris'.[32] The company had its revenge upon many of the black settlers.

Despite the failure of the company's economic goals, the religious life of the Sierra Leone settlers flourished brightly and helped them to face the realities of African colonization. While Anglicanism remained, it was the Methodists and Baptists who saw Africa as a Promised Land. Black evangelism provided them with their own leaders who began the Christianization of West Africa. Cato Perkins led this evangelism, at his death in 1805 leaving a legacy of Huntingdon churches he founded in liberated African villages.

Jamaican Maroons

To backtrack, it must be explained how the Jamaican Maroons became settlers in Sierra Leone. On August 7, 1800, 551 Maroon men, women and children had sailed from Halifax on board the navy's *Asia*, bound for Freetown. They had been accepted by the company as new black settlers, who it was hoped would quash rather than join the rebels. In this gamble, the company succeeded because the Maroons were hardened soldiers who were able to help them re-establish their authority.[33] How the Jamaican Maroons were in Nova Scotia requires explanation.

In Jamaica in 1795, one of five Trelawny Town Maroon communities initiated an uprising that became the Second Maroon War. Secure in their hidden places in central Jamaica, led by captains like Leonard Parkinson, the Trelawny Maroons engaged in guerilla warfare against government forces and raided nearby plantations. Other Maroon communities did not join them and their supplies ran low and measles began to spread. They were outnumbered and outgunned by government forces led by General George Walpole so that the rebels agreed to a truce.[34]

By March 1796, the conflict was over, although crucially Walpole promised that the surrendered Maroons would not be exiled from Jamaica. In England, their cause had not gone unnoticed by abolitionist MPs. In subduing the Maroons, British authorities had adopted the Spanish expedient of using bloodhounds and actually imported dogs from Cuba. The abolitionists saw the hounds as bloodthirsty, who ate their victims' flesh. In Parliament, Wilberforce would blame the Maroon War on the insensitivity of the Jamaican planters and the bloodhound debates favored the abolitionists in Parliament, embarrassing the Caribbean planters.

Ignoring Walpole's promise, however, the Jamaican Assembly determined to exile the Trelawny Maroons. By happenstance, the Royal Navy had a number of empty transport ships due to leave Jamaica. Jamaican authorities had discussed various destinations for the exiled Maroons, but the closest British port that these transports would pass was Halifax, so it was decided to drop them there and let Nova Scotia's governor and London authorities decide their future. The Jamaican Assembly provided a grant of £25,000 to pay their expenses and sent administrative officials and a surgeon along to watch over them.

In July 1796, the transports *Dover*, *Mary* and *Ann* landed at Halifax, carrying between 550 and 600 exiled Maroon men, women and children. With the approval of London authorities, Governor John Wentworth did his best to support the Maroons in Nova Scotia. Land and farms that had been vacated by the 1792 black Loyalist emigration to Sierra Leone was given to them. Houses were refurbished and built, a schoolmaster and clergyman employed, provisions were provided, and it was hoped the Maroons would become peaceful farmers. However, the Maroons' military reputation was determined more valuable and they were organized into a militia company, as a French invasion was feared.

The Nova Scotia winters of 1796 and 1797, however, were longer and colder than anything the Maroons had experienced. In protest at the weather and lack of familiar foods, the Maroons on occasion would withdraw their boys from school and refuse to attend church. Most of them were not Christians and they maintained their own primitive religion and customs, including polygamy. While the distribution of long-delayed clothing and supplies reversed their protests in the short term, it did not diminish their determination to leave. The majority wanted to sail from Nova Scotia and return to Jamaica, but the island government did not want them back. Otherwise, they were willing to go anywhere that was warmer. They petitioned the government in April 1798, saying that 'the Maroon cannot exist where the pineapple is not'.[35] At the same time, they secretly communicated with General Walpole, by now in Britain as an MP, for his support and he took up their cause.

After only four years in Nova Scotia, London authorities, over the objection of Governor Wentworth, decided that all the Maroons should emigrate. They were to leave in 1799, but it took a year before transport was arranged and the details were finalized. Governor Wentworth, who had been criticized for settling the Maroons as a single community rather than scattering them throughout the province, continued to ignore British authorities, delaying and ordering extra provisions for the Maroons to use during their voyage. We have seen the Sierra Leone Company decided to accept them to shore up their failing authority. This was how the Nova Scotia Maroons came to be in Sierra Leone in September 1800.

Sierra Leone belongs to the Crown

Seven years after the arrival of the Maroons, Parliament abolished the slave trade, meaning that 'Liberated Africans' taken from the slave traders by the Royal Navy or escapees from the slave factories were likely to come to Freetown. It became evident to Thornton and his directors that they could no longer handle the responsibility for the settlement. He requested that the British government assume full responsibility of the colony.

In the next year, the Union Flag was run up as Sierra Leone became a Crown colony, ending the misguided rule of the Sierra Leone Company. While it had attempted to pick up the pieces from the failed effort of the Committee for the Black Poor, its motives were much different. Its orientation was commercial, hoping that West Africa would replace the West Indies in producing staples by free black labor. It was impatient in this goal, coming to regard the free blacks settled the colony as impediments to its projects.[36]

The contrast between the governing of John Clarkson and Zachary Macaulay is one of the great dichotomies of the Emancipation Revolution. Would the Sierra Leone venture have prospered if the Royal Navy's Clarkson had been able to continue as the benevolent white leader who had the respect of the Nova Scotia black settlers? Or was the commercial view of the company's directors and their man Macaulay the most promising? From the standpoint of justifying emancipation, the answer is obviously Clarkson, but the establishment of any colony in West Africa required the resources and expectations that only the conservative company could muster.

Chapter 26

Philip Beaver at Bulama

Clarkson was not the only half-pay naval officer to devote his peacetime respite to settlement in West Africa. Besides Sierra Leone, other parts were now deemed the sites for new colonies, especially as abolitionists urged that the region replace the Caribbean as the source of sugar and other tropical commodities. A plan was developed to colonize the uncultivated island of Bulama, north of Sierra Leone, off the coast of Portuguese Guinea, with freed blacks and business associates.[1] Industrious 26-year-old Royal Navy lieutenant Philip Beaver was attracted to and ultimately led this enterprise.

Philip Beaver's career in the Royal Navy directly involved that of John Clarkson. They met each other as navy ship's boys and Clarkson would expose Beaver to the abolitionist movement. Born on February 28, 1766 at Lewknor, Oxfordshire, Beaver was the third son of a local curate.[2] His father died leaving his mother near destitute, so at the age of 11, Beaver went to sea as a ship's boy under the patronage of Captain Joshua Rowley. He and Clarkson were midshipmen aboard Rowley's 74-gun *Monarch* at the Battle of Ushant in July 1778.

In December, Beaver and Clarkson followed Rowley, who had raised his commodore's broad pennant on the *Suffolk*. Going out to the Leeward Islands, Beaver transferred with Rowley, who hoisted his rear-admiral's flag aboard the 74-gun *Conqueror*, participating in the Battle of Martinique in April 1780. Further service with Rowley followed at Jamaica aboard the *Terrible* and *Princess Royal*, both commanded by Captain John Thomas Duckworth. At the end of the war in June 1783, Rowley promoted Beaver to lieutenant.

With the war over, for the next four years Beaver lived with his impoverished mother at Boulogne out of financial necessity, attempting to learn French. It was a poor existence, broken only by the attempt of his older brother, a clergyman, to further Beaver's education. In December 1789, he resumed his naval service briefly on the sloop *Fortune* before being paid off at the end of the Spanish Armament. During the Russian Armament of 1791, he served from April to September aboard the 74-gun *Saturn*; however, these crises were momentary and Beaver was soon back on half-pay. Like Clarkson, he was inspired to be benevolent and humane towards those less fortunate. Unlike him, however, he would be impatient with blacks, whom he came to believe lacked 'habits of labor and industry'.[3]

The Bulama Association

Promoter and leader of the Bulama enterprise was retired army officer Henry Hew Dalrymple, who had served in Africa at the Goree slave station and in Grenada in the West Indies. He became involved with William Wilberforce and in 1791 he had been selected by the Sierra

Leone Company to govern their newly formed settlement at Freetown. Difficulties with him, however, led the company to dismiss him and instead chose Clarkson. The rejection led Dalrymple to create his own African colonizing expedition aimed at Bulama.

On November 2, 1791 at Old Slaughter's Coffee House in St Martins Lane, London, Dalrymple, Beaver and four other men formed a committee, 'The Bulama Association', with the intention of copying the aims of the Sierra Leone Company and developing their own island before settling free blacks upon it.[4] They saw poor blacks and whites as potential laborers hired to grow crops and build the infrastructure. They were concerned to show that 'free natives' could bring cultivation, commerce and Christianity to Africa. More well-intentioned than well-informed, they rushed hastily into the project, for Dalrymple was a man who acted first and thought later.

Meeting in a hall at Hatton Garden, London, the Bulama Association council was formed and together with subscribers, a vision was created. They promised universal male suffrage, freedom of religion, and prohibition of slavery. To London they added Manchester as a subscription center for those who wished to go to Africa. Both blacks and whites subscribed to go, numbering 275 men, women and children, probably interracial, although their exact racial division is unknown.[5] Seventeen of the fifty-eight women had been domestic servants. Many of the prospective black and white colonists had been rejected for the Sierra Leone Company's expedition. They included freethinkers, Jews, both the working class and socially elite, and Anglicized former slaves. As far as can be determined, their motives centered on the idea of bettering themselves.

The Bulama Association lacked government support and they incurred considerable cost through the purchase of stores and provisions, the hiring of ships, and charges caused by their failure to obtain a charter. Still by April 1792, the expedition sailed, consisting of three hired merchant ships, the *Hankey*, commanded by Lieutenant Beaver, the *Calypso*, commanded by Lieutenant Richard Hancorn, and a small cutter, the *Beggar's Benizon*, commanded by a Lieutenant Dobbin.[6] Aboard the vessels were the colonists, from which a council of thirteen members had been formed, although without a charter this body had no legal power over the recruited colonists. Smallpox and fever would rage on all three vessels at sea even before they arrived at Bulama. On the *Hankey*, Beaver varied his activities from maintaining order to cooking meals because the women colonists were seasick.

The reality

The realities of this African settlement would be similar to those of Sierra Leone. The *Calypso* being a better sailing ship than the *Hankey* had arrived first at Bulama and settlers had gone on shore and begun to build a modest blockhouse in which they stored their arms and munitions. Here they were surprised at night by native Africans who inflicted casualties, took their munitions and carried off four women and three children as captives. After this setback, many lost heart and the counselors, including Dalrymple, and the women and children contemplated going to Freetown.

This was the situation when Beaver arrived on the disciplined *Hankey*, finding the colonists huddled on the *Calypso*, fearing even to land. Gaining fresh supplies from the Portuguese, they returned, but soon the rainy season began and they continued on their sickly ships. To make it safe to land, Beaver negotiated with King Bellchore to purchase the island and he made effort to explore it. By July, the council led by Dalrymple had decided to abandon the colony and leave for Sierra Leone. The *Calypso* with Dalrymple and 150 refugees aboard arrived at Freetown, where Clarkson greeted the demoralized and dying colonists.[7] He feared the *Calypso*'s wretched condition would upset Freetown. After five weeks, he was able to send Dalrymple off on another ship and the rest were sent with food and medicine to England.

Beaver had refused to go when the *Calypso* left, keeping the *Hankey* and *Beggar's Benizon* at Bulama. The remaining colonists' leadership now fell upon 26-year-old Beaver's shoulders. After being elected their president, he took command of fifty-one men, thirteen women and twenty-five children. He was simply acting as the captain of a crew that was now smaller than that of a frigate. Through diligence, sheer determination and in the true character of a navy officer, he managed to redeem the captives, and instill discipline and industry into the remaining settlers. A stockade was erected to protect the settlement.[8] Still, within days his elected deputy Lieutenant Hancorn died and, despite Beaver's best effort, more of the colonists became sickly over the successive weeks and either perished under the hot African sun or resolved to go home. He found the colonists shared neither his dedication nor his work ethic. Beaver himself fell ill and whilst he lingered in what his colleagues believed to be his death throes, he heard the remaining two council members discussing the inevitability of abandonment once he had passed away. Fortunately, he recovered and within a few days was back at work, only to be confined to his cot for another two weeks in October.

As 1792 continued, the remaining Bulama colonists faced the threat from capricious local King Bellchore, who coveted the colony's arms and ammunition. Luckily, he was thwarted in his first attempt to send his warriors to attack the stockade by their fear of a couple of cannon that Beaver had deployed at the entrance. A potential attack by another tribe was then only prevented by the accidental firing of a gun – to the natives a bad omen.[9] The *Hankey* had left for more profitable waters, but thankfully the 16-gun navy sloop *Scorpion*, under Lieutenant Solomon Ferris, had been ordered to the island to render assistance. In October, Ferris had been recommissioned on the *Scorpion*, going out to Bulama in the following month on his way to Barbados. Shortly after its arrival, when King Bellchore landed 150 men, he was prevented from rushing the colonists, as the *Scorpion*'s boat spotted him and fired a warning shot.

Although the *Scorpion* departed on January 12, 1793, she left behind a midshipman by the name of Scott who volunteered for Beaver's party. The sloop's presence had allowed Beaver time and resources to strengthen the stockade, so that he was confident it could withstand a future native assault. Despite his best efforts to make a success of the colony, desertion further reduced the inhabitants to a mere nine white settlers and twenty-odd free and wage-earning blacks by the end of July, clearly insufficient to maintain the colony. Ever positive, rejoicing in the fact that there had not been a death for six months, Beaver was still anxious to attract more colonists and in correspondence home he heralded the survival of livestock, especially cattle and a tasty elephant, as well as the abundance of fresh water. He also re-stated previous assurances that in time eminently habitable Bulama would prove far superior to any settlement in the West Indies. He was at pains as war with Revolutionary France emerged to express the colony's 'attachment to our present constitution of government, by King, Lords and Commons … in the support and defence of which we will, at all times, and in any place, be ready to lay down our lives'.[10]

Sadly, Beaver's pleas for more 'good people of England' fell on deaf ears. The Bulama venture was unsupported and by November the remaining colonists decided to leave and set off for Sierra Leone aboard the *Beggar's Benizon*.[11] From there, Beaver was able to obtain a passage home, arriving at Plymouth in May 1794, where he returned to the navy, appointed to the 64-gun *Stately*, under Captain Billy Douglas, in which he immediately sailed for the East Indies.

In 1805, Beaver would find time to write his *African Memoranda*, an account of his Bulama experiences based on his journal, hoping that it would stimulate efforts to make developing Africa a national priority.[12] His zeal for the development of Africa as an alternative to the West Indies continued the efforts of abolitionists like Ramsay and the benevolent ideals of the Hanways. Like many naval officers, he came from a precarious middling background, punctuated by peacetime poverty, so that he did not see the value of personal wealth. He did see that commerce was a civilizing factor like Christianity, which could make blacks want to improve their lives by becoming industrious.

These efforts to settle West Africa would prove instructive as to what was required for planting a successful colony. The Royal Navy was the one British institution that could offer such endeavors support in Africa and it assumed a life-saving role. The actual attempts to settle blacks and whites there proved to be inadequate, considering the obstacles to their settlement. The locations chosen were not ideal as they spawned opposition from native African kings and continued to be centers of the slave trade. Clarkson, Beaver and other half-pay naval officers were aware that to save their African colonies they had to use the powers of a ship's captain, not unlike those Captain John Smith had used nearly two centuries earlier to save the desperate Jamestown colony in Virginia.

Chapter 27

Towards Abolition of the Slave Trade

By this time, the events of the War for Independence were no longer fresh, but the concern of blacks and British abolitionists for their freedom remained burning as brightly as ever. While the Sierra Leone colonists were struggling, leading to the establishment of the Crown colony, the effort to end the slave trade was paralleling them in England. The abolitionists' goal was to legally end the slave trade through Parliament. They were opposed by most slaveholders, especially in the West Indies. However, British anti-slavery efforts and imperial agendas were now tightly bound as evidenced by the colonization of Sierra Leone, inseparable from ideas of national identity that permeated the British public and made the Royal Navy crucial. The Emancipation Revolution was fulfilling the promise made during the War for Independence.

Naval rivalry in the emerging Empire

Still, British abolition of the slave trade would be played out against a background of continued European colonial rivalry. In West Africa, French and British navies had struggled for control of Goree off the Senegal Coast, the notorious if no longer flourishing slave-trading island, from which many Africans had been forced to go to the Americas. Britain had won it from France in the Seven Years' War, but returned it at the peace table. During the War for Independence early in 1779, Admiral Edward Hughes' reinforcements on the way to the Indian Ocean, returned it to British control.[1] The 1783 Peace of Paris restored Goree and Senegal to the French, who saw the abolitionists' effort to create the Sierra Leone colony as a threat to their influence and continuation of their slave trade.

This rivalry remained an outside influence on the Sierra Leone colony's precarious existence, demonstrated in 1794 when the French bombarded the Sierra Leone Company's defenseless Freetown. Citizen-Captain Arnaud received its surrender from Macaulay and occupied it, burning the company's property, although the black settlers were allowed to salvage lumber and supplies, which they regarded as their own. 'Whites and Blacks were obliged to run back into the mountains.'[2] Years later, Governor Ludlam threatened those black refugees who had salvaged during the French raid, demanding they return what they had taken during the attack. This unneeded confrontation was symptomatic of the company's inability to understand their colonists.

The rise of abolition

Immediately after the War for Independence, the success of British abolitionists can be attributed to the moral distaste brought on by religious sensitivity and humanitarian outrage associated with the evangelistic movement. In 1787, Thomas Clarkson, the elder brother of John, was sent by the

191

London Anti-slavery Society to the port of Bristol to investigate the slave trade, which, with the end of the war, had revived. A graduate of Cambridge University, he had written and published a prize anti-slavery essay, and he joined the London committee which included Granville Sharp and later the manufacturer of thousands of antislavery medallions, Josiah Wedgewood. Soon Clarkson convinced a young MP William Wilberforce to join them and ultimately bring the question of the slave trade before the Commons. In Bristol, Clarkson found many mariners who had stories to tell about their earlier slaving voyages. He gained the support of the city's Quakers and Mr Thompson, the landlord of the Seven Stars Tavern, who boarded seamen but refused association with slavers and was no crimp. At this early date, Clarkson found that 'everybody seemed to execrate [the trade], though no one thought of its abolition'.[3]

He was most concerned over what white and black seamen thought of serving on slavers. He discovered that seamen who arrived in the West Indies were paid half their wages in local currency, which was valueless once they left the islands. He also found that seamen had fallen victims to crimps, but his most shocking revelations were about the treatment of unscrupulous captains towards their crews. Clarkson described the case of free black crew member John Dean, who had been punished for a minor infraction by being fastened to the deck, burned with hot pitch, and scarred with tongs. He obtained equipment used on slave-ships, such as iron handcuffs, leg-shackles, thumbscrews, and branding irons. He would publish engravings of the tools in pamphlets and displayed the instruments at public meetings. Despite hearing and collecting such negative material, Clarkson was unable to find witnesses who were prepared to testify in public. Still, when he continued his research elsewhere, as in Manchester, forty or fifty blacks were in his audience.

John Newton

Another abolitionist was John Newton, whom we have seen was first mate on a slaver in 1748. Retiring from the slave trade in 1754, he gradually underwent a religious conversion, guided by John and Charles Wesley, who helped him to move from deism to a true Methodist conversion, putting his past behind him.[4] He returned to his native London and became the vicar of St Mary Woolnoth and dabbled in poetry that supported the faith. Woolnoth was the only City of London church commissioned from the famed Nicholas Hawksmore.

Newton had first-hand experience in the slave trade, invaluable when he met James Ramsay in 1783, followed by a meeting with William Wilberforce at his house in Hoxton. Five years later, Newton broke his long silence on the slave trade with the publication of his pamphlet 'Thoughts Upon the Slave Trade', in which he described the horrific conditions of the slave ships during the Middle Passage. He apologized for 'a confession, which … comes too late … It will always be a subject of humiliating reflection to me, that I was once an active instrument in a business at which my heart now shudders.'[5] He had copies sent to every MP, and the pamphlet sold so well that it required reprinting. Newton became an ally of Wilberforce, as he gradually became the leader of the Parliamentary campaign to abolish the African slave trade.

Edward Rushton

In Liverpool, the slave trade would thrive, yet a few dedicated abolitionists appeared. Among them, Edward Rushton was the most radical anti-slaver. Born in John Street, Liverpool, on

November 13, 1756, his father Thomas was a victualler. He was enrolled at the Liverpool Free School from the age of 6 to 9.[6] He left school and became an apprentice with Watt and Gregson, a firm that traded in the West Indies, making him an experienced sailor. At 16, he took the helm of a ship, which the captain and crew were about to abandon, and guided it safely back to Liverpool. As a result, he was promoted from apprentice to the position of second mate.

At the age of 17, he survived the sinking of a small boat dispatched to the shore on the way back from Guinea, West Africa. He swam towards the safety of a floating cask, where he discovered that a slave, Quamina, was clinging to it. He had already befriended him and had even taught him to read while on the ship. Seeing him approach, Quamina selflessly pushed the cask towards Rushton so he would be saved, bade him goodbye and sank to his death. Rushton's biographer, William Shepherd, wrote that Rushton often spoke of the incident, 'never without dropping a grateful tear to the memory of Quamina'.[7]

Working with human cargo gave Rushton first-hand experience with the ill-treatment of slaves that would cause him to become an abolitionist. In 1773, Rushton was sailing to Dominica on a slaver when a highly contagious outbreak of ophthalmia struck the slaves. The disease spread quickly and Rushton was appalled with the conditions that the slaves had to endure, so he sneaked food and water to them. He also reprimanded the captain and as a result he was charged with mutiny. In contact with the slaves, he contracted ophthalmia and became completely blind in his left eye, also developing a cataract-like condition in his right eye.

When Rushton arrived in Liverpool, his father took him to several specialists, even the king's oculist, all to no avail. To add to his problems, he was turned out of the family home, his father having remarried to a woman who could not tolerate her new stepson's presence. Fortunately, his sister took him in, and Rushton stayed with her for seven years. During that time, he lived in poverty on an allowance of 4 shillings a week given to him by his father. Out of that scanty sum he paid a young boy 3 pence a week to read to him.

Rushton studied literature, politics and philosophy. He loved to read the plays of Shakespeare and the prose and verse of Milton. Political developments in America also interested him. He went far beyond most British abolitionists when he supported the Haitian Revolution, which began in 1791. Six years later, he wrote to ex-President George Washington on the subject of slavery, questioning Washington's blatant hypocrisy in retaining numerous slaves while fighting England for independence.[8] The letter was returned by Washington without a reply. Rushton wrote a similar one to the radical Thomas Paine, author of *Rights of Man and Common Sense*, questioning the confinement of his libertarian ideals to only whites. Paine also turned a deaf ear.

Rushton held positions briefly as editor of the *Liverpool Herald* and as bookseller at 44 Paradise Street, but he made enemies for his outspoken views and lost his custom. His abhorrence of the slave trade became widely known and during the early 1780s he formed his first association with Liverpool men of similar outlook – William Roscoe, Dr James Currie, William Rathbone and the Unitarian minister William Shepherd. Thomas Clarkson sought him out while on a visit to Liverpool to credit him for his contribution to the abolitionist cause. Rushton dedicated some of his work to Beilby Porteus, then Bishop of Chester serving Liverpool. While expressing anti-slavery views, Porteus was not an abolitionist, so it is assumed Rushton was trying to pry him from his conservatism. With his friends, Rushton also formulated the idea of providing care for blind paupers, resulting in the Liverpool School for the Indigent Blind, the first of its kind in the country. He regained his sight in 1807 following an operation, thus enabling him to see his wife and children for the first time in thirty-three years.

The slave trade after the war

After the War for Independence, some historians have felt that the abolitionists were able to take advantage of a decline of the slave trade in most British ports. During the war, the trade had suffered as resources were diverted to the war effort.[9] The last slaving voyage had actually left Whitehaven in 1769. By the end of the war, the trade had also contracted in Bristol and London.

In Bristol, the decline of the slave trade had begun during the War of Austrian Succession. The city was slow to make port improvements, which contributed to rising shipping costs and increased turnabout times for vessels.[10] Merchant families that had once profited from the slave trade found that the next generations were not able to carry on the trade. By 1793, the imminent war with France caused the collapse of banks, creating a contraction of mercantile credit. Unlike London, Bristol's banks and mercantile interests were intertwined, for Bristol merchants owned their ships. There was nowhere to escape and the result was a series of bankruptcies. This forced Bristol out of the slave trade.

Even in London, the slave trade suffered a reversal. Here the decline of the trade dated from 1780. As with Bristol, London experienced delays in creating port facilities like wet docks until 1802. The silting of the Thames along with the crush of vessels of all sizes in the narrow passage led to a decline in expensive slave voyages. Still, 'the West Indies Interest' was most prominent here, where these rich, often absentee, planters were able to influence Parliament and support the continuation of the trade along the Thames.

Liverpool

These changes in the once thriving slaving ports should only be seen as shifts in the slave trade as other ports stepped in to take up the slack. Liverpool notably picked up the pieces after the war and its slave trade expanded as never before, creating a situation in which it was argued any infringement on the trade would cause widespread economic distress.

The abolitionist campaign found that the slave trade still flourished in Liverpool. While slow in the first half of the eighteenth century to be involved in the slave trade, during the second half Liverpool became Britain's leading slave-trading center. It had expanded from trade limited to the Irish Sea to being a fully fledged transatlantic port, focused on the West Indies and the Chesapeake. Liverpool grew from 7,000 inhabitants in 1708 to 34,000 in 1773 and to over 77,000 by 1801 – Britain's second largest city.[11] To accommodate its rising shipping, the Liverpool Corporation was able to fund and build six wet docks. Its more remote location allowed ships to exit by way of Northern Ireland, making it safer in wartime from raids, which also meant that its insurance rates were lower. Its proximity to the Isle of Man, a tax haven for goods, allowed it to distribute goods more cheaply. Along with shipping and shipbuilding, the city had developed an industrial base of metal manufacturing, glassworks, salt refining, potteries and cotton mills. These industries fed into an even broader manufacturing center at Manchester, which provided an array of goods for African kings and traders. Finally, the business acumen of its merchants was demonstrated as they were able to dominate specific sources of slaves in West Africa, through their good relations with African traders and their choice of attractive trade goods.

Defense of the trade

Against the abolitionists' mounting public pressure, Liverpool's merchants and slave traders would defend the slave trade. Its Rodney Street was built between 1782 and 1801, providing town houses for many elite merchants, including John Gladstone, father of future prime minister William Ewart Gladstone.[12] It was named after Admiral George Rodney, who defeated the French at the Battle of the Saints in 1782, preserving the British influence in the West Indies, and Rodney supported the slave trade. The Liverpool street immortalized by the Beatles in their song 'Penny Lane' takes its name from the slave trader James Penny, who was vocal in his opposition to the abolition movement. Eager to protect his business, he boldly claimed in evidence to the Lords Committee of Council that: 'The slaves here will sleep better than the gentlemen do on shore.' Liverpool slave traders would submit sixty-four petitions to Parliament arguing against abolition. Merchants who defended the slave trade included the Tarleton family. They were responsible for 180 slaving voyages, transporting nearly 50,000 Africans to the Americas. From 1785, John Tarleton led the business and was Liverpool's delegate to the Commons, where he protected the trade. His brother Banastre was already famous for his part in the War for Independence, and represented Liverpool in Parliament from 1790 to 1812. He made a number of speeches in defense of the odious trade based on his experience in the war.

The West Indies' planters were another source of opposition to the abolitionists. They had been hit by the wars in both America and France, fluctuating sugar prices, and higher import duties on sugar. They fought back against the abolitionists' effort in Parliament. To their credit, they did not claim that blacks were inferior to whites, disregarding racism. Instead, they felt that their slaves were not treated badly. Some argued that blacks were better off working in a Christian country than being left to their native barbarism.

You will remember the West Indies' planter Sir William Young, whose family was depicted in a portrait which supported the pro-slavery view that West Indies slaves were well treated. Italian Agostino Brunias departed London in 1770 as Young's personal painter.[13] Brunias worked and voyaged between the British-controlled Caribbean islands until his death in 1796, for the first time giving Britons a visual account of black Caribbean life. Promoting Young's imperialist mission, he portrayed the West Indies as a thriving colonial economy, a place of opportunity where the generations of deported African peoples were not resisting their enslavement. Brunias did capture the detail of diverse and joyous social gatherings of slaves, but ignored the harsh realities of slaves on the plantations.

More perceptively, the West Indies' planters argued that the economic benefits of slavery outweighed its humanitarian failings. They had been loyal in their support of men and money for the War for Independence and abolition of the trade they believed would ruin them. It was pointed out that, while the trade might be ended in the British Empire, Parliament could not legislate for foreign countries, who would continue without restrictions to prosper in the trade.

From another perspective, among the moderate supporters of the slave trade was New York-born Henry Cruger Jr. He had become his family's most renowned member because he was named Mayor of Bristol and elected their representative to the Commons. In New York, he had attended King's College and in 1759 at the age of 20 he moved permanently to the family's Bristol counting house. Cruger had embodied the sentiments of both New York's and Bristol's merchants in the era leading to the War for Independence, opposing measures that would restrict trade, but stopping short of supporting the colonies' independence.

In the 1780s, Cruger continued to be one of two Bristol representatives to the Commons. His views on the slave trade were moderate, for while he agreed it was inhumane and needed to be reformed, he felt this was to be done gradually, not overnight as William Wilberforce proposed in 1789. Cruger's family had been involved in West Indies' trade (though not the slave trade), but those Bristol merchants involved in that trade were his constituency. Such venerable organizations as the Bristol Merchant Venturers and the newer West India Society also were influential. His supporters included John Pinney and James Tobin, Nevis plantation owners, who condemned racial mixing. All of them held black slaves as servants. Like them, Cruger felt that a redirection of the African trade into new and more peaceful endeavors would be better than the abolition of the trade. He was especially concerned that the cost of abolition should not fall on West Indies' merchants, but rather the nation.[14] Thus, while recognizing the abuses of the trade, Cruger would vote against Wilberforce's bills to abolish it.

Campaign to abolish the slave trade

In May 1787, the London Anti-slavery Society morphed into the Society for Effecting the Abolition of the Slave Trade and, as seen, sent Thomas Clarkson to Bristol to gather evidence.[15] It had only twelve members, three Anglicans (Clarkson, Sharp and Philip Sansom) and nine Quakers, but the numbers would eventually rise to forty-three. It was crucial to have a printer and publisher supporting the cause. The place on the committee was filled by Quaker James Phillips, born in Cornwall, England in 1745, the son of a Quaker in the copper and iron trade. He was subsequently enrolled in a Quaker school in Rochester, Kent, and later moved to London. When his aunt, Mary Hinde Phillips, retired in 1775, she gave her business to him, thus introducing him to the field of printing and bookselling. By 1783, he was publishing dictionaries and Bibles for fellow Quakers and also account books and educational works. As the War for Independence came to an end, Quakers thought that the British economy could survive without the slave trade, which had languished during the war. When the London Society of Friends organized a twenty-three-person committee in June of 1783 to discuss the issue, Phillips was one of its members. The books, papers and pamphlets that Phillips published for the committee included the New Jersey Quaker David Cooper's *A Serious Address to the Rulers of America*, about the American injustice of tolerating slavery. Phillips was responsible for printing and distributing circular letters to the committee's possible supporters. He introduced Olaudah Equiano to Wedgwood and they corresponded with each other. The Crucial also was the London Committee's petition campaign against the slave trade. They formed a nationwide system of committees and local agents working in close connection to them. Subscription lists were published in newspapers to thank supporters. They show that the backing for abolition was predominately white and middle class. Some prominent blacks also supported the cause with their pens.

In February 1788, prime minister William Pitt announced his intention to create a Privy Council committee to bring forth a resolution on the slave trade. Granville Sharp and Thomas Clarkson promptly visited several MPs to get them to support the resolution. Both the Commons and Lords opened inquiries into the slave trade and it became a leading question to be taken up in the next Parliament. William Pitt had been educated at Cambridge University; there he met William Wilberforce and they became close friends.[16] The son of the famous William Pitt, the minister who led Britain to victory in the Seven Years' War, he had been groomed by his father for political office. He showed great political gifts and acted as prime minister in his twenties, the youngest in Britain's history. His views on the abolition of slavery were similar to those of Wilberforce, but he was too much of a political realist to believe that the trade could be done away with easily in the face of the serious opposition. While he offered government support for undertakings like the Sierra Leone colony, when the cause had failures, he remained publicly silent.

A piecemeal approach toward abolition of the slave trade remained necessary. All was not lost in 1788, as Sir William Dolben introduced a bill in Parliament to improve the conditions of slaves being transported to the West Indies, and vigorously secured its passage through the Commons.[17] Born in 1727 in Finedon, Northamptonshire, Dolben was a Tory MP, who was convinced of the 'crying-evil' of the slave trade. Support for the act also came from Sharp, Clarkson and Ramsay, but William Wilberforce feared that it would promote the idea that the slave trade was not fundamentally unjust – merely needing further regulation.

We have seen that Captain Henry Savage disbursed Dolben's Act in the Sierra Leone region. Meant to regulate the conditions on a slaver, it stated that ships could transport 1.67 slaves per ton up to a maximum of 207 tons burthen, after which only one slave per ton could be carried. The number of children was limited to two-fifths of the shipboard slaves, defining children as not exceeding 4 feet 4 inches in height. It set a limit on the number of slaves who could be dead on the arrival of the ship and it required that the slaver's master have previous experience in slaving voyages. Fines were levied for all infractions. The provisions of the act expired after one year, meaning that the act had to be renewed annually by Parliament. Dolben led the renewal effort in subsequent years, so he regularly spoke against the slave trade. The act was renewed between 1789 and 1795 and between 1797 and 1798.

As with the West Indies' planters, the abolitionists had their own artists who portrayed their cause favorably. *African Hospitality* is an anti-slavery print by engraver John Raphael Smith, after a painting by his brother-in-law George Morland. From an unsavory background, Morland was a prodigious painter, drawn to the causes of common folk. Published in 1791, the print – a companion to another called *The Slave Trade* – sold everywhere, even across the Channel in France. The image depicts the kindness of Africans ministering to a shipwrecked European family, a questionable reality, but an abolitionist ideal, showing Africans capable of noble actions.

Black support

Olaudah Equiano supported the campaign to better the conditions that slaves endured on slavers, culminating in 1788 with his leading a delegation to the Commons in support of Dolben's bill. Reading Equiano's own life story would be a powerful tool in fighting the slave trade. He first published his autobiography in 1789, following this with visits to Ireland,

Manchester, Nottingham, Sheffield, Cambridge, Stockton on Tees and Hull to support of ending the slave trade. He claimed that, 'As the inhuman traffic of slavery is now taken into consideration of the British legislature, I doubt not, if a system of commerce was established in Africa, the demand for manufactures will most rapidly augment, as the native inhabitants will insensibly adopt British fashions, manners, customs, etc.'[18] Equiano would follow his biography with a spiritual rebirth as a Wesleyan Methodist, supporting the ideal that Christianity and British manufactures would civilize Africa.

The Dolben bill was also supported by Equiano's friend Quobna Cugoano, who thanked Dolben for speaking out against slavery and enclosed several anti-slavery tracts in a letter. During the 1787 preparations for the first Sierra Leone settlement, Cugoano carefully crafted his support of a three-point plan to secure the immediate end of the slave trade. His first point was to hold days of mourning and fasting in Britain, where whites would seek God's forgiveness and gain understanding of what needed to be done. His second was much clearer but obviously premature: the total abolition of slavery. His third point interests us as a role for the Royal Navy: that 'A fleet of ships of war should be sent immediately to the coast of Africa' to intercept ships involved in the slave trade.[19] His program was sweeping as he combined the expansion of British Empire with the expansion of Christianity.

You will also remember Robert Wedderburn, the Jamaican mulatto who became an admirer of the French Revolution, more of a radical than compromising Equiano. He was among the earliest to sympathize with London's white and black working classes, writing pamphlets which combined the abolition of slavery with the need to improve working-class conditions. He looked to Parliament for reform and admired William Wilberforce, to whom in 1824 he dedicated his *Horrors of Slavery*. Two years earlier, when Wedderburn had been imprisoned, Wilberforce visited him, a meeting from which Wedderburn felt he had 'derived much ghostly consolation'.[20] He was obligated to Wilberforce for publicizing the West Indies' planters' 'lewd intercourse with their female slaves', which was his own and his mother's experience. Like the rest of the black elite, he underwent a conversion to evangelistic Christianity, becoming a licensed Methodist preacher, reflecting his talent as a better speaker than writer. From here he developed Unitarian leanings, but ultimately, he embraced a deist outlook.

Trade favoring the abolitionists

Although the slave trade was definitely expanding, support of some economic changes was useful to abolitionists. The slavers had come to depend on several commodities, not just slaves, for a profitable voyage. Shifts in African trade had forced slave-trading stations to diversify by offering exports beyond slaves. Some African slave factories had actually fallen into disuse when war interrupted the trade, leading Goree's merchants to diversify into peanuts, gum Arabic and ivory, providing a more secure future than dependence on slaves.

This trend saw slave trading replaced by what was called 'legitimate trade' between Africa and Europe. This trade was based on the usual export to West Africa of British and European manufactured goods, while imports from West Africa consisted of non-slave products, such as groundnuts, timber, rubber and, most importantly, palm oil. Liverpool traders had begun importing it in the early 1800s. It was used in West Africa instead of animal fats for cooking and making soap. Most of West Africa's oil palms grew in groves in the wild.[21] African women and children collected the loose fruits from the ground, while men harvested fruit bunches by climbing to the top of the palms. The fruit was then processed into palm oil by women, through a time-consuming and labor-intensive process involving repetitively boiling and filtering the fresh fruits with water. In England, this imported 'Red Gold' was used for making candles and soap, as well as for lamps and as an industrial lubricant.

Passage

While passage of a bill in the Commons to abolish the slave trade was much debated in 1792, 1795 and 1796 – the latter year in which Wilberforce's bill was defeated by only four votes – the abolitionists would have to wait. In January 1806, William Pitt died and Charles James Fox became the new government's leader in the Commons and, along with Wilberforce, renewed the effort to abolish the slave trade. After a bill stopping the import of slaves into conquered colonies passed Parliament, Fox moved directly to consider 'the Slave Trade to be contrary to the principles of justice, humanity and policy' and to 'take effectual measures for its abolition'.[22] It passed both houses by substantial majorities. Delay appeared as Fox followed Pitt to the grave only four months later. Wilberforce continued to push the bill and it finally passed the Commons in February 1807 and George III gave the Royal Assent. From 1808 onwards, it was unlawful for any British ship to carry slaves, nor could any be landed in other ships within the expanse of the British Empire. Of the original blacks evacuated after the war, only David George and George Liele were still alive.

Royal Navy enforces abolition

Without a method of enforcement, the noble sentiments found in Parliament's Abolition Act were no more than paper promises. When it was passed, a squadron of Royal Navy vessels was immediately sent to West Africa, tasked with suppressing the still thriving transatlantic slave trade. This was not a new duty for the Royal Navy, rather it continued the role it had played in the War for Independence – as a refuge for blacks escaping to freedom.

In West Africa, they operated at sea, boarding slave ships bound for the Americas and 'liberating' captive Africans, depositing them in Sierra Leone. On shore, naval officers resolved to 'improve' West African societies by Christianizing them. A number of African rulers were forced to sign treaties banning the slave trade. Within two years, four Liverpool slaving vessels were seized by a Royal Navy patrol off the coast of Sierra Leone.[23] In 1811, the Felony Act was passed in Parliament, which made slave trading punishable by five years' imprisonment or fourteen years' transportation. This was the beginning of a sixty-year Royal Navy operation as large numbers of French, American and Iberian slavers continued to go to Africa.

The ban on the slave trade was possible because by 1820, one quarter of the earth was devoted to the British Empire and was patrolled by the Royal Navy.

It would take until 1833 for Parliament to emancipate the estimated 800,000 enslaved men, women and children in its colonies. This was a complicated campaign that is beyond our account of the Emancipation Revolution. By 1807, the War for Independence was distant memory. It was the Napoleonic Wars in Britain and the coming of the War of 1812 in America that would provide a new testing ground for the ultimate abolition of slavery.

Chapter 28

American Epilogue

This final chapter is meant to give a brief review of what happened to the slave and free blacks who remained in the United States. After the War for Independence, overall conditions in the new republic were not conducive to freedom for slaves. It has been said, 'In those Chesapeake districts where most blacks lived, slavery was more deeply rooted when Jefferson stepped down from his presidency [in 1809] than when he composed the Declaration of Independence.'[1] Political debate in the states centered on the control of a growing number of free blacks, who were still regarded by planters as ringleaders in possible slave revolts. Even in the north, laws favored a very gradual emancipation of slaves. When legislation for abolition of the slave trade came to Jefferson, it actually enhanced the spread of existing slavery. His native Virginia had long ceased to participate in the Atlantic slave trade, as it had a surplus of slaves, which were sold for an internal market, as the Southern states expanded to the west, chiefly driven by the need for land to produce the new cotton staple.

Methodists debate slavery

As black Methodists were staging a revolt in Sierra Leone, American Methodists were moving in the opposite direction. The new Methodist Church in the United States no longer led the charge to make blacks Christians, instead becoming divided over the issue of freeing slaves. In 1780, Wesley's Bishop Francis Asbury and the conference of American Methodist preachers had condemned slavery as contrary to divine, human and natural justice, and preachers were instructed to bring about the manumission of slaves.[2] Four years later, with the war over, at the Christmas Conference of the now independent Methodist church, led by Thomas Coke and Asbury, a strong rule against slavery was adopted. While not expelled, slaveholding members were denied communion and they were required to sign a pledge to liberate their slaves within a year. New converts could not be admitted until they accepted the rule.

However, the anti-slavery effort of the two British clerics provoked such a backlash that the rule had to be suspended only six months later. For the next decade, the Methodist Church was almost silent about slavery. In 1796, officers (but not members) of the church were required to free their slaves. Four years later, Methodists would turn their back on the anti-slavery movement as the entrenched interest of slaveholders had caused their membership to decline. Methodists had to be practical and many felt that slaveholders should be members of the church, if only so that they would hear the message that would motivate them to treat their slaves well and manumit them. Methodists began to act like Episcopalians, where the values of the great planters still dominated the vestries. In the future, their black following would decline as blacks ultimately sought to establish their own separate Methodist church.

Western Lands

Before the war, only traders had gone beyond the Appalachians in Georgia, the Carolinas and Virginia, but those who returned alive told of rich soil and broad rivers. The Wilderness Road through the mountain passes was difficult and dangerous, but settlers brought their slaves with them, to cut down the forest and clear land for corn and tobacco. The War for Independence had stopped this migration. From 1782, Indians began to raid fledgling settlements and take slaves with them as they retreated.

Thanks to Benjamin Franklin, Lord Shelburne and the 1783 Peace of Paris, the new United States had acquired territories west of the Appalachian Mountains. This land was still vulnerable for Spain; Britain and even France would persist in their claims and the states themselves made conflicting claims. The new nation was still governed by the precarious Articles of Confederation, which gave the Congress no ability to tax, or act as an independent entity, or even maintain a navy.[3] The War for Independence had destroyed the Low Country's rice-plantation infrastructure. Britain blocked North American trade from its ports and imperial markets like the West Indies. Though the tobacco markets in continental Europe were still open, the price of it went into freefall in the 1780s. The development of the new western lands represented the future and can be seen as an expansion of the 'American Empire'.

Washington and the Countess

After traveling west in the autumn of 1784, George Washington, in temporary retirement in Virginia, penned a strong letter to his friend, fellow Virginian, and president of the Confederation Congress, Richard Henry Lee, in which he urged Lee and Congress to develop a definitive plan for settling the west.[4] Millions of acres of fertile farmland (quite a few of them owned by Washington himself) lay in wait, but the lack of a coherent land distribution policy blocked accelerated incorporation of the western lands and threatened to see them developed in a disorganized and chaotic manner, or worse yet in Washington's eyes, not developed at all.

Serendipitously, within a few weeks of writing to Lee, Washington received an unsolicited proposal from energetic Methodist, organizer Selina Hastings, Countess of Huntingdon. She promised to settle a large portion of the western territories in an orderly fashion with followers of her evangelistic Methodists, bringing peace to the stormy United States–Indian relations, and accomplishing the long-stated British goal of 'civilizing' native peoples.[5] She wished to purchase land for Christian colonies, which would accomplish her ecclesiastical and missionary goals, benefit the indigenous peoples of the region, and find favor in the United States as a whole. Washington communicated his immediate and enthusiastic support for her plan because it would Christianize the Indians. Through his ministrations and those of two other Americans – in London, Sir James Jay (brother of John Jay) and in Virginia, Governor Patrick Henry – the plan came before Congress in early February 1785, amid a hot debate over of western land development. Despite Washington's support, Congress's ultimate rejection of the plan sheds light on the diverging forces shaping western land policy after the war, and on the difference between British and American perspectives on new development. Rejected by Congress was the idea of a state-supported Christian colony in the United States, a not uncommon practice in British colonizing, as seen with Sierra Leone, where churches contributed to the colony's expansion.

Emancipation in the North

To compare the South's continued treatment of blacks, we need to look at the example of New York State, which still had the North's largest black population. In 1790, it had as many households with slaves as any Southern state, the difference being that each household had only one or two slaves. The war had produced no rush for emancipation; instead the process would be a very gradual. Not until 1799 did the New York Emancipation Act outline this.[6] It provided that children born to slaves after that year were to be free. However, a second law was needed in 1817 which declared that slavery would not be ended until July 4, 1827. The earlier law contained clauses that placated slaveholders, such as the use of a slave mother's children long after they reached adulthood as the children freed were required to remain in bondage until they were 28 years old for males and 25 years old for females. Thus, masters had the use of the labor of freed slaves until they reached those ages and did not necessarily have to pay for their subsistence during the extended emancipation process. Clearly, New York's emancipation laws were meant to give its masters every opportunity to dispose of their slaves without economic loss. Still, the laws were far too comprehensive to be emulated by Southern states.

Renewed Threat to Southern Planters

From 1782 to 1790 in the upper South, especially in Virginia, Maryland and Delaware, manumission laws were liberalized to allow masters to free their slaves by deed or will. In these states, the number of free blacks rose at the expense of the slave-based plantation economy. By 1810, the upper South had a free population of 94,085, compared to the Northern free black population of 78,181.[7] This was as much good management as it was altruism. Masters found it to be a convenient way of getting rid of slaves who were too old or unproductive as investments. They negotiated self-purchase agreements, allowing for manumission that was profitable. The slave was asked for money to purchase his freedom, allowing the master to enjoy his labor for a time, and as the slave used up his savings for the purchase, he might go into debt to his former master or to those whites who had loaned him money, circumscribing his freedom.

Despite the occasional acts of planters to manumit their slaves, the increase in the number of free blacks threatened them because they could no longer control them as they did their slaves. As a Maryland member of the Senate in 1793, planter John Henry raised the possibility that the black man's recollection of past injuries and the desire for revenge on his white master could lead to cruel outrages. Henry opposed efforts to renew conflict with Great Britain. He warned from his memory of the War for Independence that if they returned, 'A British Standard displayed in the heart of the Southern States, proclaiming liberty to all men, of whatever color, with professions to maintain the equal rights of all, would [succeed] in assembling an army.'[8] Black men who joined them, 'when animated with the enabling spirit of liberty, would become indeed, a very formidable enemy'.

Only the year before in Philadelphia, Henry had been warned that French refugees had arrived from Santo Domingo seeking asylum in the United States, fleeing a bloody slave revolt. While some of the refugees had actually served in the Continental army, his informant hoped that the Senate would block their asylum because the refugees had been transported to Philadelphia in British ships and, more crucially, because they were accompanied by their slaves, who 'have been trained in the use of arms, and have some arms in their possession'. Henry and his informant were haunted by the memory of armed slaves in the War for Independence supporting the British.

Planters feared the possibility of black revolt, although their fears were more apparent than real. In May 1792, a correspondent noted the people of Virginia's Northampton County 'are very much alarmed with the apprehension of an insurrection of slaves'.[9] Actually, while some blacks had manifested a desire to revolt, it turned out they had no fixed plan, nor arms or ammunition. All that they could be accused of was meeting and strolling together, while militia patrolled the county. Five slaves and a free black were jailed to undergo trial, but they were not convicted because the evidence was insufficient.

Suspicion of free blacks causing trouble remained, especially if they came from the North. When a black sea captain, Paul Cuffee of Massachusetts, docked at Vienna, Maryland on the Nanticoke in 1797, his crew was entirely made up of free blacks. Born in Africa, Cuffee had been enslaved in Massachusetts, where he decided at the age of 16 to become a sailor and during the War for Independence he and his brother refused to pay the war tax because the color of their skin disenfranchised them – to them a perfect example of 'no taxation without representation'. Cuffee now observed that Vienna's white inhabitants 'suspected that he wished secretly to kindle the spirit of rebellion and excite a destructive revolt among them'.[10] However, after a few days, realizing that all he wanted was to trade in Vienna, their hostility abated. Cuffee eventually would become an abolitionist.

Black Perspective

A mulatto slave born in Virginia in 1819, George Henry later reacted to changing Virginia laws on slaves in an account of his life. He had been a cook, then deckhand and finally captain of a Chesapeake coasting schooner that sailed out of Norfolk. He eventually escaped to Philadelphia where he became a freeman, but as he looked back to his experience in early 1800s Virginia, he claimed that free blacks were being legally forced to sell their property at a loss, as the laws now required them to leave the state. He summed up the place of slavery after the War for Independence:

> Slavery continued worse and worse under the reign of Washington than it did under the reign of Great Britain. The chains grew tighter and tighter, until at last the General Assemblies began to pass statute after statute in nearly all the Southern States, to drive out the free colored people. Owners of property amounting to from twenty-five to thirty thousand dollars, were compelled to sell it for five or six

hundred dollars, and were robbed out of all their property, amounting to millions, besides being obliged to leave the State in so many days or be made slaves. All this was done to please the slaveholders. Now I ask … is it any wonder that we should be poor men? Virginia announced in her constitution that 'All men having sufficient evidence of permanent common interest with and attachment to the community, have the right of suffrage, without distinction of color, and that they cannot be taxed or deprived of their property for public uses, without their own consent'. This was entirely worthy of the citizens who adorned that State. In the early history of Virginia, 1723, on the enactment of a statute, she undertook to disfranchise people of color, but was rebuked by legal authority in England, in admirable words as follows: 'I cannot see why one freeman should be used worse than another, merely on account of his complexion.'[11]

Here is a perspective on free blacks that explains their economic difficulties after the war. Henry was referring to an Act to Amend the Several Laws Concerning Slaves that was a reaction by the planters to the flurry of manumissions after the war, which increased the number of free blacks. The act stated that slaves freed after 1806 had to leave Virginia within a year of their manumission.[12] It sought to prevent an increase in the number of free blacks by forcing them to go to other states or countries. Free blacks now faced legal discrimination if they continued to live in Virginia.

While the act was threatening to free blacks, long term, it was neither respected nor enforced in Virginia. Instead, exemptions rose as all parties tried to avoid it. Some slaveholders did not want see free blacks leaving for other states since they wished to hire them and take advantage of their skills. Using their wills rather than deeds of manumission, slaveholders were able to continue to manumit their slaves, even though the law remained on the books until the Civil War.

While great planters like the Maryland Eastern Shore's wealthy Lloyds maneuvered to restrict free blacks, Frederick Douglas, a young slave growing up there, painted an ugly picture of their plantation and his neighborhood that bordered the Choptank River. He described it as a place known for 'the desert-like appearance of its soil, the general dilapidation of its farms and fences, the indigent and spiritless character of its inhabitants, and the prevalence of ague and fever'.[13] The white population was 'of the lowest order, indolent and drunken to a proverb, and [living] among slaves who, in point of ignorance and indolence, were fully in accord with their surroundings'. How do we explain this view of the common indolence of whites and blacks? Perhaps Douglas's memory was clouded because he was now free, convinced that life in the slaveholding South must be unbearable. But it is also possible that this condition had its roots in the racial aftermath of the War for Independence. The specter of the slow death of slavery haunts this era.

Despite Douglas's apprehension, rays of hope existed for free blacks. One of the few areas where free blacks could find employment was in the maritime field. Black seamen remained the backbone of the ferry system that was essential to Chesapeake transport. Late in 1798, Thorogood West, Captain of a Hungars Ferryboat stated in court that he was:

well acquainted with the [black] hands who are now employed at the Hungars Ferry, Virginia, [and] he knows them to be skillful Pilots and expert hands, and thinks them to be greatly superior to any white men ... Nor does [he] think that the white men who have hitherto been employed gave more satisfaction than the said negroes have given ... he has never seen the said black men drunk on board the vessels, so as to be incapable of doing their duty, that he has sometimes ... seen the said black men drunk on shore, but since the black men have commanded the boats he has not seen them drunk or more addicted to strong drink than many other seafaring men.[14]

Here was a strongly positive testimonial by a white captain.

Free blacks continued to use their maritime skills to develop a knowledge of navigating and extracting a living from the region's marshes, rivers and islands. Their ability to navigate Chesapeake Bay and the Atlantic Barrier Islands would provide them with an alternative to agricultural labor.

Still most blacks remained slaves. Before the war, only traders had gone beyond the Appalachians in Georgia, the Carolinas and Virginia, but those who returned alive told of rich soil and broad rivers. The Wilderness Road through the mountain passes was difficult and dangerous, but settlers brought their slaves with them, to cut down the forest and clear land for corn and tobacco. The War for Independence had stopped this migration. From 1782, Indians began to raid fledgling settlements and take slaves with them as they retreated.

Meanwhile in the Tidewater, as their tobacco was increasingly unprofitable, slave plantations were undergoing changes and turning to wheat for export. As noted, the slave trade in the Chesapeake had actually declined before the War for Independence – which decisively finished it off. Now slaves were healthy enough to produce their own children. This situation would spread elsewhere in the costal South.

American abolition of the slave trade

In the South, effort would be made to expand slavery without the need for the slave trade.

President Thomas Jefferson, with an eye to what was happening in Britain, urged and gained the passage of an Act 'to prohibit the importation of slaves in any port or place within the jurisdiction of the United States, from and after the first day of January [1808]'.[16] With a self-sustaining population of more than 4 million slaves already living in slave-owning states, enough Southern congressmen joined with Northerners to enact this slave trade ban. Southern entrepreneurship and Northern interest would be yoked for the future. Not realizing the implications of the act, free blacks like New York's Henry Sipkins gave orations that celebrated the event.

While the act imposed heavy penalties on international traders, the domestic sale of slaves actually boomed. As the now dominant wheat production in the Chesapeake required fewer slaves than tobacco, planters had a surplus of slaves to sell beyond the Tidewater to the west and south. Internal slave trading throughout the South was unimpeded by legislation.[17] Children of slaves became slaves, ensuring a growing slave population. A domestic or coastwise trade in slaves persisted between ports within the United States, as demonstrated by slave manifests and court records. While the slave trade was driven underground, American ships caught illegally trading were often brought into the United States and their captives sold into slavery anyway. It is estimated that up to 50,000 slaves were illegally brought into the United States after 1808, mostly through Spanish Florida and Texas, before those states were admitted to the Union. The act had not stopped either the internal or external trade in slaves.

Forced migration of slaves to the lower South

Controversial historian Edward Baptist has contended: 'the possibilities that enslaved people represented the wealth they embodied, and the way they could be forced to move themselves would actually forge links that overrode' antislavery.[18] The Chesapeake's internal slave trade expanded, offering a practical means of removing free blacks and selling bred slaves. In the early 1800s, a need for labor appeared in the lower South, especially Georgia, which included the western lands that would become Alabama and Mississippi, where an expanding economy was being created primarily by the cotton gin and foreign markets. Tidewater blacks were purchased or forcibly seized, their families broken up and they were sent to the lower South, a land they knew nothing about.

The new slave trade not only involved the great planters who sold slaves, but middle men as slave traders. Shipped by vessel or marched in an iron-bound coffle, slaves were sent from the Chesapeake to markets in Yorkville, South Carolina, Lexington, Kentucky, Montgomery Alabama, Natchez and Clinton, Mississippi, and New Orleans.From 1829 to 1831, more than two-thirds of the blacks transported to the South's largest city, New Orleans, came from Virginia, Maryland and North Carolina. Shipping by water was favored because it was faster – ensuring that the slaves arrived in better condition – but the overland coffle was cheaper; most traders used both methods depending on the season, which ran from fall to winter.

The traders who gathered and drove slaves came from respectable Southern families, which gave them options in acquiring slaves. As a young man, John B. Prentis, born in 1788 into a successful Williamsburg, Virginia family expressed genteel outrage over slavery, but by the end of his life he had transported thousands of enslaved persons from the upper to the lower South. Prentis became a Richmond, Virginia businessman, who found slave trading most profitable, even more lucrative than his interest in horses. He purchased slaves from several sources, including directly from white planters and then held them in his slave pen or jail until there were enough to be sent to the lower South. Prentis 'did his best to negotiate his conflicting class loyalties', ultimately justifying what he did as a version of white male entitlement.[18] He 'identified with the westerners' democratic aesthetic, but he was born of the old guard and depended on its members' complicity for the success of his work'. Exemplifying the process of early national expansion, he 'cherished his … ability to move fluidly from Virginia's finest parlors to the rough woods'.

Elsewhere, as slave prices rose, Cambridge and Snow Hill on Maryland's Eastern Shore became important ports for the export of slaves to the lower South. The trade involved more middling families like that of Patty Cannon, who led a gang in the 1820s from her house on the Delaware–Maryland border. She could not afford to purchase slaves, so she specialized in kidnapping free blacks and having them re-enslaved in the lower South.[19] They were seized from the streets of Philadelphia and Baltimore and then gathered at her home for shipment by water. Her gang jeopardized the security of free blacks, especially in hard times, when whites were bitter because blacks took jobs from them. In this way, free blacks disappeared, when 'pulled over the line' from the Tidewater to the lower South.

Justification for this activity was later explained in a popular novel using white dialect:

> Only a few years ago, … people around yer was a-freein' of their niggers, and it was understood that slavery would a-die out, an' everybody said, 'Let the eveil thing go.' But niggers began to go up high; they got to be wuth eight hundred dollars whair they was wurth two hundred; and all the politicians began to say: 'Niggers is not fit to be free. Niggers is bulrush, or bulwark, or bull-something of our nation.' And then kidnapping of free niggers started, and the next thing they'll kidnap free American citizens![20]

Against the prospect of being re-enslaved in the lower South or driven from Virginia, free blacks continued to find alternatives to being agricultural laborers. In the Chesapeake, participation in the earliest oyster trade was an attractive alternative.[21] As poor people, oysters were one of the mainstays of their diet and therefore they knew where to find them, a skill much in demand after the War of 1812. The oyster trade with Northern cities would enhance and protect the freedom of black men and women, well before the appearance of the Underground Railway.

Affirmations

We have followed the Emancipation Revolution's remarkable growth, focusing on the War for Independence and its effect on the eventual abolition of the slave trade. This increases the influence of the war on black history, although not in the way many would expect. As with Abraham Lincoln in the Civil War, in the War for Independence the British formulated a kind of emancipation proclamation to totally subvert what seemed to them the most hypocritical cause, with 'the loudest yelps for liberty', as Samuel Johnson famously put it, coming from 'The drivers of negroes'. At the end of the war, Britain went in one direction with emancipation while the United States went in another to retain slavery. The war had profound effect on black lives as slaves took advantage of the opportunities offered by both sides. Blacks found freedom to be their greatest goal and that it was most readily – if not perfectly – available from and protected by the British. Those blacks who became Loyalists had an important role in building a new British Empire.

The Emancipation Revolution was not inspired by the contemporary politics of the Founding Fathers in their Declaration of Independence or their concern for natural rights. The stability of British institutions made anti-slavery quite acceptable, while the abstract ideals of liberty and natural rights found in the American and French Revolutions failed to come to grips with slavery.[1] England's political and religious upheaval had been in the seventeenth century with the Glorious Revolution's Bill of Rights and the Toleration Act of 1688. In the next century, the Emancipation Revolution would essentially be based on Biblical scripture with a smattering of British constitutional and legal history. Of black writers spreading this message, some were born slaves; some had slavery thrust upon them; and some were never slaves. All were subjects of the British monarch before the War for Independence and all remained loyal afterwards. All were devoted to their freedom, spiritually as much as physically and, in this sense, all can be identified as both evangelists and abolitionists. It follows, therefore, that they were in the forefront of the anti-slavery movement.

Two aspects of the Emancipation Revolution should now be clearer, helping us to put together the structure of it. We have followed emancipation's remarkable growth, focusing on the War for Independence as the crucial event in the eventual abolition of the slave trade. This increases the influence of the war on black history, although not in the way some would expect. At the end of the war, Britain went in one direction with emancipation while the United States went in another to retain slavery. The war had profound effect on black lives as slaves took advantage of the opportunities offered by both sides, but freedom remained their foremost goal. The other aspect is that blacks found freedom most readily – if not perfectly – available from the Royal Navy and the maritime world in which it operated. Those blacks who experienced it became Loyalists and would play an important role in building a new British Empire.

The beginning of the Emancipation Revolution was in the first half of the eighteenth century, when evangelistic Christians aimed to baptize slaves, an act not welcomed by colonial plantation masters. The Great Awakening of George Whitefield advocated the better treatment of slaves, an effort which was continued under Anglicans like Bishop Porteus. In Britain and the colonies, Whitefield's preaching inspired the former African slave James Gronniosaw, while in Boston he motivated black poet Phillis Wheatley. Both of them would die in poverty but would be satisfied to praise God with their pens. The Countess of Huntingdon's acolytes David Margrett and John Marrant carried this discord a step further, asserting that freedom trumped all attempts to improve the treatment of blacks on a plantation.

After this, the trail is more complicated. It seems best to have a black guide; Quobna Cugoano was the only contemporary black writer who saw that an Emancipation Revolution was happening. You will remember he was the author who advocated the abolition of slavery as well as giving qualified support to the first effort to settle Sierra Leone with the black poor. He has been identified as the most literate black writer of the Emancipation Revolution, who justified the expansion of the British Empire into West Africa, not so much through trade as the spread of Christianity and related education. He argued that 'establishing factories and encouraging civilization on the coast of Africa, and returning some of our West Indies slaves to their original country', would 'make up for our past treachery to the natives'.[2]

Cugoano made it clear that evangelistic values were needed to inspire the creation of a new British Empire. In 1787, he penned his *Thoughts and Sentiments on the Evil and Wicked Traffic of the Slavery*, which included a history of the anti-slavery movement until then. His book was part autobiography and part political treatise based on Christian exegesis. His guide was an appreciation for reading and understanding 'the divine goodness displayed in those invaluable books the Old and News Testaments'.[3] He felt the Christian God was responsible for his freedom, while for his knowledge and ability to write he was 'highly indebted to the good people of England'.

A former African slave, Cugoano's concept of British liberty is based on his own detailed reading of the Bible. Like Daddy Moses, he was inspired for his people by 'God, the Almighty Redeemer and Savior of his people', who brought them out of bondage in Egypt, where 'they were kept under and in subjection to the whole body of this evil affections and lusts', including slavery. Cugoano also reflects on liberty as formed from his experience in Britain, depending upon the Anglican Book of Common Prayer. He has British prejudices especially against Catholics, for 'nothing in history can equal the barbarity and cruelty of tortures and murders committed under various pretences in modern slavery, except the annals of the Inquisition and the bloody edicts of Popish massacries'.[4]

Supporting the Emancipation Revolution, Cugoano dramatizes not just his own life, but the lives of early British blacks covered in our narrative, showing how Christianity sustained them. He uses the case of Gronniosaw, the African prince who lived in England, whom he felt was supported by his faith in the face of poverty and distress, claiming he would never have given up his Christianity 'for all the kingdoms of Africa'. He sees John Marrant's faith was sustained by running away to the Carolina backcountry, where he converted the king of the Cherokees to Christianity, a convert whom he met again in a British victory parade in 1780, celebrating the capture of Charleston.

Against those who claimed that West Indies' slaves were better off than the poor in the British Isles, Cugoano asserted that even 'the poorest in England would never change their situation for that of slaves.'[5] He used the Bible's Adam and Eve parable to show that all mankind sprang from one original species, that only one original creator existed, that 'all brethren descended from one father', so that 'it never could be lawful and just for any nation, or people, to oppress and enslave another'. This contradicted the slaveholders' idea that Africans were a degenerate offshoot of an original stock, inherently poor, ignorant and unsociable people.

Cugoano explained that the slave trade was incompatible with Christian government. He ignores individual nature rights, especially the rights of property, which would justify slavery and were so prevalent in the Declaration of Independence. Instead he depended upon Christian government to bring an end to the slave trade. He felt, 'the greatest depredators, warriors, contracting companies of merchants, and rich slaveholders, always endeavor to push themselves on to get power and interest in their favour; that whatever crimes any of them commit they are seldom brought to just punishment.'[6] He believed the British constitution, the finest in the world, was endangered by 'unconstitutional laws' that had reached from Britain to her colonies, which justified the slave trade. Having reaped more profit from the slave trade than any other country, Britain had to repent its wickedness before it was too late 'for God will certainly avenge himself of such heinous transgressors of his law'.

Cugoano wanted an African colony established on the principles of diplomacy with the African kings, education of the natives, and the spread of evangelistic Christianity through translations of the Bible into many languages. He was no friend of the rich merchants who directed the Sierra Leone Company's second effort to settle: 'as all men are allotted in some degree to eat their bread with the sweat of their brow; but it is evil for any people when the rich grind the face of the poor'.[7] After all, capitalistic goals had actually created the slave trade.

Cugoano was well connected to other black evangelists. In putting together his manuscript, he may have had the help of his friend Equiano or his neighbor Ignatius Sancho. Cugoano sent copies to George III, the Prince of Wales and the politician Edmund Burke. Although he would publish a condensed version of the *Evil and Wicked Traffic of the Slavery*, he died only four years later, as the Sierra Leone Company was being chartered. He had written his book as the first Sierra Leone settlement was being organized for the black poor. He predicted the difficulties that prevented both the first and second expeditions from being successful.

You also will remember Cugoano's 1787 emancipation plan had asked that the Royal Navy be sent to Africa 'with faithful men to direct that none should be brought from the coast of Africa without their consent ... and to intercept all merchant ships that were bringing them away'.[8] Here was a long-term role for the navy that had begun before the War for Independence.

The place of navy mariners in black emancipation has received emphasis, so that it is worth reviewing their role. Even before the war, blacks had found the navy to be a place of employment. We have seen that literate freeman Ignatius Sancho wrote a letter advising how to raise 20,000 seamen on a remarkable twelve-day notice. In it he identified the two chief problems in manning the navy faced: the notorious press gangs and the cut back in naval employment in time of peace. Neither problem would be definitively solved, but Sancho hoped that his own family might take advantage of the maritime possibilities offered in Britain.

Sancho and other blacks who joined a Royal Navy ship saw their condition differently from whites. Blacks found the navy to be a refuge from oppression, not just because it offered them freedom, but because the navy provided them with more security than parsimonious merchant vessels. The navy offered them abundant food, healthcare, religious services and even the possibility of a pension.

The navy had supported black aspirations for freedom. Naval officers felt themselves obligated to blacks for volunteering in various fields. As a wartime facilitator, the Royal Navy and its transports would carry blacks to freedom. Emancipation reappeared when Dunmore's Proclamation was supported by a Royal Navy squadron and private ships, attracting black recruits and even extended families and creating the first mass emancipation of slaves in British colonial history. The coordination of navy ships with those of Chesapeake Loyalists would set a precedent for raids that continued until the end of the war and were regarded by the rebels as a very cause of black and white disaffection.

Blacks rarely feared going on board a British ship because their preachers like Daddy Moses or David Margrett emphasized the Old Testament perspective that they were leaving bondage for freedom in a promised land. As slaves placed their highest value upon freedom, their appearance on a navy ship was the the moment when they first became freemen. Upon their arrival at a British-occupied port, the navy would still have to protect them from the efforts of their former masters to re-enslave them.

Rising evangelism in the Royal Navy fostered the humanitarian concerns that moved some officers to become abolitionists, especially at Barham Court. For abolitionists, Britain's post-war debate on slavery's future focused on the diminishing role of the West Indies' plantation economy in the empire. The navy's Lieutenant James Ramsay had published his views on preventing the African slave trade, by offering a tantalizing perspective on riches to be obtained from Africa. He suggested that African freemen on plantations could replace the West Indies' slaves in producing tobacco, sugar, indigo and rice. This would require abolition of the slave trade, as well as the introduction of Christianity and treatment of Africans as capable human beings, curtailing internal African wars, caused by the slave trade. These views showed the way for the navy to fully support the effort to colonize Sierra Leone.

Sailors were not choir boys, but they were increasingly capable of reading the Bible and their officers felt that evangelism improved their discipline and literacy. Reforms led to compassionate Christianity gaining wider presence among their crews. Organizations were established, aimed at serving the lower deck, like the Naval & Military Bible Society, which offered free Bibles, prayer books and tracts to the crew.

The Royal Navy was at its best in the final British evacuation, which was a logistical feat, as the navy was able to carry thousands of black and white Loyalists to widely dispersed parts of the British Empire. It fulfilled the pledge of British officers for freedom and protection of their black allies, providing them with a place in an evacuating ship. This migration would continue, even after the peace was signed, making the evacuation the turning point of the Emancipation Revolution.

It should be evident that abolitionists were never unified, especially in the attempt to colonize Sierra Leone because it tested the ability of evangelists to colonize with free blacks and whites. The first Sierra Leone expedition of 1787 was the result of benevolence towards the black poor and an effort by the government and navy to reward the service of black Loyalists. Granville

Sharp became its leading supporter. In recruiting its colonists, the Black Poor Committee of London even overlooked the miscegenation of many of the couples.

The second colonization effort of 1791 showed a fissure in the abolitionist front, as the white leadership was not willing to accept black evangelism. Critics of the shouting, clapping and dancing found in black evangelistic meetings included conservative abolitionists. William Wilberforce blamed blacks for the difficulties of the second settlement. In Sierra Leone, only Lieutenant John Clarkson gained the widespread confidence of the black settlers. Zachary Macaulay distained the Methodists' 'ridiculous bodily sensations' when worshiping. Lieutenant Philip Beaver was also not above blaming blacks for his failures in Bulama. From the African experience, some abolitionists concluded that slave and free blacks were unsuited for freedom or citizenship.

The split in the Sierra Leone abolitionists between the evangelicals and the businessmen caused a counter revolution. The latter felt that free black colonists should be redirected in Africa to trade, producing the products that had been coming from the West Indies. Their Sierra Leone Company would emphasize the need for the development of trade, along with advancing Anglican Christianity. In contrast, the evangelists had migrated from North America and would be directly involved in the hardships of establishing the colony. Cato Perkins would be the countess's leading preacher and survive the Sierra Leone Company's reprisal against black evangelist leaders, going on to establish the countess's churches in Africa that would serve as a basis for the future empire.

Throughout, I have attempted to contrast the situation of blacks in the British Isles with those in America. In British society, racism was harder to find than in America, chiefly because blacks were so few. Racism in Britain was actually a two-way street. In 1794, former slave Boston King, now a Wesleyan Methodist preacher, went to England where he commented on his treatment by the English, admitting to being prejudiced against whites because they were better educated than he. What he found was:

> more cordial love to the White People than I had ever experienced before. In the former part of my life I had suffered greatly from the cruelty and injustice of the Whites, which induced me to look upon them … as our enemies: And even after the Lord had manifested his forgiving mercy to me, I still felt at times an uneasy distrust and shyness toward them: but on that day the Lord removed all my prejudices.[9]

He was no longer prejudiced against them. In contrast, the opposition in the new United States to the Emancipation Revolution would continue. The fact that black slaves were not mentioned in the Declaration of Independence, when they numbered 20 per cent of the population, shows that they were not regarded as citizens of the new republic. Drafted four years after the war, the United States Constitution did recognize slaves, but aimed to continue the status quo. As an eminent American historian has explained, the constitution 'guaranteed state autonomy within a federal system, Southern slaveholders could count on disproportionate national power as a result of slave representation, federal assistance in the recovery of fugitive slaves or the suppression of insurrections, and interference in matters relating to race and labor'.[10] This is what the War for Independence had ultimately wrought.

Lastly, we have placed the Emancipation Revolution's participants against their late eighteenth-century background, but in concluding we must look at the revolution's legacy. In the words of the once slave trader John Newton, we find a lasting remembrance of it. In 1772, he began writing this poetry which would be published during the war in a collection of hymns.

> Amazing grace how sweet the sound
> That save'd a wretch like me
> I once was lost, but now I'm found
> Was blind but now I see
> 'Twas grace that taught my heart to fear
> And grace my fears relieved
> How precious did that grace appear
> The hour I first believed
> Through many dangers, toils, and snares
> I have already come
> This grace that brought me safe thus far
> And grace will lead me home
> When we've been here ten thousand years
> Bright, shining as the sun
> We've no less days to sing God's praise
> Than when we first begun

This hymn describes Newton's personal conversion to Anglicanism. Despite being raised a Christian, he had abandoned the faith of his childhood until March 10, 1748, when he was steering his ship through a fierce thunderstorm and he prayed to God. Having survived the storm, he attributed his safety to the grace of God. This event started his conversion and led to him eventually becoming an Anglican clergyman and abolitionist. The hymn offers the tale of a defiant man who manages again and again to escape danger, disease, abuse and death, only to revert to 'struggles between sin and conscience'.[11] He was a wretch. He was lost. He was blind in sin. It describes the joy of a soul uplifted from despair to salvation through the gift of grace. Here is the fitting legacy of the Emancipation Revolution.

Notes

Abbreviations

CVSP   *Calendar of Virginia State Papers and Other Manuscripts*. Palmer et al., eds., Richmond, 1875–1893, vols. 1–3

DCB   *Dictionary of Canadian Biography*, University of Toronto/Université Laval, 1959– to date, 15 vols.

HP   Hamond Naval Papers, 1766–1825, University of Virginia Library, Charlottesville, VA., Microfilm edition

LI   The On-Line Institute for Advanced Loyalist Studies

MA   William Brown et al., eds., *Archives of Maryland*. Baltimore, 1883–to date 864 vols.

NDAR   *Naval Documents of the American Revolution*, eds., William Bell Clark et al., Washington, DC, 1964–to date, 12 vols.

NMM   Caird Library, National Maritime Museum, Greenwich, London

RB   Red Books, 1748–1827, 33 Volumes. The Red Books are described and partially indexed in *Calendar of Maryland State Papers*. Annapolis, Md.

TNA   The National Archives, Kew, London

Preface

1. Davis, David Brion, 'American Slavery and the American Revolution', *Slavery and Freedom in the Age of the American Revolution*, Berlin, Ira and Hoffman, Ronald, eds. Urbana, Ill., 1986, 280; Brown, Christopher, *Moral Capital, Foundations of British Abolitionism*, Chapel Hill, NC, 2006, 182–5.
2. Carretta, Vincent, 'Revisiting Olaudah Equiano, or Gustavus Vassa', Gerzina, Gretchen, *Britain's Black Past*, Liverpool, 2020, 45–62.
3. Donoghue, John, *An Atlantic History of the English Revolution*, Chicago, 2013.

Introduction

1. For the sake of consistency I have chosen to use evangelism, although at times it refers to evangelicalism. The words are often used interchangeably, but it is my understanding that evangelicals are those who bear witness to having a born-again experience, while evangelists spread this gospel as missionaries to all regardless of race.

2. Sancho, Ignatius, *Letters of the Late Ignatius Sancho, An African, in Two Volumes, to which are prefixed, Memoirs of his Life*, London 1782, Carretta, ed., *Unchained Voices*, Lexington, Ky., 1996, 86.

3. Quarles, Benjamin, *The Negro in the American Revolution*, New York, 1961; Pybus, Cassandra, *Epic Journeys of Freedom*. Boston, 2006.

4. Quarles, 152.

5. Rediker, Marcus, *Between the Devil and the Deep Blue Sea*, New York, 1989; Hutchinson, John, *Press Gang, Afloat and Ashore*, Middletown, Del., 2010, 1–44, 304; Christopher, Emma, *Slave Ship Sailors and Their Captive Cargoes, 1730–1807*, New York, 2006.

6. Hawes, James, *The Shortest History of England*, Exeter, UK, 2020, 148.

7. Bailyn, Bernard, *The Ideological Origins of the American Revolution*, Cambridge, Mass., 1967, 246.

Chapter 1

1. Klein, Herbert, *The Middle Passage*, Princeton, NJ, 1978; Walvin, James, *Black Ivory, A History of British Slavery*, Washington, DC, 1994, 1–66; Tibbles, Anthony, *Liverpool and the Slave Trade*, Liverpool, 2018, 1–10.

2. Cugoano, Quobna, *Thoughts and sentiments on the Evil and Wicked Traffic of Slavery and Commerce of the Human Species*, London, 1787, Carretta, *Unchained Voices*, 146.

3. Crane, Elaine, *A Dependent People, Newport, Rhode Island in the Revolutionary Era*, New York, 1992, 16–46, 69–75.

4. Olwell, Robert, *Masters, Slaves and Subjects*, Ithaca, NY, 1998, 28, 32, 144, 167, 222–3; Littlefield, Daniel, *Rice and Slaves, Ethnicity and the Slave Trade in Colonial South Carolina*, Urbana, Ill., 1981, 25–55.

5. Tibbles, 11–78; Behrendt, Stephen, 'Human Capital in the British Slave Trade', *Liverpool and Transatlantic Slavery*, Richardson, David, Schwarz, Suzanne, Tibbles, eds., Liverpool, 2007, 66–97.

6. Walsh, Lorena, 'Liverpool's Slave Trade to the Colonial Chesapeake: Slaving on the Periphery', *Liverpool and Transatlantic Slavery*, 102–7, 111–12.

7. Elder, Melinda, Slavery and the North of England, Open University, www.open.edu › openlearn › history › heritage, accessed December 8, 2022; Routledge, Alan, *Whitehaven Harbour through Time*, Gloucestershire, 2012, 4–1; Devine, T.M., *Scotland's Empire 1600-1815*, London, 2004, 76–7.

8. Devine, 244–5.

9. Newton, John, *Memoirs of the Rev. John Newton*, London, 1813, 10–33.

10. Ibid., 34–113.

11. Newton, *Memoirs*, 114–126 and *The Journal of a Slave trader*, 1750–1754, Martin, Bernard and Spurrell, Mark, eds., London, 1962, x–xi.

12. Field, Edward, *Esek Hopkins, Commander-in-Chief of the Continental Navy During the American Revolution, 1775 to 1778*. Providence, RI, 1898.

13. Morison, Samuel, *John Paul Jones: A Sailor's Biography, Boston*, 1959, 21–3.

14. Rodger, N.A.M., *Wooden World, An Anatomy of the Georgian Navy*, New York, 1996, 268–9.

15. Christopher, 35–6, 42–4, 165–187.

16. Ibid., 143–4, 181–4, 205–7.
17. Ibid., 51–90.

Chapter 2

1. Morgan, Philip, *Slave Counterpoint.* Chapel Hill, NC, 1998, 35–57.
2. Ibid., 15–16.
3. Morgan, Philip, *Slave Counterpoint*, 80, 86, 399, 402–16, 523; Walsh, Lorena, *Motives of Honor Pleasure & Profit,* Chapel Hill, 2010, 203–4.
4. Morgan, Philip, *Slave Counterpoint*, 45–58; Walsh, 27, 416.
5. Morgan, Philip, *Slave Counterpoint*, 104–124; Russo, Jean and Elliott, *Planting an Empire, the early Chesapeake in British North America*, Baltimore, 2012, 164–71.
6. Gikandi, Simon, *Slavery and the Culture of Taste*, Princeton, NJ, 2011, 165–74; Pleasants, J. Hall, 'Justus Englehardt Kuhn, an Early Eighteenth-Century Maryland Portrait painter', *Proceedings of the American Antiquarian Society*, 46: 243–80. Kuhn's slave is thought to be the first representation in American painting of an African American subject. The angelic portrayal of young Darnall does not square with his adult life. Appointed Naval Officer of the Patuxent customs district in 1755, six years later he was accused of embezzling nearly £1,000 and he fled to Europe before he could be tried.
7. Wells, Robert, *The Population of the British Colonies in America before 1776*, Princeton, NJ, 1975, 146–51.
8. Wells, 97–107, 114–115, 123–33; Corbett, Theodore, *A Clash of Cultures on the Warpath of Nations, The Colonial Wars in the Hudson-Champlain Valley*, Fleischmanns, N.Y., 2002, 113–119, 135–8; Gerlach, Don, *Proud Patriot, Philip Schuyler and the War of Independence 1775–1783,* Syracuse, N.Y., 1987, 526.
9. Wells, 194–207.
10. Bernhard, Virginia, *Slaves and Slaveholders in Bermuda, 1616–1782*, Columbia, Mo., 1999, 148–90. 271–2.
11. Middleton, Arthur, *Tobacco Coast, A Maritime History of Chesapeake Bay in the Colonial Era,* Baltimore, 1984, 287–309, quote on 287.
12. Dawson, Kevin, *Undercurrents of Power, Aquatic Culture in the African Diaspora*, Philadelphia, 2018, 164–90.
13. Foy, Charles, 'Possibilities and Limits of Freedom: Maritime Fugitives in British North America, ca. 1713–1783', *Gender, Race, Ethnicity and Power in Maritime America*, Mystic, Ct., 2008, 43–54; Morgan, Philip, *Slave Counterpoint*, 236–7; Nash, Gary, *The Urban Crucible, Social Change, Political Consciousness and the Origins of the American Revolution*, Cambridge, Mass., 1979.
14. Morgan, Philip, *Slave Counterpoint*, 238.
15. Harris, Lynn, Patroons & Periaguas, *Enslaved Watermen and Watercraft of the Lowcountry*, Columbia, SC, 2014, 60; Olwell, 221–6.

Chapter 3

1. Morgan, Philip, *Slave Counterpoint*, quote on 386; Walsh, *Motives for Honor*, 2–6, 47.
2. Lepore, Jill, *New York Burning*, New York, 2005, 5–63; McManus, Edgar, *A History of Negro Slavery in New York*, Syracuse, NY, 1966, 121–40.

3. Hoffer, Peter, *Cry Liberty, The Great Stono River Slave Rebellion of 1739*, New York, 2012; *Stono, Documenting and Interpreting a Southern Slave Revolt*, Smith, Mark, ed., Columbia, SC, 2005.

4. Wood, Peter, *Black Majority, Negros in Colonial South Carolina*, New York, 1974, 308–26.

5. Diouf, Sylviane, *Slavery's Exiles, The Story of the American Maroons*, New York, 2016, 29–30.

6. Ibid., 33–8.

7. Wroten, William, *Assateague*, 1972, 54–5; *Pennsylvania Gazette*, December 16, 1746 in Charles, Joan, *Mid-Atlantic Shipwreck Accounts to 1899*, Hampton, VA., 1997, 18.

8. Mullin, Gerald, *Flight and Rebellion, Slave Resistance in Eighteenth-Century Virginia*, New York, 1972, 105–114, 188–9.

9. Morgan, Philip, *Slave Counterpoint*, 389–91.

10. Deal, Douglas, 'A Constricted World, Free Blacks on Virginia's Eastern Shore, 1680–1750', *Colonial Chesapeake Society*, Carr, Lois, Morgan, Philip, Russo, eds., Chapel Hill, NC, 1988, 275–305.

11. Anderson, Fred, *Crucible of War, The Seven Years' War and the Fate of Empire in British North America, 1754–1766*, New York, 2000, 160, 204.

12. 'An Act for better Ordering', May, 1740, Smith, Mark, 20–7; Wood, 324.

13. Hadden, Sally, *Slave Revolts, Law and Violence in Virginia and the Carolinas*, Cambridge, Mass., 2001, 6–40.

14. Lepore, 58–9.

15. Ibid., 56–7.

16. Ibid., 548–59.

17. Genovese, Eugene, *Roll, Jordan, Roll: The World the Slaveholders Made*, New York, 1974, 40; Schwarz, Philip, *Slave Laws in Virginia*, Athens, Ga., 1996, 9–10, 102, 125.

18. Oldmixon, John, *The British Empire in America*, London, 1741, Kelley edition, New York, 1969, 1:376–8; Dallas, R.C., *The History of the Maroons*, London, 1968, 1:35, 96–8.

19. Oldmixon, 1: 380–1; Morgan, Philip, *Slave Counterpoint*, 450–1; Chopra, Ruma, Almost Home, 18–23.

20. Chopra, *Almost Home*, 24–38.

21. Dallas, 1: 100–2.

22. Chopra, *Almost Home*, 39–57.

23. Diouf, 33–8.

Chapter 4

1. Morgan, Philip, 649–52; Patent, Anthony, *Foul Means: The Formation of a Slave Society in Virginia, 1660–1740*, Chapel Hill, NC, 2003, chap. 8; Walvin, 187–9; Olwell, 117–24, 130–3; Chater, Kathleen, *Untold Histories, Black people in England and Wales during the period of the British Slave Trade*, Manchester, 2009, 55–63, 127–8, 176–82.

2. The Fifteen Articles of the Countess of Huntingdon's Connection, 1790, www.british-history.ac.uk › vol 11, accessed January 6, 2023.

3. Linder, Suzanne, *Anglican Churches in Colonial South Carolina*, Charleston, 2000, 73–4.

4. Middleton, 'Thomas Bray' Project Canterbury; *Religious Philanthropy and Colonial Slavery, The American Correspondence of the Associates of Dr. Bray, 1717-1777*, Van Horne, John, ed., Urbana, Ill., 1985, 1–51; Nelson, John, *A Blessed Company, Parishes, and Parishioners in Anglican Virginia, 1690-1776*, Chapel Hill, NC, 2001, 265–70.

5. Bacon, Thomas, *Two Sermons Preached to a Congregation of Black Slaves, at the Parish Church of S.P. in the Province of Maryland. By an American Pastor*, London, 1749, 45–9.

6. Lepore, 184–6.

7. Kidd, Thomas. *George Whitefield: America's Spiritual Founding Father*, New Haven, 2014; Noll, Mark, *The Rise of Evangelicalism*, Downers Grove, Ill., 2003, 73–116; for a view of the Great Awakening essentially without George Whitefield or Methodists see Bonami, Patricia, *Under the Cope of Heaven*, New York, 1986, 131–60.

8. Gronniosaw, James Albert Ukawsaw, *A Narrative of the Most Remarkable Particulars in the life of James Albert Ukawsaw Gronniosaw*, Bath, 1772; Carretta, *Unchained Voices*, 36–43.

9. Ibid., 44–6.

10. Andrews, Dee, *The Methodists and Revolutionary America, 1760–1800*, Princeton, N.J, 2000, 16–9.

11. Andrews, 32–8, 40–5; Welch, Edwin, *Spiritual Pilgrim*, Cardiff, Wales, 2013.

12. Andrews, 125.

13. Welch, 142–3.

14. Harris, J. William, *The Hanging of Thomas Jeremiah, A Free Black Man's Encounter with Liberty*, New Haven, 2009, 73–7. Bethesda was started as an orphanage by Whitefield, but was given to the Countess as an academy at his death.

15. Harris, 77–9; Morgan, Philip, 424–5, 649–50; Brown, Richard, *The South Carolina Regulators*, Cambridge, Mass., 1963, 19–20.

16. Marrant, John, *A Narrative of the Lord's wonderful dealings with John Marrant*, London, 1785, Carretta, *Unchained Voices*, 110–128. According to Carretta, no corroborating evidence exists of Marrant's presence at the Siege of Charleston or the Battle of Dogger Bank: Carretta, Ibid, 131.

17. Pybus, 41–2, 215.

18. Middleton, *Anglican Maryland 1692–1792*, Virginia Beach, VA. 1992, 20–1, 57, 73–4, 101.

19. Bebbington, D.W., *Evangelicalism in Modern Britain: A History from 1730 to the 1980s*, London, 1989.

20. Tennant, Bob, 'Sentiment, Politics, and Empire: A Study of Beilby Porteus's Antislavery Sermon', in *Discourses of Slavery and Abolition: Britain and its Colonies, 1760–1838*, Brycchan, Carey, Markman, Ellis, and Salih, Sara, eds., Basingstoke, 2004, 158–74.

21. Wheatley, Phillis, *An Elegiac Poem, on the Death of ... George Whitefield*, Boston, 1770, Carretta, 59–61; Grimstead, David, 'Anglo-American Racism and Phililis Wheatley's "Sable Vail", "Length'ned Chain", and "Knitted Heart".' *Women in the Age of the American Revolution*, Hoffman, Ronald and Albert, Peter, eds. Charlottesville,

Va., 1989, 338–444; Carretta, *Phillis Wheatley, Biography of a Genius in Bondage*, Athens, Ga., 2011, 148–50

22. Davis, *The Problem of Slavery in Western Culture*, New York, 1988, 388; Morgan, Philip, 651–7.

Chapter 5

1. Chater, Kathleen, *Untold Histories*, 25–30.
2. Milton, Giles, *White Gold: The Extraordinary Story of Thomas Pellow and North Africa's One Million European Slaves*, London, 2004, 13–37, 58–61, 113.
3. Tobin, Beth, *Picturing Imperial Power*. Durham, NC, 1999, 27–55; Proctor, Alice, *The Whole Picture*, London, 2020, 112–16.
4. Mullen, Stephen, Mundell, Nelson, Newman, Simon, 'Black Runaways in Eighteenth-Century Britain', *Britain's Black Past*, Gerzina, Gretchen, ed., Liverpool, 2020, 81–98.
5. Foy, 'The Royal Navy's Employment of Black Mariners and Maritime Workers, 1754–1783', *International Maritime History Journal*, 28:1, 12–13; Rodger, The Command of the Ocean, A Naval History of Britain, 1649–1815, London, 2004, 396.
6. Bundock, Michael, *The Fortunes of Francis Barber*. New Haven, Ct., 2015, 7–77.
7. Lincoln, Margarette, *Trading in War, London's Maritime World in the Age of Cook and Nelson*, New Haven, Ct., 2018, 10–36, 48–9; Chater, 63–6.
8. Cozens, Kenneth and Morris, Derek, 'The Shadwell Waterfront in the Eighteenth Century', *Mariner's Mirror*, 99:1, 86–91.
9. Horn, James, *Adapting to a New World*, Capel Hill, N. C, 1994, 25, 39, 107; Menard, Russell, 'Immigration to the Chesapeake Colonies in the Seventeenth Century: A Review Essay', *Maryland Historical Magazine*, 68: 323–9; The date of Jane Randolph Jefferson's birth is given between 1718 and 1721 depending upon interpretation of the family bible or her baptism in St Paul's, Shadwell parish. Thomas Jefferson seems to have been embarrassed by his mother's origin on the Thames, where her modest dowry was apparently never paid to his father. Jefferson's vast correspondence scarcely mentioned her. Unlike Thomas, Jane Randolph Jefferson was a frugal and able manager of the family finances. Brodie, Fawn, Thomas Jefferson: *An Intimate History*, New York, 1974, 40–6; Kern, Susan, *The Jeffersons at Shadwell*, New Haven, Ct. 2010, 43–7.
10. Annual Register, September 6, 1763, Today in London riotous history, https://pasttenseblog.wordpress.com › 2021/09/06, accessed December 1, 2022.
11. Lincoln, 25–33.
12. Ibid., 3–4, 26, 52, 61, 70, 82.
13. Pybus, 86,103; Lincoln, 95.
14. Chater, *Untold Histories*, 55–63, 181–2.
15. Lincoln, 2–3, 15–18, 33.
16. Chater, *Untold Histories*, 55; Morris, Dereck, *Whitechapel 1600-1800*, Brentwood, Essex, 2011, 99–105; Morris, *Mile End Old Town 1740–1780*, Brentwood, Essex, 2002, 55–7.
17. *The Orthodox Churchman's Magazine*, January 11, 1802, 30; Chater, *Untold Histories*, 50–53, 178, Morris, *Mile End Old Town*, London, 2002, 2, 23, 57, 64, 68, 71–2, 91.

18. Braidwood, Stephen, *Black Poor and White Philanthropists, London's Blacks and the Foundation of the Sierra Leone Settlement 1786–1791*, Liverpool, 1994, 23–4.
19. Sharp, Granville, *Free English Territory in AFRICA*, London, 1790, 9–10.

Chapter 6

1. Wise, Steven, T*hough the Heavens May Fall, The Landmark Trial the Led to the End of Human Slavery*, Cambridge, Mass., 2005, 111–144.
2. Ibid., 200.
3. Ibid., 207–8.
4. Gerzina, Gretchen, 'The Georgian Life and Modern Afterlife of Dido Elizabeth Belle', Gerzina, 161–78.
5. Livesay, Daniel, *Children of Uncertain Fortune, Mixed-Race Jamaicans in Britain and the Atlantic Family, 1733–1833*, Chapel Hill, 2018; Karras, Alan, *Sojourners in the Sun, Scottish Migrants in Jamaica and the Chesapeake, 1740–1800*, Ithaca, NY, 1992, 46–80; Devine, 225–6.
6. Daniel Defoe described the hospital in the 1720s: A *Tour thro' the Whole Island of Great Britain*, Dutton edition, New York, 1962, 2: 250–1; Wright, Peter, *Life on the Tyne, Water Trades on the Lower River Tyne in the Seventeenth and Eighteenth Centuries, a Reappraisal*, New York, 2016, 3, 50–67, 76, 145; *The Journal of John Wesley*, November 14–28, 1742, Curnock, Nehemiah, ed., New York, 1963, 136–7.
7. Taylor, James, *Jonas Hanway, Founder of the Marine Society*, London, 1985, 139.
8. Ibid, 85–127.
9. Ibid., 70–4, 95–101, 152–8.
10. Ibid., 70–4.
11. Ibid., 8, 69–70, 131.
12. Ibid., 123–4, 131–2.
13. Grell, Ole Peter, and Israel, Jonathan Irvine, *From Persecution To Toleration: The Glorious Revolution and Religion in England*, New York, 1991.
14. Andrews, 13–9, 62–3.
15. Ibid., 15–7, 164–5.
16. *The Journal of John Wesley*, Curnock, 371, 427; Morris, *Mile End Old Town*, 56–7; Bargar, R.D., *Lord Dartmouth and the American Revolution*, Columbia, SC, 1965, 13–14.
17. Hoffman, Ronald, *Princes of Ireland, Planters of Maryland*, Chapel Hill, 2000, 150–8.
18. Bluet, Thomas, *Some Memoirs of the Life of Job ...*, London, 1734.

Chapter 7

1. Sancho, Carretta, *Unchained Voices*, 81; White, Jerry, *A Great and Monstrous Thing, London in the Eighteenth Century*, Cambridge, Mass., 2013, 125–37.
2. Rodger, *Command of the Ocean*, 395–7.
3. Williams, Gomer, *History of the Liverpool Privateers and Letters of Marque*, Montreal and Kingston, 2004, 555–60.

4. Rodger, *Wooden World*, 109, 173, 180–7.
5. Ibid., 145–56.
6. Costello, Ray, *Black Salt, Seafarers of African Descent on British Ships*, Liverpool, 2012.
7. Hammon, *Briton, Narrative of the Uncommon Sufferings, and Suprizing Deliverance of Briton*; Hammon, *A Negro Man,* Boston, 1760; Carretta, *Unchained Voices*, 20–4.
8. Hammon, 24; Black Sailors in the British Navy, Old Royal Naval College, Greenwich, https://ornc.org/black-sailors-british-navy, accessed Dec. 10, 2022.
9. Hamond to Hans Stanley, Aug. 5, 1776, NDAR 5:1119; Foy, 'Compelled to Row: Blacks on Royal Navy Galleys During the American Revolution', *Journal of the American Revolution Annual Volume 2019*, Yardley, Pa., 2019.
10. Bundock, 78–97.
11. Memorial of Benjamin Whitecuff of New York, LI, accessed June 1, 2023; Pybus, 27–30, 79, 218; Jasanoff, Maya, *Liberty's Exiles, American Loyalists in the Revolutionary World*, New York, 2011, 128, 133.
12. McCalman, Iain, 'Introduction', in Wedderburn, Robert, *The Horrors of Slavery*, London, 1824, McCalman, ed., Princeton, NJ, 2017, 3–6, 44–61.
13. Rodger, *Wooden World*, 151; Marcus, G.J., *Heart of Oak*, New York, 1975, 104–11. James Wedderburn's Scottish home, Inveresk Lodge, still exists near Edinburgh and the garden is property of the National Trust for Scotland.
14. Equiano, Olaudah, *The Interesting Narrative of the Life of Olaudah Equiano or Gustavus Vassa, the African*, London, 1794; Carretta, *Unchained Voices*, 211–3.
15. O'Riordan, Christopher, *The Thames Watermen in the Century of Revolution*, 1992. np; Emsley, Clive, *British Society and the French Wars 1793–1815*, London, 1979, 103.
16. Lincoln, 18, 42, 130, 165.
17. Williams, 238; Conway, Stephen, *The American Revolutionary War*, London, 2013, 152.
18. Governor Sharpe to Alexander Colvill, January 28, 1758, MA, 9: 137.
19. Parramore, Thomas, Bogger, Tommy, Stewart, Peter, *Norfolk, The First Four Centuries.* Charlottesville, VA, 2000, 78; Mullin, 105, 119; Wertenbaker, Thomas, and Schlegel, Marvin, *Norfolk Historical Southern Port*, Durham, NC, 1962, 17–18.
20. Matthew Squire to Lord Dunmore, September 18 1775; Journal of HM *Otter*, September 24, 1775, Condemnation Proceedings against the Brigantine Betsy, June 11, 1776, NDAR, 2:140, 195, 5:477.
21. Lord Dunmore to Lord Germain, June 26, 1776, Ibid., 5:342–3.
22. Rediker, *Between the Devil and the Deep Blue Sea*; Hutchinson, John, *Press Gang, Afloat and Ashore*. Middletown, Del., 2010, 1–44, 304.
23. Massachusetts Council, Warrant to Impress Seamen, July 3, 1779; Kevitt, Chester, ed., *General Solomon Lovell and the Penobscot Expedition,* Weymouth, Mass., 1976, 68–9; Buker, George, *The Penobscot Expedition,* Lanham, Md., 2002, 23; Gilbert, Alan, *Black Patriots and Loyalists*, Chicago, 2012, 149.

Chapter 8

1. Marcus, 118–20; Wedderburn, *The Axe laid to the Root* No. 2 [1817], McCalman, ed., 90.
2. Sancho, Carretta, *Unchained Voices*, 80.

3. Rodger, *Wooden World*, 161; Carretta, 'Naval records and Eighteenth-Century Black Biography, with Particular Reference to the Case of O Equiano (Gustavus Vassa)', *Journal of Maritime Research*, 5:1.
4. Rodger, *Wooden World*, 87–98.
5. Rodger, *Insatiable Earl, A Life of John Montagu, 4th Earl of Sandwich*, New York, 1993, 228–9; Syrett, David, *Shipping and the American War 1775–1783*, London, 1970, 9–10.
6. Hamond to Sick & Hurt Board, November 25, 1781, HP, 8: 11–13, 9: 189–91.
7. Rodger, *Wooden World*, 23–6; Blake, Richard, *Evangelicals in the Royal Navy 1775–1815*, Woodbridge, UK, 2008, 20–6, 74–81.
8. Merwe, Pieter van der, *A Refuge for All: A Short History of Greenwich Hospital*. Greenwich, 2010, 4–15; Jennings, Charles, *Greenwich, the Place Where Days Begin and End*. London, 1999, 15–29.
9. Individual Stories of Black Greenwich Pensioners, Black Greenwich Pensioners, Life in Greenwich Hospital, www. greenwichtime.com, accessed November 22, 2022.
10. Rodger, *Wooden World*, 274–88.
11. Hamilton, Douglas, 'A most active, enterprising officer: Captain John Perkins, the Royal Navy and the boundaries of slavery and liberty in the Caribbean', *Slavery and Abolition, A Journal of Slave and Post-Slave Studies*, 39: 2018, 80–100.
12. Hamilton, Douglas, 'A most active, enterprising officer: Captain John Perkins, the Royal Navy and the boundaries of slavery and liberty in the Caribbean'; John Perkins – More than Nelson, https://morethannelson.com › Biographies, accessed December 13, 2022.
13. Ibid.
14. Ibid.
15. Ibid.
16. Ibid.

Chapter 9

1. Rodger, *Command of the Ocean*, 317–18; Bernhard, 275.
2. Neff, Emily and Pressly, William, *John Singleton Copley in England*, London, 1995, 35–6, 80–5, 102–5. American-born artist John Singleton Copley painted and displayed his work in England during the War for Independence. He included blacks in heroic British military action such as *The Death of Major Peirson*. He carefully hid his political views on the war.
3. Rodger, *Wooden World*, 161.
4. Michael Henry Pascal – Equiano's World, https://equianosworld.org › associates-slavery, accessed November 25, 2022; Carretta, *Equiano the African, Biography of a Self-Made Man*, Athens, Ga., 2022.
5. Equiano, Carretta, *Unchained Voices*, 208–9.
6. Ibid., 210.
7. Equiano, *The Interesting Narrative of the life*. Norwich, 1794; Gates, Henry Lewis, Andrews, William, eds., *Pioneers of the Black Atlantic*, Washington, DC, 1998, 239–42, quote on 241.
8. Equiano, Carretta, *Unchained Voices*, 210–12.

9. Michael Henry Pascal, accessed November 25, 2002; Rodger, *Wooden World*, 268–9.
10. Michael Henry Pascal, accessed November 25, 2002.
11. Equiano, Carretta, *Unchained Voices*, 213.
12. Ibid., 214–17.
13. Ibid., 217.
14. Ibid., 218–49.
15. Ibid., 252, 257–8.
16. Rodger, *Wooden World*, 160–1.

Chapter 10

1. Pybus, *Epic Journeys*, 30, 78, 218.
2. James Howe, September 1, 1781, LI, accessed May 10, 2023; Quarles, 87–90; Rodger, *Wooden World*, 48–9.
3. Pybus, *Epic Journeys*, 31, 69, 212.
4. Morriss, Roger, *The Royal Dockyards during the Revolutionary and Napoleonic Wars*, Leicester, UK, 1983, 1–9.
5. Gwyn, Julian, *Ashore and Afloat: The British Navy and the Halifax Naval Yard before 1820*. Ottawa, 2004, 24–5, 101–121.
6. Foy, 'The Royal Navy's employment', 28: 6–35.
7. Baugh, Daniel, ed., *Naval Administration 1715–1750*, London, 1977, 326–32.
8. Charles Knowles to Navy Board, May 8, 1748, Navy Board to Admiralty Secretary, March 19, 1749/50; Ibid., 390, 398–400.
9. Charles Stewart to Navy Board, November 11, 1729; Ibid., 351; Oldmixon, 1: 378.
10. Charles Stewart to Admiralty Secretary, January 9, 1731/2; Navy Board to Admiralty Secretary, March 11, 1731/2, Baugh, 359–61.
11. Charles Stewart to Admiralty Secretary, January 9, 1731/2; Ibid., 359–60.
12. Charles Knowles to Admiralty Secretary, March 6, 1749/50; Navy Board to Admiralty Secretary, March 19, 1749/50; Ibid., 396, 398–9.
13. Charles Knowles to Admiralty Secretary, March 17, 1743/4; Ibid., 380.
14. Raymond, 25.
15. Rodger, *Wooden World*, 28, 55, 245.
16. Buckley, Roger, *The British Army in the West Indies: Society and the Military in the Revolutionary Age*, Gainesville, Fla., 1998, 125.
17. Christopher, 165–74.

Chapter 11

1. Quarles, 19–22; Selby, John, *The Revolution in Virginia 1775–1783*, Williamsburg, VA., 1989, 62–6. On Dunmore's life see David, James, *Dunmore's New World*, Charlottesville, VA., 2013, 94–130.
2. Samuel Graves to Hamond, December 25, 1775; Marriot Arbuthnot to Hamond, January 5, 1776; Hamond to Naval Captains in Virginia, February 9, 1776; Lord Dunmore to Lord Dartmouth, February 13, 1776; Lord Dunmore to Lord George Germain, June 26, 1776, NDAR, 3:235–6, 3:625; 5:756–8, 3: 1188, 1266; Selby, 66–7.

3. Members of the Virginia Committee of Safety to the Maryland Convention, December 29, 1775, *The Letters and Papers of Edmund Pendleton*, David Mays, ed., Charlottesville, VA, 1967, 1: 127–8, 145; Scharf, J. Thomas, *History of Delaware*, 1609–1888. Ann Arbor, Mich., 1972, 1:231, 2: 1335; Reese, George, 'The Court of Vice-Admiralty in Virginia and some Cases of 1770–1775', *The Virginia Magazine of History and Biography,* 88:320; the most detailed account of Dunmore's fleet before the arrival of the *Roebuck* is Long, C. Thomas, 'Britain's Green Water Navy in the Revolutionary Chesapeake: Long-Range Asymmetric Warfare in the Littoral', *International Journal of Navy History*, 8:2. The burning of Norfolk by the rebels was hidden for centuries by Virginia authorities, see Selby, 83–4.

4. Lord Dunmore to Lord Dartmouth, February 13, 1776, NDAR, 3: 1188, 1266; Selby, 85–6.

5. Hamond to Lord Dunmore, March 14, 1776; Hamond to Henry Clinton, May 4, 1776, *Maryland Gazette*, March 14, 1776, *Purdie's Virginia Gazette*, March 22, 1776, NDAR, 4: 343, 1408, 5: 1312–14.

6. Master's Log of *Mercury*, July 10, 1775, NDAR, 1: 855 and 2:42.

7. Hamond to Lord Dunmore, March 14, 1776; Hamond to Henry Clinton, May 4, 1776, Journal of *Roebuck*, May 7, 1776, NDAR, 4: 343, 1408, 5: 129, 174.

8. Hamond to Hans Stanley, August 5, 1776, HP, 1; Journal of *Roebuck*, May 22–7, 1776, Hamond to Matthew Squire, May 28, 1776, NDAR, 5:129, 223, 278, 289–90, 321–3; Edward Pendleton to Matthew Tilghman, May 26, 1776, MA, 11:446; www.blackloyalist.info/john-willoughby/, accessed January 15, 2018.

9. Thomas Hayward to Maryland Convention, June 25, 1776, MA, 16:464; Hamond to Henry Bellew, June 10, 1776, Narrative of Andrew Snape Hamond, June 1 to June 30, 1776, NDAR, 5: 462,742, 839; Scharf, 1:231.

10. Wrike, Peter, *Gwynn's Island, Virginia, During the Revolution*, Gwynn's Island, VA., 1995, 31–4, 115–19; Hamond Narrative, May 16–May 31, 1776; Hamond to George Montague, August 6, 1776; Hamond to Molyneux Shuldham, November 28, 1776; Journal of the Otter, July 8, 1776, NDAR, 5: 321–3, 669–70; 6: 66–7, 88–9, 7: 319; Journal and Correspondence of the Maryland Council of Safety, July 10, 1776, MA, 12:24.

11. Journal of *Fowey*, June 22, 1776; Dunmore Lord Germain, June 26, 1776; Narrative of Andrew Hamond, June 1–30, 1776, NDAR, 5: 686–8, 757–8, 839–41.

12. Lord Dunmore to Lord Germain, June 26, 1776, Ibid., 5:757–8.

13. Committee of Northampton County, Virginia to The President of the Congress at Philadelphia, November 25, 1775, *Revolutionary Virginia, The Road to Independence*, eds. Scribner, Robert and Tarter, Brent, Charlottesville, VA., 1978, 4: 467–9, quote on 468.

14. Narrative of Andrew Hamond, June 1–June 30, 1776; Hamond to Patrick Tonyn, June 9, 1776; Hamond to John Wright, June 10, 1776; Journal of *Fowey*, June 22, 1776, NDAR, 5: 839–41, 441–2, 463, 686–8; Journal and Correspondence of the Maryland Council of Safety, July 10, 1776, MA, 12:24; Hartley, Nick, *The Prince of Privateers, Bridger Goodrich and his Family in America, Bermuda and Britain 1775–1825*, London, 2012, 37–9.

15. Hamond to Hans Stanley, August 5, 1776, HP, 1; Jeremiah Jordan to Maryland Council of Safety, July 17, 1776, NDAR 5:1119; Journal and Correspondence of the Maryland Council of Safety, Cunningham's Examination, July 18, 1776, MA, 12:73; 'Compelled

to Row: Blacks on Royal Navy Galleys During the American Revolution', The Keep, 11/14/17, 3.

16. Lord Dunmore to Lord Germain, July 31, 1776; NDAR 6: 1324–5; Selby, 126.

17. Hammond to Matthew Squire, July 31, 1776; Hamond Narrative, August 6, 1776. NDAR, 4: 340–1, 457–8, 5:1315 and 6:174. *The Letters and Papers of Edmund Pendleton*, 1:160; Myron Smith and John Earle give several pages to this encounter, stating that it 'ranks with the Battle of the Barges as the best known in Maryland State Naval History', and yet the ships never met: Eller, Ernst, ed., *Chesapeake Bay in the American Revolution*, Centerville, Md., 1981, 215–23.

18. Hamond to Matthew Squire, July 31, 1776; Hamond Narrative, August 6, 1776, NDAR, 5:1315, 6: 172–4.

19. Dorchester Committee of Observation to Maryland Council, July 27–31, 1776, MA, 12: 151–6; Hamond to George Montague, August 6, 1776, HP, 4:41–9; Hamond Narrative, July 15–August 13, 1776, NDAR, 6:172.

20. Wrike, 121–35; Schama, 78, 180–1.

21. Hartley, 37–9; Pougher, 227.

22. Pybus, *Epic Journeys.* 15, 20, 31–4, 219.

23. Pybus, 'Washington's Revolution, Harry that is not George', *Journal of Atlantic Studies*, 3:2, 183–98.

24. www.blackloyalist.info › john-moseley-from-chesapeake bay to bay, accessed November 24, 2022.

25. Christopher Fyfe ed., *Our Children, Free and Happy: Letters from Black Settlers in Africa in the 1790s*, Edinburgh, 1991.

26. Nash, Gary, 'Thomas Peters: Millwright and Deliverer', Nash and Sweet, David, eds., *Struggle & Survival in Colonial America.* Berkeley and Los Angeles, 1981, 69–85.

Chapter 12

1. Isaac, Rhys, *The Transformation of Virginia 1740–1790*, Chapel Hill, NC, 1982.

2. Maier, Pauline, *American Scripture, Making the Declaration of Independence*, New York, 1998, 146–7, 198–200.

3. Bolster, W. Jeffrey, *Black Jacks, African American Seamen in the Age of Sail*, Cambridge, Mass., 1997, 26; Mullin, Gerald, *Fight and Rebellion, Slave Resistance in Eighteenth-Century Virginia*, New York, 1972, 94–8.

4. Reese, George, 'The Court of Vice-Admiralty in Virginia and some Cases of 1770–1775', *The Virginia Magazine of History and Biography*, 88: 320–2; Russo, Jean, 'Self-sufficiency and Local Exchange: Free Craftsmen in the Rural Chesapeake Economy', in Carr, Morgan, Russo, 389–432.

5. Mullin, 99, 110, 119–120, 143.

6. Hoffman, *A Spirit of Dissension*, Baltimore, 1973, 146–7.

7. Ibid., 148, 185.

8. Journal of HM Otter, 3 Sept., 1775; Wilson Cary to Alexander Purdie of *Virginia Gazette* and enclosed depositions, 4 Sept., 1775, NDAR, 2: 4, 17–18.

9. Ibid.

10. Schwarz, *Twice Condemned, Slaves and Criminal Laws of Virginia, 1705–1865,* Baton Rouge, La., 1988, 186–7.
11. Claims & Memorials Petition of Shadrack Furman of Virginia, LI, accessed 12 Dec., 2022.
12. Harris, 76–8, 84–6.
13. Morgan, Philip, 'Black Society in the Low Country 1760-1810', Berlin and Hoffman, 108; Harris, 97–8, 133–9, 141–9, 153–4.
14. Olwell, 222–3; Diouf, 33–4.
15. Olwell, 239–44.
16. Harris, 118, 145.
17. Claims and Memorials Petition of Scipio Handley of South Carolina, Jan. 13, 1784, LI, accessed 9 Jan., 2023; Harris, 154.
18. Harris, 154.
19. Claims and Memorials Petition of Scipio Handley
20. Ibid.
21. Ibid.

Chapter 13

1. Paine, Thomas, *The Crisis,* Albany, N.Y. 1792, Anchor Books Edition, 1973, 72–3.
2. Gruber, Ira, *The Howe Brothers and the American Revolution*, Chapel Hill, NC, 1972, 90–1, 97; Bargar, 9–10.
3. Syrett, David, *Admiral Lord Howe: A Biography*, Stroud, Eng., 2006, 7.
4. Gilbert, 198–9.
5. Gruber, 238, 243–4; Hodges, Graham, *Root & Branch, African Americans in New York & East Jersey, 1613–1863,* Chapel Hill, 1999, 140.
6. Van Buskirk, Judith, *Generous Enemies, Patriots and Loyalists in Revolutionary New York*, Philadelphia, 2002, 135.
7. Proclamation, June 30, 1779, Sir Henry Clinton, Riverton's *Royal Gazette*, July 3, 1779. Judith Buskirk, *Generous Enemies,* 135–6, speculates that Clinton may not have wanted the proclamation to include entire black families, but in practice this is how it was interpreted. King, Carretta, 356.
8. Clinton, Henry, *The American Rebellion, Sir Henry Clinton's Narrative of his Campaigns, 1775–1782, with an appendix of original documents*, Wilcox, William, ed., New Haven, Ct., 1954, 192, 237–8.
9. Clinton, 353; Wilson, Ellen, *The Loyal Blacks*, New York, 1976, 22.
10. To His Excellency Sir Henry Clinton, Commander in Chief of His Majesty's Forces in North America, January 1, 1781, LI, accessed November 30, 2022.
11. Wilson, *John Clarkson and the African Adventure*, London, 1980, 54; Nash, *Struggle and Survival*, 78–9.

Chapter 14

1. Rodger, *Insatiable Earl*, 62–3.
2. Gronniosaw, Carretta, *Unchained Voices*, 44–5.

3. Pattison to Robert Bayard, July 16, 1779 in 'Letters of Major General James Pattison', in *Collections of the New-York Historical Society.* New York, 1876, 226–7; Ubbelohde, Carl, *The Vice-Admiralty Courts and the American Revolution*, Chapel Hill, NC, 1960, 172–8; Buel, Richard, In Irons, New Haven, Ct., 1998, 135–7.

4. Gambier, James, *A Narrative of Facts, Relative to the Conduct of Vice-Admiral Gambier,* London, 1782, 14. The comment was made by William Eden of the Carlisle Peace Commission in a letter of April 27, 1779 to Gambier; Van Buskirk, 112–4.

5. Rivington's *The Royal Gazette*, March 21, 1778, NDAR, 11: 689; Adair, William, 'Revolutionary War Diary of William Adair', Harold Hancock, ed., Delaware History, 13: 161; Chopra, Ruma, *Unnatural Rebellion, Loyalists in New York City During the Revolution*, Charlottesville, VA., 2011, 127–8; Buel, *In Irons*, 136–7.

6. *The Royal Gazette*, (New York), February 6th, 1779, accessed May 28, 2023.

7. Chopra, *Unnatural Rebellion,* 129.

8. Ibid., 130.

9. Hartley, 37–9, 66–7; Pougher, 227.

10. Hartley, 90–5, 121–9, 147–91.

11. Bernhard, 222–5.

12. Jarvis, Michael, *In the Eye of All Trade, Bermuda, Bermudians, and the Maritime Atlantic World, 1680–1783*, Chapel Hill, NC, 2012.

13. Bernhard, 185–6, 219, 236–8.

14. Ibid., 246–8.

15. Ibid., 276–7.

16. McCowen, George, *The Occupation of Charleston, 1780–82*, Columbia, SC, 1972, 82–3; Coker, 125.

17. Rowland, Lawrence S., Alexander Moore, and George C. Rogers. *The History of Beaufort County, Vol. 1, 1514–1861*, Columbia, 1996, 22; McCowen, 82–3; Coker, 125.

18. Schafer, Daniel, 'The Memoir of Mary (Port) Macklin', *The Florida Historical Quarterly*, 41, 2004, 109–10; Siebert, Wilbur, 'Privateering in Florida Waters and Northwards: During the Revolution', *Florida Historical Quarterly*, 22: 2.

19. Foy, 'Eighteenth century 'prize Negroes': From Britain to America'. Slavery and Abolition, 31(3), 2010, 379–93. doi: 10.1080/0144039X.2010.504532, accessed June 12, 2023.

20. Williams, 238.

21. Rodger, *Wooden World*, 63, 127–30.

Chapter 15

1. Boyd, Julian, *Anglo-American Union, Joseph Galloway's Plans to Preserve the British Empire 1774–1788*, Philadelphia, 1941, 155.

2. Pybus, *Epic Journeys*, 25, 69, 76–7, 217.

3. Fryer, Mary and Dracott, Christopher, *John Graves Simcoe 152–1806*, Toronto, 1998, 34–6.

4. Claims and Memorials Decision on the Claim of Samuel Burke of South Carolina, Sept. 1, 1783, LI, accessed June 10, 2023; Schama, 181; Raymond, W.O., *Loyalists in Arms 1775–1783*, Bruceton Mills, W.V., 1999, 24.

5. Braisted, Todd, 'The Black Pioneers and Others: The Military Role of Black Loyalists in the American War of Independence', Pulis, John, ed., *Moving On: Black Loyalists in the Afro-Atlantic World*, New York, 1999, 3–38; Clinton, 25–7.
6. A History of the Black Pioneers – Advanced Loyalist Studies, LI, accessed January 9, 2023.
7. Chopra, *Unnatural Rebellion*, 147.
8. Nash, *Struggle and Survival*, 69–76.
9. Tyson, George, 'The Carolina Black Corps: Legacy of Revolution, 1783–1798', *Revista/ Review Interamericana* 5: 1975–1976.
10. Ibid.
11. *Virginia Gazette*, March 22, 1776. In areas of British occupation or loyal colonies, the traditional militia could be mustered as a Loyalist unit. It was usually called out by the governor or a local military authority and numbers may have temporarily been considerable. However, pay and clothing were not provided and as a result the records of Loyalist militia are sparse. Our best knowledge of them is from a few muster rolls of the Charleston militia.

Chapter 16

1. Hodges, 152, 159.
2. An authentic account of the proceedings of a body of 1783, under the Board of Directors, commanded by Captains Hubbill, Ives, Jesse Hoyt, and Charles Thomas. June 17, 1781.
3. Henry Clinton to William Luce, July 2, 1781; Return of Armed Boat Company and where engaged, March 20, 1783, LI, accessed November 30, 2022.
4. Tarleton, Banastre, *A History of the Campaigns of 1780 and 1781, in the Southern Provinces of North America*, Dublin, 1787, 92.
5. Quarles, 150–1; McCowen, 102–103.
6. John Cruden to Henry Clinton, February 19, 1782, Crary, Catherine, *The Price of Loyalty, Tory writings from the Revolutionary Era*, New York, 1973, 292.
7. Olwell, 258–9.
8. February 10, 1778, RB, no. 4, part 3.
9. Diary, June 3, 1779, Wise, Barton, ed., *Memoir of General John Cropper of Accomack County, Virginia,* Reprint Onancock, Va., 1974, 14–15, 20.
10. Joseph Dashiell to Gov. Lee, September 30, 1780, MA, 45: 127.
11. Joseph Dashiell to Thomas Sim Lee, March 4, 1781, MA, 47:104. For more on Whaland see Corbett, *A Maritime History of the American Revolutionary War,* Barnsley, UK, 2023, 207–215.
12. Wise, Barton, 30-31; George Corbin to William Davies, 18 Aug., 1781, CVSP, 2: 339–40.
13. Wise, Barton, 22.
14. Petition of Inhabitants, 3 June, 1782, Accomack legislative Petitions, microfilm, Eastern Shore Main Library, Accomac, Va.
15. Pension Application of Jonas Belote S21066, 14 April, 1834, Leon Harris, trans. and ed., 1; Hast, Adele, *Loyalism in Revolutionary Virginia, The Norfolk Area and the Eastern Shore.* Ann Arbor, Mich. 1982, 140, 142.

Chapter 17

1. Olwell, 253–7
2. Wright, Leitch, *Florida in the American Revolution*, Gainesville, Fl., 1975, 5–6, 27–8, 44, 53, 103; Mowat, Charles, *East Florida as a British Province 1763–1784*, Gainesville, Fl., 1964, 107–123.
3. Stephen DeLancey to his wife, January 14, 1779, Crary, 271–4.
4. Clinton, 116–7.
5. George, David, *An Account of the Life of Mr. David George, from Sierra Leone in Africa*, London, 1793, Carretta, 333–4; Gordon, Grant, *From Slavery to Freedom: The Life of David George, Pioneer Black Baptist Minister*, Hantsport, Canada, 1992, 7–11.
6. George, 334–5; Wilson, *Loyal Blacks*, 11.
7. George, 336.
8. George, 336–7; Documents Re David George, a Free negro, 1779, 1780, 1781, LI, accessed June 2, 2023.
9. Quarles, 154.
10. Comte d'Estaing, Journal of the Siege of Savannah, *Muskets Cannon Balls & Bombs*, ed. Kennedy, Benjamin, Savannah, 1974, 46–8, 67–8; Augustine Prévost to George Germain, November 1, 1779, Journal of the Siege of Savannah in Kennedy, 93–6.
11. Clinton, 160–161; *Roebuck* Captain's Log, December 25–26, 1779 and April 8–10, 1780, NA, ADM 51/796.
12. McCowen, George, *The British Occupation of Charleston, 1780–82*, Columbia, SC, 1972, 3; Hamond autobiography, HP, 1: 109–10; NA, ADM 1/486, f. 355.
13. Clinton, 171; Willis, Sam, *The Struggle for Sea Power: Naval History of the American Revolution*, New York, 2015, 352–5; Rodger, Command of the Ocean, 345.
14. Smith, Paul, *Loyalists and Redcoats, A Study in British Revolutionary Policy*, New York, 1972, 126–133; Marrant, Carretta, *Unchained Voices*, 126.
15. McCowen, 100–1.
16. Ibid.,
17. Diouf, 34–5.
18. Thomas Williams, Logbook of the *Roebuck*, May 15, 1780–June 2, 1781, NMM, ADM L/R 219; McCowen, 87–8. Captain James Gambier is not to be confused with his uncle Admiral James Gambier.
19. McCowen, 103–4.
20. Ibid., 64–6.
21. Quarles, 149.
22. Morgan, Philip, 'Black Society in the Low Country', Berlin and Hoffman, 109–110.
23. King, Carretta, *Unchained Voices*, 351–4. Blakeley, Phyllis, 'Boston King: A Black Loyalist', Eleven Exiles, Blakeley and Grant, John, eds., Toronto, 1982, 266–70.

Chapter 18

1. King, Carretta, *Unchained Voices*, 355–7.
2. Ibid., 356.

3. Van Buskirk, 17–27.
4. Proclamation, June 30, 1779, Sir Henry Clinton, Riverton's *Royal Gazette*, July 3, 1779.
5. John Andre to Lord Cathcart, March 4, 1780 and Disbursements for Gardiners and Labourers, Mar. 7, 1779, LI, accessed May 10, 2023; Van Buskirk, 142.
6. Chopra, *Unnatural Rebellion*, 146–7, 214.
7. Pybus, *Epic Journeys*. 31–4, 219.
8. Testimony, Murphey Steel, August 16, 1781. For Steel's possible motives see Van Buskirk, 152–3.
9. [O'Beirne, Thomas Lewis,] *Candid and Impartial Narrative of the Transactions of the Fleet: Under the Command of Lord Howe,* London, 1779, 5–10; Hamond autobiography, HP. 1: 89–90; John Bowater to Lord Denbigh, July 31, 1778, Balderston, Marion and Syrett, eds., *The Lost War, Letters from British Officers during the American Revolution*, New York, 1975, 166–7; Marine Committee to Count d'Estaing, July 17 and August 12, 1778, Paullin, 268–9, 284–5; O'Beirne, 11–31; Syrett, *Admiral Lord Howe*, 79–80; James Payne, Logbook of the *Roebuck*, August 27, 1778–May 12, 1779, NMM, ADM L/R 150.
10. James Robertson to George Germain, May 6, 1781, *The New York Letter Book of General James Robertson 1780–1783*, Klein, Milton and Howard, Ronald, eds., 190–1.
11. James Robertson to Henry Clinton, May 3, 1780, Ibid., 97–100.
12. Proposals for raising Volunteers to Man his Majesty's Ships …, October 4, 1781, Klein and Howard, 219–20; Thomas Graves to Henry Clinton, August 21, 1781; Samuel Hood to Henry Clinton, August 25, 1781, Clinton, 2.
13. Van Buskirk, 154.

Chapter 19

1. Marrant, Carretta, *Unchained Voices*, 125–6.
2. Blake, 22–3.
3. Colley, Linda, *Britons: Forging the Nation 1707–1837*, New Haven, Ct., 1992.
4. Taylor, 59–60, 70–6, 96, 120–30, 268, 274.
5. Blake, 29–33.
6. Brown, 210.
7. Burn, Andrew, *The Life of Major General Andrew Burn of the Royal Marines*, 1840, 6, 15, 17, 19, 89–92, 131, 156–72.
8. Watt, James, 'James Ramsay, 1733–1789: Naval Surgeon, Naval Chaplain and Morning Star of the Anti-Slavery Movement', *Mariner's Mirror*, 81:2, 156–70.
9. Shyllon, Forlarin, *James Ramsay: The Unknown Abolitionist*, Edinburgh, 1977, 156–70.
10. Ramsay, *An Inquiry into the Effects of Putting a Stop to the African Slave Trade, and of Granting Liberty to the Slaves in the British Sugar Colonies*, London, 1784, 13–15.
11. Ibid., 17, 31–5.
12. Blake, 67–8.
13. Ibid., 35–7.
14. Ibid., 37–40.
15. Ibid., quote on 41.
16. More, Hannah, *The Works of Hannah More*, New York, 1848, 28; Blake 40–1.

17. Talbott, John, *The Pen and Ink Sailor: Charles Middleton and the King's Navy,* 1778–1813, London, 1998, 1–28.
18. Pool, Bernard, *Navy Board Contracts 1600–1832: Contract Administration under the Navy Board,* London, 1966, 77–114.
19. Talbott, 115–44; Rodger, *The Insatiable Earl,* 159–65.
20. Talbot, 149–17.
21. Blake, 70–3, 114–23, 190–9.

Chapter 20

1. Alexander Leslie to Henry Clinton, November 30, 1781; Alexander Leslie to Henry Clinton, January 29, 1782, Clinton, 588–9, 594–5.
2. Morgan, Philip, 57–101.
3. Kulikoff, Allan, 'The Beginnings of the Afro-American family in Maryland', *Law, Society and Politics in Early Maryland,* Land, Aubrey, Carr, Lois, Panpenfuse, Edward, eds., Baltimore, 1977, 171–96.
4. Douglass, Frederick, *The Life and Times of Frederick Douglas,* Ware, Hertfordshire, 1996, 6.
5. Morgan, Philip, 93, 285, 512–19.
6. Ibid., 151–4, 340–51.
7. Ethiopian Regiment, Morning Reports, May 21, 1776, LI, accessed December 19, 2022.
8. Germain to Clinton, January 23, 1779, Clinton to Germain, May 14, 1779, Clinton, 399–400, 404–6.
9. Passport for Cato Ramsay to emigrate to Nova Scotia, April 21, 1783, African Nova Scotians in Age of Slavery and Abolition, Nova Scotia Archives, Halifax, https://archives.novascotia.ca › africanns › archives, accessed December 20, 2022.
10. The fleet returned immediately to New York with all its refugees, 'Return of Persons that came off from Virginia with General Mathew in the Fleet August 24, 1779', TNA, CO 5/52/63.
11. Simcoe, John, *Simcoe's Military Journal,* December 2, 1780, Arno ed., New York, 1968, 155.
12. Gutman, Herbert, *The Black Family in Slavery and Freedom 1750–1925,* New York, 1976, 241–6.
13. Syrett, *Shipping and the American War,* 172.
14. Ibid.

Chapter 21

1. William Smallwood to the Maryland Council of Safety, March 14, 1777, MA, 16:176.
2. Andrews, 35–55; Mason, Isaac, *Life of Isaac Mason as a Slave,* Worcester, Mass, 1893, 37–43.
3. Andrews, 15–17, 164–5.
4. Phoebus, George, *Beams of Light in Early Methodism,* New York, 1887, 13.
5. William Paca to Thomas Johnson, September 6, 1777, MA, 16:364; Rodney to George Washington, September 6, 1777, Ryden, George, ed., *Letters to and from Caesar Rodney, 1756–1784,* Philadelphia, 1933, 219; Hoffman, *A Spirit of Dissension,* Baltimore, 1973, 227.

6. Nathaniel Potter to Thomas Sim Lee, August 23, 1780, MA, 45:23; Hoffman, *A Spirit of Dissension*, 227.
7. Andrews, 54–6, 62–4.
8. Williams, William, *Garden of American Methodism: The Delmarva Peninsula*, Wilmington, De., 1984, 166.
9. Ibid., 107–9.
10. Committee of Accomack County, Virginia, to Committee of Somerset County, Maryland, August 28, 1776, NDAR, 6:340; Isaac, Rhys, *The Transformation of Virginia 1740–1790*, Chapel Hill, NC, 1982, 265.
11. Watters, William, *A Short Account of the Christian Experience and Ministerial Labor*, Alexandria, Va. 1806, 35; Wigger, John, *American Saint, Francis Asbury and the Methodists*, New York, 2009, 57–9.
12. Bangs, Nathan, *The Life of Rev. Freeborn Garrettson*, New York, 1829, 29–35, 43.
13. Straker, Ian, 'Social Status in Early American Methodism: The Case of Freeborn Garrettson', *Methodist History*, 45, 155–65.
14. Bangs, 70–1, 83–91.
15. Williams, *Garden of American Methodism*, 35–8, 41, 48.
16. Bangs, 65.

Chapter 22

1. Quarles, 158–81.
2. Hadden, 157–8.
3. Instructions to Brigadier General Arnold, December 13, 1780, Clinton, 482–3, 244; Wilcox, *Portrait of a General*, 354, 372–3; Selby, 221–3, Fallow and Stoer, 458–9, 464; Benjamin Caldwell to William Hotham, April 18, 1778, NDAR, 12:135; Kranish, Michael, *Flight from Monticello: Thomas Jefferson at War,* New York, 2010, 119–318.
4. Kranish, 141, 183–6; Selby, 223–4; Pybus, *Epic Journeys*, 44, 52, 55, 63, 78, 212; It appears that British units stopped often at Westover on their way up and down the James River, see Tarleton, 276, 300, 348.
5. Selby, 268.
6. Kranish, 219–21
7. Ibid., 222–3.
8. Ibid., 262, 327–8.
9. Council to Henry Lowes, March 16, 1778, MA, 16:537; Pybus, 31, 33–4; Truitt, Breadbasket, 94.
10. Council to George Dashiell, April 6, 1778, NDAR, 21:11–12.
11. Watters, William, *A Short Account of the Christian Experience and Ministerial Labor*, Alexandria, Va. 1806, 35; Wigger, John, *American Saint, Francis Asbury and the Methodists*, New York, 2009, 57–9.
12. Wayne to Greene, February 28, 1782; Greene to Wayne, March 6, 1782; Wayne to Greene, August 12, 1782, Ibid, 385–9, 427; Boyd, Thomas, *Mad Anthony Wayne*, New York, 1929, 206–11.

13. Greene to Wayne, June 28, 1782; Wayne to Greene, July 17, 1782, Peckham, 2: 422–5.
14. Wayne to Greene, 18 May, 1782, Ibid., 2: 408–9; Hoffman, 'The 'Disaffected' in the Revolutionary South', *The American Revolution, Explorations in the History of American Radicalism*, Young, Alfred, ed., DeKalb, Ill., 1976, 307–311.
15. Wayne congratulated Greene on his purchase of Mulbury Grove plantation. Wayne to Greene, June 15, 1782; Greene to Wayne, June 21, 1782, Peckham, 2:420, 422; Boyd, 216–28.
16. 'Account of a Conference between Washington and Sir Guy Carleton, May 6, 1783', *Founders Online*, National Archives, https://founders.archives.gov/documents/Washington/99–01–02–11217, accessed January 15, 2022; Washington to Carleton, May 6, 1783, *Founders Online*, National Archives, https://founders.archives.gov/documents/Washington/99-01-02-11218, accessed June 26, 2022; Schama, 145–6.
17. Carleton to Washington, May 12, 1783, *Founders Online*, National Archives, https://founders.archives.gov/documents/Washington/99–01–02–11252, accessed June 26, 2022.
18. Diouf, 37.
19. Ibid., 190–3.
20. Ibid., 195–203.

Chapter 23

1. Quarles, 158–63; Conway, 115–9, 166–70.
2. Talbott 90–1; Schama, 129–35.
3. G.P. Browne, 'CARLETON, GUY, 1st Baron DORCHESTER', DCB, www.biographi.ca/en/bio/carleton_guy_5E.html, accessed December 22, 2022.
4. Reynolds, Paul, *Guy Carleton, A Biography*, Toronto, 1980, 8–55.
5. Syrett, *Shipping and the American War*, 236–7.
6. Wilson, *Loyal Blacks*, 44–7.
7. Greene to Wayne, May 24, 1782; Greene to Wayne, August 2, 1782, Peckham, 2: 414, 426.
8. McCowen, 103.
9. Hamond to Robert Digby, September 24, 1782, HP, 7: 131–2; Schama, 132–6; Wilson, *Loyal Blacks*, 50–1, 68–9; McCowen, 149.
10. Liele, George, *An Account of Several Baptist Churches, Consisting Chiefly of Negro Slaves*, Carretta, *Unchained Voices*, 325–32.
11. McCowen, 147–50; Morgan, Philip, 'Black Society in the Low Country', 111.
12. Schama, 150–6; Wilson, *Loyal Blacks*, 53–5.
13. Library and Archives of Canada, Carleton Papers, Book of Negros, 1783; Schama, 150–4; Wilson, The *Loyal Blacks*, New York, 1976, 22.
14. Admiral Robert Digby's Naval Order Book, July 23 and 29, 1783, Admiral Digby Museum, Digby, Nova Scotia; *Report on American Manuscripts in the Royal Institutions of Great Britain*. London, 1909, 297; Alexr. Schraw to Oliver DeLancey, Nov. 10, 1783, LI, accessed May 10, 2023; Schama, 155, 435.
15. Van Buskirk, 179.
16. Schama, 129.

17. Samuel Hood to James Robertson, November 10, 1781, Klein and Howard, 228.
18. Schama, 129.
19. Samuel Kelly: *An Eighteenth-Century Seaman*, Garston, Crosbie, ed., London, 1925, 35–6, 53–4.
20. Wright, 125–43; Mowat, 136–40.
21. A. Deveaux to Carleton, June 6, 1783, Crary, 354–7.

Chapter 24

1. Hitchcock, Tim, *Down and Out in Eighteenth-Century London*, London, 2004, 1–22.
2. Evans, John, 'Nathaniel Wells of Piecefield and St Kitts: from Slave to Sheriff', *Monmouthshire Antiquary*, 7: 91–106; Chater, 'Genealogy and the Black Past', *Britain's Black Past*, 336; Foy, 'Unke Sommerset's' freedom: liberty in England for black sailors' *Journal of Maritime Research*, 13:1, 21–36.
3. Pybus, 79–80; Schama, 179.
4. Braidwood, 28–30.
5. Ibid., 66–9.
6. Ibid., 22–30.
7. Braidwood, 90–3; Ramsay, 14–6.
8. Ibid., 129–42
9. Wise, Steven, 31–5, 49–58; for British constitutional and legal thought see Pocock, J.G.A., *The Ancient Constitution and the Feudal Law*, New York, 1967.
10. Walvin, *The Zong: A Massacre, the Law and the End of Slavery*, New Haven, Ct. 2011.
11. Braidwood, 13–8.
12. Braidwood, 143–61; Pybus, 111.
13. Braidwood, 102–7, 142–7.
14. Equiano, Carretta, *Unchained Voices*, 283–6; Braidwood, 149–58.
15. Cugoano, Carretta, *Unchained Voices*, 175.
16. Cugoano, Carretta, *Unchained Voices*, 176; Braidwood, 158–9.
17. Braidwood does not agree, 158–61, 206–9.
18. Ibid., 152–3.
19. Ibid., 144–9.
20. Braidwood, 158–61; Thomas Boulden Thompson, *Dictionary of National Biography*, London: *Smith, Elder & Co. 1885–1900*.
21. Thompson, Thomas, Narrative of the Voyage of the Nautilus for the Purpose of Investigating the West Coast of South Africa, NMM, 1786-01-01-1786-12-31, TRN/18.
22. Braidwood, 181–92.
23. Ibid., 183–5, 198–200
24. Ibid., 204–5.
25. Ibid., 206, 229.
26. Ibid., 225–33

Chapter 25

1. Gwyn, *Frigates and Foremasts, The North American Squadron in Nova Scotia Waters 1745–1815,* Vancouver, B.C., 2003, 73–5.
2. Navy Board to Philip Stephens, December 9, 1762, NMM, ADM/B/170; Gwyn, Ashore and Afloat, 4–8, 10; Ubbelohde, 3–4, 49–53.
3. Nash, *Struggle and Survival*, 76–7.
4. Ibid, 77–8.
5. Ibid., 79–81.
6. Wilson, *John Clarkson and the African Adventure*, London, 1980, 53–6; Nash, *Struggle and Survival*, 81–3.
7. Wilson, *John Clarkson*, 6–42.
8. Schama, 116, 155, 236–7.
9. Wilson, The *Loyal Blacks*, 90–1, 101–2, 202, 208–9, 219.
10. Part 3 Cato Perkins and Nathaniel Snowball – Untold lives blog, https://blogs. bl.uk › untoldlives › 2020/11 › the-lives-a, accessed December 18, 2022; St G. Walker, James W., 'MARRANT, JOHN', in DCB, vol. 4, University of Toronto/ Université Laval, 2003, accessed March 19, 2023, www.biographi.ca/en/bio/ marrant_john_4E.html.
11. Wilson, *John Clarkson*, 72.
12. Ibid.
13. Banks, 147–89.
14. George, Carretta, *Unchained Voices*, 336–41.
15. Wilson, *John Clarkson*, 59–71.
16. Ibid., 57–91.
17. Ibid., 72–5.
18. Ibid., 76–80.
19. Ibid., 80–6, 92–7; Nash, *Struggle and Survival*, 83.
20. Wilson, *John Clarkson*, 68, 72, 98–9.
21. Ibid., 84, 87, 100, 113–4, 117–18.
22. Ibid., 115.
23. Ibid., 124–34.
24. Ibid., 138–9, quote on 178.
25. Wilson, *John Clarkson*, 133–4; Schama, 364–5; Schwarz, Susan, 'Commerce, Civilization and Christianity: The Development of the Sierra Leone Company', Richardson, Schwarz and Tibbles, 252–76.
26. Schama, 374–6; Schwarz, 'Commerce'.
27. Wilson, *John Clarkson*, 134–9.
28. Schama, 383–4.
29. Ibid., 380, 383–6, 389–91.
30. Ibid., 385–95.
31. Ibid., 390–3.
32. Ibid., 387, 394–5.
33. Chopra, *Almost Home*, 139–59; Schama, 390–7.

34. Chopra, *Almost Home*, 15–78; Grant, John, *The Maroons in Nova Scotia*, Halifax, 2002, 15–30, 117–18.
35. Chopra, *Almost Home*, 79–138; Grant, 31–145.
36. Chopra, *Almost Home*, 160–82; Schwarz, 'Commerce', 267–9.

Chapter 26

1. Smyth, W.H., *The Life and Services of Captain Philip Beaver,* London, 1829. 70–1.
2. Wilson, *John Clarkson*, 15, 32–5.
3. Smyth, 40–3.
4. Ibid., 49–54.
5. Bolton, Carol, The Bulama Colony and abolitionary reform, ResearchGate, www.researchgate.net › publication › 349348137, accessed December 27, 2022.
6. Smyth, 54–9.
7. Wilson, *John Clarkson*, 114–5; Smyth, 59–63.
8. Bolton, The Bulama Colony, accessed December 27, 2022.
9. Smyth, 90–2.
10. Ibid., 96–102.
11. Ibid., 101–7.
12. Beaver, Philip, *African Memoranda relative to an attempt to establish A British Settlement on the Island of Bulama off the West coast of Africa in the year 1792*, London 1805.

Chapter 27

1. Boubacar, Barry, *Senegambia and the Atlantic Slave Trade*, Cambridge, UK, 1998, 55–126.
2. David George to John Rippon, November 12, 1794, Carretta, 343–4; Schama. 381–3.
3. Marshall, Peter, *The Anti-Slave Trade Movement in Bristol*, Bristol, 1968, 2–4; Hochschild, Adam, *Bury the Chains, Prophets and Rebels in the Fight to Free an Empire's Slaves,* Boston, 2005, 89–97, 120–27, 182–192.
4. Newton, *Memoirs,* 39–50, 88–92.
5. Brown, 337–42.
6. 'Biographical Sketches of Edward Rushton, written by his son', *The Belfast Monthly Magazine*, 13:77, 474–85; Howman, Brian, 'Abolitionism in Liverpool', Richardson, Schwarz, Tibbles, 283–91; Tibbles, 82.
7. Howman, 283–4.
8. Ibid., 285–8.
9. Drescher, Seymour, *Econocide, British Slavery in the Era of Abolition*, Chapel Hill, NC, 2010.
10. Marshall, 21–4.
11. Morgan, Kenneth, 'Liverpool's Dominance of the British Slave Trade', Richardson, Schwarz, Tibbles, 14–42. Technically Manchester was more populous than Liverpool, but this count added the suburb of Salford to its total.
12. Hearn, David, *The Slave Streets of Liverpool*, Liverpool, 2020, np.

13. Bagneris, Mia. Colouring the Caribbean: Race and the art of Agostino Brunias, Manchester, UK, 2017.

14. Underdown, P.T., 'Henry Cruger and Edmund Burke: Colleagues and Rivals at the Election of 1774', *William and Mary Quarterly*, 15:1, 14–34.

15. Miller, Rebecca, Introduction, Basker, James, ed., *Early American Abolitionists, A Collection of Anti-Slavery Writings 1760–1820*, New York, 2005, 52–9.

16. Oldfield, J.R., *Popular Politics and British Anti-Slavery*, London, 1998, 96–154, 167–72.

17. LoGerfo, James, '"Sir William Dolben and 'The Cause of Humanity"': The Passage of the Slave Trade Regulation Act of 1788', *Eighteenth-Century Studies*, 6:4, 431–51. Oldfield, 50, 56, 63, 91, 99, 136, 173

18. Equiano, Carretta, *Unchained Voices*, 286–9; Carretta, 'Revisiting Olaudah Equiano', 47; Fryer, Peter, *Staying Power: The History of Black People in Britain*, London, 1984, 106, 102–13.

19. Cugoano, Carretta, *Unchained Voices*, 172–3; Fryer, 98–102, 111.

20. McCalman, 'Introduction', *The Horrors of Slavery*. 4–5.

21. Tibbles, 9, 39, 96–100, 107.

22. Oldfield, 173–9.

23. Wills, Mary, *Envoys of Abolition: British Naval Officers and the Campaign Against the Slave Trade in West Africa*, Liverpool, 2019; Ward, W.E.F., *The Royal Navy and the Slaves: The Suppression of the Atlantic Slave Trade*, New York, 1970; Grindall, Peter, *Opposing the Slavers: The Royal Navy's Campaign against the Atlantic Slave Trade*, London, 2016.

Chapter 28

1. Dunn, Richard, 'Black Society in the Chesapeake, 1776–1810', Berlin and Hoffman, 52.

2. Wigger, 150–5, 296–8; Raboteau, Albert, 'The Slave Church in the Era of the American Revolution', Berlin and Hoffman, 193–213.

3. Baptist, Edward, *The Half Has Never Been Told*, New York, 2014, 2–5.

4. Scott, John, 'Christian Colonization on the American Frontier in the 1780s: The Countess of Huntingdon's Plan and the American Response', *Fides et Historia*, 49:1, 2017.

5. Washington to the Countess of Huntingdon, June 30, 1785, *The Papers of George Washington, Confederation Series*, 3: May 19, 1785–March 1, 1786, Abbot, W.W., ed. Charlottesville, Va., 1994, 92–3. Welch, 169–71

6. White, Shane, *Somewhat More Independent, The End of Slavery in New York City*, 1770–1810, Athens, Ga., 1991; Hodges, 168–71.

7. Fields, Barbara Jeanne, *Slavery and Freedom on the Middle Ground, Maryland during the Nineteenth Century*, New Haven, Ct., 1985, 5–7; Dorsey, Jennifer, *Hirelings: African American Workers and Free Labor in Early Maryland*, Ithaca, NY, 2011, 17, 21–44, 82–95; Wolf, Eva, *Race and Liberty in the New Nation*, Baton Rouge, La., 2006, 43, 54–62; Berlin, Ira, *Slaves without Masters, The Free Negro in the Antebellum South*, New York, 1974, 46–7, 136–7.

8. John Henry to William Vans Murray, July 14, 1793 and General J.C. Howard to John Henry, July 3, 1792 in Henry, J. Winfield, *Traditions of Weston*, 25–6, 52–3.

9. Col. Snead, 'if there was one', Virginia Shore Slave revolt in 1792 was covered in a letter of May 5, from Col. Snead to Gov. Lee: Barnes, 46–7; Northampton Order Book 1789–1795, May 9, 1792, July 2, 1792, 207, 231; Mariner, Kirk, *Slave and Free on Virginia's Eastern Shore*, Onancock, Va., 2014, 32–3, 64–5.
10. Cuffee, Paul, *Memoir of Captain Paul Cuffee, A man of Colour, to which is subjoined The Epistle of the Society of Sierra Leone, in Africa*, London, 1812.
11. Henry, George, *Life of George Henry, Together with a Brief History of Colored People in America*, Providence, RI, 1894, 23–4.
12. Fields, 7; Mariner, *Slave and Free*, 41–2.
13. Douglas, 5.
14. Northern Legislative Petitions, December 14 (December 7), 1798, Deposition of Thorogood West.
15. Baptist, 10–11, 47–9; Deyle, Steven, *Carry me Back, The Domestic Slave Trade in American Life*, New York, 2005, 16, 19–20.
16. Baptist, 50–69. Sipkins, Henry, *An Oration on the Abolition of the Slave Trade*, New York, 1809, Basker, 276–295
17. Baptist, 4; Deyle, 15–39. Edward Baptist has been criticized by economic historians who feel he overemphasizes the role of cotton production in the lower South.
18. Winter, 81, 96–100, 112, 114; Deyle, 63–93.
19. Baptist, 176–80; Mariner, *Slave and Free*, 116–29; Morgan, Michael, *Delmarva's Patty Cannon: The Devil in the Nanticoke (True Crime)*, Charleston, SC, 2015.
20. Townsend, George Alfred, *The Entailed Hat*, New York, 1884.
21. Port of Accomack Naval Officer's Book of Entries and Clearances, 1780–1787, November 13, 1785, Accomack County Miscellaneous Records; Maddox, Lucy, 'A Liberal Share of Public Patronage': Chestertown's Antebellum Black Business', *The Key to Old Kent*, 7:2013, 77–80. Guerin, Ayasha, 'Underground and at Sea: Oysters and Black Marine Entanglements in New York's Zone A', *Shima Journal*, 2019.

Affirmations

1. Johnson, Samuel, Taxation No Tyranny, London, 1775, 454; Davis, *The Problem of Slavery in the Age of Revolution 1770–1823*, Ithaca, NY, 1975, 344; Carretta, 'Introduction', *Unchained Voices*, 1.
2. Cugoano, Carretta, *Unchained Voices*, 171.
3. Ibid., 151.
4. Ibid., 146, 179.
5. Ibid., 152, 156–7.
6. Ibid., 163.
7. Ibid., 164–5, quote on 164.
8. Ibid., 172.
9. King, Carretta, 366.
10. Davis, Berlin and Hoffman, 273
11. Blake, 185.

Index